"Thinking about and exploring media practices entail the recognition that we need another kind of gaze, other points of view, other places from which to make sense of culture and the media. *Citizen Media and Practice* provides a renewed understanding of media practices in connection to the people and the territories they inhabit. The book explores the ambiguities of media practices and charts the possibilities they open up to imagine another kind of world and connect to other ways of thinking about culture."

> **Jesús Martín-Barbero**, author of *Communication, culture and hegemony: From the media to mediations* (Sage, 1993) (Orig. edition: *De los Medios a las Mediaciones. Comunicación, cultura y hegemonía*, Gustavo Gili, 1987)

"*Citizen Media and Practice* is an outstanding contribution to practice-oriented research on citizen and activist media today. Its contributions are delicately balanced for stimulating interdisciplinary cross-fertilisation based on empirical research into a great diversity of topics related to media activism and social movements in Europe and Latin America. The book offers an up-to-date, cutting-edge overview of how practice approaches are useful for grasping contemporary activism and media processes, and how materialities, digitalities, discourses, bodies, affects and emotions are embedded into political actions that aim to change the world we live in, through our makings and aspirations, doings and sayings. This book demonstrates that practice theories are alive and kicking because they are powerful tools to understand ourselves as citizens; active agents of the world we inhabit."

> **Elisenda Ardèvol**, Professor in Social and Cultural Anthropology at UOC (Universitat Oberta de Catalunya), Barcelona. Director of the *Mediaccions Research Group in Culture and Digital Communication*.

"Stephansen and Treré have brought together a very competent and interdisciplinary collective of researchers that together have delivered an inspiring book! It builds necessary bridges between Anglo-Saxon and Latin American scholarship; it retrieves relevant and almost forgotten past research, letting it inform contemporary scholarship: and it establishes connections between research into citizen media practice with relevant and emerging fields of inquiry in the social sciences. The result is a very commendable book that challenges and pushes the boundaries of not only media scholarship but of social science more broadly."

> **Thomas Tufte**, Professor at and Director of the Institute for Media and Creative Industries, Loughborough University London. Author of *Communication and Social Change – A Citizen Perspective* (Polity, 2017)

"There is a terrific immediacy to *Citizen Media and Practice*. Reading this book feels like sneaking into an advanced seminar with leading Latin American and anglophone scholars as they debate the latest implications of the 'practice turn' for the study of media, communication and social movements."

John Postill, Senior Lecturer in Communication at RMIT University, Melbourne, author of *The Rise of Nerd Politics* (Pluto, 2018)

"This book is a timely and necessary overview of the notion of 'media as practice.' It blends insights from Latin American and Northern communication scholarship, and takes stock of the current state of the research. The chapters provide a wealth of insights to further refine the understanding of 'what citizens (and social movements) do with media'. At a time of growing concerns about the rise of anti-progressive movements around the world, this book delivers hope without rose-tinted, unrealistic promises. Amid the current obsession with data, measurement and technology, this book reminds us why organized, ordinary citizens matter in the struggle to challenge power."

Silvio Waisbord, Professor in the School of Media and Public Affairs, George Washington University, past Editor-in-Chief, *Journal of Communication* (2015-2018), author of *Communication: A Post-Discipline* (Polity, 2019).

"From data practices to video activism, this book brings together the best scholars in the field who explore the stories, the values and struggles of those working on citizen media. A must read for anyone interested in these media forms, their social importance, and their struggle for social justice."

Veronica Barassi, Senior Lecturer in Media, Communications and Cultural Studies, Goldsmiths, University of London. Author of *Activism on the Web: Everyday Struggles Against Digital Capitalism* (Routledge, 2015)

CITIZEN MEDIA AND PRACTICE

This groundbreaking collection advances understanding of the concept of media practices by critically interrogating its relevance for the study of citizen and activist media.

Media as practice has emerged as a powerful approach to understanding the media's significance in contemporary society. Bringing together contributions from leading scholars in sociology, media and communication, social movement, and critical data studies, this book stimulates dialogue across previously separate traditions of research on citizen and activist media practices, and stakes out future directions for research in this burgeoning interdisciplinary field. Framed by a foreword by Nick Couldry and a substantial introductory chapter by the editors, contributions to the volume trace the roots and appropriations of the concept of media practice in Latin American communication theory; reflect on the relationship between activist agency and technological affordances; explore the relevance of the media practice approach for the study of media activism, including activism that takes media as its central object of struggle; and demonstrate the significance of the media practice approach for understanding processes of mediatization and datafication.

Offering both a comprehensive introduction to scholarship on citizen media and practice, and a cutting-edge exploration of a novel theoretical framework, the book is ideal for students and experienced scholars alike.

Hilde C. Stephansen is Senior Lecturer in Sociology in the School of Social Sciences at the University of Westminster, London.

Emiliano Treré is Senior Lecturer in Media Ecologies and Social Transformation in the School of Journalism, Media and Culture at Cardiff University.

CRITICAL PERSPECTIVES ON CITIZEN MEDIA

Series Editors:
Luis Pérez-González, University of Manchester (UK)
Bolette B. Blaagaard, Aalborg University (Denmark)
Mona Baker, University of Manchester (UK)

Critical Perspectives on Citizen Media aims to define and advance understanding of citizen media, an emerging academic field located at the interface between different disciplines, including media studies, sociology, translation studies, performance studies, political science, visual studies and journalism studies. Titles in the series are focused on high-quality and original research, in the form of monographs and edited collections, made accessible for a wide range of readers. The series explores the relationship between citizen media and various cross-disciplinary themes, including but not restricted to, participation, immaterial work, witnessing, resistance and performance. The series editors also welcome proposals for reference works, textbooks and innovative digital outputs produced by citizen engagement groups on the ground.

Translating Dissent
Voices *from* and *with* the Egyptian Revolution
Edited by Mona Baker

Citizen Media and Public Spaces
Diverse Expressions of Citizenship and Dissent
Edited by Mona Baker and Bolette B. Blaagaard

Citizen Media and Practice
Currents, Connections, Challenges
Edited by Hilde C. Stephansen and Emiliano Treré

for more information, visit: https://www.routledge.com/Critical-Perspectives-on-Citizen-Media/book-series/CPCM

CITIZEN MEDIA AND PRACTICE

Currents, Connections, Challenges

Edited by Hilde C. Stephansen and Emiliano Treré

With a foreword by Nick Couldry

Routledge
Taylor & Francis Group

LONDON AND NEW YORK

First published 2020
by Routledge
2 Park Square, Milton Park, Abingdon, Oxon OX14 4RN

and by Routledge
52 Vanderbilt Avenue, New York, NY 10017

Routledge is an imprint of the Taylor & Francis Group, an informa business

British Library Cataloguing-in-Publication Data
A catalogue record for this book is available from the British Library

Library of Congress Cataloging-in-Publication Data
Names: Stephensen, Hilde C., editor. | Treré, Emiliano, editor.
Title: Citizen media and practice : currents, connections, challenges / edited by Hilde C. Stephensen and Emiliano Treré ; with a foreword by Nick Couldry.
Description: Abingdon, Oxon ; New York, NY : Routledge, 2020. |
Series: Critical perspectives on citizen media ; 3 |
Includes bibliographical references and index.
Identifiers: LCCN 2019024797 (print) | LCCN 2019024798 (ebook) |
ISBN 9781138571822 (hardback) | ISBN 9781138571846 (paperback) |
ISBN 9781351247375 (ebook)
Subjects: LCSH: Citizen journalism. | Social movements. | Political participation. | Internet and activism. | Mass media--Political aspects.
Classification: LCC PN4784.C615 C587 2020 (print) |
LCC PN4784.C615 (ebook) | DDC 302.23--dc23
LC record available at https://lccn.loc.gov/2019024797
LC ebook record available at https://lccn.loc.gov/2019024798

ISBN: 978-1-138-57182-2 (hbk)
ISBN: 978-1-138-57184-6 (pbk)
ISBN: 978-1-351-24737-5 (ebk)

Typeset in Bembo
by Taylor & Francis Books

Cover image: Photograph by Clemencia Rodríguez Design by Aristea Fotopoulou

MIX
Paper from
responsible sources
FSC C013985

Printed in the United Kingdom
by Henry Ling Limited

CONTENTS

ILLUSTRATIONS

Figures

Tables

ACKNOWLEDGEMENTS

This book is the outcome of many years' experience of researching, reading, thinking, and talking about citizen media and social movements' media practices. It would be simply impossible to recall all the people, events, texts, and conversations that have helped shape our vision for the collective endeavour that this collection undoubtedly is. However, some people and events deserve a special mention. First of all, we are immensely grateful to Nick Couldry, whose support for this project from conception to completion has been essential. We are also greatly indebted to Clemencia Rodríguez for helping us realize the significance of the Latin American tradition of communication theory for research on media practices.

The idea for this book emerged out of a panel we organized in 2016 at the European Communication Research and Education Association (ECREA) conference in Prague, and we drew much inspiration from the contributions to that panel from Nick, Alice Mattoni, Anne Kaun, and Tina Askanius – as well as from the ensuing discussion with several other colleagues, which continued long into the night over dinner at a Prague gastropub. Further along in the process, the International Communication Association (ICA) 2018 preconference 'Articulating voice: the expressivity and performativity of media practices', organized by Christian Pentzold, Kenzie Burchell, Olivier Driessens, Alice Mattoni, John Postill, and Cara Wallis, provided another important opportunity to refine our thinking. In particular, we would like to express our gratitude to Maria Bakardjieva, who provided very insightful feedback on an early version of our introductory chapter presented at that preconference.

We are grateful to Natalie Foster and Jennifer Vennall at Routledge for their support and patience along the way, and to our series editors, Mona Baker, Bolette Blaagaard, and Luis Pérez-González, for their faith in this project. Special thanks are due to Clemencia Rodríguez for letting us use her photograph for the book cover and to Aristea Fotopoulou for the excellent design work. Last, but by no means least, we would like to thank all the contributors to this book for the patience, enthusiasm, and intellectual rigour with which they have engaged with this project (and our sometimes rather demanding requests). Your work has been, and continues to be, a great source of inspiration for us.

Hilde C. Stephansen and Emiliano Treré

CONTRIBUTORS

Tina Askanius is Associate Professor in Media and Communication Studies in the School of Arts and Communication at Malmö University, Sweden. She holds a PhD from Lund University where she defended her thesis on contemporary forms of video activism in 2012. Her research primarily concerns social movement media practices, and she has worked extensively on these matters in the context of climate change and social justice mobilizations in Europe as well as ultra-nationalist movements in Scandinavia. Her work has been published in international journals such as *International Journal of Communication, Research in Social Movements, Conflicts and Change, Javnost – The Public, Media, Culture & Society*, and the *European Journal of Cultural Studies*.

Ángel Barbas is Associate Lecturer at the Universidad Nacional de Educación a Distancia (UNED), Spain, where he teaches in the School of Education. He holds a PhD in Education with Extraordinary Doctorate Award of the UNED (2016), an MA in Communication and Education in the Net (UNED), and a BA in Social Education (Universidad de Extremadura). His research topics are focused on the study of communication and education processes in both activist contexts and teacher training programmes. He has been awarded with fellowships to research in the UNED (Spain), The University of Texas at Austin (USA), and RMIT University (Australia). His most recent paper was published in the *Journal of Communication* (with John Postill).

Alejandro Barranquero is a Lecturer in the Department of Journalism and Audiovisual Communication at Universidad Carlos III de Madrid. He has researched and published extensively on the intersection between communication and social change processes, including approaches to the communication strategies of NGOs and social movements, alternative and community media, and education/

communication processes. He serves as the chair of the 'Communication and Citizenship' group of the Spanish Association of Communication Research (AE-IC), co-chair of the Community Communication Section of IAMCR, and is the founder and director of the Research Network in Community, Alternative and Participatory Communication (RICCAP).

Bart Cammaerts is Professor of Politics and Communication at the Department of Media and Communications of the London School of Economics and Political Science (LSE). His research focuses on the relationship between media, communication, and resistance, with particular emphasis on communication strategies of activists, media representations of protest, alternative counter-cultures, and broader issues relating to (media) participation, power, and public-ness. He publishes widely and his most recent books include *The Circulation of Anti-Austerity Protest* (Palgrave MacMillan, 2018), and *Mediation and Protest Movements* (co-edited with Alice Mattoni and Patrick McCurdy, Intellect, 2013).

Nick Couldry is a sociologist of media and culture. He is Professor of Media Communications and Social Theory at the London School of Economics and Political Science, and is a Faculty Associate at Harvard's Berkman Klein Center for Internet & Society. He is the author or editor of 14 books, including *The Mediated Construction of Reality* (with Andreas Hepp, Polity, 2016), *Media, Society, World* (Polity, 2012), and *Why Voice Matters* (Sage, 2010). His latest books are *The Costs of Connection: How Data is Colonizing Human Life and Appropriating Life for Capitalism* (with Ulises Mejias, Stanford University Press, 2019), and *Media – Why It Matters* (Polity, 2019).

Donatella Della Porta is Professor of Political Science, Dean of the Department of Political and Social Sciences and Director of the PhD programme in Political Science and Sociology at the Scuola Normale Superiore in Florence, where she also leads the Center on Social Movement Studies (Cosmos). Among the main topics of her research are social movements, political violence, terrorism, corruption, the police, and protest policing. She has directed a major European Research Council (ERC) project Mobilizing for Democracy, on civil society participation in democratization processes in Europe, the Middle East, Asia, and Latin America. In 2011 she was the recipient of the Mattei Dogan Prize for distinguished achievements in the field of political sociology. She is Honorary Doctor of the universities of Lausanne, Bucharest, and Göteborg. She is the author or editor of 90 books, 135 journal articles, and 135 contributions in edited volumes.

Lina Dencik is Reader at Cardiff University's School of Journalism, Media and Culture (JOMEC). Her research concerns the interplay between media developments and social and political change, with a particular focus on resistance. In recent years, she has moved into the areas of digital surveillance and the politics of data, and she is Co-Founder of the Data Justice Lab. Lina has written several articles and books, most recently *Digital Citizenship in a Datafied Society* (with Arne Hintz and Karin Wahl-Jorgensen, Polity Press, 2018), and is currently working as Principal Investigator on the project 'Data Justice: Understanding datafication in relation to social justice' (DATA-JUSTICE) funded by a Starting Grant from the ERC.

Aristea Fotopoulou is the author of *Feminist Data Studies: Big Data, Critique and Social Justice* (Sage, forthcoming) and *Feminist Activism and Digital Networks: Between Empowerment and Vulnerability* (Palgrave/Macmillan, 2017). She is interested in social transformations that relate to digital communication and data-driven technologies, and she currently leads ART/DATA/HEALTH: data as creative material for health an wellbeing (UKRI/AHRC Leadership Fellowship), an action research project that focuses on health inequalities, cultural participation and data science.

Andreas Hepp is Professor for Media and Communications at the ZeMKI, Centre for Media, Communication and Information Research, University of Bremen, Germany. He is involved the research network 'Communicative Figurations' and was co-applicant and principal investigator of the Deutsche Forschungsgemeinschaft (DFG) Priority Research Programme 1505 'Mediatized Worlds' (2012–2016). His main research areas are media and communication theory, media sociology, mediatization, datafication, transnational and transcultural communication, and cross-media practices.

Sigrid Kannengießer is a postdoctoral researcher at the Center for Media, Communication and Information Research at the University of Bremen, Germany. Her research interests are in media sociology, media practices, media activism and data activism, social movements and digital media, sustainability and media/communication, and gender media studies. She has published in international journals including, among others, *New Media & Society, Media and Communication*, and *Feminist Media Studies*.

Anne Kaun is Associate Professor in Media and Communication Studies at Södertörn University, Stockholm. Her research combines archival research with interviews and participant observation to better understand changes in how activists have used media technologies, and how technologies shape activism in terms of temporality and space. Furthermore, she is interested in different forms of digital and algorithmic activism, and is studying the consequences of automation in public service institutions. She also explores prison media, tracing the media practices and media work of prisoners since the inception of the modern prison system. Her work has appeared in, among others, *New Media and Society*, the *European Journal of Cultural Studies*, and *Media, Culture and Society*. In 2016 her book *Crisis and Critique* was published by Zed Books.

Helen Kennedy is Professor of Digital Society at the University of Sheffield. She is interested in many aspects of digital life, and is currently investigating the datafication of everyday life across a range of domains. This includes thinking about how datafication is experienced and perceived by non-experts; the visual dimensions of datafication; how data analytics processes discriminate and how to address this; how and whether data analytics can be accessible, transparent, accountable, fair, equitable, ethical, and just; and the relevance of all of this for data policy and practice. She has recently completed research into how non-experts relate to data through their visual representation (seeingdata.org) and what happens when social media data mining becomes widespread (published as *Post, Mine, Repeat: Social Media Data Mining Becomes Ordinary*, Palgrave Macmillan, 2016).

Dorothy Kidd worked for many years as a media activist and advocate, with practice in community newspapers, radio, film, video, and web-based social movement sites, as well as media democratization campaigns and projects in Canada and the USA. Her research project circulates investigations about the communication practices of social and political justice movements. She teaches media studies at the University of San Francisco.

Amparo Marroquín is a Professor in the Department of Communication and Culture at Universidad Centroamericana UCA, El Salvador. Her work focuses on cultural processes and communication. She is part of the coordinating team of the research group on Political Communication and Citizenship for the Latin American Council of Social Sciences (CLACSO), a researcher of the International Center for Studies on Frontier Epistemologies and the Political Economy of Culture in Chile and part of the board of the digital newspaper El Faro.

Alice Mattoni is Associate Professor in the Department of Political and Social Sciences at the University of Bologna. Her research investigates to what extent, and how, different types of media intersect with what politicians, activists, and concerned citizens do to participate in and mobilize on politics. She is the author of *Media Practices and Protest Politics: How Precarious Workers Mobilize* (Ashgate, 2012), and her work has been published in several international journals including *Communication Theory; European Journal of Communication; Information, Communication & Society; Journal of Information Technology & Politics;* and *Social Movement Studies.*

Stefania Milan is Associate Professor of New Media and Digital Cultures at the University of Amsterdam. Her work explores the intersection of digital technology, governance, and activism, with emphasis on critical data practices and autonomous infrastructure. Stefania is the Principal Investigator of the ERC DATACTIVE project exploring the evolution of citizenship and participation vis-à-vis datafication and surveillance (data-activism.net), and of the spin-off ERC ALEX project. Among others, she is the author of *Social Movements and Their Technologies: Wiring Social Change* (Palgrave Macmillan, 2013/2016) and co-author of *Media/Society* (Sage, 2011).

Elena Pavan is Senior Assistant Professor in the Department of Sociology and Social Research at the University of Trento. Her most recent research interests pertain to the relationships between collective action and digital media use. Within this area, her interdisciplinary work combines qualitative and quantitative research methods with network analysis, digital methods, and big data approaches. Her work has been published in national and international journals including *Mobilization, Social Movement Studies, Policy and Society*, and *Global Networks*.

Omar Rincón is an academic, essayist, and journalist. He holds a Doctorate in Human and Social Sciences from the National University of Colombia, and writes on mass and digital media, journalism, cultural politics, and entertainment culture for the Colombian media *El Tiempo* and *070*, and the Argentinian magazine *Revista Anfibia*. He is an Associate Professor at Universidad de los Andes (Colombia) and a communication consultant at the Friedrich-Ebert-Stiftung.

Clemencia Rodríguez is a Professor in the Department of Media Studies and Production at Temple University. In her book *Fissures in the Mediascape: An International Study of Citizens' Media* (Hampton Press, 2001), Rodríguez developed her citizens' media theory, a groundbreaking approach to understanding the role of community/alternative media in our societies. More recently she has explored how people living in the shadow of armed groups use community radio, television, video, digital photography, and the internet to shield their communities from the negative impacts of armed violence. This involved field-work in regions of Colombia where leftist guerillas, right-wing paramilitary groups, the army, and drug traffickers make their presence felt in the lives of unarmed civilians. *Citizens' Media Against Armed Conflict: Disrupting Violence in Colombia* (University of Minnesota Press, 2011) reports many of her findings. She teaches in the areas of media studies, communication and social change, and media in Latin America.

Hilde C. Stephansen is Senior Lecturer in Sociology in the School of Social Sciences at the University of Westminster, London. Her research is situated at the intersection of political sociology and media and communication studies, and focuses on social movements, citizen and alternative media, media practices, and the public sphere. Her work has been widely published in international journals including *Information, Communication & Society, European Journal of Cultural Studies*, and *Global Media and Communication*.

Emiliano Treré is Senior Lecturer in Media Ecologies and Social Transformation in the School of Journalism, Media and Culture at Cardiff University, UK. Between 2011 and 2017 he worked as Associate Professor at the Autonomous University of Querétaro, Mexico. He is also Research Fellow within the Cosmos Center on Social Movement Studies of the Scuola Normale Superiore in Italy, and serves as the vice-chair of the Communication and Democracy section of ECREA.

His research interests include protest movements and activism, media ecologies, citizen media, practice theory, and critical approaches to data and algorithms. He is the author of *Hybrid Media Activism: Ecologies, Imaginaries, Algorithms* (Routledge, 2019), winner of the Outstanding Book Award of the ICA Activism, Communication and Social Justice Interest Group. He has published widely in international journals including *New Media and Society*, *Information Communication and Society*, *Communication Theory*, *Social Movement Studies*, and *International Journal of Communication*. He is a member of the Data Justice Lab, which examines the relationship between datafication and social justice, and cofounder of the Big Data from the South Initiative, which interrogates the practices subverting the dominant narratives of datafication as narrated by the Global North.

FOREWORD

Nick Couldry

Media research in recent years has expanded continuously on many fronts, not least the study of citizens' media. In writing that, I respond to the call implied in the polemical first sentence of my 2004 article 'Theorising media as practice'. That started dismissively: 'Media research has been a thing of fits and starts'. It is an honour and a pleasure, a decade and a half later, to write a foreword to this exciting new collection which gives readers a snapshot of the fascinating debates about media, practice, and what citizens do with and around media, that has emerged, much to my surprise, from that short article.

The background to my polemic was very particular. My research project with Sonia Livingstone and Tim Markham, 'Media consumption and public engagement' (or 'Public Connection'), had just started. It was funded by the UK Economic and Social Research Council's Cultures of Consumption programme, led by Frank Trentmann, a historian of consumption with a remarkably wide vision. At the programme's opening conference in October 2003, I argued that there was something distinctive about media consumption, because it explored the consequences of circulating *representations* of the world *in that same world*, indeed, the consequences of people's relations to the *infrastructures* for such representations. I was loudly mocked by some cultural sociologists in the room, who I won't name. My first reaction was furious bewilderment: how little had media research progressed when its distinctive focus was not grasped even by its some-time friends in the academy? But later I recalled that, the very same day, I had a more positive experience, listening to a remarkable paper by Alan Warde, a sociologist of consumption (not one of those mocking me), who shocked his audience by asking whether 'consumption' was a practice at all.[1] Reading the written version of Warde's paper stimulated me to articulate a sense that I had had for some years, that media research was expanding radically, but without, yet, any narrative of what that expansion signified. Making sense of that expansion, and charting its future, was the task I set myself in that polemical article written in December 2003.

I did not expect my article to get much response. It was written fast, in something of a fury, which explains why it is less careful in outlining the context for its proposals than it might have been. So I was astonished when it began to be picked up, not just by media researchers but by anthropologists interested in media. Given the article's curious conception, I have no wish to defend here its weaknesses and gaps. But I am delighted that somehow I had managed to articulate what in 2003 was *not* being said about the field of media research. In fact, two things were left unarticulated. First, that media research was registering, indeed unfolding, a vast area of new practices with, and around, media. Second, that these practices simply did not fit into the academic 'box' that had been assigned to media studies: the box of 'production, text, audience' that left media researchers unqualified to ask wider questions about the role that media practices might play in shaping the world. In my presentation to the Culture of Consumption conference, I had sprung out of that box, only to be knocked back down by a few unfriendly sociologists. The article 'Theorising media as practice' explained what was at stake if we refused for our research to be confined within the pigeonhole of 'media studies'.

All of which is a lengthy way of saying that I am very excited to see published this collection of international research on media practices, and particularly practices in citizens' media, a field dear to my heart. In providing a few reflections to launch the book, I want to use hindsight to make clearer, 15 years later, what was at stake in defending the idea of *theorizing media as practice*. The stakes relate, very much, to what I left unsaid back in 2004.

The project for media research that I proposed in 2004 combined expansion with de-centring. I wanted to open windows onto all sorts of new research projects about media, which simply were invisible within the inherited house of 'media studies'. For example, research into the uses of media within institutional settings, such as schools, hospitals, and legal processes; or families' uses of media for their own storytelling within the family. As I explained in my article, some of this research was already going on, but could not be made sense of within an older paradigm of media studies. A new paradigm was essential to authorize research that was not tied to the production, distribution, or reception *directly* of media texts. What was important, as the wider domain of practice theory suggested, was to follow, in a more open way, what people *were doing* with or in relation to media. Inevitably, this involved looking beyond practices already tagged as 'media practices'. Far from undermining media research, this de-centring revealed how truly vast, and so far under-explored, was the domain where media research could contribute to social understanding.

Looking back, I realize I could have made more explicit why exactly this move – of both expanding and de-centring media research – was then becoming essential: I mean the revolution in media production and media consumption that already was emerging from increasingly regular use of the internet as a mode of connection. Yet that context was very much in my mind as I wrote the article and planned, at the same time, the Public Connection project.

Something even more important was also left unsaid. That concerned my personal trajectory towards writing about media as practice. In spite of its apparent breadth, the 2004 article was narrow in two respects. First, it was addressed very largely to researchers in the Anglo-American tradition and the broader European readership for that tradition. Second, it said nothing about my own engagement with earlier Latin American research, without which the article could never have been written, or even imagined. The clear reason for these omissions was the article's emotional freight: one researcher's *refusal* to be confined by media research's inherited place within the academy. Less explicit as a result was what I had already *accepted*, during my formation as a media researcher, that made this later refusal possible. I mean, as Clemencia Rodríguez notes in her introduction to Part One of this book, the long, rich tradition of media research from Latin America since the late 1970s. Above all, I mean Jesús Martín-Barbero's 1987 masterpiece *De Los Medios a las Mediaciones*, published in English as *Communication, Culture and Hegemony* in 1993.

As I describe elsewhere,[2] Martín-Barbero's book, read in English, was one of two books that turned me into a media researcher (the other was Daniel Dayan and Elihu Katz's anthropological rethinking of media studies in *Media Events*). What was so important for me as a novice, back in 1994, imagining the possibility of turning my life towards media research, was how Martín-Barbero *authorized* attention to the vast domain of uses for media – better, as he put it, 'mediations' – in everyday life, often far from the centres of media power and outside conventional definitions of media production or consumption. *That* was the 'media' that I saw around me in daily life, even from the distance of the UK, and *that* was the 'media' that seemed to be so often ignored by conventional treatments in Anglo-American media studies. And that, although I didn't frame it this way as yet, was media, theorized *as practice*.

Yet I never forgot my debt to Martín-Barbero. Indeed, I gave particular emphasis to this at the start of my first book, *The Place of Media Power*, while in another early book, *Inside Culture*, I expressed my debt to the wider Latin American tradition of thinking about culture and education, for example Paulo Freire. But by forgetting in 'Theorising media as practice' to mention those earlier inspirations, under the pressure of needing to say something even more urgent to me at the time, I unwittingly obscured the fact that Martín-Barbero's work was *itself* a rejection of his and many other Latin American researchers' sense of confinement within the Anglo-American research tradition, which in the late 1970s and early 1980s was even more oppressively dominant than it is today.

I greatly welcome therefore this new book's move to reconnect more recent research on media as practice in North America and Europe with this much longer tradition of researching media as practice in Latin America. Part One of this book brings back into view the hidden preconditions for the 'practice turn' in media research from the Anglo-American tradition which undoubtedly, and much to my delight, has taken place since 2004. In doing so, it achieves something more: it begins, in an important way, the long process of bringing back together the two 'torn halves' of global media and communications research (the dominant Anglo-American 'half' and its, in fact, *many* others).[3] Much more work is needed to restore to vision the much larger field of media research *across the world* of which Anglo-American research, we realize, is merely a fragment. The result, over time, may be to rewrite entirely the, until now rather parochial, history of 'media studies'.

There is so much else to welcome in this new book too. At the broadest level, it is highly apt that this book's focus is *citizens'* media, that is, media production outside the institutional centres of media and informational resources (mainstream television and radio). Apt, because the study of so-called 'alternative media' (media that resists the dominance of mainstream media power centres) was very much on my mind in 2004, having just co-edited, with James Curran, *Contesting Media Power*, in 2003. Once again, this was something that I omitted to mention in the 2004 piece, even though I called there for de-centring media research and for resisting the default functionalism that had entrenched the study of mainstream media as apparently the only research that was valid.

Research into what civic and political activists were doing with, and in relation to, media is now, as this new book amply demonstrates, one of the main areas where 'practice research' has expanded rapidly. One reason has been the internet's potential as a tool for speaking, commenting, mobilizing, and broadcasting, a potential whose importance was clear, but not yet banal, in 2004. This potential is explored from different angles in Parts Two and Three of this book, which address the contribution of a practice approach to studying social movements and to grasping the often-neglected role of video production in citizens' movements.

Welcome too are the debates on developing the implications of the 'media as practice' paradigm that range widely in this book. Let me select three from the many directions suggested in the pages that follow.

First, there is the contribution that exploring media practice in an open-ended way can make to understanding the deep role that *education and pedagogy* can play within civic and political movements. This has been a major focus in Latin American research, as Ángel Barbas and Alejandro Barranquero point out in their essays in Part One, although it has been important too in some Anglo-American research, for example the work of David Buckingham and Henry Giroux. Pedagogy, after all, is about unlocking the potential for imagining new worlds. Media practice, as a mode of re-presenting the world back to those within it, can play a crucial role here, but a role that is only grasped within a broad framing of what people can do with and around media (something hinted in the 2004 article).

Second, as the essays in Part Four of the book explore, there is valuable new work to be done in researching citizens' activism focused on negotiating the terms of media infrastructures themselves, perhaps building new or modified infrastructures. Once again, this is not new, and indeed it was the focus of the veritable explosion of research on alternative, radical, and citizens' media from the early 1990s. But the massive dominance today of a *new* infrastructure of connection – the increasingly privatized internet of massive social media platforms, search engines, financial platforms, and web-enabled apps and devices for literally every-thing – has brought to the fore new modes of activism *on*, that is *focused on the workings of*, this infrastructure. This is a shift that Sebastian Kubitschko has called 'acting on media'. Such activism was already anticipated in the new paradigm of media as practice as I formulated it back in 2004: that at least was what I had in mind when I wrote of practices 'related to, or oriented around, media', the word 'oriented' being intended to cover those who rejected mainstream media, but, in that rejection, remained oriented to its dominance. But, having just confessed to how much was left unsaid in that article, I can only be grateful that others have begun saying such things more explicitly than I did.

Finally, the essays in Part Five turn to the hugely important and growing area of citizens' practice in relation to 'data'. Data – the increasing dominance of data collection and processing within everyday life and as the core business model of capitalism – has become the new 'centre' around which, we are told, society and the economy coheres. Discourse on 'Big Data' provides the ideology to make this new form of power concentration seem natural. As a result, many researchers, myself included, have in the past half-decade followed the early pioneers of critical data and surveillance studies to orient their work to what is going on with data. The openness of a media practice approach has an absolutely vital role to play in uncovering the variety of practices relating or oriented to data, whether top-down (and institutionally-driven) or bottom-up (and activism-driven). One thing that is distinctive of the best of today's critical data research is that it is thoroughly inter-disciplinary and practice-focused. By adopting a de-centred perspective on a world ever more dependent on certain basic informational resources and infrastructures, practice research on data, as the authors of Part Five emphasize, is at the heart of the wider challenge to datafied capitalism now building globally.

A media practice approach, while it was offered originally as a new paradigm for media research, was never intended to be a complete theory of what goes on with and around media. How could any approach provide such a theory? Indeed, media practice research's emphasis from the start on de-centring, even dismantling, older perspectives that had simply assumed 'media' as the centre of what matters to human beings has a parallel in how actor–network theory aimed two decades before to de-centre functionalist accounts of the social world that simply assumed 'the social' to be a centripetal and integrative force. Actor–network theory was not a theory either, but its new paradigm of how to research the world has been all the more disruptive for that.

I am deeply grateful to Hilde Stephansen and Emiliano Treré for their work in bringing together this exciting collection of international essays, and for their introduction that follows. With this book, the 'media as practice' paradigm takes an important step in its development. In a time characterized by huge uncertainty, even bewilderment, at the directions of political and social change, the authors eloquently show that listening better and more openly to practices outside the academy is the only basis on which the academy can remain relevant to the chal-lenges that humanity faces today.

Please read this collection and let it inspire you to return to the world of citizens' struggle with new eyes.

Nick Couldry
London School of Economics and Political Science
March 2019

Notes

1 Published as Warde, A. (2005). Consumption and theories of practice. *Journal of Consumer Culture*, 5(2), 131–153.
2 Couldry, N. (2017). Descubriendo la realidad continua de mediaciones, o redescubriendo la historia de nuestro campo de investigación. In: M. de Moragas, J. L. Terrón and O. Rincón (eds). *De las medios a las mediaciones de Jesús Martín Barbero, 30 años después* (pp. 112–114). Barcelona: InCom-UAB Publicacions.
3 I borrow, with a major change of context, the metaphor of 'torn halves' from a letter Theodor Adorno wrote to Walter Benjamin in 1936: http://theoria.art-zoo.com/letter-to-benjamin-theodor-adorno/

1

PRACTICE WHAT YOU PREACH?

Currents, connections, and challenges in theorizing citizen media and practice

Hilde C. Stephansen and Emiliano Treré

Introduction[1]

Prompted by the rise of digital communications technologies, the past decade has witnessed an explosion of interest in citizen and activist media within a variety of fields, including social movement research, journalism studies, political communication, performance studies, and translation studies. Much commentary on citizen media has focused on how digital technologies enable non-institutionalized actors to disseminate media *content* that challenges dominant discourses or makes visible hidden realities, but there is also a growing interest in the social, material, and embodied aspects of citizen media. The concept of 'media practices' – and, more broadly, an understanding of *media as practice* (Couldry, 2004, 2012) – has become increasingly popular as a means of developing socially grounded analyses of citizen and activist media. Especially among scholars of social movements and media, among whom we count ourselves, 'media practices' has provided a productive conceptual hook for challenging the media centrism (i.e. the tendency to take media technologies and media content, rather than broader social practices and relationships, as a starting point for enquiry) of recent literature on digital media and protest.

In turning to 'practice' as a conceptual framework for studying the social movements–media nexus, scholars in this field have taken a cue from a growing interest in practice within media and communication studies more generally, which in turn has been inspired by the recent resurgence of practice approaches in social theory (e.g. Schatzki, Knorr-Cetina, & von Savigny, 2001; Reckwitz, 2002; Shove, Pantzar, & Watson, 2012; Hui, Schatzki, & Shove, 2016; Spaargaren, Weenink, & Lamers, 2016). As we will show in this chapter, much work has already been done to refine our conceptualizations of media practices. This book seeks to continue such efforts to define, problematize, and theorize media practices – with a specific focus on citizen and activist media. A key aim is to stimulate dialogue among scholars working in different fields and bridge previously separate traditions of theory and research. In doing so, we acknowledge the antecedents of the current turn to practice in areas such as audience studies, media anthropology, and alternative media, but we also want to give due recognition to a different trajectory. While much of the recent work on social movements and media has taken Couldry's (2004) call for a new practice paradigm as a starting point – and can be situated within a largely anglophone European and North American tradition of media and communications research and social theory – the notion of media practices also has a rich history within Latin American communication theory, as the contributors to the first section in this volume (Rodríguez, Rincón & Marroquín, Barranquero, Barbas) clearly illustrate. Although the interest in practices among Latin American communication scholars pre-dates the current 'turn' to practice in European and North American media scholarship by at least a couple of decades, there has been little take-up of their ideas among English-speaking academics. One important aim of this book is therefore to begin to rectify this lack of dialogue by introducing anglophone scholars to the Latin American tradition.

At the same time, we also want to help deepen engagement with practice theory as developed in the anglophone tradition. While looking 'back' at the Latin American roots of the media practice concept, the book also contributes to very current debates by exploring the utility of the media practice approach for getting to grips with urgent questions about agency, power, and social change in the context of processes of datafication and mediatization. Contributions to the book employ the practice approach to examine the complex relationship between activists' media practices and technological affordances (della Porta Cammaerts, Kaun); explore its relevance for understanding video activism as an increasingly important mode of contemporary media activism (Kidd, Askanius, Mattoni & Pavan); and consider the implications of expanding the media practice concept to include practices that involve 'acting on media' (Hepp, Kannengießer, Stephansen). Contributions to the final section of the book – on 'citizen data practices' (Kennedy, Milan, Fotopoulou, Dencik) – make a strong case for studying people's engagement with data and processes of datafication from a practice perspective.

This chapter has four parts. First, we provide an overview of different currents in research on media practices, identifying the antecedents of the media practice approach in different theoretical traditions and highlighting possible points of convergence between them. Second, we take stock of the current 'state of the art' of practice-focused research on citizen and activist media by providing an overview of how the concept of media practices has been used in recent literature and identifying key strengths and shortcomings. Third, we delineate future directions for research on citizen media and practice and reflect on some of the challenges facing this growing interdisciplinary field. Finally, we provide an outline of the contributions of the book.

Converging research paths around 'practice'?

The turn towards practice within media and communications scholarship is often attributed to Nick Couldry's (2004) article 'Theorising media as practice'. Couldry's intervention was significant in that it engaged explicitly with sociological theories of practice, and proposed an understanding of media as practice as a new paradigm in media research. The aim of this paradigm shift, for Couldry, was 'to decentre media research from the study of media texts or production structures (important though these are) and to redirect it onto the study of the open-ended range of practices focused directly or indirectly on media' (2004, p. 117). Couldry defined media practices as the 'open set of practices relating to, or oriented around, media' (2004, p. 117), later further distinguishing between 'acts aimed specifically at media, acts performed through media, and acts whose preconditions are media' (2012, p. 57). Theorizing media as practice thus involves asking what people are 'doing in relation to media across a whole range of situations and contexts' (Couldry, 2012, p. 37).

In developing this framework, Couldry took inspiration from the growing prominence of theories of practice within the social sciences. Conceived as an attempt to transcend the 'dualisms of structure and agency, determinism and voluntarism' (Shove et al., 2012, p. 3), practice theory challenges prevalent ways of thinking about subjectivity and sociality by 'shifting the research focus away from studying individuals, their motivations and background features primarily, towards a more in-depth investigation of "context" or the activities, the social practices, they engage in' (Spaargaren et al., 2016, p. 4). With long roots in social theory stretching back as far as Wittgenstein and Heidegger, practice theory comprises a variety of approaches. Bourdieu's (1977, 1990) theory of habitus and Giddens' (1984) theory of structuration – which in different ways sought to reconcile the structure/ agency dualism in social theory – are commonly thought of as 'first-generation' practice theories. The turn of the 21st century then saw the emergence of a 'second generation' of practice theorists, who have sought to systematize and extend practice theory by refining definitions of practice and elaborating on the relationship between practices, social order, and social change (Schatzki, 1996; Schatzki et al., 2001; Reckwitz, 2002; Shove et al., 2007, 2012; Hui et al., 2016; Spaargaren et al., 2016; Jonas, Littig and Wroblewski, 2017).

While there is no single, universally agreed-upon definition of 'practices', most practice theorists agree that they comprise some combination of embodied activities, shared understanding, and material or cultural objects. Schatzki, in an attempt to synthesize common understandings, defines practices as 'embodied, materially mediated arrays of human activity centrally organized around shared practical understanding' (2001, p. 11). In a slightly more elaborate definition, Reckwitz describes a practice as

a routinized type of behaviour which consists of several elements, interconnected to one another: forms of bodily activities, forms of mental activities, 'things' and their use, a background knowledge in the form of understanding, know-how, states of emotion and motivational knowledge

(Reckwitz, 2002, p. 249)

Along similar lines, Shove et al. (2012, p. 12) develop an understanding of practices as consisting of three main elements: *materials* (objects, technologies, tangible physical entities), *competences* (skill, know-how, technique), and *meanings* (symbolic meanings, ideas, aspirations). A practice, thus, can be thought of as 'a "block" whose existence necessarily depends on the existence and specific interconnectedness of these elements' (Reckwitz, 2002, pp. 249–250). These blocks, in turn, 'link to form wider complexes and constellations – a nexus' (Hui et al., 2016, p. 1) and this nexus, for practice theorists, is what makes up the social.

Placing materiality, embodiment, knowledgeability, and *process* at the centre of social analysis, practice theory thus offers a holistic framework for understanding the media's social significance. By taking practices as a starting point for enquiry, it enables open questions to be asked about what people are doing in relation to media and how these media-related practices combine and intersect with other social practices – thus facilitating an analysis of the broader social processes of which media practices form part (Couldry, 2004, 2012).

While Couldry's proposal, and most subsequent anglophone research on media practices, looked mainly to practice theory for inspiration, a shift towards practice had already taken place decades earlier in Latin American media and communication studies, and has since then profoundly defined the scholarly DNA of the discipline – as the contributors to the section on Latin American communication theory in this book make abundantly clear. The reasons why it was not properly acknowledged in the Global North until very recently can be attributed – as Clemencia Rodríguez points out in her passionate introduction to Part One – to the disregard for academic production in Spanish by scholars of the Global North, and also to the different conceptual labels that have been used. Indeed, media practice is not a term used by Latin American scholars, who favour instead a plurality of terms that connect to the concept of *lo popular*, which means 'of the people', or link it to the notion of 'mediation' developed by Martín-Barbero in the mid-1980s to counteract functionalist and media-centric approaches from North America. The shift towards the exploration and understanding of the practices of people in Latin America, and the interest in what media users do with the media in a variety of social contexts, had an inherently political nature. In one of the most unequal regions in the world, scholars such as Paulo Freire and his *comunicación popular* pointed to the centrality of communication, dialogue, and interaction to give voice to the oppressed, the marginalized, and the exploited in their own terms.

In anglophone media research, meanwhile, the more recent 'turn' to practice has antecedents in diverse traditions. Because of its ability to account for the broad range of practices that involve media, the practice framework has been understood to offer a solution to a perceived crisis in the study of audiences (Couldry, 2012, citing Ang, 1996). A concern with practices arguably has a long history within the tradition of audience research: the question of what people do with media formed the starting point for the Uses and Gratifications approach that emerged in the, 1940s (Couldry, 2012), and qualitative research on 'active audiences' became prominent following the cultural turn in the social sciences of the 1980s and 1990s. However, these frameworks remained focused on people's interactions with specific media technologies or texts (Cammaerts & Couldry, 2016) – an approach which became increasingly untenable given the growing ubiquity and embeddedness of media in everyday life. Around the turn of the 21st century, scholarship on media audiences thus moved away from a focus on direct engagement with texts toward 'a consideration of multiple articulations with media in everyday life' (Bird, 2010, p. 85; see also Bird, 2003). Practice theory offers a propitious framework for studying these multiple articulations. In a media-saturated world, where media practices cannot be reduced to 'individual usage of bounded objects called media' (Cammaerts & Couldry, 2016, p. 327), the openness of the practice approach seems better suited to capturing the diversity of everyday practices involving media (Couldry, 2012).

For similar reasons, practice theory has also been taken up within media anthropology – a field which has always taken people and their social relations (rather than texts or technology) as a starting point for analysing media as a social form (Ginsburg, 1994, p. 13). The notion of media practices has been widely used by media anthropologists as a shorthand for people's various everyday articulations with media; however, it tended until recently to be used in a mostly descriptive and unreflexive manner (Postill, 2010, 2017b). Sparked by Couldry's (2004) intervention, the edited collection *Theorising Media and Practice* (Bräuchler & Postill, 2010) sought to remedy this by bringing media anthropology into explicit conversation with practice theory. Exploring the value of practice theory for understanding diverse ways of engaging with media, contributors to this volume explored a wide range of practices, from uses of information and communication technologies by Norwegian (Helle-Valle, 2010) and Danish (Christensen & Røpke, 2010) families to practices of newspaper readers (Peterson, 2010) and news journalists (Rao, 2010) in India, amateur audiovisual production (Ardévol et al., 2010), and free software activism (Kelty, 2010). The practice framework has also been employed by digital ethnographers as a methodological framework for studying interrelated digital practices across multiple sites and platforms (Gómez Cruz & Ardévol, 2013a, 2013b; Ardévol & Gómez Cruz, 2014). Here, practice theory has been characterized as providing 'a bridge between theoretical conceptualization and empirical data, allowing us to extend our ethnographic account of mediation processes by including in our analysis a wider scope of relationships between uses, meanings, routines and technologies' (Gómez Cruz & Ardévol, 2013a, p. 33).

Most recently, the practice approach to media research has been taken up both enthusiastically and extensively in research on social movements and media activism, as a means of developing socially grounded analyses of activists' media practices. Much of this work has come as a response to a perceived 'media centrism' – i.e. a tendency to take media platforms, rather than broader social practices and relationships, as a starting point for enquiry – in recent literature on digital media and protest. Hence, the media practice approach has been seen to offer a means to develop non-media-centric analyses of activist and citizen media practices, and at the same time as a way to overcome communicative reductionism – i.e. 'the belief that media technologies' role within social movement dynamics is either not relevant or merely instrumental' (Treré, 2019, p. 1) – that plagues accounts on the relationships between media and protest movements to different extents. More specifically, it has been adopted to challenge technological determinism and instrumental visions of media as neutral communication channels (Barassi, 2015; Lim, 2018; Treré, 2019), and the one-medium fallacy, i. e. 'the tendency to focus on the use of single technologies without disentangling the whole media spectrum with which activists interact' (Treré, 2019, p. 9 – on the problematic implications of this fallacy see also Treré, 2012; Mattoni & Treré, 2014) in order to develop more nuanced analyses of the intersections between protest and media (see, for example, Barassi, 2015; Kaun, 2016; Kubitschko, 2015; Martínez Martínez, 2017; McCurdy, 2011). The endorsement of the practice approach in this subfield should also be understood as a reaction against the digital positivism (Fuchs, 2017) that largely defines many studies adopting big data/computational techniques to analyse collective action dynamics (Gerbaudo & Treré, 2015; Rodríguez, Ferron, & Shamas, 2014; Treré, 2019) that neglect the importance of social and political contexts (Fenton, 2016), and gloss over cultural nuances and specificities.

This recent surge of interest in media practices among students of social movements resonates with a longer tradition of scholarship on radical and alternative media that pre-dates current preoccupations with digital technologies – even if this influence is not always explicitly recognized. Although scholars in this field have not drawn explicitly on practice theory, they have arguably always been interested in practices, insofar as social relations and organizational processes have been central to their conceptualizations. Downing's (2001) groundbreaking study of radical media emphasized the prefigurative character of media activism, showing how activists attempt to 'practice what they preach' by implementing radical democratic principles in their mode of organizing. Atton (2002), similarly, highlighted the range of practices in which alternative media producers engage with the aim of transforming the social and economic relations involved in media production, distribution, and consumption – such as non-hierarchical, collective forms of organization and anti-copyright publishing. Rodríguez (2001) – whose work has been important in bridging the anglophone and Latin American traditions of media and communication theory (and will be discussed in more detail below) – coined the term 'citizens' media' to refer to media through which citizenship is enacted or performed. Her pioneering study *Fissures in the Mediascape* focused on how communication practices can empower individuals and communities, strengthen social bonds, and thus act as a catalyst for social change.

A concern with processes and practices has also been central within Communication for Development and Social Change, a heterogeneous field of practice and research concerned with the relationship between media and communication, and development and social change. During the 1980s and 1990s, communication came to be seen within this field as more than a tool for persuasion and behaviour change, and 'increasingly regarded as a process of democratization and empowerment and hence an end in itself' (Hemer & Tufte, 2016, p. 15). Hemer and Tufte (2016) propose that an 'ethnographic turn' is under way within Communication for Development and Social Change, which entails a focus on grassroots appropriations of media and the 'social practice which communication entails' (Hemer & Tufte, 2016, p. 18). Although Communication for Development and Social Change and scholarship on the social movements–media nexus have developed as largely separate fields, with the former focusing predominantly on policy and institutional domains and the latter on extra-institutional forms of action (Tufte, 2017; Barbas & Postill, 2017), recent developments highlight the beginnings of a process of convergence between them. The global wave of digitally-enabled protest that followed in the wake of the 2008 financial crisis prompted several calls for Communication for Development and Social Change scholars to pay closer attention to social movements (Barbas & Postill, 2017; Tufte, 2017). As Tufte (2017, pp. 80–105) shows, many of the concerns of social movements (e.g. with citizen engagement, organization, leadership, information dissemination, and the use of storytelling and performance) are very similar to those of more institutionalized communication for development actors, and the two fields face similar practical and conceptual challenges.

Practice, then, seems to constitute a potential point of convergence for a fruitful dialogue between the Latin American communication tradition and different currents in anglophone media and communications scholarship. While a concern with media practices is clearly not new, practice theory appears to offer a new way of framing 'old' questions that is better able to respond to the challenges raised by the growing ubiquity and embeddedness of media in contemporary social life. Its holistic character and concern with processes enable a more systematic analysis of media practices and deeper theoretical reflection on their significance in relation to questions of agency, structure, and social change. At the same time, one of the key aims of this edited collection is to root the media practice approach firmly within the Latin American communication tradition. We believe that the diverse disciplines and subfields that we have reviewed here have not sufficiently recognized or done justice to the primacy, richness, and conceptual power of this tradition. Furthermore, the political focus that defined the shift to media practice in Latin America has not adequately infused reflections on media practice in the Global North. In many contemporary studies of digital activism, citizen media, and social movements, the engagement with practice theory sometimes appears apolitical and unrooted. We argue, therefore, that the shift to media practice needs to rediscover its roots, and at the same time recognize the political urgency of this grounding. In times dominated by the ideology of dataism (van Dijck, 2014) and the flourishing of uncritical big data positivism and data centrism (Fuchs, 2017; Dencik and Milan, Part Five in this volume), shifting our gaze to the media practices of the marginalized and the oppressed is (again) a political act, and the Latin American communication tradition represents an essential 'guide' along this perilous path. At the same time, we contend that the strong contribution that the conceptualization of media practice in the Global North has brought forward lies in its ability to contribute to practice theory in the broader sociological realm, having the ambition to reconfigure some of the key conceptual and methodological tenets of social science itself. This powerful conceptual ambition does not equally animate the diverse studies on citizen media and practice, but it is undoubtedly a defining trait of this tradition. Thus, we believe that a strong media practice approach is one that learns its Latin American roots and inherently political nature, while at the same time aims to contribute to a broader project of reconfiguration of social theory and methodology.

Understanding citizen media from a practice perspective

Placing practices at the centre of our analysis has important implications for the study of citizen media. It enables us to expand our focus beyond media content and media technologies, to explore the broader range of socially situated practices that relate to citizen media (Stephansen, 2016). This broader concern with social relationships and processes was of course central to Rodríguez's (2001) original definition of citizens' media as media through which people *become* citizens. Questioning then-dominant framings of citizen media in terms of counter-information, Rodríguez (2001, p. 20) located the transformative effects of citizens' media in their capacity to intervene in and transform the established mediascape; 'contest social codes, legitimized identities, and institutionalized social relations'; and empower the community involved. Further developing these ideas, Rodríguez (2011) draws on theories of communication as performance to emphasize the constitutive power of citizens' media: 'Citizens' media are the media citizens use to activate communication processes that shape their local communities' (2011, p. 25). It is through the broad range of practices oriented *towards* citizens' media that collective and individual transformation is possible.

This emphasis on social relationships and processes has sometimes been forgotten in the subsequent anglophone literature on citizen media, which has celebrated the rise of web 2.0 and the opportunities this offered for 'ordinary' citizens to have their voices heard and make visible hidden realities (e.g. Gillmor, 2006). Particularly in the literature on citizen journalism, the significance of citizen media has tended to be conceptualized primarily in terms of changing news flows and the visibility such media can give to ordinary people's perspectives and experiences – even when this visibility and the place of citizen journalism within complex media ecologies are discussed in critical terms (e.g. Allan & Thorsen, 2009; Meikle, 2016). Where 'practice' figures in this literature, it is usually in relation to the practice of journalism, and the extent to which citizen journalists adopt or challenge the values and practices of professional journalists (Forde, 2011; Lievrouw, 2011; Wall, 2012).

However, practices, materiality, and sociality seem to have made a comeback in recent scholarship on citizen media. In the edited collection *Citizen Media and Public Spaces*, Baker and Blaagaard (2016, p. 16) define citizen media as encompassing

> the physical artefacts, digital content, practices, performative interventions, and discursive formations of affective sociality produced by unaffiliated citizens as they act in public space(s) to effect aesthetic or socio-political change or express personal desires and aspirations, without the involvement of a third party or benefactor.

Baker and Blaagaard's definition is important because it incorporates material objects, practices, and relationships – and the meanings invested in these. Recalling the definitions (outlined above) of practices as comprised of materials, competences, and meanings (Shove et al., 2012), such an understanding of citizen media chimes closely with the practice approach – even if Baker and Blaagaard do not engage explicitly with practice theory.

Our own understanding of citizen media, which underpins our conceptualization of this volume, draws inspiration from Baker and Blaagaard's definition but is at once broader in some respects and more specific in others. First, with regard to the *subjects* involved in citizen media, our disciplinary background leads us to question their focus on 'unaffiliated' (by which we read 'individual') citizens: in our understanding, such media are also used by collective actors such as social movements. A more appropriate term which encompasses both individuals and collectives might therefore be 'non-institutionalized actors' – recognizing that the boundaries between loosely formed activist groups and more formally organized actors such as NGOs might occasionally be blurred. Moreover, an emphasis on the collective dimension helps us recognize that citizen media include collectively organized media outlets such as alternative newspapers and activist-managed online platforms. Second, with regard to the *objects* involved in citizen media, we confine our understanding to material objects, technologies, and infrastructures that are external to the human body (recognizing that technologies such as microchips and wearables contribute to a blurring of this boundary). This does not mean we want to exclude the body from analysis – indeed, practice theory insists on the embodied nature of media practices – but we prefer a slightly more focused understanding of 'media'. While Baker and Blaagaard include the human body in their definition – which leads them to understand phenomena as diverse as parkour, protest marches, and theatrical performances as citizen media – we wish to retain some specificity to the term 'media' as involving (digital and non-digital) objects, technologies, and infrastructures through which meaning is conveyed. This slightly more restricted definition of media is important as it focuses attention on the interplay between human actors and technologies, and facilitates a critical evaluation of the appropriateness of practice theory for conceptualizing the relationship between structure and agency.

Current understandings of practice in the literature on citizen and activist media

As John Postill (2017a) has suggested in a recent review of scholarship on the media practices of social movements, it is possible to distinguish two broad camps: authors 'who use the notion of media practices as a methodological conduit to reach one or more aspects of a given social movement'; and authors 'who ask what we actually mean by "media practices" in the context of social movements research' and draw on the recent practice turn in media theory to find answers to this question (Postill, 2017a). For scholars studying media activism from the perspective of social movement research – which has always been concerned with questions of organization, collective identity, and mobilization – it makes almost intuitive sense to take media practices as a starting point, and much important work has been done in this vein, even if practice theory is not explicitly invoked.

For example, activists' daily media practices form the central focus of Costanza-Chock's (2014) rich study of the US immigrant rights movement, which develops the concept of 'transmedia organizing' to account for how community organizers 'engage their movement's social base in participatory media-making practices' (2014, p. 47) across a range of different media platforms. Lee and Ting (2015), meanwhile, draw on a broadly Marxist understanding of 'praxis' as critical–practical activity to develop the concept 'media and information praxis of social movements', referring to 'the communicative strategies that the activists use in the movement to seek, evaluate, produce, and disseminate information, as well as to mobilize participation in collective action' (2015, p. 380). 'Digital and social media activist practices' are also central to Boler et al's (2014) study of women's performance of 'connective labour' within the Occupy movement, which focuses on the 'the often hidden labor of women in sustaining the networked and affective dimension of social movements' (2014, p. 438) and highlights the 'gendered, hybrid, embodied, and material nature' of this labour. While studies such as these do not explicitly invoke practice theory, they demonstrate the value of ethnographically-inclined research that takes media practices as its central focus.

Among scholars who fall into the second of Postill's two camps, much has been done to further our understanding of citizen and activist media as practice. Within the literature on social movements and media, the media practice approach has proved incredibly productive as a methodological framework for bringing into view aspects of the movement–media relationship that would not be accessible from a more media-centric perspective. One of the first and most comprehensive studies in the social movements literature to adopt the media practice approach was Mattoni's (2012) research on the media practices of the precarious workers' movement in Italy. Mattoni (2012, p. 159) defined 'activist media practices' as

> (1) both routinised and creative social practices that; (2) include interactions with media objects (such as mobile phones, laptops, pieces of paper) and media

subjects (such as journalists, public relations managers, other activists); (3) draw on how media objects and media subjects are perceived and how the media environment is understood and known.

Blending social movement studies, media studies, and the sociology of practice, Mattoni (2012) contrasts a media-centric approach that selects a priori the types of media that will be investigated (for instance, citizen or mainstream) with a media-practice approach whose strength lies instead in exploring how activists map, understand, and then actively navigate the media environment with which they interact during their protest activities. Extending this analysis further, Mattoni (2012, 2013) also develops the concept of *repertoires of communication*, understood as the entire set of media practices that social movement actors may conceive as possible and use to reach social actors within and beyond the social movement milieu (2013, p. 50). Recognizing how activists' perception of the opportunities and constraints of the media environment informs their media choices, Mattoni's definition of activist media practices incorporates not only social movements' use of citizen and alternative media, but also their interactions and negotiations with more 'mainstream' media.

This wider emphasis and concern to situate media practices within broader social practices is shared by other scholars of media activism who draw on practice theory. For example, McCurdy (2011) uses a practice perspective to analyse activists' lay theories of media as part of a broader 'practice of activism'. Barassi (2015) – highlighting the interplay between media practices, political cultures, and imaginaries – explores how activist groups in the UK, Italy, and Spain utilize a diverse range of media outlets and networks. Kubitschko (2015) applies the notion of 'media-related practices' to German hackers' articulation of expertise through various communication channels, ranging from alternative media (such as their own in-house publication) to corporate social media (such as Twitter) and mainstream media outlets. Martínez Martínez (2017), in a study of the Marea Granate network of Spanish migrant activists, develops four categories of media practices: networking, collaborative organization and work, discursive practices, and participation in traditional media.

Focusing more specifically on *citizen* media, Stephansen (2016) draws on Couldry (2004, 2012) and Rodríguez (2001, 2011) to develop the notion of 'citizen media practices' as encompassing the broad range of practices related to citizen media beyond the production and circulation of media content. Through a case study of media activism in the World Social Forum, she identifies four types of citizen media practices – organizational practices, capacity-building practices, networking practices, and movement-building practices – and shows how such practices create the preconditions for distinct forms of agency to emerge: they generate a sense of individual and collective identity, offer lived experience of 'another communication', and help build solidarity that can provide a source of strength for activists operating in difficult contexts.

'Weak' definitions of practice

As the discussion above shows, 'practice' has emerged as a productive framework for research on activist and citizen media, allowing scholars to develop holistic analyses of people's uses and understandings of media technologies, and the broader social contexts within which these are situated. The concept of media practices has been used to develop rich accounts of the incredibly diverse ways in which activists and citizens engage with media in order to express themselves and effect cultural, social, or political change. As is clear from our brief survey of the literature on citizen and social movement media, most scholars who engage with definitions of media practices take their cue from Couldry's intervention, and draw on the anglo-European tradition of practice theory to frame their understanding (though there are exceptions: Barassi, 2015, for example, approaches activist media practices from a broader media anthropology perspective). Where scholars engage with the Latin American tradition of communication theory, this is largely confined to Rodríguez's work on citizen media. Among those who attempt to define media practices, these are mainly understood (following Couldry's definition) as what people do with, or in relation to, media, and empirical research has primarily been concerned to describe and categorize media practices and the various actors involved in such practices. The concept of media practices has thus served mostly as a methodological framework for developing empirically rich and nuanced understandings of citizen and activist media.

Nicolini (2017) distinguishes between a 'weak' and 'strong' programme within the broader practice turn in the social sciences. The weak programme, according to Nicolini, arises from the recognition that it is important to bring human activity to the centre of social analysis, but remains confined to reporting 'what people do', i.e. 'naming, describing, and listing practices' (2017, p. 23). The strong programme differs from this in that it 'strives to explain social matters, their emergence, change, disappearance and effects in terms of practices instead of simply registering what practices are performed' (2017, p. 23). The strong programme, according to Nicolini, also challenges what he refers to as 'localism' – the tendency to focus narrowly on local 'scenes of action' without exploring how such practices link to other practices in space and time. A 'strong' programme of practice research, therefore, involves situating practices in their broader social and historical context (Nicolini, 2017).

Following Nicolini, we might say that there is a tendency in the current literature on citizen and activist media practices to operate with a 'weak' definition of practice. Couldry's call for a turn to practice, and his 'disarmingly simple' proposal to treat media as 'the open set of practices relating to, or oriented around, media' (2004, p. 117), seems to have struck a chord because it spoke to an already widespread, almost intuitive, understanding that focusing on what people *do* with media offers an important corrective to the media centrism prevalent in studies of protest movements and media. However, the adoption of a practice perspective has not always been accompanied by rigorous theoretical work in relation to the concept of media practices.

Is practice enough? Integration of other concepts/approaches

Where people have sought to develop the concept of media practices theoretically, it has tended to be in conversation with other concepts and approaches. Usually, this has emerged out of a perceived necessity to address certain deficiencies in the media practices perspective, or to strengthen a specific aspect of this approach that are considered particularly relevant.

Mattoni and Treré (2014) argue that the media practice approach is particularly insightful for studying social movements at the micro-level, but less appropriate for grasping meso- and macro-level processes (cf. Postill, 2010). Hence, they propose a conceptual framework that integrates media practices with the concepts of *mediation* – 'a social process in which media supports the flow of discourses, meanings, and interpretations in societies' (Mattoni & Treré, 2014, p. 260, citing Couldry, 2008, and Silverstone, 2002) – for studying the meso-level; and *media-tization* – 'a concept used to analyze critically the interrelation between changes in media and communications on one hand, and changes in culture and society on the other' (Couldry & Hepp, 2013, p. 197) – for investigating macro-level dynamics.

Treré (2011, 2012, 2019), Mattoni (2017), and Barassi (2015) have sought to combine media practice with media/information ecology approaches that pay attention to the complex, hybrid, and multi-faceted nature of the media systems within which social movement actors operate. Treré (2011, 2012, 2019, p. 205) points out that these two conceptual lenses implicate – and reinforce – each other: on one hand, an analytical approach anchored in practice theory puts us in a position to ask holistic questions regarding the whole spectrum of media used by activists; on the other, a media ecology perspective sheds light on the complex interrelations among multiple types of media (old and new, corporate and alternative, online and offline, etc.). Mattoni (2017, p. 2) contends that, together, media practice and media ecology approaches are powerful because they recognize the wider range of technologies, actors, and contents with which activists interact, historicize social movements' use of technologies, and emphasize activists' agency vis-à-vis media technologies.

Kaun (2016; Chapter 6 in this volume), meanwhile, instead combines attention to media practices with insights from media archaeology (Ernst, 2011; Parikka, 2012) – an approach that 'considers the material properties that constitute media technologies as well as their temporal and spatial consequences' (Kaun, 2016, p. 30). Together, these two approaches, Kaun argues, allows for an analysis that takes seriously the 'temporal and spatial structuration' (2016, p. 31) of specific media technologies, while recognizing how activists resist, adapt, and politicize such technologies through their practices. In Chapter 6, she clarifies that 'while media archeologies lacks people, media practice research lacks an historically and material contextualization of what people are doing with the media'.

Several scholars have also sought to integrate the media practice approach with an attention to social and media imaginaries (Barassi, 2015; Fotopoulou, 2017;

Treré, 2018, 2019; Lim, 2018; Barassi & Treré, 2012; Treré et al., 2018), as well as technological myths and the digital sublime (Treré, 2018, 2019). While there is not a unified understanding of the ways through which practices and imaginaries can be combined in this line of work, these scholars point to the necessity of studying the discourses, meanings, beliefs, visions, understandings, and assumptions of activists in order to properly grasp what they do with media technologies. For these authors, investigating people's social imaginaries is thus an inherent component of the media practice approach. Some scholars have illustrated how the analysis of media imaginaries entails scrutinizing and critically deconstructing the rhetoric inherent in the grand narratives of progress and emancipation promoted by governments and corporations that often encapsulate the deployment and application of media and communication technologies for social change (Barassi, 2015; Fotopoulou, 2017). At the same time, it has been pointed out that we need to shed light on the concrete social imaginaries that activists and citizen media producers and consumers mobilize in specific contexts to make sense of the affordances provided by media technologies (Barassi, 2015; Treré, 2018, 2019). This means paying particular attention to the creative and collective aspects of imagination, underlining its capacity to act as a template for action and recognizing its powerful role in shaping the directions of social transformation.

Another concept with which the media practice approach has been brought into dialogue is that of the public sphere, which remains a core analytical framework for research on the relationship between media and democracy. Much recent work on the emergence and appropriation of digital networked media technologies has challenged both the spatial assumptions and model of deliberative democracy that underpin the classic Habermasian definition of the public sphere, highlighting the shifting, fluid, and fragmented character of contemporary public communication (e.g. Poell & van Dijck, 2016; Poell, Rajagopalan, & Kavada, 2018; Volkmer, 2014). Taking these changes as a starting point, contributions to the recent edited volume *Media Practices, Social Movements, and Performativity* (Foellmer, Lünenborg, & Raetzsch, 2017) use the concept of media practice to explore the relationship between everyday use of networked digital media and social change. Lünenborg and Raetzsch use the concept of media practice to 'capture and analyse quotidian routines of communication in their relevance for the emergence of publics' (2017, p. 23). Combining insights from practice theory with Judith Butler's concept of performativity, they develop the concept of 'performative publics' to propose an understanding of publics as brought into being through practices (rather than as pre-existing entities). Stephansen (2016) also deploys the media practice framework to develop an understanding of publics as constituted through media practices. Challenging a tendency within studies of citizen media to focus primarily on media content, Stephansen's practice-based understanding of publics emphasizes their social and material foundations, and draws attention to the range of organizational, capacity-building, and networking practices that form around citizen media.

The embodied and material aspects of media practices also figure centrally in Fotopoulou's (2017) study of feminist activism and digital networks, which combines a media practice perspective with insights from feminist science and technology studies. Challenging the tendency in feminist media studies to under-stand politics primarily in terms of representation, Fotopoulou emphasizes the need 'to account for bodies and practices when thinking about feminist and queer poli-tics, digital media and activism, not least because this is the site of immaterial or affective labour' (2017, p. 8). Drawing on Mattoni (2012) and Stephansen (2016), Fotopoulou uses a media practice framework to highlight the social, pedagogical, and political significance of media practices – how such practices are integral to the formation of political subjectivities and to processes of social world-making. Her feminist perspective on the embodied nature of media practices develops the con-cept of 'biodigital vulnerability' to account for the embodied and experienced aspects of the digital, and how shared experiences of corporeal vulnerability can be empowering for feminist and queer activists.

What becomes clear from this overview is the extremely productive nature of the encounters between media practice and other theoretical frameworks. While practice theory 'purists' might balk at this theoretical promiscuity, and others might take it as evidence of the weakness of the practice paradigm, we believe instead that these conceptual integrations attest to the malleable and dynamic nature of the practice perspective, as an approach that can be fortified and merged depending on the context and aims of the researcher – while preserving its strength as a framework for understanding the ways social reality and media are mutually shaped. Nonetheless, as we discuss in more detail below, we believe the media practice approach can be further strengthened through more in-depth debate about its theoretical underpinnings and more explicit engagement with practice theory.

Future directions and unresolved issues in media practice research

Where next, then, for practice-focused research on citizen and activist media? In this final section, we offer some reflections on future directions and unresolved challenges for efforts to theorize citizen media from a practice perspective.

Responding to urgent questions of our time

As this book aims to demonstrate, the media practice approach provides a highly appropriate and propitious framework for investigating the pressing challenges posed by processes of mediatization and datafication. If, as Couldry and Hepp suggest, we are now living in an age of deep mediatization when 'the very *ele-ments and building blocks* from which a sense of the social is constructed become *themselves* based in technologically based processes of mediation' (2017, p. 7, emphasis in original), an understanding of media practices becomes fundamental to understanding the social world more generally. A media practice perspective not only enables an analysis of the ways in which mediatization processes play out at the level of everyday life; it can also capture the practices of social actors who – becoming increasingly aware of the importance of media in today's world – 'take an active part in the moulding of media organizations, infrastructures and technologies' (Kannengießer & Kubitschko, 2017, p. 1). The term 'acting on media' (Kubitschko, 2018; Kannengießer & Kubitschko, 2017) has been proposed as a way to broaden the focus of media practice research to include not only practices that involve doing things *with* media but also practices that make media objects of struggle. As Hepp notes in the introduction to Part Four, deep mediatization entails the growing prominence of 'collectivities for media change' (Couldry & Hepp, 2017, p. 180) which see 'media as fundamental to contemporary societal formations' and seek to effect social transformation through media change. While the concept of 'acting on media' is relatively new, the practices it denotes have a much longer history, as Hepp points out in this volume. The 'acting on media' lens thus resonates with longer traditions of scholarship on 'emancipatory communication practices' (Milan, 2013) and media democracy movements (Hackett & Carroll, 2006; Stein, Kidd, & Rodríguez, 2009) – and these traditions could fruitfully be brought into conversation with the media practice approach to deepen our understanding of such activism. The novelty of the 'acting on media' perspective is that it draws attention to the political dimension of media practices and raises questions about the nature of agency in an age of deep mediatization.

Datafication is the process of transformation of social action into quantifiable and analysable data. In recent years, due to a blend of crucial social transformations connected with rapid technological advancements, we have witnessed a strong intensification of this process, together with the emergence of the big data phenomenon and the concomitant diffusion of reflections on the social, cultural, political, and economic implications inherent in the use and analysis of massive quantities of data. Similarly to the media centrism that has defined the literature on digital media and protest, various accounts on the role of data within contemporary societies have tended to adopt a techno-centric view of data, paying excessive attention to technical aspects to the detriment of practices and the human agency around and behind data. Recent literature, however, has urged scholars to relocate agency at the centre of the debate around the implications of datafication (Couldry & Powell, 2014; Treré, 2019; Milan & Treré, 2019) and pay attention to the specific material contexts, times, and places in which datafication plays out (Kennedy & Bates, 2017). This book follows and extends the path of these critical scholars. It makes clear that a critical practice approach to (big) data constitutes a powerful lens to overcome the prominent data centrism in studies of big data and algorithms, restoring the political dimension of datafication. It also illustrates how a practice approach to data can contribute to placing the study of data within broader sociological, ontological, and epistemological discussions on action, agency, and knowledge. Further, it demonstrates how investigating citizen data practices promotes a dialogue and builds conceptual bridges with other disciplines such as the sociology of social movements, the emerging field of critical data studies, feminist science and technology studies (STS) thinking, and Latin American media and cultural studies.

Need for deeper theoretical engagement

As suggested above, we believe there is a need for deeper debate about the theoretical underpinnings of 'media practice' in the specific context of citizen and activist media. Here, the growing field of research on citizen and activist media practices would benefit from a deeper engagement with practice theory. While we do not necessarily agree with Nicolini's (2017) assessment of the 'weak' programme of practice research as shallow and naïve – much can be, and has been, gained from studies that produce detailed, 'thick' descriptions of citizen and social movement media practices – we believe an important next step for scholars of citizen media practices would be to align themselves more closely with the 'strong' programme of practice research, which seeks to explain social phenomena and processes of social change in terms of practices (Nicolini, 2017, p. 23). This would entail engaging more explicitly with two core questions in social theory: the question of how to conceptualize the relationship between structure and agency, and the question of how to understand and explain processes of social change.

Thus far in the literature on citizen and activist media, the practice approach has been used primarily to account for citizens' and activists' *agency* vis-à-vis technological infrastructures and social institutions – an approach that is adopted by some of the contributors to this volume. Focusing on practices (what people 'do' with media) helps uncover the creativity with which activists adapt different media technologies to serve their needs and how they navigate complex media ecologies to pursue their aims. Intuitively, a focus on practices seems to entail a concern with 'micro' aspects of social reality – the situated, everyday practices of social actors as they interact with each other and with wider social structures – and indeed, a common criticism of practice theory has been that while it is useful for studying the micro-level of social interaction, it cannot adequately account for large-scale political processes (Postill, 2010; Mattoni & Treré, 2014). This criticism, however, has been challenged by recent efforts to theorize large phenomena and power through a focus on interconnections between practices (Hui et al., 2016; Nicolini, 2016; Shove, 2016; Watson, 2016). The privileging of agency and the micro-level by scholars of activist and citizen media is also complicated by Schatzki's (2016) conceptualization of practice theory as 'flat ontology': the idea that all social phenomena are constituted by practices, and that there is only one 'level' to social reality (2016, p. 31). This contrasts with conventional understandings of social reality as comprised of a micro level made up of individuals and their actions, and a macro level consisting of social systems, structures, and institutions. From Schatzki's perspective, a key premise of practice theory is that it offers a way to move beyond the structure–agency dualism in social theory by collapsing both structure and agency, macro and micro phenomena, into practices. Explaining social change (and reproduction) is therefore not a matter of understanding how agents succeed (or not) in changing social structures – it is rather a case of understanding how practices change (or persist) over time and how changes in some practices may lead to changes in others (or not).

The question of how to conceptualize social change is particularly pertinent in the context of research on citizen and activist media practices, as such practices often aim, as per Baker and Blaagaard's definition, to 'effect aesthetic or socio-political change' (2016, p. 16) – although their potential to do so is not given. A crucial question for citizen media research thus concerns the potential – as well as limitations – of citizen media to contribute to processes of social change. To address this question, a better understanding of the conditions under which, and the processes through which, citizen media practices might contribute to social change is essential. Though practice theory has been criticized for being better at accounting for social reproduction than it is at explaining social change – because it tends to conceptualize practices as 'enduring entities reproduced through recurrent performances' (Shove et al., 2012, p. 8) – efforts have been made by practice theorists to develop more convincing accounts of social change. Shove et al. (2012), who understand practices as made up of materials, meanings, and competences, argue that 'practices emerge, persist, shift and disappear when *connections* between [these] elements [...] are made, sustained or broken' (pp. 14–15). Offering further purchase on the question of social change, they employ a useful distinction between 'practices-as-entities' and 'practices-as-performances'. As entities, practices exist as a recognizable conjunction of elements that can be spoken about and drawn upon by actors enacting that practice. At the same time, practices exist as performances: 'it is through performance, through the immediacy of doing, that the "pattern" provided by the practice-as-an-entity is filled out and reproduced' (Shove et al. 2012, p. 7). It is in this 'gap' between practice-as-entity and practice-as-performance that innovation and change become possible. Enabling an understanding of changes in citizen media practices as resulting from a complex interplay between technological developments, user adaptations, and the meanings that people attach to what they do, Shove et al.'s framework is potentially fruitful for analysing the processes through which particular citizen media practices emerge, change, and disappear.

The question of how to conceptualize social change in relation to activist and citizen media needs to also take into account the role of knowledge and pedagogic practices. Education and pedagogy can play a fundamental role within social movements (Couldry, Foreword to this volume), and as contributions to Part One of this book show, a focus on the pedagogic dimension of media practice has been central in Latin American communication theory. Building on the pioneering work of Paulo Freire, whose 'liberation pedagogy' was based on a dialogic and participatory model of education, the Latin American tradition has conceptualized communication practices as pedagogical processes that enable people to come to consciousness about – and develop strategies for changing – their realities (Rodrí-guez; Rincón & Marroquín; Barranquero; Barbas – all Part One of this volume).

Within social movement studies, meanwhile, there is a growing body of literature that conceptualizes social movements as sites for knowledge production, and understands their significance in terms of their capacity to contribute new knowledge and ideas to wider society (for an overview see contributions by Stephansen, Chapter 10 and Barbas, Chapter 4 in this volume). Taken together, these perspectives point towards an understanding of critical pedagogy and knowledge production as central to processes of social change, and of media practices as central to such processes of knowledge production. To better understand the role of citizen media in processes of social change, we need to pay attention to both the pedagogic dimension of media practices (Barbas & Postill, 2017; Barbas, Chapter 4) and the knowledge that activists mobilize as part of their media practices (Mattoni, 2012; Stephansen, Chapter 10).

A further important question – arising from practice theory's understanding of social reality as a *nexus* of practices (Hui et al., 2016) – regards how citizen media practices might intersect with other social practices. This question, which was raised by Couldry (2004) but has not been taken up fully within the literature on citizen and social movement media, relates to the *ordering* of practices and the extent to which media practices might 'anchor' other practices by enacting new patterns of action that, in turn, prompt changes in other practices (Swidler, 2001). A better understanding of such connections seems crucial to understanding how citizen media practices might be implicated in broader processes of social change.

Wholesale adoption of Schatzki's flat ontology – and the idea that there is nothing 'outside' of practice – may be a step too far for citizen media scholars who wish to retain a critical analysis of agency and power relations. The popularity of approaches that combine media practice with other theoretical frameworks, as outlined above, suggests that most scholars in the field tend to see the practice approach as a powerful new conceptual and methodological lens, to be used pragmatically alongside other perspectives – rather than an overarching, general theory. There seems to be a sense that, on its own, the practice approach cannot fully account for the processes and phenomena we wish to study. For example, as Kidd (introduction to Part Three) and others have suggested, there is an urgent need for citizen media research to engage more thoroughly with questions of political economy, and it is unclear whether practice theory equips us fully to do so. We agree with this pragmatic and theoretically pluralist position. As scholars interested in the emancipatory potential of citizen and activist media, our primary concern is not to build theory for theory's sake, but rather to find the most appropriate tools for the job at hand. As long as it is well grounded in existing literature and operates with clear definitions, the integration of other conceptual frameworks enriches rather than dilutes the practice approach. However, we believe practice theory offers a rich set of conceptual tools for exploring how citizen and activist media might be implicated in broader processes of social change, and that media practice research would benefit from a closer engagement with these tools and with Nicolini's (2017) strong programme of practice research in mind.

The necessity of dialogue

From our review of the currents, connection, and challenges of theorizing media practice and citizen media, one issue has emerged with clarity: this approach flourishes only in a context characterized by dialogue, debate, and dynamism. Our book is an attempt to strengthen the conversation between the Latin American communication tradition where the roots of media practices are situated, and the plethora of mostly anglophone approaches that have experimented with the practice theory framework. We have seen that the strengths of the Latin American tradition and the anglophone visions can be fruitfully combined, retaining both the richness and the distinctly political focus of the former, and at the same time the ambitious programme of reconfiguration of social theory of the latter. We need both of these traditions in their richness and complexity to do justice to contemporary citizen media practices. At the same time, the book shows that the strength of the media practice approach lies precisely in its plasticity and suitability to be integrated, combined, and permeated by other fields of enquiry, including social movement studies, media archeology, media ecologies, critical data studies, science and technology studies, and other conceptual lenses such as social imaginaries, mediation, mediatization, performativity, and the public sphere. We believe that given the complexity of the current social and political context and the challenges we are facing in our increasingly datafied society, only a theoretically pragmatic and 'pluralist' approach to practice will be up to the task and therefore both *inter-* and cross-disciplinary dialogue are essential. Our book represents a step in this direction, but there is still a lot to do, especially considering the many insights in integrating a practice perspective coming from fields – just to name a few – as different as organizational studies (Nicolini), international studies (Bueger & Gadinger, 2014), and political economy that are only tangentially touched in this edited collection. Openness and pluralism are pivotal if we are to grasp the complexity of today's media-saturated society and media worlds, including a much needed intensification of dialogue and knowledge exchange between the Global South and the Global North in order not to fall prey to the same mistakes of the past (and of the present...).

Unresolved issues

While this book moves the debate around citizen media and practice forward in several ways, there are unresolved issues and areas that require further development. One such issue, as highlighted above, relates to the relationship between the practice approach and political economy. In line with Couldry's (2012, p. 57) point that 'a practice-based approach to media must stay close to political economy', various accounts of citizen media practices have reiterated the need to situate an understanding of media practice firmly within a political economy framework (Costanza-Chock, 2014; Gómez & Treré, 2014; Kidd, this volume; Rodríguez et al., 2014). However, such accounts remain rather underdeveloped, and it is still not entirely clear exactly how these two approaches can be integrated. More theoretical work is needed here that engages explicitly with the debate in practice theory about how to conceptualize the relationship between structure and agency. Such work is particularly urgent given the intensification of processes of datafication and rise of the 'platform' society (van Dijck, Poell, & de Waal, 2018) dominated by a small number of tech giants.

Another pressing question for media practice research is the extent to which this conceptual framework is useful or feasible for investigating the media practices of authoritarian and far-right activist collectives and protest movements. Thus far, this approach has mainly been applied to the study of progressive and radical left groups (and this is also the case for the contributions to this volume), but what can it tell us with regard to populism and activist groups that use media technologies to spread propaganda and manipulation on a large scale? What kind of changes and adjustments have to be made in order to adopt the conceptual lens provided by the practice framework to study these kinds of movements? Considering the increasing relevance of right-wing populist and authoritarian communication (Fuchs, 2018), these are important questions. We believe the media practice approach has potential to increase our understanding of such movements, but it raises methodological and ethical issues that are not easily resolved and that would require further research and conceptual development beyond the scope of this edited collection.

Linked to this latter point, there are unresolved questions about the methodological orientation adopted by media practice researchers. There seems to be an elective affinity between the exploration of media practices and ethnographic research (Ardévol & Gómez-Cruz, 2012; Pink et al., 2016; Sartoretto, 2016). The openness and non-media-centrism of ethnography make it particularly suited to explore media practices – and some insist that only ethnographically thick understandings of activist cultures will do if we want to understand the complexities of activists' negotiations with digital technologies (Barassi, 2015, pp. 19–20). However, given the proliferation of other types of digital methodologies and big data analytics, we are faced with the problem of evaluating how and under which circumstances we can integrate and complement different methodologies for studying media practices. Can practices only be studied by directly observing 'scenes of action' (Nicolini, 2017) – which would imply quite a narrow range of methodological choices – or can other approaches, such as computational methods, be used either on their own or in combination with ethnographic approaches, as Mattoni and Pavan (Chapter 8) and Milan (Chapter 11) suggest in their contributions to this volume?

Last – but by no means least – research on citizen and activist media practices needs to incorporate a critical analysis of inequalities that form around various axes of oppression including gender, sexuality, 'race', class, and (dis)ability (Kennedy, introduction to Part Five; Fotopoulou, Chapter 12 in this volume). With regard to the gender dimension, the media practice approach shares with feminist theory a concern with embodiment and materiality, but as Fotopoulou (2017, p. 7) points out, 'gender and sexuality as embodied practices, have been invisible in both research about communication systems and studies of collective action, despite their centrality'. Though there is a literature on feminist and LGBT movements, the tradition of social movement studies rarely analyses movement dynamics through a feminist lens. This is a serious oversight, which is also replicated in media and communications theory including the Latin American communication tradition (the scholarship of Martín-Barbero has been criticized for the lack of attention to gender as a key component of a better understanding of communication processes in Latin America; Lagos Lira, 2018). A media practice approach that aims to seriously do justice to the technological appropriations of citizen media producers and consumers also needs to develop an intersectional analysis that recognizes all axes of oppression and reflects deeply on their epistemological and ontological foundations. Engaging with second-generation Latin American scholars who – as Rodríguez points out in the introduction to Part One – are reflecting on the ways through which the shift to practice can evolve into an epistemology of/from/for the South is thus pivotal, as recent vivid discussions in both the Global North and South around datafication, design, and social justice testify (Escobar, 2017; Milan & Treré, 2019; Costanza-Chock, 2018).

Outline of the book

The topics, case studies, and perspectives explored in this edited collection provide a comprehensive introduction to the concerns and applications of the media practice approach across a diverse range of contexts and experiences related to activist and citizen media. Inevitably, given the size and diversity of this field, we had to make choices in terms of what topics and perspectives to include, which has left at the margins of the conversation some types of media activism and citizen media. For instance, the book does not say much about practices such as citizen journalism, community radio, DIY/hacker cultures, culture jamming, and artivism in general. Since these are covered extensively in other publications, and taking into account the impossibility of condensing the extreme richness of citizen media types in one single volume (but see on this the forthcoming *Routledge Encyclopedia of Citizen Media*), we decided to shed light on a wide spectrum of different theoretical perspectives, including more established topics (activist agency, social movement media, technological affordances, video activism), neglected explorations in the anglophone literature (Latin American communication theory and the connection to critical pedagogy), as well as original conceptual perspectives (mediatization and acting on media, citizen data practices). Partly due to our own disciplinary location as scholars of social movements and media, there is undoubtedly a 'bias' towards organized and explicitly political forms of media activism (over more individualized and 'accidental' forms of citizen media, such as citizen witnessing), but we believe this is justifiable given that it is in studies of these kinds of media activism that the media practice approach has received most attention. Another limitation of the book is that the empirical examples referred to by the contributors are all broadly left-leaning, radical, or progressive in terms of their political orientation. Again, this was a conscious choice on our part. As discussed above, the prospect of applying the media practice approach to the study of right-wing media activism raises complex methodological and ethical issues, which deserve more detailed and specific attention than would be possible in this volume. Given the growing prominence of right-wing populism and post-truth politics, this is certainly an area in urgent need of further research, but we also believe it is important in this context to develop a better understanding of the emancipatory potential of progressive forms of citizen and activist media. We believe the media practice approach, as applied and developed in the chapters that follow, provides excellent tools for this task.

Part One, Latin American communication theory, represents a powerful opener for the book. Its location at the beginning of this collection signals the relevance of Latin American thought in media and communication for laying the roots of the media practice approach. Clemencia Rodríguez's passionate introduction starts with a strong statement: 'Latin America did not have to wait until the 2004 publication of Couldry's article, "Theorising media as practice", to begin thinking about a shift to practice. In Latin America, the shift happened 40 years earlier.' Rodríguez clearly explains why this shift was not recognized by a Global North that rarely takes scholarship emerging from the South seriously. She illustrates the differences in the labels and definitions of practice between South and North, and shows that the media practice approach has always been a constitutive part of the Latin American scholarly DNA, as evidenced in the works of authors as diverse as Jesús Martín-Barbero, Paulo Freire, and Rosa María Alfaro, among others.

The Latin American shift to practice in media studies is carefully disentangled by the three contributions to this opening section. Omar Rincón and Amparo Marroquín's Chapter 2 represents a much-needed introduction to Latin American communication scholarship. The chapter explains the theoretical rupture, or how Latin American academics moved away from research questions centred on media to exploring people's experiences with media, and how those experiences are permeated by power – as domination but also as resistance. In order to illustrate the complexity of this rupture, the chapter articulates the main contributions of six key Latin American authors to 'the shift to practice': Paulo Freire, Jesús Martín-Barbero, Carlos Monsiváis, Néstor García-Canclini, Rossana Reguillo, and Bolívar Echeverría. Relying on their profound understanding and meticulous exploration of this rich body of knowledge, Rincón and Marroquín draw a vivid, nuanced portrayal of the Latin American contributions to the understanding of media as practice.

In Chapter 3, Alejandro Barranquero explores the historical development of the Latin American concept of praxis. The Spanish scholar documents how praxis emerged at the intersection of different fields, including culture and communication studies, liberation theology, and social movements. The chapter illustrates the influence of praxis on areas of inquiry in the field of communication research, such as community/citizen media, educommunication, and cultural studies centred on the notion of mediation(s). Barranquero follows the historical evolution of practice all the way to the contemporary line of inquiry around *buen vivir*, an epistemology from the South that emerges from indigenous worldviews centred on cooperative relations among living entities. Barranquero's chapter denounces the lack of interest among communication and media scholars in the Global North towards Latin America's media practice legacy, and invites media scholars and practitioners to learn from and dialogue with the Latin American scholarly legacy.

In the final contribution to this section (Chapter 4), Ángel Barbas explores an area of research little known outside Latin America: educommunication. He illustrates the evolution of educommunication in Latin America as a field that understands media and communication as educational praxis. Based on this framework, the Spanish scholar examines contemporary social movements and their use of media as educational practice. Barbas documents this Latin American tradition of educommunication that has functioned, since the early 1950s, as an incubator for hundreds of community media initiatives, and concludes by proposing an 'educommunicative diagnosis', a toolbox that includes Kaplún's 'feed-forward' methodology and Fals Borda's participatory action research, as an approach to examining activist media practices. Educommunication, concludes Barbas, 'allows us to build a bridge between media practices and media learning processes'.

The contributions to Part Two of the book make clear that the media practice approach provides a powerful lens through which we can examine and evaluate the complex interplay between activist agency and the technological affordances of media technologies. In her introduction to this section, Donatella della Porta illustrates how approaches to practices can help us go beyond traditional approaches to mass media as brokers for protest messages, but also to citizen media. A media practice approach, she argues, has the potential to bridge the focus on structure that defines the literature on mass media selectivity with the attention to agency that is key in research on citizen media. However, she concludes, in order to properly build theory, attention to media practice should be complemented by a focus on other elements of the communicative process such as technological affordances, norms, and content, as well as the knowledge that movements produce.

In Chapter 5, Bart Cammaerts develops a historical account of the various ways in which activists across time and space have appropriated traditional media as well as telecommunications and digital media to develop resistance practices. He shows how countercultures and activists have been able to shape communication technologies into tools of resistance to suit their particular needs across history. Cammaerts draws a conceptual connection between the self-mediation practices of activists, the communicative affordances of the media, and what he calls the mediation opportunity structure. He then identifies the affordances that enable activist mediation practices, situating them at the level of the three dimensions of temporality, spatiality, and resistance. Cammaerts convincingly disentangles the articulation between activist practices, technological affordances, and the constraints and opportunities of the political opportunity structure. 'The Empire always strikes back', he concludes, but 'new technologies will be developed, new affordances discovered, and new creative workarounds imagined, rejuvenating old practices as well as constituting new ones.'

In Chapter 6, Anne Kaun studies the media practices of social movements from a media archaeological perspective. Kaun combines media archeology and media practice theory, merging a materialist perspective with an experiential approach in order to foreground the material properties that constitute media technologies as well as their temporal and spatial consequences. Based on extensive archival research in combination with interviews with activists, she develops a diachronic, comparative study of the media practices of three protest movements that emerged in the context of large-scale economic crises: the unemployed workers' movement in the 1930s, the tenants' movement in the 1970s, and Occupy Wall Street in 2011. Kaun argues that activists are navigating a shift in media regimes from mechanical speed to perpetual flow towards digital immediacy, and from a space to a hyper-space bias. Her combined approach is able to shed light on the increasing desynchronization between media technologies and political practices that activists are facing in the present scenario.

Part Three of the book tackles the richness, along with the benefits and the challenges, of practice approaches to video activism. In her introduction to the section, Dorothy Kidd digs into the early roots of video activism and video practices, showing how the use of multiple digital video circuits has become a primary practice for most social and political movements in recent years, as the examples of the Indignados in Spain and the Occupy movement clearly testify. Inspired by Downing, Kidd urges combined analyses of social movement practice and political economy to reveal dynamics of exploitation, censorship, and surveillance perpetrated by corporate platforms such as YouTube and Facebook. Further, she suggests that practice theory would benefit by a brighter focus on the investigative protocols and the knowledge that social movement activists themselves adopt and generate. This, Kidd shows, also implies drawing much more deeply from the activist knowledges of the Global South to excavate the power dynamics of gender, race, class, and immigration status.

In Chapter 7, Tina Askanius synthesizes scholarship on historical and contemporary forms of video activism, identifying three distinct foci within the literature (video as technology, text, or testimony). Askanius demonstrates how the holistic, flexible, and open-ended nature of a practice-based approach allows us to appreciate this form of citizen media as being characterized by all three components. Hence, Askanius illustrates, a practice approach is able to travel beyond recurring conceptual dichotomies (online/offline, digital/analogue, old/new), addressing instead the 'rich ways in which these categories impinge and encroach on each other'. Relying on Mattoni's (2012) and Stephansen's (2016) theoretical conceptualizations, Askanius develops an understanding of video activism as 'the things activists do, think and say in relation to video for social and political change'. She concludes by exemplifying how this renewed perspective and novel definition offer a 'productive and holistic approach with which we might begin to fully understand all of the intertwined social and political practices involved in video activism and citizen media more generally'.

In Chapter 8, Alice Mattoni and Elena Pavan adopt a somewhat different perspective and demonstrate the utility of the media practice approach for studying the circulation of alternative media content through a single social media platform. Through a case study of the use of YouTube by the Italian feminist movement *Se Non Ora, Quando?* [If not now, when?] and its supporters, the authors make a strong case for the use of computational methods in the study of media practices. Through the analysis of metadata and the digital traces that movement actors and supporters leave behind when sharing YouTube videos, Mattoni and Pavan show that the 'mainstreaming' of alternative media content through this platform gave rise to hybrid forms of media practices that rested not only on the efforts of a core of organized collective actors, but also on the contributions of non-affiliated individuals. Demonstrating the utility of their platform-centred approach for capturing the dispersed nature of contemporary protest movements – and, specifically, the media practices of individual sympathizers beyond the core movement organizers – Mattoni and Pavan suggest that computational methods can fruitfully be combined with ethnographic approaches to develop more comprehensive accounts of contemporary activist media practices.

Contributions to Part Four examine, from different perspectives, the implications of expanding the media practice approach to include practices that involve thematizing and politicizing media and communication. Although, as Couldry himself points out in his foreword to this volume, such practices were implicit in his reference to practices that 'relate' to media, this dimension of media practice is made explicit by the notion of 'acting on media' (Kubitschko, 2018), which has been used to refer to 'the efforts of a wide range of actors to take an active part in the molding of media organizations, infrastructures and technologies that are part of the fabric of everyday life' (Kannengießer & Kubitschko, 2017, p. 1). In his introduction to the section, Andreas Hepp situates such 'collectivities for media change' within the broader context of *deep mediatization* – 'an advanced stage of mediatization in which, through digitalization, all elements of our social world are intricately related to digital media and their overarching infrastructures' – arguing that efforts to 'act on media' emerge as a response to these developments, but also that they must be seen as contributing to the making of deep mediatization. 'Acting on media', as an extension of the concept of media practices, involves broader practices of *doing* in relation to media beyond the *use* of media to communicate ideas, ranging from *practices of creation* (of alternative media technologies), *practices to improve and restore* existing technologies, and *practices of public discourse* that problematize issues of media regulation.

The two chapters that follow highlight the variety of practices that involve 'acting on media', showing how the concept can be applied to practices as diverse as repairing media devices and campaigning for media policy reform. In Chapter 9, 'Acting on media for sustainability', Sigrid Kannengießer develops the concept of 'consumption-critical media practices' to account for both media practices that use media to critique unsustainable consumption, and practices that involve 'acting on media' for sustainability, such as repairing media technologies or producing sustainable media devices. Individuals and collectivities involved in such practices thus 'act on media' by 'adapting, modifying and politicizing media technologies themselves [...] as part of a broader practice of striving for sustainability'. An important insight here is that by acting on media in this way, people seek to transform not just the media technologies themselves, but also wider society. Consumption-critical media practices have a strongly normative dimension as people reflect on the materiality of media technologies and media consumption, and seek to develop 'better', more sustainable alternatives.

Hilde C. Stephansen, meanwhile, is concerned in Chapter 10 with further drawing out the implications of the conceptual move to 'acting on media' by problematizing the role of knowledge in media practices. While all social practices involve cognitive processes, she argues that knowledge is brought to the fore by practices that entail acting on media because these involve not just the tacit know-how required to *use* media, but also analytical knowledge and imaginaries informed by broader visions of social change. Through critical engagement with the status of knowledge in practice theory, Stephansen proposes that we should understand knowledge practices as central to media practices, and that such knowledge practices can be studied empirically as social practices in their own right. Drawing on literature on knowledge production in social movements (Eyerman & Jamison, 1991; della Porta & Pavan, 2017), she develops a typology of activist knowledge practices, and demonstrates the utility of this typology for the study of media-related practices through a case study of the World Forum of Free Media, a global forum for NGOs and activist collectives that mobilize around media.

Finally, Part Five of the book explores the value of the practice framework for understanding processes of datafication and their consequences. The relevance of the media practice approach for this field of enquiry should be obvious, given that 'data practices are intrinsically communicative (Fotopoulou, Chapter 12 in this volume) and that 'today, media are data and media practices are data practices' (Kennedy, introduction to Part Five). However, as Helen Kennedy notes (see also the contributions by Fotopoulou and Dencik), the field of (critical) data studies has thus far been dominated by structural critique, with limited attention paid to people's *experiences* of datafication. This is a shortcoming, as our understanding of the role played by data in society 'needs to be grounded in specific material contexts, times and places' (Kennedy, this volume, citing Kennedy & Bates, 2017). The media practice framework, Kennedy suggests, offers a fruitful approach to understanding such contexts, as it brings together concerns with the emotional, the everyday, and agency through its focus on what people are 'doing in relation to *data* across a wide range of situations and contexts' (Kennedy, this volume, paraphrasing Couldry, 2012, p. 37). Beyond this, she argues – raising questions about the ability of the media practice approach to imagine new and different data practices – there is also an urgent need to consider how data arrangements can be improved to avoid 'data harms' and instead contribute to wellbeing and justice.

Citizens' efforts to impact processes of datafication for emancipatory purposes are the topic of Stefania Milan's Chapter 11 in this section, which adapts the 'acting on media' framework to the study of activism that places the politics of data and data infrastructures at its centre. Such 'data activism', she argues, can take proactive and reactive forms, involving both affirmative engagement with data for advocacy purposes, and efforts to resist surveillance and data extraction by state and commercial actors. What the diverse practices designated by 'acting on data(fication)' have in common is that they see information as a constitutive force in society and question dominant politics of representation; and that they are typically 'enabled (and constrained) by software (or lack thereof)'. This has implications for the media practice paradigm: according to Milan, we need to broaden our understanding of 'media practice' by placing software and the ontologies of information at the centre of our analysis. She suggests that the notion of 'data assemblages' may fruitfully be integrated with the media practice approach to help 'tease out the growing *complexity* of the landscape which citizen media practitioners inhabit today, and the dynamic relations between its different parts', thus helping us to give adequate consideration to the materiality of information and infrastructure.

Materiality is also a key issue in Aristea Fotopoulou's Chapter 12, though her concern is not just with information and infrastructure but also with 'labouring bodies, invisible human practices, and social relations and activities'. Exploring the relevance of practice theory for understanding citizens' data practices from a feminist perspective, Fotopoulou argues for an understanding of 'data practices' as encompassing a broader range of practices than those designated by the term 'data activism', including practices that are not explicitly political. This broader orientation, she argues, allows us to draw out the political dimension and power relations inherent in seemingly mundane everyday practices. Developing an understanding of data practices as communicative, material, and embodied, Fotopoulou draws on insights from feminist science and technology studies to argue that such practices should be understood through the lens of a feminist ethics of *care*. This involves 'accounting for the often invisible and devalued ordinary human labour involved in producing data in everyday contexts or analysing data within organizations', and asking critical questions about whose knowledge, experiences, and labour 'count'. It also entails the 'production of standpoints', i.e. actively seeking 'to incite readers to care for a more just world'.

Finally, in Chapter 13, Lina Dencik demonstrates the value of the practice framework not just for analysing the practices of 'ordinary' citizens but also for 'researching up'. Through a case study of the use of social media intelligence ('socmint') in predictive policing in the UK that highlights the relevance of organizational context and human agency, she argues for the need to overcome data centrism by situating data practices in relation to other social practices. We need, Dencik suggests, to situate datafication in the specific contexts where it is being played out and focus on the *uses* to which data are put. While police use of 'socmint' is on the one hand shaped by dominant logics of datafication, it also interacts in complex ways with values of professionalism, hesitation towards technological innovation, and continued prevalence of other forms of knowledge. Dencik's examination demonstrates the value of the practice framework for developing 'a more nuanced understanding of how citizens are governed through data systems', with implications for how we understand the potential for citizen intervention and resistance 'from below'. A practice approach to datafication, Dencik argues, 'shifts the focus away from data as the entry point for citizen intervention and resistance' towards an understanding of the relationship between data practices and other social practices within institutional contexts as itself a site of struggle and intervention.

Together, the contributions to this book provide an introduction to the broad range of debates and concerns that animate practice-oriented research on citizen and activist media today. By critically reflecting on and demonstrating the relevance of approaches that place *media practices* at the centre of analysis, they make an important theoretical contribution to the development of the media practice framework, and open up new avenues for research by pointing to its relevance for understanding and responding to some of the key issues of our time. It is our hope that, by bringing together contributions from scholars in diverse areas – and particularly by reuniting the Latin American and anglophone traditions of media practice research – this book will stimulate inter- and intra-disciplinary dialogue paving the way for further theoretical work and empirical research on citizen media practices. With its emphasis on sociality, materiality, experience, and meanings, the media practice framework has the potential to illuminate not only the complex ways in which contemporary processes of mediatization and datafication play out in specific contexts, but also the myriad ways in which ordinary citizens and activists respond to, engage with, and resist such processes. A better understanding of such citizen media practices, in all their complexity and diversity, is essential to the conceptualization and development of media infrastructures and institutions that place justice, equality, and wellbeing over profit and financial benefits.

Note

1 Both authors contributed equally to this chapter; names are listed in alphabetical order.

References

Allan, S., & Thorsen, E. (eds) (2009). *Citizen Journalism: Global Perspectives* (Vol. 1). Bern: Peter Lang.

Ang, I. (1996). *Living Room Wars*. London: Routledge.

Ardévol, E., & Gómez Cruz, E. (2014). Digital ethnography and media practices. In *The International Encyclopedia of Media Studies* (Vol. 7, Research Methods in Media Studies). Oxford: Wiley-Blackwell.

Ardévol, E., Roig, A., San Cornelio, G., Pagés, R., & Alsina, P. (2010). Playful practices: theorising 'new media' cultural production. In B. Bräuchler & J. Postill (eds), *Theorising Media and Practice*. New York: Berghahn Books.

Atton, C. (2002). *Alternative Media*. London: Sage.

Baker, M., & Blaagaard, B. (2016). Reconceptualising citizen media: a preliminary charting of a complex domain. In M. Baker & B. Blaagaard (eds), *Citizen Media and Public Spaces: Diverse Expressions of Citizenship and Dissent* (pp. 1–22). London: Routledge.

Barassi, V. (2015). *Activism on the Web: Everyday Struggles against Digital Capitalism.* London: Routledge.

Barassi, V., & Treré, E. (2012). Does Web 3.0 come after Web 2.0? Deconstructing theoretical assumptions through practice. *New Media & Society,* 14(8), 1269–1285.

Barbas, A., & Postill, J. (2017). Communication activism as a school of politics: lessons from Spain's Indignados Movement. *Journal of Communication,* 67(5), 646–664.

Bird, S. E. (2003). *The audience in everyday life: living in a media world.* New York: Routledge.

Bird, S. E. (2010). From fan practice to mediated moments: the value of practice theory in the understanding of media audiences. In B. Bräuchler & J. Postill (eds), *Theorising Media and Practice* (pp. 85–104). New York: Berghahn Books.

Bodrozic, S., & Paulussen, S. (2018). Citizen media practices at the digital startup Mvslim. *Journalism Practice,* 12(8), 1061–1069.

Boler, M., Macdonald, A., Nitsou, C., & Harris, A. (2014). Connective labor and social media. *Convergence: The International Journal of Research into New Media Technologies,* 20(4), 438–460.

Bourdieu, P. (1977). *Outline of a Theory of Practice.* Cambridge: Cambridge University Press.

Bourdieu, P. (1990). *The Logic of Practice.* Stanford: Stanford University Press.

Bräuchler, B., & Postill, J. (eds) (2010). *Theorising Media and Practice.* New York: Berghahn Books.

Bueger, C. (2014). Pathways to practice: praxiography and international politics. *European Political Science Review,* 6(3), 383–406. https://doi.org/10.1017/S1755773913000167

Bueger, C., & Gadinger, F. (2014). *International Practice Theory.* Basingstoke: Palgrave Macmillan.

Cammaerts, B., & Couldry, N. (2016). Digital journalism as practice. In T. Witschge, C. W. Anderson, D. Domingo, & M. Hermida (eds), *The Sage Handbook of Digital Journalism* (pp. 326–340). London: Sage.

Christensen, T. H., & Røpke, I. (2010). Can practice theory inspire studies of ICTs in everyday life? In B. Bräuchler & J. Postill (eds), *Theorising Media and Practice.* New York: Berghahn Books.

Costanza-Chock, S. (2014). *Out of the Shadows, Into the Streets!: Transmedia Organizing and the Immigrant Rights Movement.* Cambridge, MA: MIT Press.

Costanza-Chock, S. (2018). Design justice, AI, and escape from the matrix of domination. *Journal of Design and Science.* https://goo.gl/e1qitt

Couldry, N. (2004). Theorising media as practice. *Social Semiotics,* 14(2), 115–132.

Couldry, N. (2008). Mediatization or mediation? Alternative understandings of the emergent space of digital storytelling. *New Media & Society,* 10(3), 373–391.

Couldry, N. (2012). *Media, Society, World: Social Theory and Digital Media Practice.* Cambridge: Polity.

Couldry, N., & Hepp, A. (2013). Conceptualizing mediatization: contexts, traditions, arguments. *Communication Theory,* 23, 191–202.

Couldry, N., & Hepp, A. (2017). *The Mediated Construction of Reality.* Cambridge: Polity.

Couldry, N., & Powell, A. (2014). Big data from the bottom up. *Big Data & Society,* 1(2), 2053951714539277.

van Dijck, J. (2014). Datafication, dataism and dataveillance: Big Data between scientific paradigm and ideology. *Surveillance & Society,* 12(2), 197–208.

van Dijck, J., Poell, T., & de Waal, M. (2018). *The Platform Society: Public Values in a Connective World.* Oxford: Oxford University Press.

Downing, J. D. H. (2001). *Radical Media: Rebellious Communication and Social Movements.* London: Sage.

Ernst, W. (2011). Media archaeography: method and machine versus history and narrative of media. In E. Huhtamo & J. Parikka (eds), *Media Archaeology: Approaches, Applications, and Implications* (pp. 239–255). Berkeley, CA: University of California Press.

Escobar, A. (2017). *Designs for the Pluriverse: Radical Interdependence, Autonomy, and the Making of Worlds.* Durham, NC: Duke University Press.

Eyerman, R., & Jamison, A. (1991). *Social Movements: A Cognitive Approach.* Cambridge: Polity.

Fenton, N. (2016). *Digital, Political, Radical.* New York: Wiley.

Foellmer, S., Lünenborg, M., & Raetzsch, C. (eds) (2017). *Media Practices, Social Movements, and Performativity: Transdisciplinary Approaches.* London: Routledge.

Forde, S. (2011). *Challenging the News: The Journalism of Alternative and Community Media.* London: Macmillan Education.

Fotopoulou, A. (2017). *Feminist Activism and Digital Networks: Between Empowerment and Vulnerability.* Basingstoke: Palgrave Macmillan.

Fuchs, C. (2017). *Social Media: A Critical Introduction.* London: Sage.

Fuchs, C. (2018). *Digital Demagogue: Authoritarian Capitalism in the Age of Trump and Twitter.* London: Pluto Press.

Gerbaudo, P., & Treré, E. (2015). In search of the "we" of social media activism: Introduction to the special issue on social media and protest identities. *Information, Communication & Society*, 18, 865–871.

Giddens, A. (1984). *The Constitution of Society: Outline of the Theory of Structuration.* Cambridge: Polity.

Gillmor, D. (2006). *We the Media: Grassroots Journalism by the People, for the People.* Sebastopol, CA: O'Reilly Media.

Ginsburg, F. (1994). Culture/media: a (mild) polemic. *Anthropology Today*, 10(2), 5–15.

Gómez, R., & Treré, E. (2014). The #YoSoy132 movement and the struggle for media democratization in Mexico. *Convergence*, 20(4), 496–451.

Gómez Cruz, E., & Ardévol, E. (2013a). Ethnography and the field in media(ted) studies: a practice theory approach. *Westminster Papers in Communication and Culture*, 9(3), 29–46.

Gómez Cruz, E., & Ardévol, E. (2013b). Performing photography practices in everyday life: some ethnographic notes on a Flickr group. *Photographies*, 6(1), 35–44.

Hackett, R. A., & Carroll, W. K. (2006). *Remaking Media: The Struggle to Democratize Public Communication.* London: Routledge.

Hemer, O., & Tufte, T. (2016). *Voice Matter: Communication, Development and the Cultural Return.* Gothenburg: Nordicom.

Helle-Valle, J. (2010). Language-games, in/dividuals and media uses: what a practice perspective should imply for media studies. In B. Bräuchler & J. Postill (eds), *Theorising Media and Practice.* New York: Berghahn Books.

Hui, A., Schatzki, T., & Shove, E. (2016). *The Nexus of Practices: Connections, Constellations, Practitioners.* Abingdon: Taylor & Francis.

Jonas, M., Littig, B., & Wroblewski, A. (2017). *Methodological Reflections on Practice Oriented Theories.* Cham: Springer International.

Kannengießer, S., & Kubitschko, S. (2017). Acting on media: influencing, shaping and (re) configuring the fabric of everyday life. *Media and Communication*, 5(3), 1–4.

Kaun, A. (2016). *Crisis and Critique: A Brief History of Media Participation in Times of Crisis.* London: Zed Books.

Kelty, C. (2010). Theorising the practices of free software: The Movement. In B. Bräuchler & J. Postill (eds), *Theorising Media and Practice.* New York: Berghahn Books.

Kennedy, H., & Bates, J. (2017). Data power in material contexts: Introduction. *Television & New Media*, 18(8), 701–705.

Kitchin, R., & Lauriault, T. (2015a). Small data in the era of big data. *GeoJournal*, 80(4), 463–475.

Kubitschko, S. (2015). Hackers' media practices: demonstrating and articulating expertise as interlocking arrangements. *Convergence*, 21(3), 388–402.

Kubitschko, S. (2018). Acting on media technologies and infrastructures: expanding the media as practice approach. *Media, Culture & Society*, 40(4), 629–635.

Lagos Lira, C. (2018). Jesús Martín Barbero and communication studies. In *Oxford Research Encyclopedia of Communication*. Oxford: Oxford University Press.

Lee, A. Y. L., & Ting, K. W. (2015). Media and information praxis of young activists in the Umbrella Movement. *Chinese Journal of Communication*, 8(4), 376–392.

Lievrouw, L. (2011). *Alternative and Activist New Media*. Cambridge: Polity.

Lim, M. (2018). Roots, routes, and routers: communications and media of contemporary social movements. *Journalism & Communication Monographs*, 20(2), 92–136.

Lünenborg, M., & Raetzsch, C. (2017). From public sphere to performative publics: developing media practice as an analytic model. In S. Foellmer, M. Lünenborg, & C. Raetzsch (eds), *Media Practices, Social Movements, and Performativity: Transdisciplinary Approaches* (pp. 13–35). London: Routledge.

Martínez Martínez, M. J. (2017). Prácticas mediáticas y movimientos sociales: el activismo trasnacional de Marea Granate. *Index.Comunicación*, 7(3), 31–50. Retrieved from http://journals.sfu.ca/indexcomunicacion/index.php/indexcomunicacion/article/view/340/305

Mattoni, A. (2012). *Media Practices and Protest Politics: How Precarious Workers Mobilise*. Abingdon: Taylor & Francis.

Mattoni, A. (2013). Repertoires of communication in social movement processes. In B. Cammaerts, A. Mattoni, & P. McCurdy (eds), *Mediation and Protest Movements* (pp. 39–56). Bristol: Intellect.

Mattoni, A. (2017). A situated understanding of digital technologies in social movements. Media ecology and media practice approaches. *Social Movement Studies*, 16(4), 494–505.

Mattoni, A., & Treré, E. (2014). Media practices, mediation processes, and mediatization in the study of social movements. *Communication Theory*, 24(3), 252–271.

McCurdy, P. (2011). Theorizing 'lay theories of media': a case study of the Dissent! Network at the, 2005 Gleneagles G8 Summit. *International Journal of Communication*, 5, 619–638.

Meikle, G. (ed.) (2016). *The Routledge Companion to Media and Activism*. London: Routledge.

Milan, S. (2013). *Social Movements and their Technologies: Wiring Social Change*. Basingstoke: Palgrave Macmillan.

Milan, S., & Treré, E. (2019). Big Data from the South(s): beyond data universalism. *Television and New Media*, in press.

Nicolini, D. (2016). Is small the only beautiful? Making sense of 'large phenomena' from a practice-based perspective. In A. Hui, T. Schatzki, & E. Shove (eds), *The Nexus of Practices: Connections, Constellations, Practitioners*. London: Routledge.

Nicolini, D. (2017). Practice theory as a package of theory, method and vocabulary: affordances and limitations. In M. Jonas, B. Littig, & A. Wroblewski (eds), *Methodological Reflections on Practice Oriented Theories* (pp. 19–34). Cham: Springer International.

Parikka, J. (2012). *What is Media Archaeology?* Cambridge: Polity Press.

Peterson, M. A. (2010). 'But it is my habit to read The Times': metaculture and practice in the reading of Indian newspapers. In B. Bräuchler & J. Postill (eds), *Theorising Media and Practice*. New York: Berghahn Books.

Pink, S., Horst, H., Postill, J., Hjorth, L., Lewis, T., & Tacchi, J. (2016) *Digital Ethnography: Principles and Practice*. London: Sage.

Poell, T., & van Dijck, J. (2016). Constructing public space: global perspectives on social media and popular contestation. *International Journal of Communication*, 10, 226–234.

Poell, T., Rajagopalan, S., & Kavada, A. (2018). Publicness on platforms: tracing the mutual articulation of platform architectures and user practices. In Z. Papacharissi (ed.), *A Networked Self and Platforms, Stories, Connections* (pp. 43–58). New York: Routledge.

della Porta, D., & Pavan, E. (2017). Repertoires of knowledge practices: social movements in times of crisis. *Qualitative Research in Organizations and Management*, 12(4), 297–314.

Postill, J. (2010). Introduction: theorising media and practice. In B. Bräuchler & J. Postill (eds), *Theorising Media and Practice* (pp. 1–32). New York: Berghahn Books.

Postill, J. (2017a). The media practices of social movements: a critical overview of the literature. Lecture at the Summer School on Media in Political Participation and Mobilization, Centre on Social Movement Studies, Institute of Humanities and Social Sciences, Scuola Normale Superiore, Florence. Retrieved from https://johnpostill.com/2017/06/23/the-media-practices-of-social-movements-a-critical-overview-of-the-literature/

Postill, J. (2017b). *The Rise of Nerd Politics: Digital Activism and Political Change*. London: Pluto Press.

Rao, U. (2010). Embedded/embedding media practices and cultural production. In B. Bräuchler & J. Postill (eds), *Theorising Media and Practice*. New York: Berghahn Books.

Reckwitz, A. (2002). Toward a theory of social practices: a development in culturalist theorizing. *European Journal of Social Theory*, 5(2), 243–263.

Rodríguez, C. (2001). *Fissures in the Mediascape: An International Study of Citizens' Media*. Cresskill, NJ: Hampton Press.

Rodríguez, C. (2011). *Citizens' Media against Armed Conflict: Disrupting Violence in Colombia*. Minneapolis, MN: University of Minnesota Press.

Rodríguez, C., Ferron, B., & Shamas, K. (2014). Four challenges in the field of alternative, radical and citizens' media research. *Media, Culture & Society*, 36(2), 150–166.

Sartoretto, P. (2016). Exploring inclusive ethnography as a methodology to account for multiple experiences. In S. Kubitschko & A. Kaun (eds), *Innovative Methods in Media and Communication Research* (pp. 189–203). Cham: Springer International.

Schatzki, T. R. (1996). *Social Practices: A Wittgensteinian Approach to Human Activity and the Social*. Cambridge: Cambridge University Press.

Schatzki, T. R. (2001). Introduction: practice theory. In T. R. Schatzki, K. Knorr Cetina, & E. von Savigny (eds), *The Practice Turn in Contemporary Theory* (pp. 1–14). London: Routledge.

Schatzki, T. (2016). Practice theory as flat ontology. In G. Spaargaren, D. Weenink, & M. Lamers (eds), *Practice Theory and Research: Exploring the Dynamics of Social Life* (pp. 28–42). Abingdon: Taylor & Francis.

Schatzki, T. R., Knorr Cetina, K., & von Savigny, E. (eds) (2001). *The Practice Turn in Contemporary Theory*. London: Routledge.

Shove, E. (2016). Matters of practice. In A. Hui, T. Schatzki, & E. Shove (eds), *The Nexus of Practices: Connections, Constellations, Practitioners*. London: Routledge.

Shove, E., Watson, M., Hand, M., & Ingram, J. (eds) (2007). *The Design of Everyday Life*. Oxford: Berg.

Shove, E., Pantzar, M., & Watson, M. (2012). *The Dynamics of Social Practice: Everyday Life and How it Changes*. London: Sage.

Silverstone, R. (2002). Complicity and collusion in the mediation of everyday life. *New Literary History*, 33(4), 761–780.

Spaargaren, G., Weenink, D., & Lamers, M. (2016). *Practice Theory and Research: Exploring the Dynamics of Social Life*. Abingdon: Taylor & Francis.

Stein, L., Kidd, D., & Rodríguez, C. (2009). *Making our Media: Global Initiatives toward a Democratic Public Sphere. Vol. 2: National and Global Movements for Democratic Communication.* Cresskill, NJ: Hampton Press.

Stephansen, H. C. (2016). Understanding citizen media as practice: agents, processes, publics. In M. Baker & B. Blaagaard (eds), *Citizen Media and Public Spaces: Diverse Expressions of Citizenship and Dissent* (pp. 25–41). London: Routledge.

Swidler, A. (2001). What anchors cultural practices. In T. R. Schatzki, K. Knorr Cetina, & E. von Savigny (eds), *The Practice Turn in Contemporary Theory*. London: Routledge.

Treré, E. (2011). Social movements and alternative media. The "anomalous wave" movement and the ambivalences of the online protest ecology. PhD thesis, University of Udine, Italy.

Treré, E. (2012). Social movements as information ecologies: exploring the coevolution of multiple Internet technologies for activism. *International Journal of Communication*, 6, 2359–2377.

Treré, E. (2018). The sublime of digital activism: hybrid media ecologies and the new grammar of protest. *Journalism & Communication Monographs*, 20(2), 137–148.

Treré, E. (2019). *Hybrid Media Activism: Ecologies, Imaginaries, Algorithms*. London and New York: Routledge.

Treré, E., Jeppesen, S., & Mattoni, A. (2017). Comparing digital protest media imaginaries: anti-austerity movements in Spain, Italy & Greece. *Triple C*, 15(2), 404–422.

Tufte, T. (2017). *Communication and Social Change: A Citizen Perspective*. New York: Wiley.

Volkmer, I. (2014). *The Global Public Sphere: Public Communication in the Age of Reflective Interdependence*. New York: Wiley.

Wall, M. (2012). *Citizen Journalism: Valuable, Useless, Or Dangerous?* Brussels: International Debate Education Association.

Watson, M. (2016). Placing power in practice theory. In A. Hui, T. Schatzki, & E. Shove (eds), *The Nexus of Practices: Connections, Constellations, Practitioners*. London: Routledge.

PART I

Latin American communication theory

INTRODUCTION

Clemencia Rodríguez

Since the 1980s, 'the practice paradigm' has been central to the work of Latin American media and cultural studies scholars. Latin America did not have to wait until the 2004 publication of Couldry's (2004) article, 'Theorising media as practice', to begin thinking about 'a shift to practice'. In Latin America, the shift happened 40 years earlier. The question of why the Latin American shift failed to cross the Atlantic or the Mexico–US border has predictable answers. Scholars in the Global North rarely take scholarship emerging from the Global South seriously, and English-speaking academics seldom read studies published in Spanish. Nor do academics from the Global North frequently attend Latin American media studies conferences, such as the Latin American Federation of Faculties of Communication (FELAFACS) or the Latin American Communication Researchers Association (ALAIC). There are exceptions, though. Nick Couldry immersed himself in the work of Jesús Martín-Barbero early on (in fact, the introductory chapter of Couldry's *Place of Media Power* states: 'We need, as Jesús Martín-Barbero has proposed, to place the media in a wider historical "field of mediations" (1993: 139)' (Couldry, 2000, p. 7). More importantly, Couldry learned Spanish to gain more in-depth access to scholarly work coming from Latin America. Couldry took his commitment to Latin American scholarship so seriously that, after more than three years of Spanish instruction in London, in 2017 he was able to present a paper about Jesús Martín-Barbero in Spanish at the International Association for Media and Communication Research (IAMCR) conference held in Cartagena, Colombia.

Three of the five authors in this section are Latin American (counting myself); we were trained in Latin American universities, in communication and media studies schools. Omar and I were freshmen together at Universidad Javeriana in Bogotá in 1979, where we were fed Freire and Gramsci from day one. Jesús Martín-Barbero occasionally visited our campus; our professors assigned Martín-

Barbero's then-unpublished writings in our courses on communication theory, media and society, and research methods. Works such as *Prácticas de comunicación en la cultura popular: mercados, plazas, cementerios y espacios de ocio* [Communication practices in popular culture: markets, squares, cemeteries and leisure spaces] were photocopied time and again by professors and students; the conditions could be precarious, but the intellectual activity was not (the library at Universidad Javeriana stores an exceptional collection of these photocopied texts, authored by Martín-Barbero and many other Latin American authors). By the time we graduated with bachelor degrees in media studies, 'the shift to practice' was part of our scholarly DNA. We have never studied media any other way. Omar and I represent that first generation of Latin American media scholars who were driven by the need to explore 'how media are embedded in the interlocking fabric of social and cultural life' (Couldry, 2004, p. 129). Amparo Marroquín represents the second generation. Marroquín completed a doctoral degree in philosophy with a dissertation focused on the work of Jesús Martín-Barbero. This second generation is pushing the boundaries of what it means to *pensar desde el Sur* [think from the South]; that is, how the shift to practice can evolve into an epistemology of the South, from the South, and for the South, anchored in the realignments initiated by Freire, Martín-Barbero, Rosa María Alfaro, Néstor García Canclini, and others.

Among Latin American media scholars, 'the practice paradigm' does not have the same labels as those used by scholars in the Global North. 'Media practice' is not a term used by Latin American media scholars. Instead, in the 1980s, Latin American research and academic circles began using terms such as *práctica popular* [popular practice], *prácticas de la cultura popular* [popular culture practices], or *prácticas de la comunicación popular* [popular communication practices] very similarly to the ways Stephansen and Treré define 'media practice' in this volume's introduction. In the Latin American context, *popular* means 'of the people,' and has nothing to do with 'pop culture' or entertainment industries. Thus, *práctica popular, prácticas de la cultura popular*, and *prácticas de la comunicación popular* refer to people's activities and agency as they use and interact with technologies and create their own representations and meanings. Over the years, these terms evolved into *lo popular*, and the term 'practice' was mostly dropped. In the mid-1980s, Martín-Barbero invited us to leave behind the smoke screen of studying media as 'texts plus audiences' and to explore instead 'mediations', or the material and symbolic performances of people using media. In light of this, I invite English readers of this section on Latin American communication theory to think 'media practice' when Marroquín and Rincón use the terms 'popular', 'mediation', or '*lo popular*'.

How new is the new media practice theory paradigm? In 1982, when I was a second-year college student in the School of Communication at Universidad Javeriana, one of the plenary speakers for International Communication Week was a professor from Universidad del Valle named Jesús Martín-Barbero. Addressing a hall full of students and faculty, Martín-Barbero told us about the 'epistemological shiver' he recently experienced while watching a Mexican film at a local theatre in Cali. Martín-Barbero had finished a dissertation in semiotics from the University of

Louvain in Belgium. He came to the field of media studies as a philosopher and a semiotician, and as such, he approached the study of media as texts, discrete social phenomena to be dissected in search for meaning. However, these theoretical frameworks proved limiting when trying to understand what Colombian audiences were *doing* with *La ley del monte* [*The Law of the Mountain*] (Mariscal, 1976), the Mexican film that had taken Colombians by storm. In the theatre, surrounded by audiences who interacted with the text in ways that spilled over his European training in semiotics, Martín-Barbero's 'epistemological shiver' led him to realize that a shift to practice was necessary. Five years later, in 1987, Jesús Martín-Barbero published *De los medios a las mediaciones* [published in English in 1993 as *Communication, Culture and Hegemony: From the Media to Mediations*], a book that sanctioned and documented the shift toward practice in Latin American media studies. In 2017, after cancelling his keynote presentation at the IAMCR conference, to be held that year in Cartagena, Colombia, Martín-Barbero wrote a letter to Amparo Cadavid, the main organizer of the conference. In his letter, Martín-Barbero mentions Foucault's analysis of art as the 'practice of seeing'; he reminds us of the need for 'a nocturnal map' to understand not things or texts, but 'situations as constituted by subjects and mediations'. We need a map to explore the practices of media users, practices constituted by their political cultures, resistances, complicity with domination, and popular aesthetics. Martín-Barbero says that his mode of thinking emerged at the intersection between the work of Antonio Gramsci and Paulo Freire.

As I mentioned, chapters of Freire's *Pedagogy of the Oppressed* (1970) and *Education, The Practice of Freedom* (1976) were required reading in our media theory courses. The original Portuguese version of *Pedagogy of the Oppressed* was published in Brazil in 1968, at a time when the Cold War was establishing military dictatorships and brutal regimes around the world and making Latin America one of its main battlegrounds. Freire's book, like Martín-Barbero's, was a trailblazer, marking the emergence of a new Latin American way of thinking about communication, language, and power. According to Freire, the impact of poverty, injustice, and oppression extends well beyond issues of access to material resources, plunging individuals and communities into states of isolation that he called 'a culture of silence' (Freire, 1970). According to Freire, people subjected to experiences of oppression and exploitation lose their own voices and learn to mimic the voice of domination; they internalize stigmatized notions of themselves and their environment; and they adopt visions of their neighbourhoods and communities coined by the powerful. Freire's analysis shifted the focus from issues of class identity or simplistic political economy to the centrality of communication and interaction. From Freire we learned that interaction constitutes identities, not the other way around. We read Freire as a brutal indictment of our societies and the economic and political systems that bred the most unequal region in the world, but also as a breath of fresh air. Freire opened a new door to social change and social justice, and it was a door that did not patronize the poor with notions of 'false consciousness'. Instead, Freire proposed communication and dialogue as critical tools to break through the culture of silence; he thought that people would be able to overcome alienation, isolation, and silence by appropriating their own languages and using this new fluency 'to speak the world in their own terms'. Freire's ideal communication – known in Latin America as *comunicación popular* [popular communication] – transforms people into subjects who acquire their own languages, use those languages to re-signify their reality, and develop ways to move those interpretations of reality into the public sphere. According to Freire, popular communication can transform people from passive objects of others into self-determining subjects, individuals with agency. The ultimate goal of *comunicación popular* is 'conscientization', a process that begins and ends in practice – from language to action.

The three chapters in this section, by Rincón and Marroquín, Barranquero, and Barbas, reflect the Latin American shift to practice in media studies. Omar Rincón and Amparo Marroquín's 'The Latin American *lo popular* as a theory of communication' (Chapter 2) constitutes an excellent introduction to Latin American communication scholarship. The chapter explains the theoretical rupture, or how Latin American academics moved away from research questions centred on media to exploring people's experiences with media and how those experiences are permeated by power – as domination and also as resistance. This chapter by Rincón and Marroquín embodies the authors' profound understanding and meticulous exploration of this body of knowledge. It articulates the main contributions of six Latin American authors to 'the shift to practice', including Freire, Martín-Barbero, Monsiváis, Canclini, Reguillo, and Echeverría.

In Chapter 3, Alejandro Barranquero explores the historical development of the Latin American concept of praxis. Barranquero documents how praxis emerged from different fields, including culture and communication studies, liberation theology, and social movements. The chapter explains the influence of praxis on areas of inquiry in the field of communication research, such as community/citizens' media, educommunication, and cultural studies centred on the notion of mediations. Barranquero follows the historical evolution of practice all the way to today's line of inquiry around *buen vivir* [good living], an epistemology from the South that emerges from indigenous worldviews centred on cooperative relations among living entities. Barranquero's chapter denounces the lack of interest among communication and media scholars in the Global North towards Latin America's media practice legacy, and invites media scholars and practitioners to learn from the Latin American scholarly legacy.

Finally, Ángel Barbas contributes a chapter on an area of research little known outside Latin America: educommunication. In Chapter 4, Barbas explains the evolution of educommunication in Latin America as a field that understands media and communication as educational praxis. Based on this framework, Barbas examines contemporary social movements and their use of media as educational practice. Barbas documents this Latin American tradition of educommunication that has functioned, since the early 1950s, as an incubator for hundreds of community media initiatives, and concludes with an educommunication toolbox to be applied in analyses of activist media practices. The toolbox includes Kaplún's 'feed-forward' methodology and Fals Borda's participatory action research.

These three chapters are a solid introduction to the Latin American scholarly tradition of media, communication, and cultural studies. The section makes an important contribution to a field that has been greatly neglected in the Global North and rarely circulates in English publishing circles. For readers who want to explore this field further, I recommend Atwood & McAnany's *Communication and Latin American Society* (1986), Yúdice, Franco, & Flores's *On Edge: The Crisis of Contemporary Latin American Culture* (1992), García Canclini's *Transforming Modernity: Popular Culture in Mexico* (1992), and Martín-Barbero's *Communication, Culture and Hegemony: From the Media to Mediations* (1993). We wait with excitement for the soon-to-be-published *Media Cultures in Latin America: Key Concepts and New Debates* edited by Juan Salazar and Anna Pertierra. The two editors selected a group of renowned Latin American scholars to curate sections on Mediations, Epistemologies of the South, Popular culture, Citizens' media, and Memory and human rights, among others. This book, which should have been published 20 years ago, will finally do justice to Latin America's scholarly contribution to how we understand the complex interaction between people, media, culture, and power.

References

Atwood, R., & McAnany, E. (1986). *Communication and Latin American Society: Trends in Critical Research, 1960–1985.* Madison, WI: University of Wisconsin Press.

Couldry, N. (2000). *The Place of Media Power: Pilgrims and Witnesses of the Media Age.* London: Routledge.

Couldry, N. (2004). Theorising media as practice. *Social Semiotics*, 14(2), 115–132.

Freire, P. (1970). *Pedagogy of the Oppressed.* New York: Herder and Herder.

Freire, P. (1976). *Education, The Practice of Freedom.* London: Writers and Readers Publishing Cooperative.

García Canclini, N. (1992). *Transforming Modernity: Popular Culture in Mexico.* Austin, TX: University of Texas Press.

Mariscal, A. (dir.) (1976). *La ley del monte.* https://www.imdb.com/title/tt0308503/

Martín-Barbero, J. (1981). Prácticas de comunicación en la cultura popular: mercados, plazas, cementerios y espacios de ocio. In M. Simpson Grinberg (ed.), *Comunicación alternativa y cambio social.* Mexico City: Universidad Nacional Autónoma de México (UNAM).

Martín-Barbero, J. (1987). *De los medios a las mediaciones. Comunicación, cultura y hegemonía.* Barcelona: Gustavo Gili.

Martín-Barbero, J. (1993). *Communication, Culture and Hegemony: From the Media to the Mediations.* Newbury Park, NJ: Sage.

Salazar, J., & Pertierra, A. (forthcoming). *Media Cultures in Latin America: Key Concepts and New Debates.* London: Routledge, in press.

Yúdice, G., Franco, J., & Flores, J. (1992). *On Edge: The Crisis of Contemporary Latin American Culture.* Minneapolis, MN: University of Minnesota Press.

2

THE LATIN AMERICAN *LO POPULAR* AS A THEORY OF COMMUNICATION

Ways of seeing communication practices

Omar Rincón and Amparo Marroquín

Introduction

Stuart Hall once said in an interview that the feeling of living in a colonialized space is like feeling that important things happen somewhere else, in a distant centre. Everything that is important is said far away from our place. This feeling brought about new reflections in some fields of communication in Latin America. The Latin American studies that gave birth to reflections on the relations between mass media, culture, and politics inherited the anglophone tradition that was born in another place, in another language. Therefore, in the 1950s and 1960s research studies focused on a media-centred paradigm that highlighted the power of the media through the effect theory that was in line with the empirical approaches of Lazarsfeld and Berelson (Lazarsfeld, Berelson, & Gaudet 1948), Lasswell's behaviourism (Smith, Lasswell, & Casey, 1946), and Elihu Katz's proposal of uses and gratifications (Katz & Lazarsfeld, 1956). We were also enthusiastic about the European Marxist and structuralist critical thinking of Adorno (1944) and the Frankfurt School, on the so-called Cultural Industry and the ways of building mass culture and turning culture into merchandise, as well as the ideological denunciations of the media empire made by French scholar Armand Mattelart (Mattelart & Dorfman, 1971). Finally, we were trapped in Eco's (1965) idea of dividing media scholars into two groups: the apocalyptic and the integrated. In all cases, media were considered almighty, and addressees were passive and unprotected against the power of media and capitalism.

In the 1960s, under the influence of the Cuban Revolution and liberation theology, a new way of seeing communication beyond media emerged, aiming at being closer to cultures and putting people's practices into perspective. A movement of thinkers (Brazilian Paulo Freire, Spanish-Colombian Jesús Martín-Barbero, Venezuelan Antonio Pasquali, Bolivian Luis Ramiro Beltrán, Argentine-Mexican

Néstor García Canclini, Mexican Carlos Monsiváis, Argentinians Héctor Schmucler, Anibal Ford, Marita Mata, and Eliseo Verón, and Peruvian Rosa María Alfaro,
amongst others)[1] criticized communication theories for being media-centred and
began to 'think from the South'. Rather than the media, citizens' media practices
and ways of seeing and feeling became the focus of research. The importance of
this rupture lies in the fact that it forced experts to 'abandon' media-centred analysis, North Americanism, and right- and left-wing moral dualisms. It led scholars
to change the place where questions (and observations) are made and to 'look from
the other side': that of the people. This rupture invited us to move from imperialist
hegemonies to people's processes and uses of mass communication; to dilute the
power of semiology and information; and to move towards the study of social-
exchange problems and operations in concrete experiences. This has made communication in Latin America *something different* since the 1970s; it became a way of
thinking whereby the presence of *the others* is discovered, and other logics of
communication, politics, and culture – what we call 'the popular' – are read,
understood, and revealed.

This mutation implied decentralizing studies and moving from media communication to the social practices and mediations that articulate the experiences of
individuals with media and political power. Thus, research studies moved their
attention from media to practices and social uses. This epistemological turn also
challenged the limitations of the empiricist effects approach and the Marxist
approach, which were focused on media structure and power. The key issue was to
broaden the understanding of media to cultures and to popular communication
practices. The idea was to challenge and criticize media hegemony from the practices of individuals located in the territory.

This break is similar to Couldry's (2004) proposal for the European scenario: a
new paradigm of media research that understands media not as texts or production
structures, but as practice; that is to say, the study of the whole range of practices
oriented towards media, and the role of media in ordering other practices in the
social world. The only difference is that, in Latin America, the so-called 'media
practices' are located in popular cultures. In other words, we believe that communication's potential in terms of meaning, narration, and politics can be found in
people's local lives (not in Anglo-Saxon pop, since communication is not limited
to the cultural industry or show business). What we, in Latin America, name as *lo
popular* (popular culture, popular practices) recounts *other ways of knowing* focused
on *narratives* rather than on concepts and argumentation; on *corporeality* expressed
through dancing, celebrations, and rituals rather than on ideas and thoughts; on
humour and *sarcasm* as a form of criticism of power, made from the bottom up.
Thus, when media practices are studied and analysed, what we really understand is
people's ways of narrating, of exposing their bodies and politicizing their lives from
and in communication.

This Latin American way of conceiving communication is focused on the
following: recognizing the knowledge of our territories and identities (thinking
from the bottom up); knowing that we are inhabitants of our historical exclusions

of class and race (thinking from and as *lo popular*); assuming that we have inherited Western culture and the Anglo mainstream (thinking of and from pop); believing that we are developed and progressive countries wilfully in our own multi-temporal chaos (thinking from and in heterogeneous modernity); and recognizing that we express ourselves through aesthetic and sentimental variegation (thinking from our baroque nature).

Within this context, this chapter presents six Latin American communication researchers who we consider pioneers of the study of media practices from and with the South. Brazilian Paulo Freire says that ordinary people have their own knowledge and ways of saying that should be listened to; therefore, media practices or popular practices are seen as a dialogue between popular knowledges and cultures whereby they enter into conversation with the knowledge of media cultures and the enlightened. Through his ideas and work on the genealogy of 'the popular', Spanish-Colombian Jesús Martín-Barbero invites us to think about mediations and how media practices are articulated with the cultural industry and the various political expressions. Mexican Carlos Monsiváis assumes that popular practices in and with the media express modes of cultural migration and new ways of reaffirming sentimental identities. Argentine-Mexican García Canclini holds that popular practices can only be understood by considering their temporal heterogeneity, their cultural hybridity, and their coming in and out of modernity. In her studies on media practices, Mexican Rossana Reguillo shows that young people are insurrectionist subjects that become visible through their corporal, musical, and political fights and struggles to survive in the context of injustice and generalized exclusion of the continent. Ecuadorian Bolívar Echeverría describes popular practices as a powerful field of expression where it can be confirmed that we, Latin Americans, are and make ourselves from the baroque. What follows is an outline of how each of these authors understands popular practices as experiences whereby media become a part of people's daily life, and how such practices reflect submission and resistance against the power, economy, and pretensions of the media's political hegemony.

Paulo Freire: media practices as a critical dialogue between knowledges

From Mexico to Argentina, community radio stations, territorial projects, and digital movements still find in Paulo Freire an inspiration for their communication practices. This Brazilian thinker (1921–1997) continues to be revolutionary by virtue of proposing dialogue as a strategy for developing critical awareness of one's place in the world. It is not Plato's dialogue in search of knowledge; it is a dialogue between the knowledges of several individuals whereby each one can learn and make proposals from his/her world, experiences, and aesthetics. It is a dialogue for transformation, made not only of words but also of practices. Freire changed our point of view with his theories built on experiences from and with the oppressed by recognizing that they have their own knowledge, aesthetics, and narratives of enunciation. He generates and promotes a pedagogy stemming from the oppressed so that they find their place in the world and develop a critical awareness of it (Freire, 1970). This is where communication and a policy of hope and liberation come from. This assumption of people having their own knowledge, language, and culture finds in media practices a space to play, to struggle, and to converse; where other ways of being present in the public sphere can be made visible and recognized. This dialogue of knowledges finds in media practices an existential and political scenario of expression in people's own codes, symbols, and rituals. Speaking from themselves and with their own words makes it possible for the subjects of communication to abandon passivity before the media, and to develop the capacity of enunciation and a critical awareness of their voice, their presence in the media, and their ways of resisting and imagining social life.

Popular practices emerge from individual awareness of one's existence, conditions, codes, and knowledge in order to converse with civilized, scriptural, and media-related ones. This dialogue is made from people's oral and visual practices. Knowledge is built from popular experience and is expressed in narratives that act as a strategy to have control over one's own destiny with a critical perspective on life, in total respect for the social, cultural, and natural environment. Freire invites us to recognize that in people's cultures there is knowledge; for culture is not exclusive to the bourgeoisie, the enlightened, the modern, or the elites. Those ignored, those at the bottom, ordinary people are rich in their own right; the point is that they have been denied the right to express themselves and, therefore, have been forced to live in a 'culture of silence'. Freire suggests that media practices be anchored in the territory, in experience, in the people. This is the origin of what has been called *comunicación para el vivir bien/buen vivir* [communication for good living] (Contreras, 2016). In the 21st century, it has inspired insurgent community media such as *La Garganta Poderosa* [The Powerful Throat] in Argentina, *Mídia Ninja* in Brazil, *El colectivo de comunicación Wayuu* [The Wayuu Communications Collective] in Colombia, and other rural communications collectives.

Freire enters into dialogue and shares ideas with authors of the Anglo academy, like Clemencia Rodríguez (2011) and her hypothesis that communicative citizenships are built in community radio or other media as a strategy to gain power and to make politics in public life; or with John Downing (2001) and his idea of media practice diversity ranging from dance, music, or graffiti to video, radio, and the internet.

Freire argues that popular culture becomes political in media practices when individuals and their collectives gain consciousness, become citizens, fight for their rights, and reach public enunciation in cultural movements whereby they seek to be free with their own voices. Freire shares with Downing (2001), Rodríguez (2011), and Couldry (2006) the idea that citizens gain political agency in media activism when they express their own ideas and points of view. This is how Latin American communication studies recognize the existence of popular politics, politics from the bottom up, on the left wing and with the land, as expressed by Arturo Escobar (2016), who brings American cultural studies into dialogue with Afro-Latin cultures to enunciate a feeling–thinking theory.

At present, Freire's proposal continues to be linked to his idea of dialogue, of listening to others, of recognizing that people's knowledge is the clue to understanding digital communication practices (Jenkins, 2006) as collaborative and community experiences. In the same line of thought, Couldry (2012) vindicates the popular habits, practices, and rituals with which people shape their relationships with media and technology. In line with Freire, Jenkins, and Couldry, we should not let ourselves be blinded by technology, but should rather be fans (Jameson, 1993) of the communities under study, of shared knowledge, and of critical and political awareness of life.

Jesús Martín-Barbero: media practices as the place of popular culture and mediations

Popular communication practices in Latin America take the form of melodrama in soap operas, music, films, and art. These sentimental popular practices have never been well received by intellectuals, scholars, and the enlightened. It was not until Martín-Barbero's 1987 publication of *De los medios a las mediaciones* [published in English as *Communication, Culture and Hegemony: From the Media to Mediations,* 1993] that the centrality of melodrama and *lo popular* in communicative practices began to be seriously considered. Martín-Barbero puts forward the concept of mediations as a way of thinking about what happens 'in between' and 'in articulation'; a way of understanding the simultaneous occurrence of resistance and complicity, challenge and obedience, ancestral and modern issues; a better way of understanding what people do with the media and what the media do with people.

The great epistemological contribution of Jesús Martín-Barbero in *De los medios a las mediaciones* was his invitation to change the place from which questions and observations are made, and to see with and from the citizens' point of view. This change of perspective makes everything look different because it takes us to play in the field of *re-cognition*, a matter of culture (and identity) and not of 'knowledge' (and concepts). What really matters here is not 'what' but 'how', the narration, the tone, the style... What is important is that which identifies us as being from a territory, a language, a history, a set of rituals, an identity. The value of Martín-Barbero's contribution lies in recognizing that there is a mass-popular cultural logic that can be found in media practices, a dense place where we can understand what audiences do with what they see and enjoy. This change of perspective was shared by Stuart Hall (1980) in his famous essay 'Encoding/decoding', where he holds that television and media are decoded and interpreted in different ways according to the cultures, economies, and experiences where communicative practices take place. Like Martín-Barbero, Hall suggests that people play an active role in their relations with the media because they articulate what they see and enjoy in them within their social-cultural contexts, and this enables them to resist and intervene in media messages in their own forms of collective action.

Martín-Barbero identifies *lo popular* as the subject of action, as those *other* ways of seeing, narrating, and giving meaning, those *other* uses of massive media. Popular practices of communication become, then, a matter of *seeing with the others* (Martín-Barbero & Corona, 2016) from the bottom up and in the territory. In the same line of thought, Couldry (2006) suggests that we are witnessing an intensification of mediation in the various forms of social life, and proposes a more critical view of what the media do and what is done with the media in everyday life. The author also shares Martín-Barbero's proposal of analysing how media transform the knowledges and actions of popular subjects in daily life.

In this context, Martín-Barbero understands the communication process as mass popular culture establishing a tension between the industrial and the cultural, political, and quotidian rituals of pleasures involved in consuming media products. In the prologue to the second edition of *De los medios a las mediaciones* (Martín-Barbero, 1998), this map of communication, only feasible on a cultural and political horizon, was made explicit.

This map has allowed us to analyse media practices on a deeper and more complex level, by de-instrumentalizing the media communication process so that the opacities, ambiguities, and tensions in people's cultures can be observed. On the one hand, there is a changing tension between *industrial formats* and *cultural matrices*. Formats account for the arrangements and production of the communication machine; they are empty signifiers since, in order to produce meaning, pleasure, and recognition, they must be in tension with the cultural matrices made up of territory, identity, history, and memories. Therefore, it is not enough to know about industrial and technical issues; one should be familiarized with the ritual and social practices of the communities, with the flavour of popular tastes, in order to witness the miracle of connection, to make sense and to provide citizens with pleasure. The map shows clearly Martín-Barbero's assumption that, in order to understand what happens with the media, one must look at cultural issues and see what people do with the media; that is, media practices.

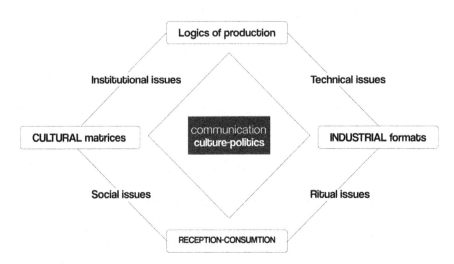

FIGURE 2.1 Martín-Barbero's map of communication
Adapted from Martín-Barbero (1998, p. xvi)

The second tension occurs between the *logics of production* and the *logics of enjoyment (reception, consumption, uses)*. The former are determined by the industry and the level of specialization of technical processes, by hegemonic projects and public policies, and by the knowledge and conditions of producers. Here, the problem is not the know-how but the issue of public policies that may seek larger audiences or more money, more concentration or more diversity, more freedom and plurality, or more control and surveillance. However, it is not enough to have public policies or industrial knowledge to determine production. It is also necessary to know how people receive, consume, enjoy, and use media, and what they do with what they see, read, listen to, and are connected to. This is an ambiguous, porous, and evolving realm; so much so that we have passed from being audiences to being programmers of our pleasures. Once again, the call is to understand media practices in and with people, to decentralize our way of looking at the media and their production logics, and to turn to what people do in daily life with what they consume and enjoy.

Mediations become researchable in popular communication practices that go beyond media and inhabit music, dancing, singing, celebrations, stories, and rituals, along with indigenous people, Afro descendants, women, and young people (Rincón, 2005, 2010). Many Latin American researchers working in this field are worth mentioning, including the following: Pablo Vila (1995, 1996; Semán & Vila, 2011) and his particular approach to music through the articulation of identity with politics; Pablo Alabarces (1993; Alabarces & Rodríguez, 2008) and his contributions in the fields of rock music, soccer, and *cumbia*; George Yúdice (2007) and his studies of music as a form of resistance against the industry, made from the bottom up; Ángel Quintero (2009, 2014) and his study of the ways in which dance resists colonialism; and Clemencia Rodríguez (2001, 2008, 2011) and her research on popular practices as a political construction of resistance.

This is not an idealization of either *lo popular* or people, but rather a critical, strategic action to unveil our ambiguities and contradictions as social individuals. Popular, Afro-descendant, indigenous, and peasant cultures are not being idealized, nor are the resistance and creativity of the weak being exalted, nor are the aberrations and manipulations of media, businessmen, and industry being maximized. Everything is being put into context; contradictions are assumed and the density of political power is taken into account. *Mediations*, as a category, account for the complexity of miscegenation, resistance, submission, and deformation of urban, massive, popular, political, and cultural issues found in popular media practices.

Carlos Monsiváis: media practices as cultural migrations

Cities are, by far, the Latin American places that expel. Latin America continues to be a violent region and cities are spaces defined by escapes and misunderstandings, where other ways of seeing and understanding are produced. In order to be named, cities give rise to hip-hop, graffiti, bodily expressions, and performance. If Martín-Barbero and Freire changed our perspective to understand how popular culture practices are seen by the others, with the people and from the bottom up, then Monsiváis analysed media practices as cultural migrations from the rural-ancestral side to the pop-urban side. Carlos Monsiváis (1938–2010) brought together people and the cultural industry, rural worlds and urban lives, bodily sentimentalities and showbiz emotions. In this way, he described, explained, and made visible the various forms of urban popular culture, which is different from that of Hollywood but whose existence cannot be denied, a USA pop-mainstream that in popular practices becomes Latin American. Even though Hollywood establishes the protocols of entertainment, it is not hegemonic because 'the poor do not trust Hollywood with their image and their sentimentalism'; that is what 'Mexican cinema, and to a lesser extent, Argentine and Brazilian cinema' are for (Monsiváis, 1999, p. 6). Monsiváis sees media practices as a dialogue between the popular nature of Latin issues and the pop essence of mass culture.

Juan Villoro (2017, p. 48) says that as early as 1955,

> before the publication of Roland Barthes' *Mythologies* and a decade before Umberto Eco's *Apocalyptic and Integrated* came out, Monsiváis spoke overtly about cult and popular cultures […] in order to understand a country and an era, it is essential to know how such country and such era represent themselves. This applies to the fine arts and romantic songs, comics, advertising, journalism, photography, gastronomy, and all other resources used by a society to define itself through senses.
>
> *(Villoro, 2017, p. 48)*

As we can see, when analysing media practices, Monsiváis examines the expressive contradictions that reveal the sentimental cultures of Latin America.

Monsiváis (1999) assumes media practices as 'cultural migrations' that lead ordinary people to adopt, with both conformity and disagreement, fashions and attitudes that travel in a sort of 'journey of habits' whereby they keep their faith in the Virgin Mary but proclaim free love and sexual ease. Monsiváis suggests that radio manages to negotiate the melodic rhythm of daily life; television gets stragglers closer to avant-garde cultural and social manifestations, disseminates (very simple) fantasies of consumption, and re-elaborates the hierarchies of taste.

Monsiváis led us to imagine that media practices create *cooltures* that can only be described and interpreted as *bastard cultures* (Rincón, 2013), or as what Baricco (2014) calls 'barbarians'. In other words, media and digital practices change our experience of the world and make us all cultural 'tastemakers' of experiences extending from the media and the digital world to wine, football, music, travel, food. Along the same line, new Latin American ways arise to understand how citizens want to participate in pop worlds with their expressive practices in media, music, dance, food, and ancestral rituals, as shown by Brazilian Micael Herschmann (2009; Herschmann & Fernandes, 2014).

Néstor García Canclini: media practices as multi-temporal modernity

When large migrant protests took place in the United States on 1 May 2006, the media, especially the radio, played a key role. Eduardo Sotelo, better known as 'Piolín', was an announcer from Los Angeles who led, made visible, and gave voice to the cause of Hispanics. During those same protests, the band called *Los Tigres del Norte* [The Northern Tigers] led a march that drew almost a million people. For many of the spectators, *Los Tigres* was a very peculiar folk music group; however, they are a communication phenomenon of the cultural industry. They are a hybrid cultural practice that links media with popular culture, the music industry with migrants, the Mexican identity with globalized pop.

Argentine-Mexican anthropologist Néstor García Canclini (1939–) has been a key author in research studies on the cultural industry and popular practices. In his first book, *Arte popular y sociedad en América Latina* [*Popular Art and Society in Latin America*], published in 1977, García Canclini already wondered about popular art in Latin America. In 1982 his book *Culturas populares en el capitalismo* [*Popular Cultures in Capitalism*] was published, and in 1989 one of his most famous essays: *Culturas híbridas, estrategias para entrar y salir de la modernidad* [*Hybrid Cultures: Strategies to come in and out of Modernity*]. García Canclini invites us to think how popular culture (people's practices) transforms media experiences that can no longer be thought of without people's gestures and bodies; without craftwork; without popular festivals and carnivals; without meeting and market places that are produced and transformed by technology, from the logic of capitalism. Thus, hybrid culture is, as Silvia López (2018, p. 94) would say, 'a term to name ways of approaching the visibility regime that modernity was at that time in Mexico'. It accounts for those individuals and popular practices by assuming a multi-temporal and cultural heterogeneity, and the games played in consumption and media use.

García Canclini proves that thinking of *lo popular* implies approaching national and transnational markets. In other words, *lo popular* is not to be found in a pure, ancestral, and original environment. Popular culture is also a commodity. It is easy to say so but, at the time, it was this anthropologist's perspective that allowed us to see how crafts circulated in global markets while being anchored in specific territories where they have been part of alternative and diffuse settings. García Canclini also noted that 'The era of globalization, which seeks to unify the ways of naming the world, does not allow the popular to be named with the enormous variations suggested by folklorists, English leftists, Gramscians, or Latin American nationalisms, populisms or tropicalisms' (García Canclini, 2002, p. 25). Therefore, instead of looking for impossible syntheses, the author invites us to think why, even in a globalized era, it is still necessary to speak of and return to *lo popular*, as an expression of the subaltern, something that 'cannot be eliminated by globalization' (2002, p. 30).

García Canclini's proposal allows us to do research and to think of popular practices and their ways of expressing multiple temporalities. In the same line of thought, we find Argentinians Pablo Semán (2006, 2008; Semán & Vila, 2011) and Alejandro Grimson (2011) who have analysed the ways of crossing borders and discovering ironic divergences in religion, music, territories, and politics. Bolivian Rivera Cusicanqui (2006) suggests the notion of *ch'ixi* to demonstrate the parallel coexistence of multiple cultural differences that do not merge, but are rather antagonistic or complementary; each one reproduces itself from the depths of the past and relates to the others contentiously.

Rossana Reguillo: technopolitical practices as insurgent landscapes

While we, Westerners, were discussing (again) why young people are incapable of making commitments and why political practices are out of fashion, in Mexico the hashtag #YoSoy132 [#Iam132], which later became #FueElEstado [#ItwasThe State], showed a new way of doing politics that goes from disenchantment to new forms of hope (Reguillo, 2012; Treré, 2013). It is a way of doing politics that goes through pop media referents but also through ancestral practices, poetry, music, and corporality. To make matters worse, the hashtag #OccupyWallStreet in New York challenged one of the foundational institutions of current neoliberalism. From #RenunciaYa [#ResignNow] in Guatemala to #MeToo used by global women's movements, a new ghost runs through hegemonic thought: that of the new insurrections that move calmly from the intimate world of networks and cellphone screens, to the street where different collectives gather. As pointed out by Toret (2013, p. 19), insurrection – as a popular practice of techno-politics – implies that cultural practices are made in three layers in the social context: the digital layer, the media layer, and the physical layer. Young people and women become activists with digital resources (social networks, cellphones), media (visibility and denunciation in the traditional spaces of journalism), and finally gain political agency (in the physical layer, on the street, in common spaces).

Rossana Reguillo, one of the most original Latin American thinkers, has been mapping the reality of Mexico for the past 30 years. From her extensive work and rigorous reflection, we highlight two important elements of regional communication practices. First, the overwhelming violence classified in the *narco-machine* category (Reguillo, 2011), a context where social-cultural processes are carried out in more media-oriented, more pop, more digital structures whose basic traits are dissidence, anarchy, and illegality. As Reguillo has pointed out, Mexico is the paradigmatic place to think about this, but Latin America as a whole must be read in the same key. Media and pop culture resources are both perpetrators and victims of the violence and communication practices of fear societies.

Reguillo's second contribution is her work on 'insurgent landscapes' (2017), which allows us to better understand the new youth movements and their political performances 'made' in media and entertainment cultural referents. These protest movements are led by young people who denounce in media, digital, and street practices a dehumanized, violent landscape that leaves little room for a dignified life but, at the same time, makes it possible to have 'inscription surfaces' where different opinions are expressed using the particular features of social networks. These surfaces, which Reguillo thinks of globally, also permit revisiting popular counter-hegemonic practices that are constantly self-reinvented. They allow us to understand not only Latin American fear practices but also how young people are using their bodies and their symbolic resources in politics, with hashtags such as #Yosoy132 [#Iam132] in Mexico, #esto apenas comienza [#this has just begun] in Guatemala, #me pongo la ruana [#I put my ruana on] in Colombia, and #Niunamenos [#Notevenoneless] in Argentina.

Bolívar Echeverría: media practices from our baroque nature

Latin American media practices include melodrama, but also comprise particular aesthetic proposals such as that of *love in the time of cholera* that *Calle 13* – a rap fusion band – has referred to so well and in so many ways in their song *Latinoamérica*. Our last 'recovered' thinker talks about these aesthetics and holds that popular practices in Latin America are baroque. Bolívar Echeverría (1941–2010) did his academic work in Mexico, was a critical thinker and translator of Walter Benjamin, and an expert on Marx and several thinkers of the Frankfurt School. This Ecuadorian philosopher felt the need to think of culture as something that, though 'apparently accessory, is indispensable for the essential' (2010, p. 20). Just like other Latin American authors, Bolívar Echeverría thought that although Marxism was experiencing a sort of exhaustion, it was crucial to use creativity to find alternatives to capitalism. His proposal was made from the philosophy of culture, and was anchored in Latin America and in what he called the baroque ethos.

Echeverría's proposal lies in reviewing, against the general trend (as suggested by Benjamin), the 17th Century, which in Latin America was characterized by inhabiting the modern project from a different place: the place of popular culture. To this end, Echeverría holds that while modern capitalism consists of a Protestant mentality and a Calvinist perspective whereby work is the blessing of men (Weber), it is possible to find in the baroque a new proposal. This proposal is characterized by ambiguity; it assumes the chaotic reality of growing capitalism and, although not denying it, it seems to refuse accepting it: 'It is not abstention or irresolution what characterizes baroque behaviour. It is rather deciding or taking sides for the two opposites at the same time' (Echeverría, 2000, p. 176).

Echeverría reminds us that Latin America has managed to build its own modernity, challenging the idea of an abstract and individualistic utopia, and suggests a baroque *ethos*: a Catholic, *mestizo*, Latin American one; a faithful modernity. This is Echeverría's contribution and with it, the picture is complete: if we want to understand Latin American media practices, we must do so from a baroque aesthetic. It is from Echeverría that the expressive modes of Latin American popular practices, so often depreciated, make sense. That taste becomes researchable in the cinema, in religion, in music, and in the various ways that we, people from the South, have of organizing ourselves on stage. Research studies like those of Rodríguez (2001) and Rivera Cusi-canqui (2006) show a productive appropriation of how people express themselves and create meaning with their own aesthetics and formats.

Conclusions: the Latin American proposal of popular culture as enunciation of media practices

What characterizes Latin America is a baroque, multi-temporal variegation, a cultural mutation in permanent flow. This fact makes us desire and actually be a *coolture* (Rincón, 2013) without losing *lo popular*, our territory, our identity. We have also created a pop, popular, and subaltern theory of communication, though modern and progressive, that aims at producing knowledge and making politics from the bottom up. We are not one thing or the other: we are both pop and popular, submissive and subaltern. Thus, we have taken up some fundamental discussions from European, Western, and modern thought: Nietzsche and his suspicion about the place we should assign to the Dionysian after a long exile; Freud and his question about the place of the collective and oneself; Gramsci and that ungraspable place where hegemony is built. We, Latin American thinkers, depart from these and other dialogues with afterlife but are inscribed in our territory.

The six authors discussed in this chapter have made contributions to understanding communication practices from a Latin American perspective: a baroque view that is, at the same time, faithful and full of bodies, rituals, daily life, symbols, and practices; a way of thinking that comes from the popular without ignoring the market, intervening modernity by telling and narrating; an imagination that inhabits the fantasy of ancestral sounds and images; an experience whereby we dream, tell, and dance melodrama and carnival to produce insurgent practices which are reinvented by young people and women from the territory, and social networks to build communication capable of giving meaning back to the best modernity: the one inhabited by utopia and celebration.

Latin America's proposal for thinking about media practices is focused on popular subjects and communities; on what people do with the media; on the expressive and political use of media resources to gain visibility and public voice; on the intercultural dialogues always present in the negotiation between media and people's lives; on the expansion of media communication to music, food, festivals, and rituals of identity. We propose seeing media practices as a critical *dialogue* between knowledges and cultures (Freire); as mediations between popular culture, the cultural industry, and political power (Martín-Barbero); as media-aided cultural migrations (Monsiváis); as heterogeneity of temporalities and practices (García Canclini); as insurrection performed by women, youth, indigenous people, Afro-descendants, and the digital world (Reguillo); as baroque aesthetics (Echeverría); as a bastard experience of *coolture* (Rincón); as a field where communication for good living is possible (Contreras). The Latin contribution to the study of media practices is a popular, tasty, and carnal culture, narrative and humorous, not short of emotions: seeing, understanding, explaining from and with the people; going beyond media; thinking about the people rather than the media.

Note

1   The list would be endless, but our biased selection includes other key thinkers like Juan Díaz Bordenave from Paraguay; Ismaer de Oliveria, Immacolata Vasallo de Lopes, Renato Ortiz, and Arlindo Machado from Brazil; Mario Kaplún from Uruguay; Valerio Fuenzalida from Chile; Guillermo Orozco, Jorge González, and Rossana Reguillo from Mexico.

References

Adorno, T., & Horkheimer, M. (1944). La industria cultural. Iluminismo como mistificación de masas. In *Dialéctica del iluminismo*. Buenos Aires: Edit. Sudamericana.

Alabarces, P. (1993). *Entre gatos y violadores: el rock nacional en la cultura argentina*. Buenos Aires: Colihue.

Alabarces, P., & Rodríguez, M. (eds) (2008). *Resistencias y mediaciones. Estudios sobre cultura popular*, Buenos Aires: Paidós.

Baricco, A. (2014). *The Barbarians: An Essay on the Mutation of Culture*. New York: Rizzoli Ex Libris.

Contreras, A. (2016). *La palabra que camina. Comunicación popular para el Vivir Bien/Buen Vivir*. Quito: Ciespal.

Couldry, N. (2004). Theorising media as practice. *Social Semiotics*, 14(2), 115–132.

Couldry, N. (2006). *Listening Beyond the Echoes: Media, Ethics and Agency in an Uncertain World*. Boulder, CO: Paradigm Press

Couldry, N. (2012). *Media, Society, World: Social Theory and Digital Media Practice*. Cambridge: Polity.

Couldry, N., & Curran, J. (eds) (2003). *Contesting Media Power: Alternative Media in a Networked World*. Boulder, CO: Rowman & Littlefield. Downing, J. (2001). *Radical Media. Rebellious Communication and Social Movements*. Thousand Oaks, CA: Sage.

Echeverría, B. (2000). *La modernidad de lo barroco*. México DF: ERA.

Echeverría, B. (2010). *La definición de la cultura*. México DF: Fondo de Cultura Económica.

Eco, U. (1965). *Apocalípticos e integrados*. Barcelona: Lumen.

Escobar, A. (2016). Desde abajo, por la izquierda y con la tierra. *El País*, 17 January.

Freire, P. (1970). *Pedagogía del Oprimido*. Montevideo: Tierra Nueva.

García Canclini, N. (1977). *Arte popular y sociedad en América Latina*. México DF: Grijalbo.

García Canclini, N. (1989). *Culturas híbridas. Estrategias para entrar y salir de la modernidad*, 6th edition. México DF: Grijalbo.

García Canclini, N. (2002). *Culturas populares en el capitalismo*. Sixth Edition. México DF: Grijalbo.

Grimson, A. (2011). *Los límites de la cultura. Crítica de las teorías de la identidad*. Buenos Aires: Siglo XXI editores.

Hall, S. (1980). Encoding/decoding. In S. Hall, D. Hobson, A. Lowe, & P. Willis (eds), *Culture, Media, Language* (pp. 128–138). London: Hutchinson.

Herschmann, M. (2009). Ciudadanía y estética de los jóvenes de las periferias y favelas de los países latinoamericanos. In *Entre saberes desechables y saberes indispensables [agendas de país desde la comunicación]*. Bogotá: C3FES.

Herschmann, M., & Fernandes, C. S. (2014). *Música nas ruas do Rio de Janeiro*. Sao Paulo: Intercom.

Jameson, F. (1993). On 'cultural studies'. *Social Text*, 34, 17–52.

Jenkins, H. (2006). *Convergence Culture: Where Old and New Media Collide*. New York: New York University Press.

Katz, E., & Lazarsfeld, P. (1956). *Personal Influence: The Part Played by People in the Flow of Mass Communications*. Glencoe: The Free Press.

Lazarsfeld, P., Berelson, B., & Gaudet, H. (1948). *The People's Choice: How the Voter Makes Up His Mind in a Presidential Campaign*. New York: Columbia University Press.

de Lopes, I. V. (2004). *Telenovela: internacionalização e interculturalidade*. São Paulo: Edições Loyola.

López, S. (2018). Tiempos a destiempo: la posvida de un libro. In O. Rincón (ed.), *Pensar desde el Sur* (pp. 90–105). Bogotá: Fescomunicación.

Martel, F. (2011). *Cultura Mainstream*. Madrid: Taurus.

Martín-Barbero, J. (1998). *De los medios a las mediaciones. Comunicación, cultura y hegemonía*. 2nd edition. Bogotá: Convenio Andrés Bello.

Martín-Barbero, J., & Corona, S. (2016). *Ver con los otros*. México: Fondo de Cultura Económica.

Mattelart, A., & Dorfman, A. (1971). *Para leer al Pato Donald. Comunicación de masa y colonialismo*. Valparaíso: Ediciones Universitarias de Valparaíso.

McBride, S. et al. (1980). *Un solo mundo, voces múltiples. Comunicación e información en nuestro tiempo*. México DF: Fondo de Cultura Económica.

Monsiváis, C. (1999). *Del rancho al internet (las migraciones culturales)*. México: Colección biblioteca del ISSSTE.

Monsiváis, C. (2008). *Pedro Infante. Las Leyes del Querer*. México DF: Edit. Aguilar.

Orozco, G. (2002). *Recepción y mediaciones*. Buenos Aires: Norma.

Quintero, A. (2009). *Cuerpo y cultura. Las músicas <mulatas> y la subversión del baile*. Madrid: Iberoamericana.

Quintero, A. (2014). Sensibilidades y comunicación en las músicas populares afrolatinoamericanas. In Sánchez, A. (ed.), *Sensiblidad de frontera.Comunicación y voces populares*. Lima: PUCP.

Reguillo, R. (2011) La narco máquina y el trabajo de la violencia: Apuntes para su decodificación. In *E-misférica. 8.2 #narcomachine. Julio-diciembre de 2011*. New York: Hemispheric Institute of Performance and Politics.

Reguillo, R. (2012). *Culturas juveniles. Formas políticas del desencanto*. Buenos Aires: Siglo XXI.

Reguillo, R. (2017). *Paisajes insurrectos. Jóvenes, redes y revueltas en el otoño civilizatorio*. Barcelona: Nuevos Emprendimientos Editoriales.

Rincón, O. (2005). Comunicar entre lo techno y lo retro: activismo y estéticas en experimento. *Revista Signo y Pensamiento* 47(24).

Rincón, O. (2010). estos/medios/apropiados: cuentos indígenas de la paciencia, la identidad y la política. Revista Folios, Universidad de Antioquia.

Rincón, O. (2013). Las identidades y las sensibilidades como innovación mediática y narrativas colabor-activas. *Revista Dixit* 19. Universidad Católica del Uruguay.

Rivera Cusicanqui, S. (2006). Ch'ixinakax utxiwa. Una reflexión sobre prácticas y discursos descolonizadores. In M. Yupi (ed.), *Modernidad y pensamiento descolonizador. Memoria del seminario internacional*. La Paz: U-PIEB/IF EA.

Rodríguez, C. (2001). *Fissures in the Mediascape: An International Study of Citizens' Media*. Cresskill, NJ: Hampton Press.

Rodríguez, C. (ed.) (2008). *Lo Que le Vamos Quitando a la Guerra. Medios Ciudadanos en Contextos de Conflicto Armado en Colombia*. Bogotá: Centro de Competencias en Comunicación, Fundación Friedrich Ebert.

Rodríguez, C. (2011). *Citizens' Media against Armed Conflict: Disrupting Violence in Colombia*. Minneapolis, MN: University of Minnesota Press.

Schmucler, H. (1984). Un proyecto de Comunicación/cultura. *Revista Comunicación y Cultura*, 12.

Semán, P. (2006). *Bajo Continuo: Exploraci ones descentradas sobre cultura popular y masiva*. Buenos Aires: Editorial Gorla.

SemánP. (2008). *La religiosidad popular: Creencias y vida cotidiana*, Buenos Aires: Capital Intelectual.

Semán, P., & Vila, P. (eds) (2011). *Cumbia. Nación, etnia y género en Latinoamérica*. Buenos Aires: Gorla y Ediciones de Periodismo y Comunicación (UNLP).

Smith, B., Lasswell, H., & Casey, R. (1946). *Propaganda, Communication, and Public Opinion: A Comprehensive Reference Guide*. Princeton, NJ: Princeton University Press.

Toret, J. (ed.) (2013). *Tecnopolítica: La potencia de las multitudes conectadas. El sistema red 15M, un nuevo paradigma de la política distribuida*. Barcelona: Universidad Abierta de Cataluña/ Internet Interdisciplinary Institut (IN#).

Treré, E. (2013). #YoSoy132: la experiencia de los nuevos movimientos sociales en México y el papel de las redes sociales desde una perspectiva crítica. *Educación Social. Revista de Intervención Socioeducativa*, 55, 112–121.

Vila, P. (1995). El rock nacional: género musical y construcción de la identidad juvenil en Argentina. In N. G. Canclini (ed.), *Cultura y Pospolítica. El debate sobre la modernidad en América Latina* (pp. 231–271). México: Consejo Nacional para la Cultura y las Artes.

Vila, P. (1996). Identidades narrativas y música. Una primera propuesta para entender sus relaciones. *TRANS 2* (1996) revista cultural de música.

Villoro, J. (2017). *El género Monsiváis*. México DF: Instituto Nacional de Antropología e Historia.

Yúdice, G. (2007). *Nuevas tecnologías, música y experiencia*. Barcelona: Gedisa.

3

PRAXIS IN LATIN AMERICAN COMMUNICATION THOUGHT

A critical appraisal

Alejandro Barranquero

The value of praxis in Latin American communication research

In the 20th century, Latin American social scientists began constructing a new and independent epistemological framework that was *from* and *for* the region but also oriented to the rest of the world (Fals Borda, 1973; Kush, 1962). This movement sought to create a model for conducting research informed by the particular values and needs of the 'oppressed' (Freire, 1970). To this end, many authors explored the concept of praxis, marking a move away from positivism and its rigid separation between knowledge and ethical values. Since the 1970s, the concept of praxis has been a major influence in communication theory, becoming one of its most defining features. This is especially true when we compare the influence of praxis in the region with its prevalence in other academic communities, at least since the generally agreed 'turn to practice' in recent years (Couldry, 2012).

In the second half of the 20th century, Latin American communication thinking expanded the concept of praxis in three directions. First, the search for an autonomous communication science brought a departure from US and European theoretical frameworks, and praxis was adopted as a liberating principle with the capacity to integrate communities and research. Second, many communication pioneers combined theory and activism, basing their analyses on the innovative grassroots media projects under way in the region (Díaz Bordenave, 1985; Gerace, 1973; Kaplún, 1998). Third, praxis was understood as a way to apply theory to improving the standard of life for the most impoverished and vulnerable sectors, whether through large-scale projects (e.g. communication policies promoted by the state) or by means of popular communication.

Practice has determined the development of different communication subfields that made major advancements in Latin America, including communication for development, media literacy, media reception, and alternative media. These different areas were closely connected in their earliest incarnations in the 1960s and 1970s because of their shared pioneers and main theoretical referents. One of these pioneers is Brazilian educator Paulo Freire (1970), who believed that communication could become a central tool to create critical awareness by incorporating the imaginaries and expectations of the 'oppressed'. Starting in the 1980s, the dialectical relationship between theory and practical community solutions became an important issue for Latin American Cultural Studies, a field led by Jesús Martín-Barbero, Néstor García Canclini, and others. These authors articulated a cultural theory based on the idiosyncrasies of the Latin American context and the region's complex relations with Western modernity. Early Latin American Cultural Studies represented not only an academic position but also a political project to decolonize the social sciences and situate the region in international academic circuits.

The idea of praxis is not exclusive to communication thought, but rather represents a central tenet of several autonomous and self-generated proposals including dependency theory and liberation theology (Flores-Osorio, 2009). In fact, the word 'liberation' was added as a qualifier to connect theory with social change in fields such as liberation philosophy (Cerruti, 1983; Dussel, 1996), liberation sociology (Fals Borda, 1973), pedagogy (Freire, 1970), psychology (Martín-Baró, 1983), and liberation communicology (Beltrán, 1974b). The idea of praxis also inspired a new methodological paradigm called participatory action research that acts as a critique of positivism and its strict separation between subjects and research objects. Inspired by Marxism, participatory action research promotes the use of dialogical techniques to make researchers participants in their own research and to decentralize science from its usual academic and intellectual arenas (Bosco Pinto, 1976; Rahman, 1993). This new methodological approach owes much to Paulo Freire (1970) and especially to Colombian sociologist Orlando Fals Borda, who developed concrete participatory action research applications based on his work with poor farmers and rural populations (Fals Borda, 1973, 1986, 2006).

This chapter reviews the origin and evolution of praxis as a central component of Latin American communication research. We will first trace its historical and theoretical roots by looking at the significant influence of certain conceptual debates. Second, we will reconstruct the importance of the notion of praxis in the work of a few pioneers who strongly influenced later developments. Third, we will explore a number of paradigmatic experiences that demonstrate that media practice did not evolve out of a strict application of theory, but rather from fieldwork engaged in combating injustice in contexts such as social movements and indigenous rights struggles. Finally, we will connect regional Latin American advancements with the more recent 'media practice' literature in the European/US context, focusing on what media scholars and practitioners can learn from the Latin American praxis tradition.

Tracing back the theoretical roots of praxis in communication thought

During the second half of the 20th century, Latin America witnessed a period of profound upheaval marked by the dialectical tension between oppression and freedom (Barranquero, 2011). Consequently, social sciences in the region began to reflect the influence of reformist and revolutionary movements such as the Cuban revolution (1959) and the reformist government of Salvador Allende in Chile (1970–1973). Ideas of praxis and liberation determined the construction of the first communication theories, which were identified as the '(Critical) Latin American Communication School' at the end of the 20th century. Although the thesis that the School represented a unified research programme is highly controversial,[1] Marques de Melo (2009) claims that the theories that fell under the purview of the label share at least three features. First, a consistent concern for Latin American identity and its communication problems, including cultural dependence on other countries, the absence of public media services, elite-oriented private broadcasters, concentration and monopolies, etc. Second, a preoccupation with constructing a critical communication science guided by ethical and political values and challenges to theories and methods imported from the USA and Europe. Third, a trend toward theoretical and methodological hybridization. Latin American theory often combines re-appropriations of Western theories with original contributions from popular sectors, social movements, indigenous groups, etc.

There is much evidence that the notion of praxis was central to pioneering Latin American communication research. Various scholarship has recognized that Latin America's contributions to communication studies have been substantially different from those of the regions where communication research was born: Europe and the USA. For example, Everett M. Rogers (1982) postulated that Latin American communication research functioned as a 'hinge school' that provided a bridge between the strong experimental and positivist accent of US administrative research and the more philosophical and speculative nature of European critical theory. Other authors have observed that Latin American thought is characterized by its emphasis on the connection between theory and practice and its search for political and social change (Atwood & McAnany, 1986; Huesca & Dervin, 1994; Dervin & Huesca, 1997). The following ideas are highly visible in debates and reflections within the field of Latin American communication research at the end of the 20th century: horizontal communication, dialogue, right to communicate, and communication policies. As a result of this common background, Latin American researchers shared a unified position in the 1970 UNESCO summit focused on developing a 'New Information and Communication Order (NWICO)'. These talks led to the publication of the McBride Report (1980), which promoted State policies to encourage media pluralism and combat media concentration and unbalanced information flows. Furthermore, two praxis-based frameworks comprise the main theoretical foundations of Latin American communication thought: Marxism and liberation theology (Marques de Melo, Gobbi, & Kunsch, 2002). Also known as 'philosophy of practice', Marxism understands practice in two ways: as a revolutionary activity to transform the material conditions of existence, and as the dialectical unit between theory and practice. For its part, liberation theology tried to articulate new theological models based on connections between theory and a practical commitment to the poor (Berryman, 1987).

The concern for practice in Latin American communication research owes much to the works of Paulo Freire, who proposed a conceptualization of praxis as a liberation principle influenced by Marxism and liberation theology. Based on Freire's previous experience as an adult education instructor, *Pedagogía del oprimido* [*Pedagogy of the Oppressed*, 1970] launched a critique of traditional education, which he believed acted to reproduce inequality and a 'culture of silence'. He argued that traditional authoritarian models of education undervalued the inherent capacities of students to discover reality by themselves. He referred to traditional education as operating according to a 'banking' model because it was based on a vertical model that transferred information ('deposits') from the minds of the teachers (or 'bankers') to the students, who were deemed 'poor', ignorant, and in need of the paternalistic guide of the 'oppressors'. These 'deposits' contributed to perpetuating the status quo since they contained the ideas and norms that the 'oppressed' are supposed to internalize in order to move up in the socio-political structure.

As an alternative, Freire suggested a 'liberation pedagogy' based on free dialogue and aimed at eliminating power differences between the educator and the educated, creating a situation in which both teachers and students become learners. Liberation pedagogy hinged on the concept of 'conscientization', a process that invited teachers and learners to critically approach reality in order to discover the myths that maintain oppression and dehumanizing structures (Freire, 1975: 225). Conscientization is based on praxis, understood as the unity between what human beings do (practice) and how they think about what they do (theory). Freire claimed that reflection and action are inseparable: neglecting action leads to mere 'verbalism', which is synonymous with pure intellectualism and wordiness; neglecting reflection results in superficial and vain activism: 'I never advocate either a theoretic elitism or a practice ungrounded in theory, but the unity between theory and practice' (Freire in Macedo, 1995, p. 377).

Paraguayan Juan Díaz Bordenave and his colleague Bolivian Luis Ramiro Beltrán were the first Latin American scholars to earn PhDs in communication studies at US institutions. While working as a development consultant, Díaz Bordenave, who was strongly influenced by Freire and liberation theology, became inspired by the proliferation of Latin American emancipatory movements. He used his experiences with these movements as a basis for his critiques of the modernization paradigm (Rogers, Lerner and others) and his proposal that participatory communication should form a central component of democracy. According to Díaz Bordenave, communication and participation are not just methodological tools for furthering development, they are also human rights and organic parts of a much larger and more important process: the construction of a participatory society (Díaz Bordenave, 1985). The Freirean concept of praxis was at the root of Díaz Bordenave's new society. He believed that the quality of public participation increases when people appropriate their right to communicate, learn to construct their own judgments, and are able to handle conflicts and coordinate actions for social change: 'Education for participation is based on the concept of praxis: where practice, technique and theory are combined as reflection' (Díaz Bordenave, 1985, p. 28).

In the late 1960s, Latin American communication scholars also initiated a process of self-reflection that led to a denunciation of the region's cultural and scientific dependence. The author who best represents this trend is Bolivian Luis Ramiro Beltrán, who wrote two interrelated papers that questioned the influence of US functionalism in Latin America and called for a new 'communicology of liberation', based on popular practices in the field and regional concerns (Beltrán, 1974a, 1976). Beltrán's interest in practice and cultural independence influenced the (national) communication policies he proposed, which spurred debates on political economy (Beltrán, 1974b) and inspired progressive State policies such as the Ratelve project in Venezuela (1974–1975) (Capriles, 1996). Inspired by Paulo Freire (1970), Frank Gerace (1973), and regional alternative media projects, Beltrán proposed a model of 'horizontal communication' grounded in participatory, egalitarian, and dialogic premises. Both Beltrán's communication policies and his notion of horizontal communication influenced the 1970s NWICO debates; his 'Farewell to Aristotle: "horizontal communication"' (Beltrán, 1979) was even included as an annex in the McBride Report (1980).

Outside the academy, regional institutions were central to the articulation of a new research program for Latin America. Founded in 1959 in Quito under the sponsorship of UNESCO, the International Centre for Higher Studies in Journalism for Latin America (Centro Internacional de Estudios Superiores de Periodismo para América Latina, CIESPAL) was the first large-scale institution devoted to the promotion of media education and research. This organization had long acted as the entryway to Mass Communication Research in the region,[2] but in the 1970s CIESPAL (1973) itself denounced the intellectual dependency of the region in a report and advocated for the creation of an autonomous science. In conjunction with other national associations,[3] CIESPAL worked to construct new theoretical frameworks that led to the birth of two major regional institutions: the Latin American Association of Communication Researchers (Asociación Latinoamericana de Investigadores de la Comunicación, ALAIC, 1978) and the Latin American Federation of Social Communication Faculties (Federación Latinomericana de Facultades y Programas de Comunicación Social, FELAFACS, 1981).

Praxis as educommunication, mediations, and citizenship

In the final quarter of the 20th century, a new generation of authors began to expand reflections on praxis in the communication field. Influenced by strong Christian convictions, Uruguayan Mario Kaplún worked for many years as a teacher and a promoter of innovative radio formats in Venezuela, Uruguay, and Argentina. His work formed the point of departure for one of the most quoted works in media literacy, alternative media, and communication for development in Latin America: *The Popular Communicator* (Kaplún, 1985a). [4] This book was conceived as a practical toolkit to promote grassroots communication, so it is notable for its clear and didactic style: 'We develop theoretical notions by applying them, showing how they are translated in the concrete tasks' (Kaplún, 1998: 13). He wrote about the importance of 'listening to communities' as the first step of any real communication process, a process he referred to as 'feed-forward'. Inspired by Freire and Díaz Bordenave, he argued that traditional education put too much emphasis on content and effects, neglecting the potential for conscientization through dialogue and grassroots participation in the media (Kaplún, 1998).

Praxis and dialogue became central tools in the innovative educational methodologies he developed, which included radio drama, cassette-forum, and other group and edutainment methodologies (Kaplún, 1984, 1985a, 1985b). The Uruguayan also helped to popularize the concept of 'educommunication', a term used in Latin America as interchangeable with media literacy.[5] Compared with the more aseptic and apolitical US and European media literacy approaches, Latin American educommunication emphasizes media literacy's relationship with praxis and politics. Kaplún argued that, like Europe, the region had emphasized a pedagogy that unveils media ideology and processes, while also insisting that no educational process is complete until students critically create their own communication content as a way to express their own world. All educommunication strategies, however, are connected to a progressive or conservative view of the world, so critical reflection is needed to verify the ideological constraints that determine educational processes in practice.

During this same period, Spanish-Colombian scholar Jesús Martín-Barbero acknowledged Paulo Freire and Antonio Gramsci as the main influences of his most famous work, *De los medios a las mediaciones* (1987) [*Communication, Culture and Hegemony*, 1993]. In this book, Martín-Barbero invited scholars to shift from media to 'mediations', provoking an epistemological turn in the region, which was, at the time, very much trapped in discussions about ideology and cultural dependence. Mediations served as a way out of this dialogic impasse and a fruitful path forward to unveil the complex relationship between popular communication, mass media culture, and social practices. For Martín-Barbero, popular communication is a space for cultural determination but also a platform to promote creativity and intentional actions. Thus, the popular culture is interpenetrated by the influence of mass media, but it also provides oppositional elements from collective memory, social action, and a 'dense variety of strong, living, popular cultures which provide a space for profound conflict and unstoppable cultural dynamism' (Martín-Barbero, 1983, p. 2). Echoes of Martín-Barbero are readily apparent in the important tradition of Latin American reception studies, which focuses on the active and creative role of information receivers in negotiating mass media messages and meanings.[6]

Mexican scholar Guillermo Orozco (1987) posited that the interactions between audiences and television were a routinized 'communicative praxis', since audiences interact with media according to different combinations of mediations or *multimediaciones*. Orozco's work moved away from the overly individualistic 'uses and gratifications' approach to explore the affective reception of popular media products such as telenovelas (Martín-Barbero & Muñoz, 1992; González & Mugnaini, 1986). Another Mexican scholar, Rossana Reguillo, initiated a long tradition of studies on youth and media. She proposed that young people's practices cannot be analysed through any normative or institutionalized approach, and called for exploring the 'terrain of structures and actions', or how young people 'make the institutions speak' through their multiple mediations (Reguillo, 2000, p. 69).

Understanding praxis as synonymous with cultural agency, Martín-Barbero's mediations helped Latin American research break away from the media-centric approaches and rigid dualistic perceptions – vertical versus horizontal; information versus dialogue; structure versus process – that had limited and defined it in the 1970s and 1980s (Dervin & Huesca, 1997; Huesca & Dervin, 1994). In the early 2000s, inspired by mediations as well as European authors (e.g. Chantal Mouffe), Colombian scholar Clemencia Rodríguez published a very influential book that built bridges between Latin American and European/US scholarship on alternative media, *Fissures in the Mediascape* (Rodríguez, 2001). Her work connected notions of praxis and citizenship, and proposed the concept of 'citizens' media' to move the conversation away from mass media, concentrating instead on the cultural processes that are triggered when citizens appropriate information technologies to create their own representations. Rodríguez's move from media to mediations brought nuance to the field as she invited a focus on the multiple contradictions and tensions involved in any citizens' media appropriation. She encouraged the use of contextual perspectives to understand how citizens' media allow the exercise of citizenship outside any legal or State-imposed definition. Like many other authors in the region, Rodríguez places her work at the service of praxis, understanding that 'the knowledge we produce within academia is most valuable if and only if it becomes useful for those in the field trying to make our societies better places to live' (Rodríguez, 2010a, p. 133).

Her reflections are in line with other contemporary authors who notably contributed to enlarging alternative media studies. Although the list is endless,[7] we can quote the work of Peruvian scholar Rosa María Alfaro (1993, 2006), who in 1984 founded Calandria, a very influential association for popular communication. Alfaro criticized the 'socialization' of alternative media projects at the expense of their original 'political' or 'macro-social' purposes. When these projects became larger or more organized, she argued, many began to serve rationalism at the expense of entertainment and emotion, uncritically venerating participation without acknowledging that civil society organizations and their practices are spaces of aggregation but also of conflicts based on the expression of identities. To overcome this impasse, Alfaro proposed underlining creativity and reconnecting theory and practice, since 'praxis itself has been and is richer than our older discourses and systematizations' (Alfaro, 1990, p. 65).[8] In addition to Rodríguez and Alfaro, the beginning of the 21st century saw the emergence of many other authors who emphasized the value of praxis as a mechanism for building citizenship and decentralizing power. For example, Argentinian scholar María Cristina Mata suggests that citizenship can be equated with praxis, since both serve to question the unequal organization of social relations and define politics outside the confines of State legitimacy. She advocates for a new politics,

> the one of women who affirm the political nature of private life; that of the native peoples who denounce the existence of national states that still preserve the mark of colonial exclusion; that of migrants who reject being placed at the margins of public affairs and are only accepted as an over-exploited labour force
>
> *(Mata, 2011, p. 18).*[9]

The value of practical grassroots experiences

Praxis in Latin American communication research does not just involve the intersection of theory and practice; scholars tend to use the term to refer to a long-standing tradition of regional alternative media projects, probably the largest such tradition in the world (Gumucio, 2001, p. 7). Reconstructing the history of alternative media, Beltrán (1993) demonstrated that practice always precedes theory in the field of communication for development. This is especially noticeable in the case of Latin America, where many alternative media experiences started to blossom at the end of the 1940s as a result of pure intuition and creativity, and not from any previous theoretical framework.

During the second half of the 20th century, many grassroots practices were used to resist post-colonial dependency and confront the dominance of oligarchic media ownership over public service media. The pioneering initiatives were the work of two major groups of actors: the reformist sectors of the Catholic Church, and unions and citizens' associations representing the interests of workers and popular cultures (Vinelli, 2010). The Second Vatican Council (1959) did much to open up the Church to the outside world. This resulted in the Second Meeting of the Latin American Episcopal Council (Consejo Episcopal Latinoamericano, CELAM) in Medellín in 1968, initiating an increased focus on communication research and action in the official strata of the Catholic Church (Peppino, 1999). More radical were the efforts of liberation theology and the so-called ecclesial grassroots communities (*comunidades eclesiales de base*) in Brazil and Chile, comprised of progressive priests who promoted horizontal education and communication strategies to combat the injustice and violence of the military governments. At the same time, Bolivian mining unions promoted a large number of radio stations from the late 1940s to the 1980s, which challenged the cultural dominance of the mining oligarchies in the Andean region and represented one of the first community media projects in the world. Completely designed, operated, and even financed by the miners, these stations offered autonomous programming in local languages and aimed to represent indigenous sectors whose voices were totally absent in the private media (Gumucio, 2001; Herrera, 2006).

In a media context dominated by private broadcasters, several meaningful initiatives took on the public service functions neglected by both public and private broadcasters in the second half of the 20th century. Some initiatives were educational, such as Radio Sutatenza in Colombia, which started as a small rural radio station but later became one of the largest informal education projects in Latin America. Led by Popular Cultural Action (Acción Cultural Popular, ACPO), this Catholic project combined radio shows with in-person education to promote literacy among farmers and in rural areas. Other initiatives were more politically militant and served as tools to oppose dictatorships and corrupt governments. This was the case for the guerrilla radio stations in Central America during the 1980s and 1990, such as the Salvadorian Radio Venceremos (1981–1994). Finally, many projects emphasized culture, representing the values and civil rights demands of popular movements, voices that were absent or poorly represented in the mainstream media. Community video and the so-called Third Cinema in countries such as Bolivia (well represented by Jorge Sanjinés), Colombia (Marta Rodríguez), and Argentina (Fernando Birri, Octavio Getino, Fernando Solanas) are examples of this cultural turn (Gumucio, 2014).

At the end of the 20th century, the Zapatista movement in Mexico surprised the world with its innovative use of digital technologies for cultural resistance; the actions became known as the 'first informational guerrilla movement' (Castells, 2004). Since the groundbreaking broadcasts of Subcomandante Marcos, the uses of digital technologies as tools of resistance have multiplied. In fact, the internet, mobile devices, and technological networks have strongly contributed to the organization and visibility of Latin American uprisings in recent years, as seen in the cases of Yosoy132 and #1Dmx in Mexico, the Chilean student protests, and the Brazilian Movimento Passe Livre, among others. Praxis remains essential to new social movements and their relationships with community radio (Gumucio & Herrera, 2010), video-activism (Sierra & Montero, 2015), and digital technologies (Restrepo, Valencia, & Maldonado, 2017; Sierra & Gravante, 2018). Various authors writing about ICTs have recently adopted the expression 'technopolitical praxis' to refer to the increasing intersection between political activism and information technologies, since these realms are mutually constitutive and interdependent. The concept of technopolitics has also been useful in understanding the interactions between online and offline participation, as well as the innovative praxis of social collectives that co-produce practical actions based in cooperation and collective reflection (Treré & Barranquero, 2018).

Since the end of the 20th century, indigenous activism has been an emerging topic in communication studies. This focus continues and builds on established intellectual threads such as concern for indigenous media appropriation and communication policies (Arcila, Barranquero, & González Tanco, 2018). Inspired by the critical response to the 500th anniversary of Spanish colonization (1992) and the success of the Zapatistas in Mexico (from 1994), many indigenous organizations strengthened their structures and started to fight and win legal battles for the recognition of cultural rights. After the arrival of the first indigenous governments in Bolivia (2006) and Ecuador (2007), communication research on indigenous communication practices multiplied exponentially, starting a dialogue around issues important to the lives of indigenous people: environmental protection, territorial rights, traditional epistemologies, decolonization, etc. In accordance with these new conversations, an emergent research line is exploring the interaction between communication and *Buen Vivir* [Good Living], an indigenous worldview that emphasizes the construction of a good life based on cooperative relations among humans, and between humans and nature (Barranquero & Sáez, 2017; Contreras, 2016; De Souza Silva, 2011; Magallanes & Ramos, 2016).

The social philosophy of *Buen Vivir* calls for the (re)construction of integral and operative knowledge systems that challenge positivism and modern science. For indigenous thinking, praxis is not merely a dialectical dimension of empirical work. Instead, it is a perspective inherent to traditional indigenous knowledge, which integrates belief systems, knowledge corpuses, and productive practices (Toledo & Barrera-Bassols, 2008). The concept of praxis has also been used to emphasize the role of indigenous ancestral and contemporary practices in constructing culturally specific multiple epistemologies (*pluriverse*) from the diversity of existing cultures in Latin America (Gudynas, 2016). Both social movements and indigenous studies have been important influences on the so-called Modernity/Coloniality movement that claims to decolonize social science through a critique of the implicit universalism that characterized the project of modernity. The movement also advocates the recovery of knowledge and praxis from Latin American marginalized sectors (Escobar, 2010). Within this framework, scholars have conceptualized communication as a thread of connection between diverse actors and social fights, positioning it as a space where it is possible to deconstruct the project of modernity and build new ways of thinking aimed at progressive social change (Restrepo et al., 2017, p. 27).

Citizens' appropriations of media and ICT technologies demonstrate that experience always comes first in the field of alternative communication studies. Rather than arising from existing theoretical frameworks, instances of Latin American communicology are usually the result of applying imagination to solve the injustices and address urgent issues in different historical contexts. This explains Latin American communication scholarship's critical view of the way Western scholarship often constructs universalist models that ignore the significance of local cultures and the systematization of experiences and case studies. Cultural pluralism, the revision of historical texts, and the recognition of marginalized communities have motivated recent calls to 'decolonize' communication science from a Latin American perspective (Torrico, 2015; Sierra & Maldonado, 2016; Restrepo et al., 2017). Influenced by former efforts to create an autonomous communication science (Beltrán, 1974a, 1976), a new generation of scholars are denouncing the domination of communication studies by a modern/colonial matrix, characterized by the dominance of 'European and North American authors, but also by what the Western world wants, desires and needs' (Karam, 2016/2017, p. 158). This decolonizing project also rejects traditional media-centric approaches to interpreting media from the wider perspective of culture and citizens' praxis, understanding both as dynamic and contested: 'De-westernizing means ceasing to see communication and its field with the eyes of technocracy and the market [...] and recover the liberating content of its meaning and praxis' (Torrico, 2015, p. 18).[10]

Conclusions

The turn of the 21st century brought burgeoning practice-based approaches to European and North American media research, especially after 2004 when Nick Couldry invited researchers to focus not on media as objects, text, or production process, but on 'what people [are] doing in relation to media across a whole range of situations and contexts' (Couldry, 2004, p. 119). In his 'Theorising media as practice' (2004) and later writings, Couldry argued that it is essential to explore the human needs and contextual conditions that give rise to media-related actions. He advocated this approach as a way 'to think normatively' in order to solve the question of 'how we should live with the media in the contemporary world' (Couldry, 2012, pp. 33–34). He located the beginning of this paradigm shift in the 1990s, with the work of a group of researchers 'who sought to move beyond the specific contexts of media consumption', mentioning influential scholars such as Ien Ang, Faye Ginsburg, and Roger Silverstone (Couldry, 2012, p. 39). Although he acknowledged the influence of Martín-Barbero's 'mediations' (1987/1993), many of the scholars who have responded to Couldry's call so far have systematically neglected the Latin American media-practice legacy. This omission is unsurprising since contact between European and North American and Spanish-speaking academic communities has been limited and very much constrained by the barriers of language, culture, and a particular 'geopolitics of knowledge' (Escobar, 2010). This disconnection is worth attention, though, because European and US researchers have much to learn from Latin American scholars' perspectives on praxis. Of particular significance are the emphasis Latin American authors have placed on contextual and historical approaches, and their regard for media as a basic human need and right.

In Latin America, the concept of practice has historically acted as an antidote to media instrumentality, technological determinism, and ahistorical and apolitical attitudes because media was regarded as a human process, whether at an individual, group, or technologically mediated level. The ideas of decentralizing power and developing cultural agency are essential to understanding that media studies' 'turn' toward practice had important antecedents in Latin America, as we have seen in reviewing the contributions of scholars from different fields such as alternative media, educommunication, reception studies, and communication for development. Practice-based media approaches also owe much to anthropology, which has been a major influence in Latin American communication research. This can be traced to Brazilian scholar Luiz Beltrão's (1980) explorations of the influence of popular groups and cultures in media appropriations in the early 1960s and the long lineage of research on the potential of the practice-based 'theatre of the oppressed', developed by another Brazilian scholar, Augusto Boal (1979). Media anthropology has influenced a wide range of contemporary studies. For instance, Clemencia Rodríguez (2010b) used a 'performance' approach to argue that citizens' media do not exclusively send messages but rather surround and infiltrate audiences, since grassroots groups perceive media as a lived experience enacted through praxis, the body, and the senses.

John Postill (2010) posits that praxis has not been adequately defined or problematized in European and US communication scholarship; we believe this is also true in the case of Latin American scholarship. Over time, the term has become an 'empty signifier' (Barassi, 2016) in communication research, used to refer to different and even opposing understandings. To fill this gap in research, we have outlined four practice-oriented approaches to communication: praxis understood as a liberating principle; praxis as the focus of diverse media studies that connect theory with case studies; praxis as a way receivers interact with media; and praxis as a methodology that moves from action to theory and then back to action. Regardless of the way it is defined, praxis is part of the DNA of Latin American communication thinking, and it is still encouraging scholars to act in the space where academia and activism meet, connecting knowledge with social change.

Notes

1 This thesis was proposed by Brazilian pioneer José Marques de Melo during the period 1998–2005 and it guided an ambitious project to reconstruct and project the history of Latin American communication thought. Nevertheless, the existence of a School has been questioned. Some authors consider that Latin American thinking in the period was more heterogeneous than homogeneous, so the School is mostly a utopic projection launched by Marques de Melo and his team, which is far from occupying a dominant position in academia today (Fuentes, 1999; León Duarte, 2007).

2 CIESPAL supported the visit of leading Functionalist scholars Harold D. Lasswell and Everett M. Rogers to the region. Their theories shaped the first Latin American empirical works.

3 CEREN, Chile (Centro de Estudios de la Realidad Nacional / National Reality Center); ICINFORM, Brazil (Instituto de Ciências da Informação / Institute of Information Sciences); INTERCOM, Brazil (Sociedade Brasileira de Estudos Interdisciplinares da Comunicação / Brazilian Society of Interdisciplinary Communication Studies); ININCO, Venezuela (Instituto de Investigaciones de la Comunicación de la Universidad Central de Venezuela / Communication Research Institute of the Central University of Venezuela).

4 This book was later reviewed and published by a Spanish editor under the title *A Pedagogy of Communication* (Kaplún, 1998). With the support of UNESCO, Kaplún also developed a systematization of participatory development projects undertaken throughout Latin America (Sullivan-Ryan & Kaplún, 1978).

5 However, international recognition of the Latin American educommunication legacy is still scarce given that most of its referents – Francisco Gutiérrez, Daniel Prieto, Delia Crovi, Jorge Huego, María Teresa Quiroz, etc. – are not translated into English.

6 Similarly to the case of educommunication, reception studies in Latin America are practically unknown in the Anglo-Saxon academia, although they constitute an important research line in Chile (Valerio Fuenzalida), Perú (Teresa Quiroz), Brazil (Carlos Lins da Silva), and Argentina (Alejandro Grimson).

7 To name just a few we can refer to Argentinian Natalia Vinelli, Claudia Magallanes, Máximo Simpson and María Soledad Segura, Colombian Omar Rincón, Amparo Cadavid and Pilar Riaño, Venezuelan Jesús María Aguirre, Antonio Pasquali and Elizabeth Safar, Mexican Claudia Magallanes, Antoni Castells i Talens and Guiomar Rovira, Brazilian Regina Festa and Cicilia Krohling Peruzzo, Bolivian Erick Torrico, Alfonso Gumucio, Karina Herrera and José Luis Aguirre, Peruvian Rafael Roncagliolo and Juan Gargurevich, and Chilean Fernando Reyes Matta and Chiara Sáez Baeza.

8 Author's own translation from the original in Spanish.

9 Author's own translation from the original in Spanish.

10 Author's own translation from the original in Spanish.

References

Alfaro, R. M. (1990). ¿Participación para qué? Un enfoque político de la participación en la comunicación popular. *Diálogos de la Comunicación*, 22, 59–78.

Alfaro, R. M. (1993). *Una comunicación para otro desarrollo*. Lima: Calandria.

Alfaro, R. M. (2006). *Otra brújula: innovaciones en comunicación y desarrollo*. Lima: Calandria.

Arcila, C., Barranquero, A. & González Tanco, E. (2018). From media to *buen vivir*: Latin American approaches to indigenous communication. *Communication Theory*, 28(1). doi: 10.1093/ct/qty004

Atwood, R. & McAnany, E. G. (eds) (1986). *Communication and Latin America Society. Trends in Critical Research, 1960–1985*. Madison, WI: University of Wisconsin Press.

Barassi, V. (2016). Contested visions: digital discourses as empty signifiers from the 'network' to 'big data'. *Communication and the Public*, 1(4), 423–435.

Barranquero, A. (2011). Rediscovering the Latin American roots of participatory communication for social change. *Westminster Papers in Communication and Culture*, 8(1), 154–177. http://doi.org/10.16997/wpcc.179

Barranquero, A., & Sáez, C. (2017). Latin American critical epistemologies toward a biocentric turn in communication for social change: communication from a good living perspective. *Latin American Research Review*, 52(3), 431–445. https://doi.org/10.25222/larr.59

Beltrán, L. R. (1974a). Communication research in Latin America: the blindfolded inquiry? Paper presented at Conference on the Contribution of the Mass Media to the Development of Consciousness in a Changing World, International Association for Media and Communication Research, Leipzig, pp. 1–23.

Beltrán, L. R. (1974b). National communication policies in Latin America (Com. 74/conf. 617/2). Report prepared for the Meeting of Expression Communication Policies and Planning in Latin America, Bogota (Colombia). Paris: UNESCO.

Beltrán, L. R. (1976). Alien premises, objects and methods in Latin America communication Research. In E. M. Rogers (ed.), *Communication and Development: Critical Perspectives* (pp. 14–42). Beverly Hills, CA and London: Sage.

Beltrán, L. R. (1979). *Farewell to Aristotle: 'horizontal communication'*. International Commission for the Study of Communication Problems No. 48. Paris: UNESCO.

Beltrán, L. R. (1993). Communication for development in Latin America: a forty-year appraisal. In D. Nostbakken & C. Morrow (eds), *Cultural Expression in the Global Village* (pp. 9–31). Ottawa: International Development Research Center.

Beltrão, L. (1980). *Folkcomunicação: a comunicação dos marginalizados.* São Paulo: Cortez.

Berryman, P. (1987). *Liberation Theology: Essential Facts about the Revolutionary Movement in Latin America and Beyond.* Philadelphia, PA: Temple University Press.

Boal, A. (1979). *The Theatre of the Oppressed.* New York: Urizen Books.

Bosco Pinto, J. (1976). *Educación Liberadora. Dimensión teórica y metodológica.* Buenos Aires: Búsqueda.

Capriles, O. (1996). *Poder político y comunicación.* Caracas: Universidad Central de Venezuela, Consejo de Desarrollo Científico y Humanístico.

Castells, M. (2004). *The Information Age: Economy, Society and Culture. Vol. 2. The Power of Identity,* 2nd edn. Malden, MA: Blackwell Publishing.

Cerruti, H. (1983). *Filosofía de la Liberación Latinoamericana.* México: Fondo de Cultura Económica.

CIESPAL (1973). Seminario sobre 'La investigación de la comunicación en América Latina. Informe Provisional'. *Chasqui,* 4, Primera Época, 11–25.

Contreras, A. (2016). *La palabra que camina. Comunicación popular para el Vivir Bien/Buen Vivir.* Quito: CIESPAL.

Couldry, N. (2004). Theorising media as practice. *Social Semiotics,* 14(2), 115–132.

Couldry, N. (2012). *Media, Society, World: Social Theory and Digital Media Practice.* Cambridge, UK: Polity.

De Souza Silva, J. (2011). *Hacia el 'día después del desarrollo': descolonizar la comunicación y la educación para construir comunidades felices con modos de vida sostenibles.* Asunción: ALER-SICOM.

Dervin, B., & Huesca, R. (1997). Reaching for the communicating in participatory communication: A meta-theoretical analysis. *Journal of International Communication,* 4(2), 46–74.

Díaz Bordenave, J. (1985). *Participación y sociedad.* Buenos Aires: Búsqueda.

Díaz Bordenave, J., & Martins de Carvalho, H. (1978). *Planificación y comunicación.* Quito: CIESPAL.

Dussel, E. (1996). *Filosofía de la liberación.* Bogotá: Nueva América.

Escobar, A. (2010). Worlds and knowledges otherwise: the Latin American modernity/coloniality research program. In W. D. Mignolo & A. Escobar (eds), *Globalization and the Decolonial Option* (pp. 33–64). New York/London: Routledge.

Fals Borda, O. (1973). *Ciencia propia y colonialismo intelectual.* México: Nuestro Tiempo.

Fals Borda, O. (1986). *Conocimiento y poder popular. Lecciones con campesinos de Nicaragua, México y Colombia.* Bogotá: Siglo XXI. [(1988). *Knowledge and people's power: Lessons with peasants in Nicaragua, Mexico and Colombia.* New Delhi, India: Indian Social Institute.]

Fals Borda, O. (2006). Participatory (action) research in social theory: origins and challenges. In P. Reason & H. Bradbury (eds), *Handbook of Action Research* (pp. 27–37). London: Sage.

Freire, P. (1970). *Pedagogía del oprimido.* Montevideo: Tierra Nueva. [(1970). *Pedagogy of the Oppressed.* New York: Continuum.]

Freire, P. (1975). A few notions about the word 'conscientization'. In R. Dale et al. (eds), *Schooling and Capitalism* (pp. 224–227). London: Oxford University Press.

Flores-Osorio, J. M. (2009). Praxis and liberation in the context of Latin American theory. In M. Montero & C. C. Sonn (eds), *Psychology of Liberation. Theory and Applications* (pp. 11–36). New York: Springer.

Fuentes, R. (1999). La investigación de la comunicación en América Latina: condiciones y perspectivas para el siglo XXI. *Comunicación y Sociedad,* 36, 105–132.

Gerace, F. (1973). *Comunicación horizontal.* Lima: Librería Studium.

González, J., & Mugnaini, F. (1986). Para un protocolo de observación etnográfica en los usos diferenciales y los modos de ver las telenovelas. *Culturas Contemporáneas,* 1, 149–176.

Gudynas, E. (2016). *Derechos de la naturaleza. Ética biocéntrica y políticas ambientales.* Quito: Abya-Yala.

Gumucio, A. (2001). *Making Waves: Stories of Participatory Communication for Social Change.* New York: Rockefeller Foundation.

Gumucio, A. (2014). *El cine comunitario en América Latina y el Caribe.* Bogotá: Friedrich Ebert Stiftung.

Gumucio, A., & Herrera, K. (eds) (2010). *Políticas y legislación para la radio local en América Latina.* La Paz: Plural.

Herrera, K. M. (2006). *Del grito pionero al silencio? Las radios sindicales mineras en la Bolivia de hoy.* La Paz: Friedrich Ebert Stiftung.

Huesca, R. (2007). Tracing the history of participatory communication approaches to development: a critical appraisal. In J. Servaes (ed.), *Communicaton for Development and Social Change* (pp. 180–200). London: Sage.

Huesca, R., & Dervin, B. (1994). Theory and practice in Latin American alternative communication research. *Journal of Communication,* 44(4), 53–74.

Kaplún, M. (1984). *Comunicación entre grupos: El método del cassette-foro.* Bogotá: CIID.

Kaplún, M. (1985a). *El comunicador popular.* Quito: CIESPAL.

Kaplún, M. (1985b). *Un taller de radiodrama: Su metodología, su proceso.* Quito: CIESPAL.

Kaplún, M. (1998). *Una pedagogía de la comunicación.* Madrid: Ediciones de la Torre.

Karam, T. (2016/2017). Tensiones para un giro decolonial en el pensamiento comunicológico. Abriendo la discusión. *Chasqui,* 133, 247–264.

Kush, R. (1962). *América profunda.* Buenos Aires: Hachette.

León Duarte, G. A. (2007). *La nueva hegemonía en el pensamiento latinoamericano de la comunicación. Un acercamiento a la producción científica de la Escuela Latinoamericana de la Comunicación.* Hermosillo, Sonora: Universidad de Sonora.

Macedo, D. P. (1995). A dialogue: culture, language, and race. *Harvard Educational Review,* 65(3), 377–402.

Magallanes, C., & Ramos, J. M. (eds) (2016). *Miradas propias: Pueblos indígenas, comunicación y medios en la sociedad global.* Quito: CIESPAL.

Marques de Melo, J. (2009). *Pensamiento comunicacional latinoamericano. Entre el saber y el poder.* Sevilla: Comunicación Social.

Marques de Melo, J., Gobbi, M. C., & Kunsch, W.L. (eds). (2002) *Matrizes comunicacionais latino-americanas. Marxismo e Cristianismo.* São Bernardo do Campo. São Paulo: UNESCO-UMESP.

Martín-Barbero, J. (1983). Comunicación popular y los modelos transnacionales. *Chasqui,* 8, 4–11.

Martín-Barbero, J. (1987). *De los medios a las mediaciones. Comunicación, cultura y hegemonía.* Barcelona: Gili. [(1993). *Communication, Culture and Hegemony. From the Media to Mediations.* London: Sage.]

Martín-Barbero, J. (2006). A Latin American perspective on communication/cultural mediation. *Global Media and Communication,* 2(3), 279–297.

Martín-Barbero, J., & Muñoz, S. (eds.). (1992). *Televisión y melodrama.* Bogota, Colombia: Tercer Mundo Editores

Martín-Baró, I. (1983). *Acción e ideología. Psicología social desde Centroamérica.* San Salvador: UCA.

Mata, M. C. (2011). Comunicación popular. Continuidades, transformaciones y desafíos. *Oficios Terrestres,* 1(26), 1–22.

McBrideSean (ed.) (1980). *Many Voices, One World,* Paris, Unesco.

Obregón, R., & Singhal, A. (2005). A conversation with Everett Rogers. *MAZI,* 2 February.

Orozco, G. (1993). Dialéctica de la mediación televisiva. Estructuración de estrategias de recepción por los televidentes. *Anàlisi*, 15, 31–44.

Orozco, G. (1987). Research on cognitive effects of non-educational television: an epistemological discussion. In P. Drummond & R. Patterson (eds), *TV and its Audience. International Research Perspectives*. London: British Film Institute.

O'Sullivan-Ryan, J., & Kaplún, M. (1978). *Communication Methods to Promote Grass-Roots Participation: A Summary of Research Findings from Latin America, and an Annotated Bibliography*. Communication and Society, 6. Paris: UNESCO.

Peppino, A. M. (1999). *Radio educativa, popular y comunitaria en América Latina: origen, evolución y perspectivas*. México: UAM & Plaza y Valdés.

Postill, J. (2010). Introduction. Theorizing media as practice. In B. Bräuchler & J. Postill (eds), *Theorising Media and Practice* (pp. 1–19). New York: Berghahn Books.

Rahman, M. A. (1993). *People's Self Development: Perspectives on Participatory Action Research*. London: Zed Books.

Reguillo, R. (2000). *Estrategias del desencanto. Emergencia de culturas juveniles*. Buenos Aires: Norma.

Restrepo, P., Valencia, J. C., & Maldonado, C. (eds) (2017). *Comunicación y sociedades en movimiento. La revolución sí está sucediendo*. Quito: CIESPAL.

Rodríguez, C. (2001). *Fissures in the Mediascape. An International Study of Citizens' Media*. Cresskill, NJ: Hampton.

Rodríguez, C. (2010a). Knowledges in dialogue. A participatory evaluation of citizen's radio stations in Magdalena Medio, Colombia. In C. Rodríguez, D. Kidd, & L. Stein (eds), *Making our Media: Global Initiatives towards a Democratic Public Sphere* (pp. 131–154). Cresskill, NJ: Hampton Press.

Rodríguez, C. (2010b). Communication and the power of performance. *Media Development*, 57(4), 26–29.

Rogers, E. (1982). The empirical and critical schools of communication research. In M. Burgoon (Ed.), *Communication Yearbook* (Vol. 5, pp. 125–144). New Brunswick, NJ: Transaction Books.

Sierra, F., & Gravante, T. (eds) (2018). *Networks, Movements and Technopolitics in Latin America. Critical Analysis and Current Challenges*. Cham: Palgrave Macmillan and International Association for Media and Communication Research.

Sierra, F., & Maldonado, C. (eds) (2016). *Comunicación, decolonialidad y buen vivir*. Quito: CIESPAL.

Sierra, F., & Montero, D. (eds) (2015). *Videoactivismo y movimientos sociales. Teoría y pracis de las multitudes conectadas*. Barcelona: Gedisa.

Toledo, V. M., & Barrera-Bassols, N. (2008). *La Memoria Biocultural. La importancia ecológica de las sabidurías tradicionales*. Barcelona: Icaria.

Torrico, E. (2015). La comunicación 'occidental'. *Oficios Terrestres*, 32, 3–23.

Treré, E., & Barranquero, A. (2018). Tracing the roots of technopolitics: towards a North–South dialogue. In F. Sierra & T. Gravante (eds), *Networks, Movements and Technopolitics in Latin America. Critical Analysis and Current Challenges* (pp. 43–63). Cham: Palgrave Macmillan and International Association for Media and Communication Research.

Vinelli, N. (2010). Alternative media heritage in Latin America. In J. D. Downing (ed.), *Encyclopedia of Social Movement Media* (pp. 27–30). Thousand Oaks, CA: Sage.

4

EDUCOMMUNICATION FOR SOCIAL CHANGE

Contributions to the construction of a theory of activist media practices

Ángel Barbas

Introduction

Communication for social change (CfSC) is a domain of knowledge concerned with studying the relations between communication processes and the socio-political conditions of human beings. CfSC began at the end of the 1960s, in a socio-political context marked by development paradigms and the emergence of critical theories (Beltrán, 1979, 2005). This period saw the simultaneous publication of a series of studies in the United States (see e.g. Lerner, 1958; Rogers, 1962; Schramm, 1964) and Latin America (see e.g. Pasquali, 1963; Freire, 1969; Beltrán, 1970) based on practices and experiences that were developed across differing cultural and geographical contexts. These two strands of scholarship correspond to the primary approaches that informed the development of CfSC: the 'diffusionist' approach, linked with the US context and the 'participatory' approach, associated with a Latin American perspective (Barranquero & Sáez, 2010; Gumucio, 2011; Huesca, 2007).

Importantly, CfSC's epistemological framework was rooted in social practice. These practices arose through different communication experiences and processes at the end of the 1940s in the United States and Latin America. CfSC emerged from the communication practices that originated after World War II. These were developed by campaigns designed by international organizations – such as the United States Agency for International Development, the World Bank, and the Food and Agriculture Organization of the United Nations, among others – to decrease poverty and improve the lives of those in the most disadvantaged countries. In this chapter, however, my arguments are based in community and grassroots communication practices developed by various social collectives in Latin American countries since the mid-1940s (Gumucio, 2001; O'Sullivan-Ryan & Kaplún, 1978; Kaplún, 1985, 1992) and subsequently in other countries in Europe, Africa, and Asia (Alumuku &

White, 2005; Landáburu, 2017). Despite the variety of these experiences, which are framed by unique social and political contexts, a review of the literature demonstrates many common elements. These include their shared communication model, community-based character, openness to citizen participation, and orientation to transforming the lives of the people and communities with whom they are involved (Alfaro, 2000; Barranquero & Sáez, 2010; Beltrán, 2005; Gumucio, 2011; Rodríguez, 2001). The personal and social transformational element of these Latin American communication initiatives explicitly relates to the educational dimensions of the experiences and practices that have traditionally been the subject of study of CfSC. For this reason, scholars and activists began to consider 'educommunication' one of the branches of CfSC.

I frame my work within a flourishing field of research emerging around activist media practices. I believe the educational orientation of CfSC in general, and the educommunication paradigm more specifically, can contribute significantly to enriching discursive resources as well as methodologies of analysis for studying the relations between media practices, communication activism, and citizens' media. My objective is to contribute to knowledge of activist media practices. To this end, I outline the educommunication paradigm and explore some of the most relevant theoretical approaches to media practices from a pedagogical perspective, analysing their characteristics and arguing for the need to incorporate educommunication knowledge into the study of these phenomena. Finally, I propose and elaborate on the concept of 'educommunicative diagnosis' as a toolbox for analysing activist media practices.

The paradigm of educommunication

In the late 1960s and early 1970s, educommunication emerged as a subfield of CfSC focused on the pedagogical dimensions of citizens' and community media, as well as communication processes more generally. Communication and education began to be seen as constituent parts of the same process of media and socio-political training. In this paradigm, an educational act is viewed a communicational act, and a communicational act as an educational act. Consequently, Educommunication, Educational Communication, and Pedagogy of Communication, among other categories, were born based on the tenet that communication educates and that one is educated through communication (see e.g. Kaplún, 1985, 1992; Gutiérrez, 1973, 1975; Prieto, 1999; Oliveira, 2009).

The work of Freire (1965, 1970) is fundamental to these developments. In response to the 'diffusionist' approach, in which communication was understood as the hierarchical transmission of knowledge from one to many, Freire proposed a 'participatory' and 'dialogical' approach, in which communication was understood as the democratic production of knowledge. Further, in response to the 'banking' model, in which education was understood as an instrument of domestication and oppression of subjugated groups by dominant groups, Freire suggested 'problematizing' and 'liberatory' models of education. Freire established a reciprocal relationship between communicative and educative practices and interpreted communication and education processes as 'circles of culture', which generated consciousness raising and the politicization of participants. Later, authors such as Gutiérrez (1973, 1975), Kaplún (1985, 1992), and Prieto (1999) laid the foundation for an educational model of communication characterized by favouring participation, empowerment, and consciousness raising to generate individual and collective transformation. This model was intended to promote processes of 'conscientization' that permit the development of processes of 'politicization' (Freire, 1970).

Accordingly, educommunication is understood as a form of critical pedagogy that studies communication practices as pedagogical processes. It is distinguished by its determined historical conjuncture and specific sociocultural context. As educommunication came on the scene in Latin America, similar movements in countries such as the United Kingdom, France, USA, and Canada, began to emerge at the end of the 1960s and beginning of the 1970s. These efforts were driven by authors such as McLuhan (1960), Vallet (1968), and Porcher (1974), who analysed the growing influence of communication media in society, reflecting on the role of media as educational agents. This marked the beginning of what we know today as 'media education' (Masterman, 1985; Buckingham, 2003, 2015), an academic discipline officially recognized by national and international educational institutions (e.g. British Film Institute, European Union, UNESCO) that has seen important developments in recent years due to the wave of ICTs and the mass use of the internet.

The terms educommunication and media education are often used interchangeably, but it is important to remember that these concepts grew out of different epistemological traditions. While educommunication is a paradigm or philosophy that can support the development of actions or research in different educative and communicative contexts, media education is a technical discipline with concrete procedures, focused on training citizens in media competencies. In the Ibero-American context, educommunication and media education have converged in recent years to address the study of the relationships that exist between educational and communicational processes and, as is more relevant to the proposal of this chapter, to analyse media practices as a means of learning. We must therefore ask what the epistemology of educommunication can contribute to the theory of media practices in activist contexts. Answering this question requires us to first explore some theoretical approaches to media practices from a pedagogical perspective.

Media practice theory in activist contexts: a pedagogical perspective

Theories of practice form a branch of social theory that addresses the study of 'practice' as an alternative to focusing on structures, systems, or individuals. It emerged as an intermediate path between attributing social phenomena exclusively to individual actions, and attributing them exclusively to social structures (Postill, 2010). When we talk about 'social practices', we refer to individual interactions, but also to activities of the mind and body, as well as objects and 'things'. These 'things' can include the knowledge individuals obtain through their life experiences, their mental schema and frameworks, their understanding of social reality, and their procedural knowledge, as well as their emotional states and the motivations that lead them to act in determinate moments (Schatzki, 2001; Reckwitz, 2002; Shove et al., 2012). Studying social practices from the perspective of practice theory implies considering a social practice as a 'block' composed of these elements, the nature of which depends on the coexistence, interdependence, and specific interconnection established between these elements when a person interacts with their environment (Postill, 2010; Reckwitz, 2002; Schatzki, 2001).

Communication processes developed in social movements should be observed as 'complex socio-technical institutions' (Downing, 2008), so the theory of practice offers a propitious framework with which to approach the study of communication processes in activist contexts. This theoretical approach allows us to focus on what people do with the media beyond functionalist media-centric approaches. This section seeks to analyse the theoretical approaches that focus on the ways media practices are organized and combined, as well as how they intersect with other social practices, specifically educational and activist learning processes (Couldry, 2004). This analysis involves considering some theoretical approaches to media practices in activist contexts and addressing the implicit pedagogical dimensions of these practices. These are, in my view, key to understanding how educommunication supports the construction of a theoretical-conceptual framework that allows us to analyse media practices developed in contexts of communicational activism.

Theoretical approaches to practice in activist contexts

In this chapter I focus on two theoretical approaches to practice in activist contexts, which are complementary and mutually reinforcing. First, there are theoretical approaches that focus attention on the richness of activist interactions with the media and the people who are engaged in those communication processes, beyond the production or circulation of content (Mattoni, 2012; Mattoni & Treré, 2014; Stephansen, 2016). Second, there are those approaches that explore how social movements, through their political, social, and cultural practices, generate significant knowledge for activist groups and society as a whole (Casas-Cortés et al., 2008; Chesters, 2012; Cox & Flesher Fominaya, 2009; Cox, 2014; Della Porta & Pavan, 2017).

In her work on precarious workers in Italy, Mattoni (2012) defines 'activist media practices' as social practices that include interactions with media-objects (mobile phones, computers, and print media) and interactions with media-subjects (journalists, public administrators, and other activists). This definition is important because it posits that media are more than discrete artefacts. According to Mattoni, people and the networks of interactions between media artefacts and people are also essential to the definition of media. Mattoni and Treré (2014) similarly extend Martín-Barbero's (1987) concept of mediation to articulate a proposal specific to the context of communication activism. For these authors, 'processes of mediation' are circular and include media practices and social activities in which members involve themselves in social movements, using communication media to achieve their objectives.

Research conducted by Stephansen (2016), based on her fieldwork at the World Social Forum, further explores these issues and offers new approaches. Building on the concept of 'citizens' media' developed by Rodríguez (2001), the author proposes the term 'citizen media practices' to explain the repertoire of media practices developed by activists, constructing a taxonomy of media practices composed of organizational practices, capacity-building practices, networking practices, and movement-building practices. Stephansen (2016) defines some of these practices as 'processes of informal pedagogy' for the empowerment of activists; ultimately, she contends, citizens' media practices can contribute to the emergence of a civic culture supported by emancipatory processes of knowledge production.

Also addressing the production of knowledge, Della Porta and Pavan (2017) argue that social movements form collective spaces of knowledge production that are true laboratories for innovation. The work by Casas-Cortés et al. (2008) explores those ideas, arguing that social movements perform epistemological work by analysing, imagining, and developing new ways of knowing and being in the world. In the same sense, Chesters (2012) defines these processes as a form of phenomenological epistemology in the specific context of activist practices. Cox & Flesher Fominaya (2009) necessarily ask both how and what type of knowledge is developed by social movements. They refer to the pedagogical approach of Paulo Freire – one of the pioneers of educommunication – to argue that, through consciousness raising, people can come to know reality and challenge the structures of oppression. Further, Cox (2014) develops the concept of 'movement spaces of self-education' to explain how social movements are constituted in learning environments as well as why they use the methodology of participatory action research (PAR) to produce knowledge.

The approaches to media practices outlined above provide valuable conceptual tools for understanding the complex communication ecosystems in which activists operate. These ecosystems include the relationships of interdependence that are established between the media practices activists develop and the totality of social practices in which they are involved. They also highlight the importance of these processes for the production and management of knowledge. Activist media practices have consequences in the lives of participants, affecting their individual and collective identities, modifying their mental patterns, transforming their understandings of the world and their position in relation to others. Here, we return to Couldry (2004), whose focus on media practices allows us to understand how these practices are organized and combined, and how they intersect with other social practices. We must also ask, however, how these practices intersect with educational practices. How do media practices relate to the educational processes developed by social movements? What can pedagogical knowledge contribute to the theory of media practices in activist contexts?

Practice-oriented theory can open up space for thinking about the relationship between media practices and learning, but the connection is largely implicit in the literature on activist media practices. The epistemology of educommunication leads us to consider media practices explicitly as a means of learning – a perspective largely overlooked by communication and media studies scholars, with notable exceptions (Barbas & Postill, 2017, Kellner & Kim, 2010, Lema, Rodríguez & Barranquero, 2016). An educommunication perspective enables us to see that social movements develop a range of different educational practices in relation to the media practices deployed by participants. For this reason, I focus on social movements that have emerged in recent years, as they have deployed an important repertoire of communication and education practices. The following section is dedicated to the pedagogical dimension of activist media practices.

The pedagogical dimension of activist media practices

Social movements can be observed as informal education environments, insofar as their actions are aimed at training activists and promoting citizenship as a whole. We could even say that social movements function as pedagogical-political actors because they educate society toward a different way of understanding the world (Della Porta & Diani, 2011; Marí, 2005). Many of the communication practices developed by the alter-globalization movement, as well as some groups from the World Social Forum (Juris, 2004, 2006; Milan, 2013; de Sousa, 2007; Stephansen, 2016) and more recently, anti-austerity movements (Barranquero, 2014; Candón, 2013; Costanza-Chock, 2012; Postill, 2014), are characterized by the importance placed on the media empowerment of activists and society as a whole. In some cases, social movements have organized and developed substantial repertoires of teaching and learning to achieve such empowerment. In other cases, media practices act as *de facto* processes of learning.

While doing fieldwork among the movement of the Spanish Indignados in Madrid in 2014 and 2015, I was able to see the pedagogical dimension of the movement in general, and the actions that supported media practices in particular (Barbas & Postill, 2017). The movement was characterized by the creation of various communication projects of different types and the frequent incorporation of media training. Some training actions were part of an explicit pedagogical plan, designed to teach participants to use digital media and technologies for coordination, the dissemination of messages, or the production of content. Outside of these organized seminars, workshops, and courses, however, the interactions and social practices that activists developed in their daily lives had an influence on their learning, as documented in participant interviews. The importance given to communication and media empowerment meant media practices acted as *anchoring practices*, or elements that structure social practices (Couldry, 2004; Swidler, 2001). These include the dynamics of daily life as well as pedagogical actions, whether formal or informal. We framed the media practices of activists as a school of politics and identified three pedagogical principles: first, the principle of pedagogical sovereignty, originating in the hacker idea of technological sovereignty; second, the principle of pedagogical action, which regards communication activists as political educators; and third, the principle of networked pedagogy, based on the notion of communication activists as producers of open networks of political education (Barbas & Postill, 2017).

In sum, studying activist media practices from the perspective of educommunication involves considering the media ecosystem as a pedagogical environment that can accommodate more or less systematic educommunicative projects aimed at communicational empowerment. This means the pedagogical dimension of media practices can be more or less visible and more or less explicit, depending on the degree of systematization; nevertheless, a pedagogical dimension is always present in the communication ecosystem of activists. For this reason, we need to introduce the paradigm of educommunication to theories of media practices. We need to make use of tools that allow us to observe and analyse educational phenomena that occur in activist communication ecosystems. The educommunication approach can provide valuable analytical-conceptual tools for this project.

I use the term 'diagnosis', viewed from the perspective of educommunication, as an instrument of analysis. I propose the concept of educommunicative diagnosis as a toolbox that will allow us to explore and discover the pedagogical dimension of activist media practices.

The educommunicative diagnosis: a toolbox for the analysis of activist media practices

In the social sciences, the term diagnosis refers to the analysis of systematically collected data with the aim of identifying a particular social situation (Ander-Egg & Aguilar, 1995). An educommunicative diagnosis of activist media practices will contribute data in relation to the situation of a collective from the paradigm of educommunication. Accordingly, it is important to remember that educommunication requires a certain methodological flexibility; as Barranquero (2007, p. 118) articulates, 'the method is built in community and is modified according to the concrete problems that arise during the process'. Among the wide variety of educommunicative experiences found in Latin American literature, I would like to emphasize two methods that emerged from different practices and then joined into one conceptual tool. These two practices include the concept of feed-forward (as opposed to feedback) and the method of PAR.

Mario Kaplún coined the term 'feed-forward' to describe 'the initial search we do among the recipients of our media messages so that our messages represent them and reflect them' (Kaplún, 1978, pp. 120–123). Although Kaplún applied this term to radio programme production, a close reading of this concept permits us to amplify its interpretation and consider its application as a diagnosis. For example, Kaplún and his collaborators used it as a research method to discover the social problems of the communities in which they worked, asking questions, living in the community, and having discussions with them to help them problematize their lives. The researchers involved community members in educommunicative projects with the goal of transforming their reality. Feed-forward is a way to analyse reality that emerges from educommunicative practices, in which the distances and distinctions between producers and receivers are removed, as well as those between educators and learners, with the objective of engaging the community in resolving their own problems. Kaplún's feed-forward concept connects directly with PAR as a method of analysis in social inquiry.

Participatory action research is a qualitative research and action strategy that seeks to analyse and understand social situations with the goal of developing solutions that contribute to improving the quality of life of the community or group being studied. Using the feed-forward concept, PAR makes the collectives themselves participants in the investigation process. The collective is the protagonist of the investigation, becoming 'subject' rather than 'object' of the study. Participatory action research has its origins in the work of Kurt Lewin (see Lewin, 1946), but it has been fully realized in the work of Latin American researchers, including the Colombian Orlando Fals Borda, who constructed a methodological framework based on a PAR approach. Fals Borda's approach was inspired by a confluence of thinking around community-based education and alternative communication in Latin America at the end of the 1960s and beginning of the 1970s (Bonilla, Castillo, & Fals Borda, 1972; Fals Borda, 1985). This approach uses a mode of PAR rooted in the Latin American socio-critical research paradigm, which studied community development through the improvement of communication and education. Accordingly, PAR was used as a principal method of research in the field of educommunication. Combined with Kaplún's feed-forward concept, PAR is a tool for developing diagnostic procedures in the context of activist media practices.

This theoretical foundation means educommunicative diagnoses should be made with the participation of activists and using qualitative techniques framed in methodological procedures such as the feed-forward approach or PAR. Techniques such as participant observation, discussion groups, ethnographic conversations, and in-depth interviews may be used, along more systematic techniques, such as surveys and standardized questionnaires, when needed. Regardless, it is essential to emphasize that, in the educommunication paradigm, the diagnosis must be inserted into the dynamics of daily life of the collective. It can be oriented to the production of knowledge for the academic world, but it must also take into account the production of knowledge for the improvement of activist media practices.

An educommunicative diagnosis provides information on media competencies, training needs, and action planning as well as impact evaluation. I will now elaborate on these diagnostic categories with the aim of expanding our analytical toolbox, suggesting guided questions that can be used to analyse the pedagogical dimension of activist media practices.

The study of media competence and training needs

The educommunicative diagnosis of social movements' media practices can provide valuable information about activists' need for training in media skills and communication empowerment. For this, it is essential to consider the concept of 'media competence', which has emerged in recent years in media education research in different parts of the world. Media competence is defined as the conceptual, procedural, and attitudinal knowledge that individuals need to responsibly and critically use communication media from the point of view of both production and reception (Ferrés, 2007, Ferrés et al., 2011, Ferrés & Piscitelli, 2012).

The educommunicative diagnosis can help us assess levels of media competence and the training needs of activists. Standardized criteria and indicators have been developed as a reference point (Ferrés et al., 2011); however, following the paradigm of educommunication and educommunicative diagnosis that I propose here, the active participation of the group under study is essential to collaboratively define criteria and indicators of analysis. We will also need to answer some of the following questions: What media competencies do activists need to achieve their social and political objectives? How do they perceive these needs? Have they made any systematic identification of these training needs? What kind of media practices should be developed to meet these needs?

Action planning

As has been mentioned in previous sections, studying activist media practices from the perspective of educommunication involves considering the media ecosystem as a pedagogical environment that can accommodate educommunicative projects with varying degrees of specificity and systemization. The goal is enhancing media-based learning and the development of communicational empowerment. This implies prior planning of such projects, although this planning may not be explicit or manifest. An educommunicative diagnosis can provide valuable information in this regard.

Social movements that develop communication projects and produce citizens' media have strategies and planning models with varying degrees of systematization. 'Systematic planning' refers to the degree to which the stages, phases, and activities of a project are planned out ahead of time. More systematic projects develop a plan in advance that remains more or less stable throughout the development process. Non-systematic planning, or planning with a more flexible degree of systematization, emerges as the project unfolds. Activists continuously collect data from the project's results and make adjustments as they go along (Ander-Egg, 1978).

Some authors define this model as 'planning without a plan' (Díaz Bordenave & Martins de Carvalho, 1978), which does not imply the absence of organizational strategies for action. It does, however, imply adapting planning to reality in a process divided into three principal phases: action, reflection, and action. These should not be understood as rigid divisions, but as different moments of a permanent self-reflexive cycle, in which action generates knowledge of the situation and new knowledge informs the redesign of action in order to continue with the planning process on a continuum.

The educommunicative diagnosis can help us analyse how media competency training is conducted. Questions we can ask include: How have the formative training actions been planned and how systematic is the planning? To what extent is the planning consistent with the training needs of the activists? How does planning or non-planning influence the learning of new media competences and, more generally, the development of media empowerment among activists to achieve their social and political objectives?

Impact evaluation

The educommunicative diagnosis can also provide data on the impact that training actions have on activists' learning. Media practices must be understood as a means of learning, particularly when considering training projects that are not rigidly systematized. Further, as mentioned earlier, standardized criteria and indicators have been developed for analysing activists' learning (Ferrés et al., 2011); however, in the paradigm of educommunication and the proposed educommunicative diagnosis, we cannot forget the need to promote the active participation of the collective that we are investigating in defining the criteria and indicators of analysis.

Questions to guide evaluation of the learning of activist media practices include: How have activists learned the media practices they develop? What are the characteristics of these practices? What influence does systematic planning of formative media practice training actions have on learning? How do activists translate media practices for use in different contexts and for different purposes? How do the media practices learned by activists relate to their capacity for social and political action?

Conclusions

In this chapter, I have tried to contribute to knowledge of activist media practices from the paradigm of educommunication. To this end, I have explored some of the theories of media practices from a pedagogical perspective, arguing that, although such perspectives open up space for thinking about the relationship between media practices and learning, they rarely pay explicit attention to how activist media practices combine and intersect with the educational practices developed within social movements (Couldry, 2004). I have focused on those theoretical approaches that highlight the rich interactions that activists establish with media and the people who engage in these communication processes (Mattoni, 2012; Mattoni & Treré, 2014; Stephansen, 2016), as well as those approaches that affect how social movements generate knowledge (Casas-Cortés et al., 2008; Chesters, 2012; Cox & Flesher Fominaya, 2009, Cox, 2014; Della Porta & Pavan, 2017).

This review shows that theories of media practices provide us with valuable conceptual tools for understanding the complex communication ecosystem deployed by activists, as well as the rich interdependent relationships established between the constituent elements of this ecosystem and the potential that activist practices have as engines for knowledge production. However, these theories do not address the pedagogical dimension of social movements, despite having significant relevance in social movements emerging in recent years in different parts of the world (Castells, 2012; Della Porta & Diani, 2011, Marí, 2005; Sousa, 2007).

Using an educommunication epistemology, I have focused on activist media practices understood as a means of learning and on the implicit or explicit pedagogical dimension of the social movements' media practices. This focus supports my argument that there is a theoretical gap in scholarly explanations of the confluence between media practices and learning processes. I contend that social movements that have emerged in recent years have articulated an important repertoire of media practices to achieve their social and political objectives. This has made processes of teaching and learning to achieve media and communication empowerment increasingly important (see e.g. Candón, 2013; Costanza-Chock, 2012; Milan, 2013; Postill, 2014). In making these arguments, I build on the ethnographic fieldwork I conducted in Madrid in 2014–15 with the Indignados movement (Barbas & Postill, 2017). That fieldwork led me to conclude that the study of activist media practices from the perspective of educommunication requires considering the media ecosystem as a pedagogical environment that can accommodate a range of educommunicative projects.

Examining some of the theories of media practices and confirming the pedagogical dimensions of social movements has led me to introduce the paradigm of educommunication. I propose using analytical tools that allow us to understand the pedagogy of activist media practices. In other words, we should ask what kinds of relationship are established between media practices and educational processes, and how these relationships affect activist learning.

I propose the concept of educommunicative diagnosis as a toolbox for analysing activist media practices. I developed this proposal based on methodological procedures that are part of the epistemology of educommunication, such as the feed-forward approach and PAR. Educommunicative diagnosis includes tools for analysing activist media practices from the perspective of educommunication, such as the study of media competence and training needs, the planning of actions, and impact evaluation. I have included guided questions for each of these conceptual tools, which can be used to analyse the pedagogical dimensions of activist media practices.

We must make explicit the fundamental pedagogical dimension of social movements' media practices. It is the activists themselves who are continuously systematizing and developing their media practices based on varyingly explicit or implicit pedagogical planning. If we want to understand and theorize about the impact of media practices, their pedagogical dimensions and an epistemology of educommunication must frame our approach.

To continue advancing the construction of a theory of activist media practices, I advocate theory that integrates diverse academic disciplines and analytical perspectives to account for the fact that our object of study – dynamic and often imprecise – emerges directly from experiences that do not develop according to the laws of academic orthodoxy. We will be able to overcome limitations to the extent that we are able to construct a transdisciplinary theoretical framework based on a dialogue between the academic world and the world of communication activism. The proposal elaborated in this chapter represents a call to continue working in this direction. We need conceptual links that allow us to expand our capacity to understand the complex repertoire of media practices developed within social movements. Educommunication, already a bridge that connects education and communication, allows us to build another bridge between 'media practices' and 'media learning processes'.

References

Alfaro, R. M. (2000). Culturas populares y comunicación participativa: en la ruta de las rededini- ciones. *Razón y Palabra*, 18. http://www.razonypalabra.org.mx/anteriores/n18/18ralfaro.html
Alumuku, P., & White, R. (2005). La radio comunitaria para el desarrollo en África. *Redes. com: Revista de Estudios para el Desarrollo Social de la Comunicación*, 2, 405–413. http:// revista-redes.hospedagemdesites.ws/index.php/revista-redes/article/view/65
Ander-Egg, E. (1978). *Introducción a la planificación*. Buenos Aires: El Cid Edit.
Ander-Egg, E., & Aguilar, M. J. (1995). *Diagnóstico social. Conceptos y metodología*. Buenos Aires: Lumen.
Barbas, Á., & Postill, J. (2017). Communication activism as a school of politics: lessons From Spain's Indignados movement. *Journal of Communication*, 67(4), 646–664.
Barranquero, A. (2007). Concepto, instrumentos y desafíos de la edu-comunicación para el cambio social. *Comunicar*, 29, 115–120. https://www.revistacomunicar.com/index.php? contenido=detalles&numero=29&articulo=29-2007-19
Barranquero, A., & Sáez, C. (2010). Comunicación alternativa y comunicación para el cambio social democrático: sujetos y objetos invisibles en la enseñanza de las teorías de la comunicación. In *Comunicación y Desarrollo en la era Digital*. Proceedings of the II Congreso Internacional AE-IC, Universidad de Málaga, Spain. https://orecomm.net/wp-con tent/uploads/2010/01/AEIC-Barranquero-Saez.pdf
Barranquero, A. (2014). Comunicación, cambio social y ONG en España. Pistas para profundizar en la cultura de la cooperación desde los nuevos movimientos comunicacionales. El caso del 15M. *COMMONS: Revista de Comunicación y Ciudadanía Digital*, 3(1), 6–28. http://dx.doi.org/10.25267/COMMONS.2014.v3.i1.01
Beltrán, L. R. (1970). Communication in Latin America: persuasion for status quo or for national development? PhD thesis, Michigan State University, USA.
Beltrán, L. R. (1979). *Farewell to Aristotle: Horizontal Communication*. International Commission for the Study of Communication Problems, 48. Paris, France: UNESCO. https:// unesdoc.unesco.org/ark:/48223/pf0000039360
Beltrán, L. R. (2005). La comunicación para el desarrollo en Latinoamérica. Un recuento de medio siglo. Proceedings of the III Congreso Panamericano de la Comunicación, Universidad de Buenos Aires, Argentina. https://www.infoamerica.org/teoria_textos/lrb_ com_desarrollo.pdf

Bonilla, V., Castillo, G., & Fals Borda, O. (1972). *Causa popular, ciencia popular. Una metodología del conocimiento científico a través de la acción.* Bogotá, Colombia: La Rosca.

Buckingham, D. (2003). *Media Education: Literacy, Learning and Contemporary Culture.* Cambridge, UK: Polity.

Buckingham, D. (2015). La evolución de la educación mediática en Reino Unido: algunas lecciones de la historia. *Revista Interuniversitaria de Formación del Profesorado,* 82, 77–88. http://aufop.com/aufop/uploaded_files/articulos/1507479351.pdf

Candón, J. (2013). *Toma la calle, tomas las redes. El movimiento #15M en Internet.* Andalucía, Spain: Atrapasueños.

Casas-Cortés, M., Osterweil, M., & Powell, D. (2008). Blurring boundaries: recognizing knowledge-practices in the study of social movements. *Anthropological Quarterly,* 81(1) 17–58. https://www.countercartographies.org/wp-content/files/Blurring_Boundaries.pdf

Castells, M. (2012). *Redes de indignación y esperanza.* Madrid: Alianza.

Chesters, G. (2012). Social movements and the ethics of knowledge production. *Social Movement Studies,* 11(2), 145–160.

Costanza-Chock, S. (2012). Mic check! Media cultures and the Occupy Movement. *Social Movement Studies: Journal of Social, Cultural and Political Protest,* 1(11).

Couldry, N. (2004). Theorising media as practice. *Social Semiotics,* 14(2), 115–132.

Cox, L. (2014). Movements making knowledge: a new wave of inspiration for sociology? *Sociology,* 48(5), 954–971.

Cox, L., & Flesher Fominaya, C. (2009). Movement knowledge: what do we know, how do we create knowledge and what do we do with it? *Interface,* 1(1), 1–20. http://www.interfacejournal.net/wordpress/wp-content/uploads/2010/11/interface-issue-1-1-pp1-20-Editorial.pdf

Della Porta, D., & Diani, M. (2011). *Los movimientos sociales.* Madrid, Spain: CIS.

Della Porta, D., & Pavan, E. (2017). Repertoires of knowledge practices: social movements in times of crisis. *Qualitative Research in Organizations and Management,* 12(4), 297–314.

Díaz Bordenave, J., & Martins de Carvalho, H. (1978). *Planificación y comunicación.* Quito: CIESPAL.

Downing, J. (2008). Social movement theories and alternative media: an evaluation and critique. *Communication, Culture & Critique,* 1, 40–50.

Fals Borda, O. (1985). *Conocimiento y poder popular: lecciones con campesinos de Nicaragua, México y Colombia.* Bogotá: Siglo XXI.

Ferrés, J. (2007). La competencia en comunicación audiovisual: dimensiones e indicadores. *Comunicar,* 29, 100–107. https://www.revistacomunicar.com/index.php?contenido=detalles&numero=29&articulo=29-2007-17

Ferrés, J., & Piscitelli, A. (2012). La competencia mediática: propuesta articulada de dimensiones e indicadores. *Comunicar,* 38, 75–82. https://doi.org/10.3916/C38-2012-02-08

FerrésJ., García, A., Aguaded, J. I., Fernández, J., Figueras, M., & Blanes, M. (2011). *Competencia mediática: Investigación sobre el grado de competencia de la ciudadanía en España.* Madrid: Instituto de Tecnologías Educativas, Ministerio de Educación. http://rabida.uhu.es/dspace/bitstream/handle/10272/6876/Competencia_mediatica.pdf?sequence=2

Freire, P. (1965). *La educación como práctica de la libertad.* Montevideo: Tierra Nueva.

Freire, P. (1969). *¿Extensión o Comunicación?* Santiago de Chile: ICIRA.

Freire, P. (1970). *Pedagogía del oprimido.* Montevideo: Tierra Nueva.

Gumucio, A. (2001). *Haciendo olas. Historias de comunicación participativa para el cambio social.* New York: Rockefeller Foundation.

Gumucio, A. (2011). Comunicación para el cambio social: clave del desarrollo participativo. *Signo y Pensamiento,* 30(58), 26–39. https://revistas.javeriana.edu.co/index.php/signoypensamiento/article/view/2454

Gutiérrez, F. (1973). *El lenguaje total. Una pedagogía de los medios de comunicación.* Buenos Aires: Humanitas.

Gutiérrez, F. (1975). *Pedagogía de la comunicación.* Buenos Aires: Humanitas.

Huesca, R. (2007). Siguiendo el rastro de la historia de los enfoques de Comunicación Participativa en Desarrollo: Un acercamiento crítico. *Redes.com: Revista de Estudios para el Desarrollo Social de la Comunicación,* 4, 21–42. http://revista-redes.hospedagemdesites.ws/index.php/revista-redes/article/view/115

Juris, J. (2004). Indymedia. De la contra-información a la utopía informacional. In Marí, V. (ed.), *La red es de todos. Cuando los movimientos sociales se apropian de la Red* (pp. 154–177). Madrid: Editorial Popular.

Juris, J. (2006). Movimientos sociales en red: movimientos globales por una justicia global. In Castells, M. (ed.). *La sociedad red: Una visión global* (pp. 415–439). Madrid: Alianza.

Kaplún, M. (1978). *Producción de programas de radio. El guión-la realización.* Quito: CIESPAL.

Kaplún, M. (1985). *El comunicador popular.* Quito:CIESPAL/CESAP/Radio Nederlad.

Kaplún, M. (1992). *A la educación por la comunicación.* Quito:CIESPAL.

Kellner, D., & Kim, G. (2010). YouTube, critical pedagogy, and media activism. *Review of Education, Pedagogy, and Cultural Studies,* 32(1), 3–36.

Landáburu, A. (2017). Modelo y escenario de las radios comunitarias en India. *Telos: Revista de Pensamiento, Sociedad y Tecnología,* 107. https://telos.fundaciontelefonica.com/archivo/numero107/modelo-y-escenario-de-las-radios-comunitarias-en-india/

Lema, I., Rodríguez, E., & Barranquero, A. (2016). Jóvenes y tercer sector de medios en España: Formación en comunicación y cambio social. *Comunicar,* 48, 91–99.

Lerner, D. (1958). *The Passing of Traditional Society: Modernizing the Middle East.* New York: The Free Press.

Lewin, K. (1946). Action research and minority problems. *Journal of Social Issues,* 2(4), 34–46.

Marí, V. (2005). Movimientos sociales y educación popular en tiempos de globalización. *Revista de Educación,* 338, 177–192. http://www.educacionyfp.gob.es/dam/jcr:dc78c4dc-e419-421a-bf17-07db23f0c052/re33812-pdf.pdf

Martín-Barbero, J. (1987). *De los medios a las mediaciones.* México DF: Gustavo Gili.

Masterman, L. (1985). *Teaching the Media.* London: Comedia.

Mattoni, A. (2012). *Media Practices and Protest Politics: How Precarious Workers Mobilise.* London: Routledge.

Mattoni, A., & Treré, E. (2014). Media practices, mediation processes, and mediatization in the study of social movements. *Communication Theory,* 24(3), 252–271.

McLuhan, M. (1960). *Report on Project in Understanding New Media.* Washington, DC: National Association of Educational Broadcasters. http://blogs.ubc.ca/nfriesen/files/2014/11/McLuhanRoPiUNM.pdf

Milan, S. (2013). *Social Movements and their Technologies: Wiring Social Change.* London: Palgrave Macmillan.

Oliveira, I. (2009). Caminos de la educomunicación: utopías, confrontaciones, reconocimientos. *Nómadas: Revista de Ciencias Sociales,* 30, 194–207. http://nomadas.ucentral.edu.co/nomadas/pdf/nomadas_30/30_14D_Caminosdelaeducomunicacion.pdf

O'Sullivan-Ryan, J., & Kaplún, M. (1978). *Communication Methods to Promote Grassroots Participation: A Summary of Research Findings from Latin America, and an Annotated Bibliography.* Paris: UNESCO. https://unesdoc.unesco.org/ark:/48223/pf0000043552

Pasquali, A. (1963). *Comunicación y cultura de masas.* Caracas: Universidad Central de Venezuela.

Porcher, L. (1974). *La escuela paralela.* Buenos Aires: Kapelusz.

Postill, J. (2010). Introduction: Theorising media and practice. In Bräuchler, B. & Postill, J. (eds), *Theorising Media and Practice* (pp. 1–32). Oxford and New York: Berghahn Books.

Postill, J. (2014). Freedom technologists and the new protest movements. A theory of protest formulas. *Convergence*, 20(4), 402–418.

Prieto, D. (1999). *La comunicación en la educación*. Buenos Aires: La Crujía.

Reckwitz, A. (2002). Toward a theory of social practices: a development in culturalist theorizing. *European Journal of Social Theory*, 5(2), 243–263.

Rodríguez, C. (2001). *Fissures in the Mediascape. An International Study of Citizens' Media*. New York: Hampton Press.

Rogers, E. (1962). *Diffusion of Innovations*. New York: The Free Press.

Schatzki, T. R. (2001). Introduction: Practice theory. In Schatzki, T. R., Knorr-Cetina, K., & von Savigny, E. (eds), *The Practice Turn in Contemporary Theory* (pp. 1–14). London: Routledge.

Schramm, W. (1964). *Mass Media and National Development. The role of Information in the Developing Countries*. Palo Alto, CA: Stanford University Press.

Shove, E., Pantzar, M., & Watson, M. (2012). *The Dynamics of Social Practice: Everyday Life and How it Changes*. London: Sage.

de Sousa, B. (2007). El Foro Social Mundial y el autoaprendizaje. La Universidad Popular de los Movimientos Sociales. *Revista Theomai*, 15, 101–106. http://revista-theomai.unq.edu.ar/numero15/artsantos_15.pdf

Stephansen, H. C. (2016). Understanding citizen media as practice: agents, processes, publics. In Baker, M. & Blaagaard, B. (eds), *Citizen Media and Public Spaces: Diverse Expressions of Citizenship and Dissent* (pp. 25–41). London: Routledge.

Swidler, A. (2001). What anchors other practices. In Schatzki, T. R., Knorr-Cetina, K., & von Savigny, E. (eds), *The Practice Turn in Contemporary Theory* (pp. 74–94). London: Routledge.

Vallet, A. (1968). *Du ciné-club au langage total: Pédagogie et culture pour notre temps*. Paris: Ligel.

PART II

Activist agency and technological affordances

INTRODUCTION

Donatella Della Porta

About 50 years ago, the student movement I experienced directly as a teenage activist in Sicily was dense in communication practices. In terms of production, we were intensively involved in writing documents for internal use and leaflets for circulation, but also journal articles for sympathetic outlets, and even books for 'movement-near' publishers. The network of student collectives of which I was part also engaged in artistic production (at times, even of good quality): we had a 'musical commission' that staged various tours, a 'photographic commission' that documented sufferance and resistance to it; and a 'cinema commission' that even rented a cinema theatre to screen political movies and documentaries. After an important protest event, we would write a sort of press release that we dutifully delivered to the local (right-wing) daily, which almost never published even a small part of it (a fact that annoyed us a bit but was not really considered very important, as we did not aim to impress what we considered the conservative audience of that newspaper). While we did not call them graffiti, we did write our slogans on the walls (especially in front of schools and universities).

The various products of our communicative activities were distributed using existing technologies, with some creativity. We usually typed our texts on stencil to be used with mimeographs, which we had pushed university administrators to put at the disposal of the students for self-organized cultural activities (I did this, but so did other male comrades – so I am not really convinced by the image of the female comrades as *angeli del ciclostile* – angels of the mimeograph). Our posters were written by hand using multi-coloured marker pens. Only occasionally, we collected money to have our leaflets or posters printed by (sympathetic) professionals. Calls for meetings and protest events circulated by posters and/or telephone chains – each of us calling another five comrades, usually from our parents' telephones. The mail system was used sparingly, mainly for sending movement journals that we then sold in our schools, at the risk of being charged with 'unauthorized selling'. As censorship was frequent, the distribution of propaganda materials such as written texts of artistic performances often brought about police charges for attacks against morality and apology of crime (I collected a few of these, but fortunately there was then an amnesty). Only a few cars – often small and on short loan from relatives – were available to take leaflets, musical instruments, or documentaries around. Motorbikes (small ones) were used creatively to transport posters, buckets full of glue, and brushes for wild posting all around the city. We ourselves travelled to do 'political work' at the periphery of the city and in the province mainly by bus, train, or hitchhiking.

We then consumed much of what we produced within the alternative circuits – our own, or in the broader counterculture. With no cellphone and no internet, we were nevertheless creative in our communication practices, even if distribution was quite challenging. In the collective production of communication, rhythms were slow but intense, with activists contributing in different communicative streams with different competences and skills.

I was reminded of all this while reading the two contributions to this section of the book that show brilliantly how the concept of practices allows us to move beyond several stereotypes coming from conventional approaches to both mass media and digital media, allowing for a historical account of the evolution of different practices. As I am going to argue in this short introduction, the more traditional approaches – to mass media as brokers for protest messages, but also to alternative media – would have some problems in capturing the richness and complexity of communicative activities in and around social movements like the ones I have just recalled. In this sense, the reference to practices could be useful in bridging the focus on structures present in the literature on mass media selectivity with that on agency developed in research on alternative media. My account would certainly resonate with Nick Couldry's call to focus attention on:

> 1. New ways of consuming media, which explicitly contest the social legitimacy of media power; 2. New infrastructures of production, which have an effect on who can produce news and in which circumstances; 3. New infrastructures of distribution, which change the scale and terms in which symbolic production in one place can reach other places.
>
> (Couldry, 2003, p. 44)

At the same time, however, this very complexity of activities of production, distribution, and consumption, as well as the presence of various actors, seem to indicate that practice as a sensitizing concept needs to be bridged with others in order to provide for theoretical understanding of a quickly moving field.

A main approach in previous research on communication in social movements has paralleled the attention to political opportunities in social movement studies by focusing on media (or discursive) opportunities (as well as the interaction between the two). In doing this, research has pointed in particular at the selectivity of mass media towards movement actors, the limitations on media freedom and pluralism that discourage media coverage of contestation, along with the increasingly negative effects of tendencies of concentration, commercialization, and deregulation in the mass media system. If research has repeatedly confirmed the limited capacity of social movements to influence the mass media, with selection but also descriptive biases when covering protest, the practice approach would allow us to investigate the ways in which mass media are perceived and handled.

While certainly mass media can work as important gatekeepers for social movements and might shape public sensibilities, social movement activists and organizations pay limited (and perhaps declining) attention to the established media in their everyday activities. Digital media have instead been seen as favouring movements through the multiplication of information producers, as well as of information available for consumption – their pluralism allowing for the development of multiple, critical public spheres with increasing capacity for citizens to oversee their governments. However, as concerns remain about the unidirectional (top-down) use of new technologies, the presence of a digital divide, and the very quality of communication online, a focus on practices allows us to single out how activists respond to these challenges. This moves attention from the abstract 'power of the media' to the relations between media and publics (Couldry, 2006). Media practices therefore become central, not only as the practices of media actors, but more broadly in terms of what various actors do in relation to the media, including activist media practices.

Practice approaches can also help to go beyond research on activist media, stressing the communicative agency of activism in connecting various media. If analysis of media opportunities has tended to pay particular attention to structural constraints, agency emerges especially in research that, in the tradition of resource mobilization approaches, has looked at alternative media as strategic instruments for mobilization, but also as arenas for the prefiguration of horizontal and participatory visions of production and communication. Studies of alternative media especially stress the differences in their contents and style as well as in the ways they produce news, pointing to their capacity to improve participatory democracy by expanding the range of information and ideas, being more responsive to the excluded, and impacting on participants' sense of self (Downing, 2001). Together with their critical, counter-hegemonic contents, they have the capacity to involve not only (or mainly) professional journalists but also ordinary citizens in news production, given their horizontal links with their audience (Atkinson, 2010). As my memories confirm, alternative communicative practices have long overcome the distinction between audience and producers, readers and writers. An approach to activists' media practices that goes beyond specific alternative media allows us to understand the ways in which members of social movements deal with the challenge for alternative (on- and offline) media of reaching beyond those who are already sympathetic to their cause.

Research on social movements and their communication practices has started to move beyond a vision of alternative media as separated from the broader media field. For instance, attention to media practices as 'practices of resistance in their own right' (Cammaerts, 2012; Mattoni & Treré, 2014) addresses the ways in which 'people exercise their agency in relation to media flows' (Couldry, 2006, p. 27). While new technologies might have facilitated a blurring of the boundaries between news production and news consumption, producers and the public, the historical accounts that the two chapters in this section (as well as my own memories) present show that the very logic of communication in progressive social movements has always aimed (even if with varying results) at producing alternative public spheres, giving citizens a right to speak that also means a right to communicate and 'be the media'. The innovation is therefore not so much in the growing blurring of boundaries between production, distribution, and consumption in activist milieus, but rather in how the layering out of different means of communication (production, distribution, and consumption) affects the potential for creativity in challenging technological affordances.

If attention to practices as a sensitizing concept seems very useful to map what activists do with media, in order to properly build theory, it is however important to combine attention to practices with attention to other elements that affect the communicative practices – technological affordances, norms, and content being central ones.

First of all, as the two chapters that follow highlight, technical affordances – the materiality of practices as described by Anne Kaun (Chapter 6) and the temporality, spatiality, and resistance embedded in certain means of communication as described by Bart Cammaerts (Chapter 5) – remain relevant in defining constraints and opportunities for media production, distribution, and consumption. Digital media have deeply transformed the media opportunities for movements by their very limited costs, immediacy, and global spread. Hence, digital media shape the modes in which individuals can express themselves in public (Gerbaudo & Treré, 2015) even if activists 'purposively and strategically create, select, juxtapose, and publicly display digital contents of all types (photos, video, texts, animated gifs etc.) that, altogether, define their public presence' (della Porta & Pavan, 2018 p. 33) The 'material agency' of digital media certainly impacts upon the modes and forms of online protest and activism (Pavan, 2014). The very fast time of technological change also has a relevant impact on practices

> [b]ecause digital media are tools designed to be in a 'permanently beta' version, that is, to be constantly in evolution, also their interplay with collective endeavours is very likely to remain fluid and ever-evolving. All possible transformative effects that digital media may exert on social movement dynamics are played out at the crossroads between material and social factors and thus are inherently sociotechnical.
>
> (della Porta & Pavan, 2018, p. 34)

Beyond the materiality of the media, movement practices are – like other repertoires of action – also led by norms. New technologies have been said to resonate with social movements' vision of democracy at the normative level. Fast and inexpensive communication allows for flexible and more participatory organizational structures. Research on contemporary movements has confirmed the importance of normative visions in determining the use of new technologies. Differences, and even tensions, in the use of new technologies by various social movement organizations and activists reflect different conceptions of democracy and communication. Conceptions of democracy inside and outside groups tend to filter the technological potentials of technological innovations. Different social movement organizations thus tend to exploit different technological opportunities, producing communication endowed with different qualities that apparently reflect different organizational models (Mosca & della Porta, 2009). Interactions between platform providers and online creative communities are subject to different types of governance that are related to different conceptions of democratic decision making (Fuster, 2010). Activists involved in community radio and radical internet projects use old and new technologies differently as the repertoires of action, networking strategies, and organizational forms are filtered through the activists' motivations and ideological/cultural backgrounds with a particular attention to the normative meanings of internal democracy as well as relations with users (Milan, 2013).

Finally, and related to this, the content of alternative political imaginaries is important, as social movement activism has per se a high capacity for innovation. Movements focused on media policy are particularly interesting in the development of normative (and ethical) debates on issues of censorship and accountability. Thus, 'accounting more systematically for the knowledge that movements produce in the current digital mediascape appears to be a necessary step to comprehend how fluid and ever evolving communication networks can become *agents of democratization*' (della Porta & Pavan, 2018, p. 35).

More generally, attempts to develop a theory of practice have pointed to the potential to combine a focus on practices with attention to concepts such as technological affordances, norms, and knowledge. In particular, Andreas Reckwitz (2002) has linked together various streams of thought that address practices as main explanations of social order. Contrasting them with theories that stress either interest or norms, he has located practice theory within cultural approaches, distinguishing it however from mental, textual, and intersubjective versions of the latter. In this version, a practice is 'a routinized type of behaviour which consists of several elements, interconnected to one another: forms of bodily activities, forms of mental activities, 'things' and their use, a background knowledge in the form of understanding, know-how, states of emotion and motivational knowledge' (ibid., p. 249). Practice theory then regards agents as 'carriers of routinized, oversubjective complexes of bodily movements, of forms of interpreting, knowing how and wanting and of the usage of things' (ibid., p. 259). While the emphasis on routines seems useful to understand how a certain social order is reproduced, research on media practices would need to address the breaking of routines, which is a central focus of social movement activism. With more of a focus on societal changes, Shove, Pantzer, & Watson (2012) have defined practices as consisting of three main elements: materials (objects, technologies, tangible physical entities); competences (skill, know-how, technique); and meanings (symbolic meanings, ideas, aspirations). Change is thus explained as resulting from processes of innovation that develop through reconfigurations of practices. As activists reconfigure their communicative practices to adapt them to transformed material conditions but also emergent norms, the need to understand the motivations of the (individual but especially collective) agents would benefit from engagement with other theories of action.

In conclusion, while it is no longer true that there is little research on movements and media, certainly development within the two main traditions of media studies and social movement studies have remained largely separate, with limited attempts at bridging them. The concept of practices is potentially able to facilitate dialogues across borders, enabling understanding of the interaction between structure and agency, technical and social, habitus and strategies, the past and present. Especially, reflection on the media practices of activists allows us to expand the attention to media systems as structural constraints and opportunities to include creative ways through which those constraints are addressed. At the same time, they allow us to map different ways to communicate, beyond alternative media outlets. Considering materiality but also knowledge, practice theory also helps to go beyond technological determinism, but without losing sight of technological affordances.

Not by chance, parallel moves to the growing attention to practices can be singled out in social movement studies. First of all, the concept of practices resonates with the attention to social movement performances as routinized forms of contention (Tilly, 2008). Moreover, the conceptualization of a media environment in which not only different spokespersons intervene, but also different types of media interact (Mattoni, 2009), can be considered in parallel with approaches in social movement studies that have pointed to the importance of looking at broader fields (or arenas), which involve social movements, activists, and organizations, but also other players with different and mutable roles and strategies (e.g. Jasper & Duyvendak, 2015). Finally, resonant with the concept of 'practice movement' (Eckert, 2015), which aims at singling out the various forms of resistance in everyday life, the concept of media practices also sensitizes us to the importance of looking at what activists do when they are not protesting in the streets.

References

Atkinson, J. D. (2010). *Alternative Media and Politics of Resistance.* New York: Peter Lang.

Cammaerts, B. (2012). Protest logics and the mediation opportunity structure . *European Journal of Communication,* 27(2), 117–134.

Couldry, N. (2003). Beyond the Hall of Mirrors? Some theoretical reflections on the global contestation of media power. In N. Couldry & J. Curran (eds), *Contesting Media Power: Alternative Media in a Networked World* (pp. 39–55). Lanham. MD: Rowman & Littlefield.

Couldry, N. (2006). *Listening Beyond the Echoes: Media, Ethics and Agency in an Uncertain world.* New York: Paradigm.

Downing, J. D. H. with Villareal Ford, T., Gil, G., & Stein, L. (2001). *Radical Media: Rebellious Communication and Social Movements.* London: Sage.

Eckert, J. (2015). Practice movements: the politics of non-sovereign power. In D. della Porta & M. Diani (eds), *Oxford Handbook of Social Movements* (pp. 567–577). Oxford: Oxford University Press.

Fuster, M. (2010). Governance of online creation communities: provision of infrastructure for the building of digital commons. PhD thesis, European University Institute, Florence.

Gerbaudo, P., & Treré, E. (2015). In search of the 'we' of social media activism: introduction to the special issue on social media and protest identities . *Information, Communication & Society*, 18(8), 865–871.

Jasper, J., & Duyvendak, J. W. (eds) (2015). *Players and Arenas: The Interactive Dynamics of Social Movements*. Amsterdam: Amsterdam University Press.

Mattoni, A. (2009). Multiple media practices in Italian mobilizations against precarity of work. PhD thesis, European University Institute, Florence.

Mattoni, A., & Treré, E. (2014). Media practices, mediation processes, and mediatization in the study of social movements. *Communication Theory*, 24, 252–271.

Milan, S. (2013). *Social Movements and their Technologies: Wiring Social Change*. London: Palgrave Macmillan.

Mosca, L., & della Porta, D. (2009). Unconventional politics online. In D. della Porta (ed.), *Democracy in Social Movements* (pp. 194–216). London: Palgrave.

Pavan, E. (2014). Embedding digital communications within collective action networks: a multidimensional network perspective. *Mobilization: An International Journal*, 19(4), 441–455.

della Porta, D. (2013). Bridging research on democracy, social movements and communication. In B. Cammaerts, A. Mattoni, & P. McCurdy (eds), *Mediation and Protest Movements* (pp. 21–37). Chicago, IL: Intellect.

della Porta, D., & Pavan, E. (2018). The nexus between media, communication and social movements. In G. Meikle (ed.), *The Routledge Companion to Media and Activism* (pp. 29–37). London: Routledge.

Reckwitz, A. (2002). Towards a theory of social practices: a development in culturalist theorizing. *European Journal of Social Theory*, 5(2), 243–263.

Shove, E., Pantzar, M., & Watson, M. (2012). *The Dynamics of Social Practice*. London: Sage.

Tilly, C. (2008). *Contentious Performances*. Cambridge: Cambridge University Press.

5

A GENEALOGY OF COMMUNICATIVE AFFORDANCES AND ACTIVIST SELF-MEDIATION PRACTICES

Bart Cammaerts

Introduction

Many scholars, including many contributors to this edited collection, have in recent years made valuable contributions to building conceptual bridges between media and communication studies and social movement studies. In doing so, the central role of media, of communication tools, and of self-mediation practices in the context of contentious politics has been foregrounded and better theorized. Media and communication are deemed to be crucial to assert a collective identity and circulate movement discourses, either independently or through the mainstream media, but they are equally important in terms of mobilizing efforts for direct actions and organizing a movement.

In this chapter, I will provide a historical overview of the various ways in which activists and social movements have appropriated, used, and above all shaped media and communication technologies to fit a set of self-mediation practices in support of their broader movement goals. At the same time, we can observe persistent attempts by the powers that be to limit and constrain the emancipatory potentials of media and communication technologies to act as tools of resistance.

The broader theoretical argument that I will be making is that media and communication technologies, through their appropriation by agentic actors, enable a wide variety of self-mediation practices, which implicates on one side material affordances and innovations through the creative social shaping of technology, and on the other side regulation and the dynamic interplay between the State and activists. This in turn relates to the permanent struggle as well as dialectic between structure and agency. Furthermore, there is a spatial and a temporal dimension to this, whereby the precise nature of this interplay between agentic opportunities and structural constraints varies over time as well as in different (political) contexts. I will link this to a dialectic between the political opportunity structure and the mediation opportunity structure.

Self-mediation practices, communicative affordances, and the mediation opportunity structure

Couldry (2004, p. 118) calls media practices the 'things that people do with the media'. Along the same lines, in the context of activism and social movements, self-mediation practices denote what activists do with media and communication tools in the context of their struggle. I deliberately emphasize both media *and* communication in this context as movements indeed produce their own media, as well as aim to be represented in 'the media'. At the same time, they are highly active communicators, directed internally within the movement and externally to the world outside of the movement. Elsewhere I have argued that activists' self-mediation practices are pivotal in the constitution of a movement and the construction of a collective identity (see Cammaerts, 2018). Furthermore, the self-mediation practices of social movements fit and map onto a set of communicative goals and mediation needs, which I have suggested include the need to disseminate movement frames, to mobilize for actions, to coordinate actions, to organize the movement, to manage its public visibility, to record protest events, and to archive protest artefacts potentially leading to movement spillovers.

Practice theory is a highly useful theoretical resource in this context precisely because it presents a distinctly dialectical theorization of the relationship between structure and agency. It sought to avoid the over-privileging of one over and above the other, which fits the study of social movements and ultimately of social change. Here, the work of Ortner (2006) and her critiques of 'classic' practice theory are important. She highlighted the importance of Raymond Williams' Gramscian approach in relation to practice theory, underlining the importance of (cultural) hegemony and denying the possibility of total domination and closure. Equally relevant to activism and to the possibility of agency is Rao's evocation of tactics in the context of practices. Relying on de Certeau's famous distinction between the strategic and the tactical, Rao defines tactics as:

> cunning combinations of possible practices, an opportunity that is seized upon to create an advantage. It is the act itself, ephemeral and situational, which is not in line with a dominant order. When accumulated, such acts may render structure ineffective. They are the fuzziness of everyday life that carries the *potential for transformation*.
>
> *(Rao, 2010, p. 151; emphasis added)*

Ortner's work also boosted the historical and politico-culturalist perspective in practice theory: 'a theory of practice is a theory of history', she argued (1989, p. 192), and thus a theory of change. A historical approach stresses the importance of a temporal dimension, of memory and tradition, and at the same time of renewal with regard to practices. The impact of culture on practice then foregrounds the inevitability of the political and how practices are always shaped by power, inequalities, and asymmetries.

While at first focused on audiences and ordinary citizens, a practice theory approach can also be very useful to study and analyse media production or meaning making. Media practice, Ipsen argues, is 'an activity that constitutes media meaning' (2010, p. 174). This opens up the possibility to apply a practice theory approach to what activists do with media and communication technologies in their efforts to disseminate their movement discourses and frames and to mobilize for direct action (Mattoni and Treré, 2014; Cammaerts, 2018).

It is, however, impossible to theorize the self-mediation practices of activists and social movements without acknowledging the distinct materialities of the various media and communication technologies at their disposal. Objects and technologies that enable communicative practices have a set of affordances embedded in them that are amenable to certain practices and less to others. Self-mediation practices are, however, not only circumscribed by the affordances of media and communication technologies, but also by the persistent efforts to limit the emancipatory potentials of these technologies and objects by the powers that be.

Let me first address 'affordances' and how they impact self-mediation practices. Gibson (1977), an ecological psychologist, coined the notion of affordances to explain how the environment surrounding an animal constitutes a given set of affordances. Affordances represent opportunities or rather potentialities for a set of actions, and thus for a set of practices.

Affordances can be objective and subjective, recognized and hidden. This means that objects can hold affordances that have hitherto not yet been recognized as such. Furthermore, what is technologically possible is not always intended when technologies are designed. As social constructivist perspectives on technological innovation have repeatedly pointed out, this very fact opens up a space for user resistance, for innovation and creativity, uncovering hidden affordances (Silverstone & Hirsch, 1992). This requires skills, knowledge, and know-how, although serendipity can also play a role in this regard. The appropriation of the affordances of new media and communication technologies and the potential for uncovering hidden affordances leading to innovative mediation practices is one aspect of what I have called the *mediation opportunity structure* (Cammaerts, 2012)

Whether activists are able to exploit the communicative affordances, known as well as hidden, is dependent not only on the mediation opportunity structure, but also on the political and regulatory context in which activists operate. In other words, the political opportunity structure impacts on the mediation opportunity structure and shapes the horizon of the possible. What is a distinct option for activists to do or use in one context might not be possible in another, giving rise to both differential activist practices and innovative circumventions in different contexts. As such, the appropriation of media and communication technologies by activists situates itself at the 'intersection between social context, political purpose and technological possibility' (Gillan, Pickerill, & Webster, 2008, p. 151).

In what follows I will address a number of communicative affordances relevant to activists, as well as the ways in which states tend to intervene to limit or thwart the emancipatory potentials of media and communication technologies.

Activist affordances, communicative practices and state interventions

The communicative practices afforded by media and communication technologies are varied and mainly situated at three levels of analysis: i) temporality – linked to the affordances of asynchronous and real-time communicative practices; ii) spatiality – related to the affordance of media and communication technologies to collapse distance and enable both private and public communicative practices; and iii) resistance – implicating the affordance to circumvent state-imposed limitations and to hack technologies in order to enable this.

The latter set of affordances, circumvention and hacking, is necessary precisely because state and corporate actors tend to put in place structural constraints geared towards limiting the emancipatory mediation opportunities afforded by media and communication technologies. This also refers to what is commonly called the *political opportunity structure*. As Meyer points out:

> The wisdom, creativity, and outcomes of activists' choices – their *agency* – can only be understood and evaluated by looking at the political context and the rules of the games in which those choices are made – that is, *structure*.
>
> *(Meyer, 2004, p. 128; emphasis in original)*

If we interconnect the political with the mediation opportunity structure we can observe various structural interventions that aim to limit the agentic opportunities, but this relationship is dialectical and dynamic. As such, we point towards evidence that agency leads to clever and creative workarounds, circumventing the limitations put in place by the state or the market. Below, I discuss various historical examples of this dialectic in the context of different media and communication technologies and their specific affordances.

Print

The first media and communication technology enabling self-mediation practices by activists and movements was the printing press. Print cultures had both temporal and spatial affordances as they enabled the asynchronous and gradual spread of movement discourses and ideas through society. With technological improvements over time, printed material could be produced in vast quantities, more cheaply, and it could be distributed more easily and more widely.

In pre-revolutionary France, for example, a vibrant print culture existed, producing an array of incendiary pamphlets and publications. It acutely demonstrated the 'dangerous power of the written word to subvert social order by entering into collective processes of political contestation', as Baker (1987, p. 208) put it. However, in order to reach the urban and rural working classes or *Sansculottes*, visual representations of movement frames, for example through satirical cartoons (see Figure 5.1), were often more important than the printed word, because those who were literate represented a minority at that time.

Print has remained an important form of public communication for activists and social movements throughout history as print technologies improved through numerous innovations. As evidenced by the emergence of a 'proletarian public sphere' (Negt & Kluge, 1993), these print technologies were appropriated by new movements in order to have full control over the means of communication.

This appropriation of printing technologies by both revolutionary and reformist forces did not go uncontested. States did their utmost to control the use of and access to printing technologies. In many countries, access to paper was controlled by the state and printers required a state licence to operate. Censorship was also commonplace. On the eve of the French Revolution almost 200 censors were working for the *Ancien Régime* and all publications needed a royal stamp of approval before they could be published officially (Darnton, 1982, p. 6; Roche, 1989, p. 5). Besides this, there were mechanisms in place to censor and repress content post-publication.

FIGURE 5.1 The 1789 print 'The Awakening of the Third Estate'
Source: Anonymous (1789) Reveil Du Tiers Etat. France, 1789. Retrieved from: Library of Congress, https://www.loc.gov/item/2009633461/

Even after the demise of absolute monarchies, political and moral censorship remained firmly in place in the emerging liberal democracies, for example through seditious libel, anti-heresy, *lèse-majesté*, and obscenity laws. After reviewing 500 years of printing history, Steinberg (1955[1996], p. 195) concluded that in terms of print, 'governments have continuously and usually successfully tried to introduce some kind of censorship while shamefacedly avoiding the odious name'.

At the same time, resistance against state control of print cultures was rife. Despite the fervent efforts of the French State to contain subversive revolutionary content, circumvention was widespread. Printers in the Netherlands, living in a more liberal 'protestant' regime, made a fortune printing content destined to be smuggled into France (Eisenstein, 1997). This material would subsequently be distributed through clandestine shops and book-peddlers across France (Darnton, 1982, p. 184).

Another common way of circumvention was DIY production, by-passing official printers altogether through cheap means of self-reproduction. For example, in Soviet Russia, we could observe a revival of *Samizdat*, a tradition of clandestine distribution of censored content which harked back to the anti-tsarist movement of the 19th Century. Rather than printing presses, typewriters were the main technology used to reproduce subversive texts. Thin and brittle carbon copy paper would be used to enable the typing of several copies at once. *Samizdat* is both private and public at the same time, representing 'a dialogical meeting of subjectivities, of the author with reader-publishers' (Komaromi, 2012, p. 89).

The need for low-cost, fast production and independence from official printers led the student activists of May '68 to resort to the centuries-old silk-screen printing technique (Rohan, 1988). Screen printing or serigraphy was subsequently appropriated by many movements, and for a long time it constituted the preferred way to reproduce textual and visual content in various underground and sub-cultures across the world. This tradition of DIY printing persists until today, aided by the invention of photocopying, desktop publishing, and laser printers, which together have greatly democratized the production of printed material, making state control of printed content much more difficult.

Postal services and telecommunication

The emergence of postal services and their affordance of sending letters 'made it possible to mobilize opinion' across large distances (Briggs & Burke, 2009, p. 131). Furthermore, postal services afforded internal communication with a view to assess and discuss the (political) context, to coordinate the movement, to organize direct actions, and to exchange sensitive information.

Letters were an important means to distribute news and gossip in the run-up to the French Revolution (Funck-Brentano, 1905). They played a crucial role during the American Revolutionary War (1775–1783), when political and military leaders used letters as their main mode of communication to discuss strategies and tactics to win their independence struggle against the British (Nagy, 2011). The importance and relevance of letters in the context of activism and political struggles can also be deduced from the publication of letters written by political and intellectual leaders throughout history. A good example is the vast archive of letters sent by Karl Marx and Friedrich Engels to each other and to others within the burgeoning anarchist and socialist movement (Marx & Engels, 1934).

With the emergence of first the telegraph and later on the telephone, real-time mediated communication over longer distances became a distinct possibility. Especially the telephone, with its affordance to enable real-time, one-to-one communication across large distances, was ideal for coordinating a social movement across distance. The protagonists of the US civil rights protests in the 1950s and 1960s, such as Martin Luther King, used the telephone amply to coordinate actions and to distribute information amongst themselves. For the US civil rights movement, the telephone 'functioned [...] to build decentralized social formations' (Adams, 1996, p. 434). Here, we can observe how mediated communication technologies became instrumental in terms of building and sustaining movement networks.

In the case of both the postal services and telecommunication, one of the most prevalent ways in which the state attempted to control interpersonal communication was through interception and surveillance practices. Across Europe, so-called black chamber (or *cabinet noir*) operations were set up inside central post offices. They specialized in opening, reading, and re-sealing correspondence. During the US Revolutionary War, it was estimated that about half of the correspondence between revolutionary leaders was intercepted by the British (Nagy, 2011). This practice continued well into the 19th and 20th centuries. In their letters to each other and to others, Marx and Engels regularly discuss the interception of letters by police and secret services.

The telephone, however, made covert surveillance much easier and less detectable. In 1963, then US Attorney General Robert Kennedy authorized the FBI to wiretap Martin Luther King Jr's telephones, both at his home and in his office, transcribing everything that was said (Garrow, 1986). In the post-9/11 era, anti-terrorism laws have enabled law enforcement agencies in Western countries to expand their surveillance practices massively. In the US context, '[a]nti-war protestors, the occupy movement, Greens, and others from the left and right opposing governmental policies are surveillance targets with post-9/11 tools' (Price, 2013, np). A similar tendency can be observed in the UK (Flesher Fominaya & Wood, 2011).

As a result of these state practices, many communicative counter-practices emerged geared towards circumventing or mitigating surveillance by the state. Letters written by leaders during the US Revolutionary War were often written with invisible ink (Nagy, 2011). Coded language, which ultimately led to the development of encryption, was another common response to surveillance. In one of his letters, Marx mentions the use of secret addresses, unknown to police and secret services, to which letters could be sent safely (Marx & Engels, 1934).

When it comes to telephones, activists suspicious of eavesdropping by the state would avoid saying sensitive things over the telephone, use public telephones, or turn to coded language. In the context of the US civil rights struggle, Wide Area Telephone Service (WATS) lines were used to distribute sensitive information safely (Stephen, 2015). These were similar to 0800-lines but paid for by organizations that were part of the movement. These lines would then be used by activists from the South who wanted to report aggression towards black citizens or arrests of militants, circumventing white switchboard operators. The reported information would then be conveyed further through so-called WATS-Reports.

As this example points out, real-time telecommunication was not only used in the context of private forms of communication to coordinate decentralized movements; the telephone was also instrumental in terms of distributing alternative information and counter-discourses. Another illustration of this is how the telephone, in conjunction with audio-cassette tapes, played a key role in the run-up to the 1979 Iranian revolution. Khomeini's speeches were transmitted through the telephone from Paris, recorded on cassette tapes in Tehran, and subsequently copied, distributed, and even amplified to large crowds. Sreberny-Mohammadi & Mohammadi (1994) spoke in this regard of 'small media' which expose the complex interconnections of private and public forms of communication, and illustrate how the use of these small media could serve as a kind of gigantic megaphone.

In recent times, the emergence of the mobile phone has yet again offered activists new and different real-time communicative affordances in support of their various struggles. In a very short time, mobile technologies 'have evolved beyond simple mobile chatting devices into tools for political activity, organisation and mobilisation' (Hermanns, 2008, p. 74). These are, however, vulnerable to surveillance and jamming practices by the state. During the 2014 pro-democracy protests in Hong Kong, the affordances of mobile technologies were mobilized by the digital native protesters of the Umbrella movement, but this did not go uncontested. In response, the Chinese and Hong Kong authorities waged cyber-warfare against the pro-democracy activists, surveilling their communication and censoring online content (Tsui, 2015). Furthermore, the use of smartphones was seriously hampered in the occupied spaces, which led protesters to download FireChat, an app enabling mesh networking through Bluetooth (Monachesi & Turco, 2017). As such, they could bypass the internet and the mobile network while still being able to communicate with each other, amounting to yet another creative workaround in the ongoing standoff between protesters and the powers that be.

Radio broadcasting

The emergence of broadcasting ushered in a new era of public real-time communication, and radio especially proved to be a powerful tool in the hands of activists.

Radio has the affordance of immediacy and, just as with audio or visual prints, literacy is not necessary. In this regard we could refer to the role of radio during the Cuban revolution (1953–1959). Radio stations in Havana and Santiago, under the control of the Batista regime, were targeted and occupied to distribute a call for a national strike (Sweig, 2002, p. 136). Furthermore, in the winter of 1958, Che Guevara set up Radio Rebelde, a short-wave radio station located in the Sierra Maestra, a mountain range in the south of the island. Later, Castro (2012, p. 38) wrote that the station was 'an essential tool and vehicle for the dissemination of information and, secondly, a means of communicating with the outside world'.

In the same period, the Algerian independence struggle appropriated radio as a tool to reach mass audiences. In a very short time, radio was transformed from a hegemonic instrument in the hands of the French colonizers to an instrument of resistance. La Voix de l'Algérie Libre et Combattante, which started broadcasting in December 1956, brought 'to all Algeria the great message of the Revolution' (Fanon, 1965, p. 82). Owning a radio all of a sudden became a patriotic duty. In 20 days, all the radio sets in the whole of Algeria were sold out.

The Cuban and French authorities did everything they could to disrupt the broadcasts of Radio Rebelde and the Voice of Free Algeria, respectively, from jamming their radio signal to banning batteries and battery chargers, as well as seizing radio sets, or setting up black-propaganda stations (Moore, 1993; Downing et al., 2001). Censorship is, however, not always blatant and direct as was the case in Cuba and Algeria, but can occur indirectly through regulation, through the issuing or denying of radio licences. The physical limitations inherent in the frequency spectrum gave state actors the opportunity to control access to the airwaves, which led in many countries to state monopolies on broadcasting or commercial networks controlling the airwaves.

This was contested in many European and US cities by pirate radio stations circumventing regulation, with some establishing themselves as central nodes in the local ecology of counter-cultural activities providing an important platform for a wide variety of political struggles, be they local or global (Cammaerts, 2009). It has to be acknowledged that most, but not all, of these alternative initiatives were yet again silenced through repression, the confiscation of transmitters, or co-optation by the market. At the same time, the emergence of the internet and podcasts has enabled broadcasting for a new and much broader array of actors without needing expensive equipment or a frequency to transmit.

The internet

As a convergent technology, the internet has presented itself as a very powerful tool enabling both real-time and asynchronous (semi-)independent communicative practices, as well as private and public communicative practices. One of the very first examples of the resistant affordances of the internet was its use by the Zapatista Army of National Liberation (Ejército Zapatista de Libéracion Nacional, EZLN) in its fight against large land-owners and the dreadful exploitation of the indigenous Maya population in Chiapas. With the help of NGOs such as the Association for Progressive Communication and activist academics, the Zapatistas built what Cleaver (1995, np) called 'an electronic fabric of struggle' (see Figure 5.2 for one of the many Zapatista-related websites).

Ejército Zapatista de Liberación Nacional

Año 13 de la lucha y cuarto de la guerra contra el olvido y la mentira

LA TORMENTA...

Nacerá del choque de estos dos vientos, llega ya su tiempo, se atiza ya el horno de la historia. Reina ahora el viento de arriba, ya viene el viento de abajo, ya la tormenta viene... así será...

LA PROFECIA...

Cuando amaine la tormenta, cuando lluvia y fuego dejen en paz otra vez la tierra, el mundo ya no será el mundo, sino algo mejor.

Subcomandante Marcos, August 1992

As an unperfect actor on the stage,
Who with his fear is put besides his part,
Or some fierce thing replete with too much rage,
Whose strength's abundance weakens his own heart;
So I for fear of trust forget to say
The perfect ceremony of love's rite
And in mine own love's strength seem to decay,
O'ercharged with burthen of mine own love's might.
O let my books be then the eloquence
And dumb presagers of my speaking breast,
Who plead for love and look for recompense
More than that tongue that more hath more expressed.
O learn to read what silent love hath writ,
To hear with eyes belongs to love's fine wit.

William Shakespeare, Sonnet XXIII

✴ ¡Bienvenidos! ✴

These pages are dedicated to all the courageous women and men who make up the Ejército Zapatista de Liberación Nacional

¡Ya Basta! has been accessed **101178** times since the counter was reinstalled on 6 October 1996.

FIGURE 5.2 Screenshot of http://www.ezln.org (10 December 1997)
Source: Site capture by the Internet Archive – Wayback Machine on 10 December 1997. Retrieved from: https://web.archive.org/web/19971210190555/http://www.ezln.org/

The Zapatista case demonstrated how the internet could be used by the powerless to resist and to communicate their struggle, thereby spatially extending the scope of conflict from the local to the global (Martinez-Torres, 2001). Their informational net-war not only led to a global movement in solidarity with the plight of the Maya population, it also invited an international gaze upon the conflict in Chiapas and their struggle for indigenous rights, which arguably led to caution when it came to repression by the Mexican State.

Moreover, the internet proved to be potent in terms of coordinating and mobilizing for direct actions in the offline world. We could refer here to the profuse use of online forums, chat and mailing lists to organize and coordinate the so-called 'Battle of Seattle' in 1999 (Kahn & Kellner, 2004). To the great surprise of security forces, about 50,000 protesters managed to disrupt and even shut down an official World Trade Organization (WTO) summit. This successful protest 'became a symbol and battle cry for a new generation of activists, as anti-globalization networks were energized around the globe' (Juris, 2005, p. 195). The anti-WTO protests in Seattle gave rise to the Independent Media Center, commonly known as Indymedia – a network of semi-independent entities providing informational infrastructures for a variety of struggles to represent themselves and to mobilize for direct action (Cammaerts, 2005).

The emergence and success of proprietary social media platforms has in the meantime significantly altered the ways in which activists and social movements communicate, organize, and mobilize online (see e.g. Gerbaudo, 2012). Whereas websites and independent means of communication still exist, much of this has shifted to social media platforms such as Twitter and Facebook, which combine real-time and asynchronous communicative affordances within their platforms and enable the transnationalization of struggles. The Arab Spring protests (2010), the Indignados and Occupy movement (2011), as well as the Gezi Park protests in Turkey (2013) are all examples of how activists have used social media platforms in a very productive manner to mobilize and coordinate mass protests, replacing mailing lists and movement platforms such as Indymedia or ProtestNet. This is an example of what could be called spatially mediated movement spillovers.

The reactions against the enormous emancipatory potential of the internet by states, and increasingly by corporate actors controlling the means of communication, are unsurprisingly very similar to those discussed in the historical examples above: censorship, surveillance, jamming, repression, disruption, and counter-propaganda. Today, almost all countries, along with corporate actors and public institutions such as schools, filter the internet and censor content online in some way or another. Many bloggers worldwide have been prosecuted, fined, and/or jailed for what they have written online.

It is common in this regard to single out authoritarian regimes, especially in Asia and the Middle East, for their filtering and repressive practices (Zittrain et al., 2017), but similar practices, albeit less extreme and with different justifications, are enacted in the so-called liberal West. We could refer here to the blocking of Pirate

Bay and similar sites enabling peer-to-peer sharing of copyright-protected digital content, or the repression against members of Anonymous (Wesselingh, 2014; Earl & Beyer, 2014). Besides this, corporate actors are increasingly implicated in efforts of Western states to limit access to what is called 'online terrorist content'. In June 2017, Facebook, Microsoft, Twitter, and YouTube formed the Global Internet Forum to Counter Terrorism, formalizing ongoing collaborations between these companies, governments, and supra-national bodies to 'make our hosted consumer services hostile to terrorists and violent extremists' (Twitter, 2017). But just as with the surveillance practices mentioned above, more legitimate activists and movements are the victims of these hostile environment policies. We could refer here again to the repression against WikiLeaks/Anonymous, or the sudden removal of several anti-austerity groups by Facebook in 2011 (see Cammaerts, 2018).

Just as has been the case throughout history, activists have been creative and innovative in terms of hacking technologies to enable circumvention in an online context. This has given rise to the notion of hacktivism or 'activism gone electronic' (Jordan & Taylor, 2004, p. 1). Hacktivismo, a sub-division of the hacker collective The Cult of the Dead Cow, for instance, developed several tools based on onion routing technology (Tor open-source software) to enable activists to conceal their identity and IP address when browsing, chatting, or emailing. Virtual private network (VPN) connections enable activists to bypass local censorship of content in some contexts, and they can rely on powerful encryption technologies to protect content they wish to keep secret when communicating online.

This shows that the internet is not merely facilitative, but is constitutive of protest and direct action. In this regard, we could refer to the ways in which the internet itself has become a versatile weapon in the hands of activists. The above-mentioned hacker collective Anonymous, for example, connects dispersed members and organizes distributed denial-of-service attacks against a common target, or hacks servers to extract information. They have targeted a variety of ideological enemies such as Scientology, European fascist parties, the Klu Klux Klan, and more recently Daesh.

Finally, we can discern a burgeoning movement which explicitly focuses on internet rights and advocates for a radical freedom of information, unfettered communication, and strong privacy protections. We could refer in this regard to the emergence of Anonymous, WikiLeaks, and Pirate Parties (Beyer, 2014).

Conclusion

Distinct media and communication technologies and infrastructures, such as print presses, postal services, telephone, broadcasting, and more recently the internet, have afforded a variety of mediation practices to activists relevant to their various struggles and in line with a set of mediation needs. These mediation practices thus link up with a set of mediation logics, such as the need to distribute movement discourses, mobilize for direct actions, coordinate internally, produce and archive protest artefacts, as well as circumvent state regulation and repression. The temporal, spatial, and resistant affordances of media and communication technologies enable a set of agentic opportunities which impact differentially on the various mediation logics.

However, these agentic opportunities are not merely circumscribed by the affordances inherent in technologies, and by technological innovations giving rise to new affordances. The political context, and how it reacts to limit the agentic opportunities that media and communication technologies afford, should also be taken into account. This political opportunity structure has a temporal/historical and a spatial/contextual dimension. Activists in certain contexts have to contend with different kinds of constraints and opportunities from those in other contexts, but at the same time, it is clear from our analysis that all nation states, and increasingly corporate actors, have always intervened, in subtle as well as less subtle ways, when it comes to media and communication technologies.

The political opportunity structure never fully controls or contains the mediation opportunity structure, but the mediation opportunity structure is not fully autonomous either – the Empire always strikes back. In spite of this, when considering the history highlighted above, we can be certain that new technologies will be developed, new affordances discovered, and new creative workarounds imagined, rejuvenating old practices as well as constituting new ones. These might be temporal or short-lived, but they will facilitate and shape political struggles across the world. Furthermore, let us not forget that '[t]he power of the media resides in the capacity to reactivate memories of the revolutionary past' (Briggs & Burke, 2009, p. 88). Long may it continue!

References

Adams, p. C. (1996). Protest and the scale politics of telecommunications. *Political Geography*, 15(5), 419–441.

Baker, K. M. (1987). Politics and public opinion under the old regime: some reflections. In J. R. Senser & J. D. Popkin (eds), *Out of Print: Press and Politics in Pre-Revolutionary France* (pp. 204–246). Berkeley, CA: University of California Press.

Beyer, J. L. (2014). The emergence of a freedom of information movement: Anonymous, WikiLeaks, the Pirate Party, and Iceland. *Journal of Computer-Mediated Communication*, 19(2), 141–154.

Briggs, A., & Burke, p. (2009). *A Social History of the Media: From Gutenberg to the Internet.* Cambridge: Polity Press.

Cammaerts, B. (2005). ICT-usage among transnational social movements in the networked society – to organise, to mobilise and to debate. In R. Silverstone (ed.), *Media, Technology and Everyday Life in Europe: From Information to Communication* (pp. 53–72). Aldershot: Ashgate.

Cammaerts, B. (2009). Community radio in the West: A legacy of struggle for survival in a state and capitalist controlled media environment. *International Communication Gazette*, 71(8), 1–20.

Cammaerts, B. (2012). Protest logics and the mediation opportunity structure. *European Journal of Communication*, 27(2), 117–134.

Cammaerts, B. (2018). *The Circulation of Anti-Austerity Protest*. Basingstoke: Palgrave Macmillan.

Castro, F. (2012). *La victoria estratégica. La contraofensiva estratégica*. Madrid: Ediciones Akal.

Cleaver, H. (1995). The Zapatistas and the electronic fabric of struggle. Retrieved from: http s://la.utexas.edu/users/hcleaver/zaps.html. Accessed 15 February 2019.

Couldry, N. (2004). Theorising media as practice. *Social Semiotics* 14(2): 115–132.

Darnton, R. (1982). *The Literary Underground of the Old Regime*. Cambridge, MA: Harvard University Press.

Downing, J. D., with FordV. T., Gil, G. and Stein, L. (2001). *Radical Media: Rebellious Communication and Social Movements*. London: Sage.

Earl, J., & Beyer, J. L. (2014). The dynamics of backlash online: Anonymous and the Battle for WikiLeaks. In L. M. Woehrle (ed.), *Intersectionality and Social Change* (pp. 207–233). Bingley: Emerald Group Publishing.

Eisenstein, E. L. (1997). *The Printing Press as an Agent of Change: Communications and Cultural Transformations in Early-Modern Europe*. Cambridge: Cambridge University Press.

Fanon, F. (1965). *The Wretched of the Earth*. New York: Grove Press.

Flesher Fominaya, C., & Wood, L. (2011). Repression and social movements. *Interface: A Journal For and About Social Movements*, 3(1), 1–11.

Funck-Brentano, F., with P. d'Estrée (1905). *Les Nouvellistes*. Paris: Hachette.

Garrow, D. (1986). *Bearing the Cross: Martin Luther King Jr. and the Southern Christian Leadership Conference*. New York: Harper Collins.

Gerbaudo, p. (2012). *Tweets and the Streets: Social Media and Contemporary Activism*. London: Pluto Press.

Gibson, J. J. (1977). The theory of affordances. In R. Shaw & J. Bransford (eds), *Perceiving, Acting, and Knowing: Toward an Ecological Psychology* (pp. 67–82). Hillsdale, NJ: Lawrence Erlbaum Associates.

Gillan, K., Pickerill, J., & Webster, F. (2008). *Anti-War Activism: New Media and Protest in the Information Age*. Basingstoke: Palgrave Macmillan.

Hermanns, H. (2008). Mobile democracy: mobile phones as democratic tools. *Politics*, 28(2), 74–82.

Ipsen, G. (2010). Communication, cognition and usage: epistemological considerations of media practices and processes. In B. Bräuchler & J. Postill (eds), *Theorising Media and Practice* (pp.171–190). Oxford and New York: Berghahn Books.

Jordan, T., & Taylor, p. A. (2004). *Hacktivism and Cyberwars: Rebels with a Cause?*London: Routledge.

Juris, J. S. (2005). The new digital media and activist networking within anti-corporate globalization movements. *Annals of the American Academy of Political and Social Science*, 597, 189–208.

Kahn, R., & Kellner, D. (2004). New media and internet activism: from the 'Battle of Seattle' to blogging. *New Media & Society*, 6(1), 87–95.

Komaromi, A. (2012). Samizdat and Soviet dissident publics. *Slavic Review*, 71(1), 70–90.

Martinez-Torres, M. E. (2001). Civil Society, the Internet, and the Zapatistas. *Peace Review: A Journal of Social Justice*, 13(3), 347–355.

Marx, K., & Engels, F. (1934). *Correspondence 1846–1895: A Selection with Commentary and Notes*. London: Lawrence & Wishart.

Mattoni, A., & Treré, E. (2014). Media practices, mediation processes, and mediatization in the study of social movements. *Communication Theory*, 24(3), 252–271.

Meyer, D. S. (2004). Protest and political opportunities. *Annual Review of Sociology*, 30, 125–145.

Monachesi, p. , & Turco, M. (2017). New urban players: stratagematic use of media by Banksy and the Hong Kong Umbrella movement. *International Journal of Communication*, 11, 1448–1465.

Moore, D. (1993) Revolution! Clandestine radio and the rise of Fidel Castro. *Monitoring Times*, April.

Nagy, J. A. (2011). *Invisible Ink: Spycraft of the American Revolution*. Yardley, PA: Westholme Publishing.

Negt, O., & Kluge, A. (1993). *The Public Sphere and Experience: Toward an Analysis of the Bourgeois and Proletarian Public Sphere*. Minneapolis, MN: University of Minneapolis Press.

Ortner, S. B. (1989). *High Religion: A Cultural and Political History of Sherpa Buddhism*. Princeton, NJ: Princeton University Press.

Ortner, S. B. (2006). *Anthropology and Social Theory: Culture, Power and the Acting Subject*. Durham, NC: Duke University Press.

Price, D. (2013). A social history of wiretaps. *Counterpunch*, 9 August. Retrieved from: http s://www.counterpunch.org/2013/08/09/a-social-history-of-wiretaps-2/

Rao, U. (2010). Embedded/embedding media practices and cultural production. In B. Bräuchler & J. Postill (eds), *Theorising Media and Practice* (pp. 147–168). Oxford and New York: Berghahn Books.

Roche, D. (1989). Censorship and the publishing industry. In R. Darnton and D. Roche (eds), *Revolution in Print: The Press in France, 1775–1800* (pp. 3–26). Berkeley, CA: University of California Press.

Rohan, M. (1988). *Paris '68: Graffiti, Posters, Newspapers and Poems of the Events of May 1968*. London: Impact.

Silverstone, R., & Hirsch, E. (1992). *Consuming Technologies: Media and Information in Domestic Spaces*. London: Routledge.

Sreberny-Mohammadi, A., & Mohammadi, A. (1994) *Small Media, Big Revolution: Communication, Culture, and the Iranian Revolution*. Minneapolis, MN: University of Minnesota Press.

Steinberg, S. H. (1955 [1996]). *Five Hundred Years of Printing*. London: The British Library.

Stephen, B. (2015). Social media helps Black Lives Matter fight the power. *Wired*, November. Retrieved from: http://www.wired.com/2015/10/how-black-lives-matter-uses-social-m edia-to-fight-the-power/

Sweig, J. E. (2002). *Inside the Cuban Revolution: Fidel Castro and the Urban Underground*. Cambridge, MA: Harvard University Press.

Tsui, L. (2015). The coming colonization of Hong Kong cyberspace: government responses to the use of new technologies by the Umbrella movement. *Chinese Journal of Communication*, 8(4), 447–455.

Twitter Public Policy (2017). Global internet forum to counter terrorism. *Twitter Public Policy*, 26 June. Retrieved from: https://blog.twitter.com/official/en_us/topics/compa ny/2017/Global-Internet-Forum-to-Counter-Terrorism.html

Wesselingh, E. M. (2014). Website blocking: evolution or revolution? 10 years of copyright enforcement by private third parties. *Revista de Internet, Derecho y Política*, 19 October, 35–47.

Zittrain, J., Faris, R., Noman, H., Clark, J., Tilton, C., & Morrison-Westphal, R. (2017). *The Shifting Landscape of Global Internet Censorship*. Cambridge, MA: Berkman Klein Center for Internet & Society.

6

TIME OF PROTEST

An archaeological perspective on media practices

Anne Kaun

Introduction[1]

Media technologies play a vital role in the mobilization and organization of protest and social movements. Many studies have emphasized this point, sometimes slightly overstating their importance. Lately, more critical approaches that point to the dialectical and at times ambivalent relationship between media practices, media technologies, and political practices have emerged (see for example Dencik & Leistert, 2015). Within these critical studies, the media practice perspective plays a crucial role in pointing out the ambivalent relationship between technologies' inherent properties and the role of active appropriation by activists (Barassi, 2013, 2015; Velkova, 2017). Although there is a growing field of media practice studies (see the introduction to this volume for a review), it is still rare to engage with media practices from a historical perspective and discuss the *longue durée* of the role of media technologies for political organizing. A historical perspective is, however, crucial in examining current developments of citizen media and their importance for political organizing over time.

Media historical approaches, on the other hand, have emphasized changing imaginaries related to media technologies, as well as exploring how media are experienced and studied as historical subjects (Gitelman, 2008). Carolyn Marvin, for example, engages with imaginaries and discourses of 'new' technologies in history and argues that

> people often imagine that, [...] new technologies will make the world more nearly what it was meant to be all along. Inevitably, both change and the contemplation of change are reciprocal events that expose old ideas to revision from contact with new ones. [...] The past really does survive in the future.
>
> *(Marvin, 1988, p. 235)*

Media history has so far, however, shown little interest in media practices and their politics.

In order to introduce a historical approach, this chapter investigates media practices of protest movements from a media archaeological perspective. The combination of media archaeology and media practice theory is fruitful as it combines a materialist perspective on media with experiential aspects of media as practice. Rather than analysing media as discourse or narratives, media archaeology considers the material properties that constitute media technologies as well as their temporal and spatial consequences. According to Jussi Parikka, media archaeology is interested in 'materialities of cultural practice, of human activity as embedded in both cognitive and affective appreciations and investments, but also embodied, phenomenological accounts of what we do when we invent, use and adapt media technologies' (Parikka, 2012, p. 163). In this chapter I investigate the temporal properties of media technologies employed by activists. Empirically, I am drawing on a diachronic, comparative study of media practices of protest movements of the dispossessed. The three movements examined – the unemployed workers' movement in the 1930s; the tenants' movement in the 1970s; and Occupy Wall Street in 2011 – emerged in the context of large-scale economic crises and represent attempts at filling the discursive void that the crisis situations induced. Based on extensive archival research in combination with interviews with activists, I argue elsewhere that activists are navigating shifts in media regimes, from mechanical speed to perpetual flow towards digital immediacy, and from a space to a hyper-space bias (Kaun, 2016a). Based on these shifts, activists today are experiencing an increasing desynchronization between media and political practices.

Historicizing media practices through media archaeology

The media practice approach has emerged as a vital and increasingly diverse field of inquiry within the study of social movements and the media (McCurdy, 2012). John Postill (2010) argues that media practices' background can be traced to different epistemological and ontological traditions within social theory (e.g. Schatzki's or Bourdieu's notion of social practice) or media anthropology. The specific approach applied for the purposes of this chapter can be situated in the field of socially oriented media theory (in contrast to textual analysis, medium theory, and the political economy of the media) as suggested by Nick Couldry (2012). Central to socially oriented media theory is the analysis of media in its context rather than in isolation (also referred to as a non-media-centric approach). Following Couldry (2006), I regard media usage as part of a complex sphere of social practices. In that sense 'the media sphere is an inseparable part of the social, interacts with many already-existing discourses, and competes with many other discursive machineries' (Carpentier, 2011, p. 146).

Developing ideas of a contextualized analysis of media usage, following David Morley and Roger Silverstone (1990), Couldry argues against the 'fallacy' of media-centrism in the study of media. Whereas Morley and Silverstone argue for an analysis of media as a domesticated practice alongside and embedded within other practices, Couldry takes the reasoning one step further; he deconstructs the myth that media are the exclusive access point to the social world, since 'to assume that media are more consequential than other institutions that structure the social world (economic, material, spatial, and so on)' (2006, p. 12) might be misleading. The myth of the mediated centre that Couldry describes is built on the assumption that centralized media are *the* access point to 'central realities of the social world, whatever they are. This myth builds on an underlying myth that society has a centre' (2006, p. 16). This assumption needs to be deconstructed in order not to re-manifest the power that centralized media already wield. There-fore, it is argued, research needs to understand media alongside other social practices and institutions. At the same time, media studies need to look at alter-native points of connection within society to broaden the understanding of media's importance to the social sphere. Guided by that premise, Couldry is interested in alternative media (Couldry & Curran, 2003) and alternative media practices (Couldry, 2000) as an expression and realization of decentred media studies. In that sense, he touches upon the question of the 'object of media studies', which has been a highly debated issue since the institutionalization of media and communication studies as a discipline (cf. Schramm, 1983, Noelle-Neumann, 1975). Following this approach, this chapter focuses on critical media practices that are directed towards centralized mainstream media and question their role for sense-making processes in contemporary societies.

Nick Couldry (2012) develops the notion of media practices, and defines practices as concerned with regularity of action. Media practices in turn are concerned with specific regularities in actions that relate to media, and regula-rities of context and resources that enable media-related actions. Practices are social and linked to possibilities, constraints, and questions of power. Further-more, practices are related to needs. Media practices, then, are concerned with the need for coordination, interaction, community, trust, and freedom. Taking media practices as a theoretical backdrop also enables us to think normatively about the media and the question of how we should live with them. Ultimately media practices stand in for 'what people are doing in relation to media in the contexts in which they act' (Couldry, 2012, p. 35). Following Couldry's under-standing, this encompasses, first, practices that are directed to media (e.g. letter to the editor); second, actions that involve media, but do not necessarily have them as object or major aim (e.g. everyday talk that takes media content as a starting point); and, third, actions that depend on the prior existence, presence, or func-tioning of media (e.g. Facebook communities).

Raymond Williams already in 1974 pointed to material aspects of media prac-tices, namely that '[p]ractice (…) has always to be defined as work on a material for a specific purpose within certain necessary social conditions' (p. 160). In order to extend and strengthen this argument of considering material aspects of media, I draw on media archaeology. Emphasizing the materiality of media artefacts, media archaeology shifts the focus of analysis slightly. Rather than analysing media as discourse or narratives, media archaeology considers the material properties that constitute media technologies as well as their temporal and spatial consequences. Media archaeology's aim is to provide a 'rediscovery of cultural and technical layers of previous media' (Ernst, 2011). It focuses therefore on the materiality of media, establishing nonlinear histories and considering forking paths in media technologies' development. Media archaeology, however, lacks a coherent object of study or method. It rather constitutes a disparate field of inquiry that ranges from studies interested in forgotten, unsuccessful, or imaginary media to questions of machine time (Ernst, 2011) or deep time of the media (Zielinski, 2006), and geological properties of media (Parikka, 2015). What these inquiries have in common, however, is that they turn away from questions of representation and hermeneutics, and towards questions of the material object media in order to challenge discourses of newness that are often put forward in media studies (Mattern, 2017). Wolfgang Ernst gives the following example to illustrate the media archaeological approach:

> While a Greek vase can be interpreted by simply being looked at, a radio or a computer does not reveal its essence by monumentally being there but only when being processed by electromagnetic waves or calculating processes.
>
> *(Ernst, 2011, p. 241)*

According to Jussi Parikka, media archaeology is interested in 'materialities of cultural practice, of human activity as embedded in both cognitive and affective appreciations and investments, but also embodied, phenomenological accounts of what we do when we invent, use and adapt media technologies' (Parikka 2012, p. 163). The 'techno-epistemological configurations underlying the discursive surface of mass media' (Ernst, 2011, p. 239) in connection with questions of adaptation and resistance against hegemonic media regimes through activist practices are therefore at the heart of analysis. Considering what Ernst has called the *Eigenzeit* of media technologies vis-à-vis temporalities of political, organizational, and spatial practices of activists who are engaged in the movements contributes a fresh perspective on protest.

While media archaeology lacks people, media practice research lacks a historical and material contextualization of what people are doing with media. The suggestion here is to approach media practices through a media archaeological lens and ask what are the consequences of employing certain media technologies for political mobilization, and how do these engagements change over time? Instead of considering representations or discourses of and about protest movements, the analysis focuses on their relationship to hegemonic regimes of temporality that emerge as properties of media technologies. The combination of media archaeology and media practice theory is fruitful as it allows for linking a materialist perspective on media with experiential aspects of media as practice. According to Raymond Williams, it is the concrete practice that gives meaning to media technology and its particular properties as 'the new technology is itself a product of a particular social system, and will be developed as an apparently autonomous process of innovation only to the extent that we fail to identify and challenge its real agencies' (Williams, 1974, p. 135).

Archaeologies of media practices of the dispossessed

The analysis builds on three case studies that are considered – according to the their appearance in mainstream news media and secondary sources (Castells, 1977, 1980; Gitlin, 2012; Gould-Wartofsky, 2015; Piven & Cloward, 1977) – to be the most relevant protest movements that emerged in the context of major economic crises in the US. The idea of considering crisis-related protest movements draws on Walter Benjamin and Bertolt Brecht's collaborative, unfinished project *Krise und Kritik* (Wizisla, 2004). They argued that crisis situations constituting crucial turning points in history both make possible and require new forms of critique. For them, these new forms of critique should be formulated by intellectuals and artists to turn the transitional moment or critical juncture into positive social change. Similarly, I consider protest movements as direct reactions to crisis situations that aim to fill the crisis-induced void with new meaning and promote social change. Following ideas of media archaeology, I trace media practices of protest movements over time in order to engage with shifts and continuities, through the lens of temporal regimes that are inherent in dominant media technologies.

For the analysis, I draw on archive and interview material related to i) the Great Depression of 1929 and the unemployed workers' movement; ii) the oil and fiscal crisis in the early 1970s and new urban movements, particularly the rent strike and squatters' movement; and iii) the Great Recession of 2007/2008 and the Occupy Wall Street movement. The interviews were conducted with activists within the Occupy movement based in Philadelphia and New York. They had different roles within the movement, ranging from central positions in the core organizing groups and subgroups to more peripheral roles. All have, however, spent considerable amounts of time in encampments in Manhattan and Philadelphia. In total, eight different activists were interviewed. For historical contextualization, members of the Interference Archive in Brooklyn were interviewed on the role of history writing from below. Furthermore, I participated in workshops and seminar series on community archiving, and volunteered as part of the community cataloguing initiative. The selected movements are organizationally and ideologically diverse. It is, however, not my aim to reconstruct their genealogy in detail. Instead their media practices figure as empirical entry points to analyse changes in media technologies over time. Furthermore, considering the role of social media vis-à-vis previous mobilizations allows us to historically contextualize the role of media technologies in protest movements.

Unemployed workers and mechanical speed

The unemployed workers' movements emerged in the context of the 1930s Great Depression in the United States. Following the crash of the stock exchange in 1929, the number of unemployed people exploded, increasing from half a million in October 1929 to more than 4 million in January 1930 and 9 million in October 1931 (Piven & Cloward, 1977). Unemployment and shrinking salaries of those still in employment had devastating effects on the daily lives of people, going hand in hand with growing malnutrition and diseases such as tuberculosis. There were numerous organizations and political groups that aimed to organize the unemployed and mobilize them for direct actions such as marches, demonstrations, and occupations of relief offices. The main aims and approaches of the organizations were very diverse. While the Labor Research Association, for example, focused mainly on gathering information on unemployment and its conditions, the Socialist and Communist parties aimed to establish organizational structures and advocated for improved relief programmes. Smaller local organizations, such as the Greenwich House in New York City, focused specifically on local conditions, housing meetings of the unemployed from Greenwich Village as well as the National Unemployment League. The League for Industrial Democracy (out of which Students for a Democratic Society – the SDS – emerged in the 1960s) organized nationwide lectures, lecture circuits, and chapter meetings. In order to organize and mobilize unemployed workers, these organizations used a sophisticated set of different media, ranging from shop papers written by unemployed workers and distributed in the factories to radio talks, as Harold Lasswell and Dorothy Blumenstock (1939) show in their comprehensive study of communist media in Chicago. Although the radio gained importance, the main way to inform members and non-members remained printed outlets. From 1932, for example, clip sheets containing major news were introduced for the purpose of being reprinted by approximately 500 farmers' and workers' newspapers.

In the 1930s, then, organizers of the unemployed workers' movement relied predominantly on printed outlets that were reproduced with the help of low-cost printing presses – so-called mimeographs. The employment of machines to reproduce brochures, pamphlets, and shop papers helped to speed up the process, and consequently it was possible to reach out to more people. At the same time, media practices relying on technologies such as the mimeograph were still characterized by collective approaches on the level of production, distribution, and consumption. There were, for example, often three to four workers operating mimeographs in an efficient manner. Distribution was often organized by smaller groups of workers, who distributed pamphlets, factory papers, and leaflets in the streets or in the factories, often under threat of being arrested and fired. The content was also consumed in groups rather than individually, in cafés and on street corners. In that sense, even if reproduction added to the speed of production and number of copies, it was still an 'effortful' speed that needed the work and engagement of a collective rather than individuals.

For Walter Benjamin, reproducibility meant that media images no longer had a unique place in time, which coincided with their increased mobility. He suggests that 'technical reproduction can place the copy of the original in situations which the original itself cannot attain. Above all, it enables the original to meet the recipient halfway' (Benjamin, 1936/2008, p. 21). This argument suggests a democratization of the image through its reproduction, but also the political potential to spread it to the masses for resistance against fascism. Benjamin's arguments resonate with the experience of acceleration of speed with the possibilities of mechanical reproduction in the 1930s. Although Benjamin points out the dangers of immature usage of technology and the increasing alienation of recipients, he remains hopeful of the potential that comes with reproducibility for political mobilization of the masses in the age of mechanical speed, which was the dominant temporal regime that the unemployed workers navigated.

The tenants' movement and perpetual flow

The early 1970s were also marked by economic crisis, specifically the oil crisis. New York in particular was also faced with a fiscal crisis, which resulted in austerity measures and strict budget cuts that left many unemployed. Manuel Castells (1980) discusses in his book *The Economic Crisis and American Society* why there were no mass protests comparable to those in the 1930s, although the economic situation was similarly severe. Castells argues that growing police violence with new special units, an ideological delegitimization of political protest post-1968/69 radicalization, and the absence of an immediate political alternative led to a shift from mass mobilization to individual violence, visible in increasing crime rates. However, he had hopes for what he called new urban movements, one of which was the tenants' movement in New York that advocated for tenants' rights against increasingly hostile housing conditions. The scarcity of low-cost housing resulted from a combination of austerity measures and deregulation of the housing market. A paradoxical housing situation emerged, with empty units abandoned by the owners while large numbers of people were desperately in search of affordable housing. After considerable decay of housing facilities, however, owners often turned the vacant units into high-end housing or office spaces (Gold, 2014).

From 1959, the Metropolitan Council on Housing was the central organization for tenants in New York. Over the years, the Met Council continuously professionalized its work and support of local tenants' organizations, particularly in terms of media practices. It arranged television training and workshops on publicity and press releases, held lists of press and television contacts, and documented the appearance of questions related to the tenants' movement in mainstream media. Especially after 1973, numerous new activists and organizations aimed to organize aggrieved tenants, which led to the emergence of multiple federations that constituted an increasing diversification of strategies, mirroring the diversifying socioeconomic backgrounds of participants in the tenants' movement.

The organizers of the tenants' movement in the 1970s navigated an increasingly complex media ecology, ranging from mainstream newspapers to community radio and papers and television news. Hence, in the 1970s there was a further acceleration of speed in the (re)production process of media content that intersects with the increased commercialization and globalization of the media technologies employed. Analysing television as the dominant media technology of the 1970s, Raymond Williams (1974) was especially concerned with a change from sequence as programming to sequence as flow. Referring to flow, he aims to capture the integration of previously separate segments, for example a theatre play or musical piece, through commercial breaks and trailers. Commercial breaks and trailers for future programmes create a constant flow of parallel narratives, capturing the viewer for the whole evening. Writing at the threshold of the 24-hour news cycle, Raymond Williams already captures the experience of a constant stream of new experiences that television offers, while diminishing real beginnings and endings of the presented programme elements. Organizers in the 1970s had to apply tactics to insert their messages in this perpetual flow of commercial television and other formats. The tenants' movement and the Metropolitan Council on Housing chose an events-based approach to intercept the dominant temporal regime of *perpetual flow*.

One of the most prominent examples of this approach is the Housing Crimes Trial that an activist coalition organized on the 6 December 1970 at Columbia University. The organizing coalition, headed by the Metropolitan Council on Housing, consisted of I Wor Kuen, the Black Panthers, the Young Lords, the City Wide Coordinating Committee of Welfare Rights, Social Service Employees, and several smaller community organizations. The event attracted between 1,000 and 2,000 spectators. The nine-hour trial was headed by seven peoples' judges, including representatives from the Young Lords, the Black Panthers, and the Metropolitan Council on Housing, who invited tenants, squatters, and community organizers to share their experiences of outrageous housing conditions, landlords, and the ignorance of city officials. The two main aims of the event were to establish a platform for shared experiences related to the precarious housing situation in New York at that time, and to attract wider attention with the help of mainstream media, in particular television. In order to reach the latter goal, the Met Council provided media training workshops and handbooks to professionalize the activist media practices adopting the dominant media logic. Through professionalization, as well as establishing events-based, spectacular direct actions, the activists hoped to be able to intercept the perpetual flow of television and to receive broader attention and consequently support for their cause.

Occupy Wall Street and digital immediacy

The third movement considered here – the Occupy Wall Street (OWS) movement – emerged in the aftermath of the so-called Great Recession (Foster & McChesney, 2012). Although OWS has been explicitly multi-voiced and there exist a variety of narratives concerning the movement, I will try to briefly provide an overview of the major formative events of the movement and in that way partly reconstruct the dominant narrative told about OWS. In July 2011, Adbusters, the notorious facilitator of anti-consumerism campaigns, launched a call to occupy Wall Street by introducing the hashtag #occupywallstreet on Twitter. After online mobilization, a few dozen people followed the call on 17 September 2011. Since Wall Street was strongly secured by police force, the occupiers turned to nearby Zuccotti Park. The small, privately owned square became the place for camping, campaigning, and deliberating for the upcoming weeks until the first eviction in November 2011 (Graeber, 2013). The number of activists in the camp grew surprisingly quickly and developed into a diverse group of occupiers based on what has been characterized as leaderlessness and non-violence (Bolton et al., 2013), but even these two notions were contested. Hence, the movement was and is characterized by a non-consensus about ethics and advocated for a diversity of tactics, while particularly stressing the importance of space through linking the movement to the long tradition of occupation and reclaiming of public spaces.[2]

While OWS, similarly to the two earlier movements, created a rich media ecology including printed outlets like flyers, fanzines, and a newspaper, as well as video and live streaming, there was a strong focus on participation and visibility in corporate social media. Aiming for broad attention to the movement and its discussions, the occupiers contributed to the production of digital media content despite being critical of the corporate background and business models of these platforms. The contribution and use of corporate social media can be analysed in terms of communicative capitalism that predominantly builds on the circulation of messages and the logic that the 'exchange value of the messages' dominates, rather than the 'use value' (Dean, 2008, 2012). Dean suggests that network communication technologies, which are based on ideals of discussion and participation, intertwine capitalism and democracy. Communicative capitalism expanding with the growth of global telecommunications hence becomes the single ideological formation (Dean, 2012). Content or the use value of the messages exchanged becomes secondary or even irrelevant. Hence, any response to them becomes irrelevant as well, and any political potential disperses into the perpetual flow of communication (Dean, 2009, 2010). One of the major principles of communicative capitalism is furthermore to accelerate the speed of circulation in order to minimize turnover time and increase the production of surplus value (Manzerolle & Kjøsen, 2012). As digital media enhance personalization, they enable new trajectories and pathways between production, exchange, and consumer. In that sense, personalization as an organizational principle of digital media enhances the already accelerated speed of exchanges, which is taken to its extreme, namely the suspension of circulation in the age of digital immediacy. For the case of OWS, the focus on exchange value rather than use value becomes particularly apparent when considering the overemphasis on quantifications of social media visibility in terms of uploads, clicks, likes, and followers by both academics and commentators. DeLuca and co-authors suggest, for example, that social media were quickly filling up with Occupy Wall Street: on the first day of occupation more than 4,300 mentions of OWS were counted on Twitter, exploding to 25,148 until 2 October 2011. After three months there were 91,400 OWS-related videos uploaded on YouTube (DeLuca, Lawson, & Sun, 2012). This overemphasis on metrics is partly reflected among the activists involved in working groups that focused on social media. There was a shared understanding that visibility and presence in social media were crucial for the movement. Sasha[3] of the Media Working Group, for example, reflects on the entanglement of offline direct action and online mobilization, painting a picture of a closely intertwined ecology of media practices including live streams on social media:

> And of course, the marches they kept doing. There was a ton of marches all the time and there were always live streams. And having the convenience of having a live stream capability in your cellphone, which is about the most user-friendly thing I have ever seen in my life [...]. But everything that was being streamed was also tweeted out. By like all the people in the park and other people who were following people in the park. [...] They tweet that out and it gets tweeted and retweet and others start watching it as well.
>
> *(Interview with Sasha, Media Working Group, OWS)*

At the same time, it is important to emphasize the diversity of media practices within OWS. Aaron, a central member of the Tech Ops working group, mentioned during our interview, for example, that there was a clear distinction between what he calls 'social media people' within the Media Working Group and the technically oriented group that built the administrative digital infrastructure for the General Assembly and the working groups. While the 'social media people' focused on playing according to the logic of social media, that was in turn producing an acceptable narrative for mainstream news media as well, the Tech Ops Working Group tried to implement an open source infrastructure that resembled the ideals of horizontal and participatory decision-making. Both groups rarely shared any overlaps in terms of concrete projects or personnel.

Hence, while there were attempts to build a digital infrastructure that resembled the principles of OWS's political organizing, there was a strong focus on following social media logics, including the need to constantly update and produce content for different streams and accounts. This need to permanently produce media content comes to stand in a stark contrast with the time-consuming meetings to build collective and participatory decisions. Hence in a way, social media practices and practices of political decision-making became desynchronized (Kaun, 2015).

Media regimes and media practices

As argued above, activists have to navigate a dominant temporality established by – among other social forces and institutions – media technologies, which is here defined as time regime. Veronica Barassi (2015) refers in this context to a current hegemonic construction of social time – in her case more specifically immediacy – that produces potential conflicts with other layers of temporality in everyday life and particularly protest practices. I choose the notion of regime to emphasize the hegemonic character of a dominant temporality that is established through media technologies and discursive practices. Regimes have not only a political meaning referring to a form of government or period of rule, but also describe a regular pattern of occurrence or action, and characteristic behaviour and orderly procedure. In that sense, temporal regimes of media establish particular regularities and orders of process that are most often taken for granted. In the analysis, I have investigated the taken-for-granted time regimes with which protest movements are grappling. In a certain sense, time regimes describe a discursive closure that stands in contrast to struggles about the meaning and purpose of media technologies, for example on a regulatory level (Jakobsson & Stiernstedt, 2010; Pickard, 2015). However, as I have shown elsewhere, through their media practices, activists relate in different ways to dominant temporal regimes. They either attack, adapt, formulate alternatives, or abstain from the dominant media regime (Kaun, 2016a and 2016b). For example, the Archiving Working Group within OWS collected both physical objects and digital artefacts in order to preserve the history and development of the movement on their own terms. In that sense, they tried to counter the dominant regimes of digital immediacy and ephemerality of social media. This example shows the dialectical relationship between a temporal regime that dominates public discourse and practices, and the agentic potential of renegotiating and questioning specific aspects of the dominant regime.

Crises, such as the Great Recession, give new meaning and visibility to these ongoing struggles about media technologies and potentially unlock the established discursive closure of media regimes. In connection with protest practices, they hence become an entry point and empirical lens to analyse and make sense of social change. In terms of the historical foundations of the struggles, I have identified both continuities and shared features of protest movements in moments of economic crisis, especially when it comes to the hope connected with media innovations for furthering social change. In the 1930s, intellectuals such as Bertolt Brecht and Walter Benjamin had high hopes for the radio to give new voice to the struggles of the working class. In the 1970s, the Metropolitan Council on Housing considered engaging with cable television in order to attract broader attention and support. In both cases, the media innovation was considered as a harbinger for more democratization of the public sphere and discourse. However, the three movements are also characterized by fundamental changes when it comes to their media practices and the structuring of time. There is a fundamental change from mechanical speed and perpetual flow towards digital immediacy. While digital immediacy emerges as such a hegemonic force, it makes accounting for the different temporalities of political protest difficult.

Conclusion

The suggestion to combine the media practice perspective with a media archaeological approach does not seem straightforward, particularly thinking of the dispute between Raymond Williams and Marshall McLuhan (Fuchs, 2017; Jones, 1998) in which Williams considered McLuhan a technological determinist disregarding questions of power and ideology in the analysis of media. Williams, instead of focusing on the character of media technologies as such, considered media in their broader societal context as forms of social practices. Media archaeology, with strong links to medium theory and a partly anti-humanist tendency, has very little to do with an interest in media practices that is inspired and informed by cultural studies. This chapter is, however, not about dissolving this fundamental schism. Instead, it aims to show how a focus on media practice adds to our understanding of how media technologies configure time and space, which media archaeology has been interested in. My analysis is an attempt to balance a material perspective that emphasizes the properties of media technologies with an acknowledgement of agency. In many ways, the media practices approach often overemphasizes the agency of, for example, activists in choosing and adopting media for their purposes, while the media archaeological approach foregrounds properties inherent in technology that shape possible practices. On the one hand, media archaeology often disregards the role of agency; on the other hand, media practice research often lacks a historical and material contextualization of what people are doing with media. At the same time, the media practice approach adds to the analysis the perspective of active shaping of media technologies by practices. It is hence the intertwinement of both approaches that fruitfully allows for a dialectical analysis of the relationship between media technologies' properties and media practices.

This is achieved here by focusing on the temporal dimension in media practices and media archaeology. Focusing on the temporality of media and practices related to them allows us to excavate how media technologies function in the context of political participation and mobilization. Developing the notion of temporal regimes of media brings media practices and the perspective of media archaeology together. Time regimes are defined here as discursive, hegemonic formations that activists have to relate to and navigate.

Notes

1 Parts of the chapter have been previously published in Kaun, A. (2017). 'Our time to act has come': desynchronization, social media time and protest movements. *Media, Culture and Society*, 39(4), 469–486.
2 Michael Gould-Wartofsky (2015) links the occupation of Zuccotti Park, for example, to the Landless Workers' Movement in Brazil that emerged in the 1980s, and the squatters' movement of the 1970s reclaiming affordable housing through occupation.
3 The author uses pseudonyms for interviewees throughout the text.

References

Barassi, V. (2013). When materiality counts: the social and political importance of activist magazines in Europe. *Global Media and Communication, 9*(2), 135–151.
Barassi, V. (2015). Social media, immediacy and the time for democracy: critical reflections on social media as 'temporalizing practices'. In L. Dencik & O. Leistert (eds), *Critical Perspectives on Social Media and Protest: Between Control and Emancipation* (pp. 73–90). London and New York: Rowman & Littlefield.
Benjamin, W. (1936/2008). The work of art in the age of its technological reproducibility: Second version. In M. Jennings, B. Doherty, & T. Levin (eds), *The Work of Art in the Age*

of Its Technological Reproducibility and Other Writings of Media (pp. 19–55). Cambridge and London: Belknap Press.

Bolton, M., Welty, E., Nayak, M., & Malone, C. (2013). We had a front row seat to a Downtown revolution. In E. Welty, M. Bolton, M. Nayak, & C. Malone (eds), *Occupying Political Science. The Occupy Wall Street Movement from New York to the World* (pp. 1–24). New York: Palgrave Macmillan.

Bray, M. (2013). *Translating Anarchy: The Anarchism of Occupy Wall Street.* Winchester and Washington, DC: Zero Books.

Carpentier, N. (2011). *Media and Participation. A Site of Ideological–Democratic Struggle.* Bristol and Chicago, IL: Intellect.

Castells, M. (1977). *The Urban Question. A Marxist Approach.* Cambridge, MA: MIT Press.

Castells, M. (1980). *The Economic Crisis and American Society.* Princeton, NJ: Princeton University Press.

Couldry, N. (2000). *The Place Of Media Power: Pilgrims and Witnesses of the Media Age.* London: Routledge.

Couldry, N. (2006). *Listening Beyond the Echoes. Media, Ethics, and Agency in an Uncertain World.* Boulder, CO and London: Paradigm.

Couldry, N. (2012). *Media, Society, World. Social Theory and Digital Media Practice.* Cambridge, MA: Polity.

Couldry, N., & Curran, J. (2003). *Contesting Media Power: Alternative Media in a Networked World.* Lanham, MD and Oxford: Rowman & Littlefield.

Dean, J. (2008). Communicative capitalism: circulation and the foreclosure of politics. In M. Boler (ed.), *Digital Media and Democracy* (pp. 101–121). Cambridge, MA and London: MIT Press.

Dean, J. (2009). *Democracy and Other Neoliberal Fantasies: Communicative Capitalism and Left Politics.* Durham, NC: Duke University Press.

Dean, J. (2010). *Blog Theory: Feedback and Capture in the Circuits of Drive.* Cambridge, MA: Polity.

Dean, J. (2012). *The Communist Horizon.* London and New York: Verso.

DeLuca, K., Lawson, S., & Sun, Y. (2012). Occupy Wall Street on the public screens of social media: the many framings of the birth of a protest movement. *Communication, Culture & Critique, 5*(4), 483–509.

Dencik, L., & Leistert, O. (2015). Introduction. In L. Dencik & O. Leistert (eds), *Critical Perspectives on Social Media and Protest* (pp. 1–12). London and New York: Rowman & Littlefield.

Ernst, W. (2011). Media archaeography: method and machine versus history and narrative of the media. In E. Huhtamo & J. Parikka (eds), *Media Archaeology: Approaches, Applications and Implications.* Berkeley, CA: University of California Press.

Foster, J. B., & McChesney, R. (2012). *The Endless Crisis. How Monopoly-Finance Capital Produces Stagnation and Upheaval from the USA to China.* New York: Monthly Review Press.

Fuchs, C. (2017). Raymond Williams' communicative materialism. *European Journal of Cultural Studies, 20*(6), 744–762.

Gitelman, L. (2008). *Always Already New. Media, History, and the Data of Culture.* Cambridge, MA: MIT Press.

Gitlin, T. (2012). *Occupy Nation.* New York: HarperCollins.

Gold, R. (2014). *When Tenants Claimed the City: The Struggle for Citizenship in New York City Housing.* Urbana, Chicago, Springfield, IL: University of Illnois Press.

Gould-Wartofsky, M. (2015). *The Occupiers: The Making of the 99 Percent Movement.* Oxford and New York: Oxford University Press.

Graeber, D. (2013). *The Democracy Project. A History, A Crises, A Movement*. New York: Spiegel and Grau.

Jakobsson, P., & Stiernstedt, F. (2010). Pirates of Silicon Valley: State of exception and dispossession in Web 2.0. *First Monday*, 15(7).

Jones, P. (1998). The technology is not the cultural form? Raymond William's sociological critique of Marshall McLuhan. *Canadian Journal of Communication*, 23(4), 423–454.

Kaun, A. (2015). Regimes of time: media practices of the dispossessed. *Time & Society*, 24(2).

Kaun, A. (2016a). 'Our time to act has come': desynchronisation, social media time and protest movements. *Media, Culture and Society*, 39(4), 469–486.

Kaun, A. (2016b). *Crisis and Critique. A History of Media Participation in Times of Crisis*. London: Zed Books.

Lasswell, H. D., & Blumenstock, D. (1939). *World Revolutionary Propaganda: A Chicago Study*. New York: Knopf.

Manzerolle, V., & Kjøsen, A. M. (2012). The communication of capital: digital media and the logic of acceleration. *TripleC*, 10, 214–229.

Marvin, C. (1988). *When Old Technologies Were New. Thinking About Electric Communication in the Late Nineteenth Century*. New York: Oxford University Press.

Mattern, S. (2017). *Code and Clay, Data and Dirt: Five Thousand Years of Urban Media*. Minneapolis, MN: University of Minnesota Press.

McCurdy, P. (2012). Social movements, protest and mainstream media. *Sociology Compass*, 6(3), 244–255.

Morley, D., & Silverstone, R. (1990). Domestic communication – technologies and meanings. *Media, Culture & Society*, 12(1), 31–55.

Noelle-Neumann, E. (1975). Publizistik- und Kommunikationswissenschaft: Ein Wissenschaftsbereich oder ein Themenkatalog? [*Publizistik* and communication studies: a research area or a catalogue of topics?] *Publizistik*, 20(3), 743–748.

Parikka, J. (2012). *What is Media Archaeology?* Cambridge, Malden, MA: Polity.

Parikka, J. (2015). *A Geology of Media*. Minneapolis, MN and London: University of Minnesota Press.

Pickard, V. (2015). *America's Battle for Media Democracy: The Triumph of Corporate Libertarianism and the Future of Media Reform*. Cambridge: Cambridge University Press.

Piven, F. F., & Cloward, R. A. (1977). *Poor People's Movements. Why They Succeed, How They Fail*. New York: Vintage Books.

Postill, J. (2010). Introduction: Theorising media and practice. In B. Bräuchler & J. Postill (eds), *Theorising Media and Practice* (pp. 1–34). New York and Oxford: Berghahn Books.

Roberts, A. (2012). Why the Occupy Movement failed. *Public Administration Review*, 72(5), 754–762.

Schramm, W. (1983). The unique perspective of communication: A retrospective view. *Journal of Communication*, 33(3), 6–17.

Velkova, J. (2017). Repairing and developing software infrastructures: the case of Morevna Project in Russia. *New Media and Society*, 20(6).

Williams, R. (1974). *Television: Technology and Cultural Form*. New York: Schocken Books.

Wizisla, E. (2004). *Benjamin und Brecht. Die Geschichte einer Freundschaft. [Benjamin and Brecht. The Story of a Friendship]*. Frankfurt am Main: Suhrkamp.

Zielinski, S. (2006). *Deep Time of the Media: Toward an Archaeology of Hearing and Seeing by Technical Means*. Cambridge, MA and London: MIT Press.

PART III

Practice approaches to video activism

INTRODUCTION

Dorothy Kidd

In October 2018, I sat with young video-makers in their Potocine theatre, located high up in the hills of Ciudad Bolívar, a barrio in Bogotá created by people displaced by Colombia's decades of violent conflict. Together we watched the opening video of the *Ojo al Sancocho* (*Eyes on Sancocho*) International Festival of Film.[1] Shot from the point of view of three teenagers, we move through the neighbourhood as they run headlong into class prejudice and police harassment, meet up with friends, and raise money to buy a camera to tell the stories of their neighbourhood. As I looked at Ciudad Bolívar through the eyes of those young video-makers, I was struck again by the power of film and video to engage us intimately and connect across space, time, language, and culture.

The self-managed Potocine theatre and film festival is part of the larger project of Sueños [Dreams] Films, which also includes intensive video-making training (Rodríguez, 2018). The videos they produce provide far more granular and visceral representations of the complexity of their lives and neighbourhood than the unknowing classist stereotypes propagated about them. Sueños Films then brings people together in their theatre to watch and discuss the videos, and the issues and concerns they raise, as a vital part of weaving a stronger social fabric.

Ojo al Sancocho is part of a long historical legacy of film and video activism, the focus of this section. From the 1930s onwards, film-makers in many regions of the world have used the moving image to bring to life the lives of communities seldom represented in the dominant public service or commercial media, and, as importantly, to assemble audiences to collectively discuss critical social, cultural, and political issues and mobilize for change.[2] In the late 1960s, my generation of activist producers adopted a new technology, the portable video recorder, for many of the same goals. A little bit cheaper, and much more user-friendly, video was quickly taken up by movements of women, Indigenous peoples and racialized groups, LGBTQ people, and working class urban and rural citizens who realized the importance of making their own media to counter the systematic disinformation about them, and to generate new collective visions.[3]

Most film and video activists operated with little support from academic or public service media institutions, and instead adopted a do-it-ourselves approach. Much like Sueños Films, they built their own media organizations: forming training, production, and exhibition spaces, and creating national, regional, and international networks to circulate the videos and share aesthetics, training, production, and distribution techniques. They also shared research, analyses, and political strategies for democratizing the programming of state and commercial media outlets (Thede & Ambrosi, 1991; Kidd, 2008). For as sociologist and activist Gary Kinsman points out, 'activists are [always] thinking, talking about, researching, and theorizing about what is going on, what they are going to do next, and how to analyze the situations they face' (2006, p. 134).

Some of these earlier practices, as Stephansen and Treré note in Chapter 1 of this book, have been analysed through the lens of the alternative and social change communication fields, with especially strong contributions from Latin America.[4] Another school draws on Marxist, autonomist Marxist, and anarchist analyses to underscore the role of video practice in anti-capitalist social and political formations.[5] Indigenous communities around the world have also adapted video tools to re-insert themselves and their histories, and challenge the racist and colonialist erasures and mis-representations of Hollywood and of national film cultures, educational institutions, and state-controlled publicity.[6] Many of these experiences and analyses have never been published, or translated into the dominant language of academic English, or brought into conversation across academic silos.

The current cycle of video activism

The turn to practice theory, which this volume examines, breaks down some of these earlier silos of knowledge. The authors in this section have all conducted considerable research about social justice movement communication practices, collaborated on studies that bridge disciplines, and produced reflective new theorizations. Mattoni and Askanius have already brought some of the contributions of earlier generations of video activists into these conversations (Mattoni & Teune, 2014; Askanius, 2012). As their chapters in this section outline, the scope and scale of social movement video production and circulation has not only increased, but has changed the composition of video-makers and the kinds of social, cultural, and representational practices that they undertake.

In previous historical cycles, as discussed above, many movements incorporated video practices as part of their repertoire, circulating them horizontally among their own constituencies and local allies as part of the constitution of new imaginaries, and social and political demands. Nevertheless, the video production capacity of many organizations was extremely limited, and continues to be so; more importantly, movements were seldom able to break through the control of distribution held tightly by the commercial and public service media and circulate videos beyond their local contexts.

In the current cycle of movement practice, and especially since the movements of 2011 and the examples set by los Indignados in Spain and the Occupy movement, video has become a primary practice for most social and political movements (Askanius, 2012; Doerr, Mattoni, & Teune, 2014; Treré & Mattoni, 2016).

Many movements, especially in the Global North, use multiple digital video circuits, from their own websites to corporate-controlled social media platforms, to mobilize supporters within and far beyond their normal circles, survey and challenge state and corporate authorities, and provide regular news reports and analyses. The speed and nimbleness of activist video-makers during uprisings, amidst the weakening of the commercial media's monopoly control, has allowed movements, for short periods, to effectively challenge the reach and framing of the dominant commercial and public service media's gate-keepers (Martini, 2018). In addition, as discussed by Mattoni and Pavan (Chapter 8 in this volume), many individual activists use these same circuits to distribute their videos, which, while largely supportive of movement goals, are produced without direction from any centralized organization.

What's at stake?

In 2012, John Downing, the veteran social movement media researcher, addressed the Union for Democratic Communication conference (Downing, 2013). He sketched a dire environmental, political, and social panorama in which none of the existing political leadership or their proposals would suffice to ensure planetary survival. However, rather than a gloomy ending, Downing called on researchers to actively support the development of social movement media, which, he argued, were some of the better forms of economic, political, and cultural organization available as they open up channels of reflection and knowledge exchange and intervention into public debate for ever-expanding numbers of people. Researchers, he suggested, needed to contribute to making social change by combining political economy and cultural approaches to social movement media, and he outlined ten questions to address (2013, pp. 25–27).[7]

Downing's call to combine analyses of social movement practice and political economy is imminently necessary in the case of social movement video. Of course, the tilt to video on social media platforms, which has vastly expanded movement reach, was not only due to smart activists: a political economy analysis reveals that Facebook and Google's YouTube, which together dominate the digital advertising market, promoted video content as a more effective medium for delivering social media users to advertisers (Tandoc & Maitra, 2018). However, these two global corporate giants have also stepped up censorship of video and other posts, negatively impacting alternative news sites, marginalized communities, social justice movements, and individual posters alike (Gourarie, 2016; York, 2018). Keeping clear eyes on the shifting economics and politics of digital capitalism is in fact one of the practices of media activists, advocates, and civil libertarians, essential to find and help keep open the cracks in the media-scape for the production and circulation of social justice content.

The renewed attention to the communications practices of social and political justice movements that this volume engages is very welcome. One important approach that would strengthen practice theory considerably is to pay greater attention to the investigative protocols which social movement activists themselves use. This approach parallels Askanius's call (Chapter 7 in this volume) for researchers to 'leave their desk and screens behind' and, whenever possible, place themselves 'in the midst of the scene of action'. For, as activist researcher Aziz Choudry argues, 'it is not knowledge that challenges power structures, but how it is used' (2015, p. 149). Choudry points out that effective activism requires the synthetic and systemic analysis of the everyday practices of social movement actors, as well as the analytical knowledge of the contexts within which everyday practices occur (2015, p. 123). Attention to these contexts would mean, as Choudry illustrates, drawing much more deeply from the activist knowledges of the Global South, and investigating the power tensions between non-governmental organizations and grassroots groups, as well as the power dynamics of gender, race, class, sexuality, and immigration status. Finally, practice theory adherents might better support social movements by addressing questions put forward by della Porta and Pavan (2017) and Kinsman (2006, p. 135): how can we build research into the everyday organizing of social movements, making the research more participatory, dialogical, and multi-voiced?

Notes

1 Arquitectura Expandida. Potocine – Self-managed Cinema Room, Ciudad Bolívar, Bogotá. http://arquitecturaexpandida.org/potocine/.
2 The list of counter-cinema movements is very long, and would, for a start, include the New York Film and Photo League of the 1930s, California Newsreel in the 1960s and 1970s, Cinema de la Base during the Allende pre-Pinochet coup period in Chile, Grupo Chaski in Peru in the 1980s (Santiváñez Guarniz, 2010), the work of Anand Patwardhan and others in the 1970s and 1980s in India (Deprez, 2015; Kishore, 2017), Paper Tiger TV and Deep Dish in the 1980s and 1990s in the USA (Halleck, 2002), and MediAct in South Korea in the 2000s (Hadl & Jo, 2008).
3 For a glimpse into the practice of film activists, see Burton (1978), Schiwy (2009), Santiváñez Guarniz (2010); for the USA, see Downing (1984), Halleck (2002), Tripp (2012), Robé (2017); for India, see Sinha (2010), Deprez (2015), Kishore (2017); for Korea, see Hadl and Jo (2008).
4 Among many others, see Riaño (1994), Gumucio Dagron (2001), Gumucio Dagron & Tufte (2006), Garcés & Jiménez (2016).
5 Delcourt, Mattelart, & Mattelart (1983), Hadl and Jo (2008), Berardi, Jacquemet, & Vitali (2009), Wolfson and Funke (2014), Robé (2017), Kidd (2020), Robé & Charbonneau (2020).
6 Stewart (2007), Salazar & Cordova (2008), Schiwy (2009), Marubbio (2010), Roth (2010), Smith (2012), Monani (2013), Magallanes-Blanco and Ramos Rodríguez (2016), Ginsburg (2016), Valencia, Restrepo & Cardona (2017).
7 Nick Dyer-Witheford (2008) has outlined a series of similar questions from the autonomist Marxist protocols that can be used to analyse anti-capitalist communications practices.

References

Askanius, T. (2012). Radical online video: YouTube, video activism and social movement media practices. *Lund University Studies in Media and Communication*, 17.

Berardi, F., Jacquemet, M., & Vitali, G. (2009). *Ethereal Shadows: Communication and Power in Contemporary Italy*. New York: Autonomedia.

Burton, J. (1978). The camera as 'gun': two decades of culture and resistance in Latin America. *Latin American Perspectives*, 5(1), 49–76.

Choudry, A. (2015). *Learning Activism: The Intellectual Life of Contemporary Social Movements*. Toronto: University of Toronto Press.

Delcourt, X., Mattelart, M., & Mattelart, A. (1983). *La culture contre la démocratie? L'audiovisuel à l'heure transnationale*. Paris: Éditions La Découverte.

Deprez, C. (2015). A space in between: the legacy of the activist documentary film in India. In C. Deprez & J. Pernin (eds), *Post-1990 Documentary: Reconfiguring Independence*. Edinburgh: Edinburgh University Press.

Doerr, N., Mattoni, A., & TeuneS. (2014). Visuals in social movements. In D. della Porta & M. Diani (eds), *Oxford Handbook of Social Movements*. Oxford: Oxford University Press.

Downing, J. (1984). *Radical Media: The Political Experience of Alternative Communication*. Boston: South End Press.

Downing, J. D. (2013). Towards a political economy of social movement media. *Democratic Communiqué*, 26(1), 17–28.

Dyer-Witheford, N. (2008). For a compositional analysis of the multitude. In W. Bonefeld (ed.), *Subverting the Present, Imagining the Future: Insurrection, Movement, Commons*. New York: Autonomedia.

Garcés, A., & Jiménez, L. (2016). *Comunicación para la movilización y el cambio social*. Medellín: Universidad de Medellín.

Ginsburg, F. (2016). Indigenous media from U-Matic To YouTube: Media sovereignty in the digital age. *Sociologia & Antropologia*, 6(3), 581–599.

Gourarie, C. (2016). Censorship in the social media age. *Columbia Journalism Review*, 21 January. Retrieved from: https://www.cjr.org/analysis/censorship_in_the_social_media_age.php

Gumucio Dagron, A. (2001). *Making Waves: Stories of Participatory Communication for Social Change*. New York: Rockefeller Foundation.

Gumucio Dagron, A., & Tufte, T. (eds) (2006). *Communication for Social Change Anthology: Historical and Contemporary Readings*. Livingston, NJ: CFSC Consortium.

Hadl, J., & Jo, D. (2008). New approaches to our media: general challenges and the Korean case. In M. Pajnik & J. D. Downing (eds), *Alternative Media and the Politics of Resistance* (pp. 81–109). Ljubljana: Peace Institute.

Halleck, D. (2002). *Hand-Held Visions: The Impossible Possibilities of Community Media*. New York: Fordham University Press.

Kidd, D. (2008). The global movement to transform communications. In K. Coyer, T. Dowmunt, & A. Fountain (eds), *The Alternative Media Handbook* (pp. 239–248). London: Routledge.

Kidd, D. (2020). Mobilizing with video in the extractive zone. In C. Robé and S. Charbonneau (eds), *InsUrgent Media from the Front: A Global Media Activism Reader*. Bloomington, IN: Indiana University Press, in press.

Kinsman, G. (2006). Mapping social relations of struggle: activism, ethnography, social organization. In C. Frampton, G. Kinsman, A. K. Thompson, & K. Tillecsek (eds), *Sociology for Changing the World*. Halifax: Fernwood Publishing.

Kishore, S. (2017). The promise of portability: CENDIT and the infrastructure, politics, and practice of video as little media in India 1972–1990. *BioScope*, 8(1), 124–145.

Magallanes-Blanco, C. & Ramos Rodríguez, J. M. (eds) (2016). *Miradas Propias: Pueblos indígenas, comunicación y medios en la sociedad global*. Puebla, Mexico: Editorial Universidad Iberoamericana.

Martini, M. (2018). Online distant witnessing and live-streaming activism: emerging differences in the activation of networked publics. *New Media & Society*, 20(11).

Marubbio, E. (2010). Introduction to Native American indigenous film. *Postscript*, Summer.

Mattoni, A., & Teune, S. (2014). Visions of protest. A media-historic perspective on images in social movements. *Sociology Compass*, 8(6), 876–887.

Monani, S. (2013). Indigenous film festival as eco-testimonial encounter: the 2011 Native Film + Video Festival. *NECSUS – European Journal of Media Studies*, 2(1), 285–291.

della Porta, D. & Pavan, E. (2017). Repertoires of knowledge practices: social movements in times of crisis. *Qualitative Research in Organizations and Management*, 12(4), 297–314.

Riaño, P. (ed.) (1994). *Women in Grassroots Communication: Furthering Social Change*. Thousand Oaks, CA: Sage.

Robé, C. (2017). *Breaking the Spell: A History of Anarchist Filmmakers, Videotape Guerillas, and Digital Ninjas*. Oakland, CA: PM Press.

Robé, C., & Charbonneau, S. (2020). *InsUrgent Media from the Front: A Global Media Activism Reader*. Bloomington, IN: Indiana University Press, in press.

Rodríguez, G. (2018). Ojo al Sancocho. Retrieved from: http://www.ojoalsancocho.org/festival/.

Roth, L. (2010). The social movement of Indigenous media in Canada. In J. D. Downing (ed.), *Encyclopedia of Social Movement Media*. London: Sage.

Salazar, J. F., & Cordova, A. (2008). Imperfect media: the poetics of indigenous video in Latin America. In M. Stewart & P. Wilson (eds), *Global Indigenous Media: Cultures, Poetics, and Politics* (pp. 39–57). Durham, NC: Duke University Press.

Santiváñez Guarniz, S. (2010). La generación del 60 y el cine del grupo Chaski. *Debates en Sociología*, 35, 95–106.

Schiwy, F. (2009). *Indianizing Film: Decolonization, the Andes & the Question of Technology*. New Brunswick, NJ: Rutgers University Press.

Sinha, M. (2010). Witness to violence: documentary cinema and the women's movement in India. *Indian Journal of Gender Studies*, 17(3), 365–373.

Smith, L. (2012). Decolonizing hybridity: indigenous video, knowledge, and diffraction. *Cultural Geographies*, 19(3), 329–348.

Stewart, M. (2007). The Indian film crews of challenge for change: representation and the state. *Canadian Journal of Film Studies/Revue Canadienne d'Études Cinématographiques*, 16(2), 49–81.

Tandoc, E. & Maitra, J. (2018). News organizations' use of native videos on Facebook: tweaking the journalistic field one algorithm change at a time. *New Media & Society*, 20(5), 1679–1696.

Thede, N. & Ambrosi, A. (eds) (1991). *Video the Changing World*. Montréal: Black Rose Books.

Treré, E., & Mattoni, A. (2016). Media ecologies and protest movements: main perspectives and key lessons. *Information, Communication & Society*, 19(3), 290–306.

Tripp, S. (2012). From TVTV to YouTube: a genealogy of participatory practices in video. *Journal of Film and Video*, 64(1–2), 5–16.

Valencia, J. C., Restrepo, P., & Cardona, L. F. (2017). Activistas de Película: apropiación tecnológica, aparición y desaparición del pueblo Wiwa en el conflict armado colombiana.

In F. S. Caballero & T. Gravante (eds), *Tecnopolítica in América Latina y el Caribe*. Quito: Ediciones CIESPAL.

Wolfson, T. & Funke, P. (2014). Communication, class and concentric media practices: developing a contemporary rubric. *New Media & Society*, 16(3), 363–380.

York, J. (2018). Introducing Offline Online: a series of infographics demonstrating how offline inequities are replicated online. *Onlinecensorship.org*, 7 March. Retrieved from https://onli necensorship.org/content/infographics.

7

VIDEO ACTIVISM AS TECHNOLOGY, TEXT, TESTIMONY – OR PRACTICES?

Tina Askanius

Introduction

Recent years have seen a theoretical turn towards practices within both media studies (Couldry, 2004, 2012; Bräuchler & Postill, 2010) and social movement studies (Andrews, Cox, & Wood, 2015; Haluza-DeLay, 2008; Juris & Khasnabish, 2015). At the intersections of these fields, scholars have probed media(-related) practices within and as part of social movements (Mattoni, 2012; Mattoni & Treré, 2014). By situating debates on the virtues and limitations of practice theory in relation to the specific field of video activism, this chapter inscribes itself into this burgeoning area of scholarship on what might be referred to as social movement media practices.

Over the past decades, digital video has become ubiquitous to the extent that it has fundamentally changed practices of political protest, activism, and social movements (Eder & Klonk, 2016). With its increased availability, video technology plays an ever more important role, for example in exposing state violence and organizing collective action, as most recently illustrated by the Black Lives Matter movement, in which video has been used strategically to catalyse debates about the US prison–industrial complex and racism in general (Robé, 2016); or in the explosion of video emerging out of popular uprisings and conflict zones such as Syria (Wessels, 2017). The uptick of this mode of citizen media over the past two decades – due to digital, mobile, and social media – has generated a significant body of literature; this chapter directs critical attention to its theoretical and methodological starting points.

I propose a practice-based framework as a means of bringing a non-media-centric perspective into the analysis of the role of moving images (their production, circulation, and consumption) in social movement politics, by positioning video activism in relation to a range of social and political practices performed by social movement actors today. This chapter demonstrates how a practice approach helps us address one of the most common shortcomings in contemporary media research, that of isolating our objects of analysis in single case studies that prioritize the analysis of one platform (e.g. Twitter, YouTube, or Facebook) while neglecting to address the interlaced workings of these platforms within a broader media ecology. Taking a specific interest in YouTube as a corporate 'honeypot' for contemporary online video culture, including activist video, much of my own work in this area (Askanius, 2013b, 2014; Askanius & Uldam, 2013) is biased towards this one-platform approach, and so partly fails to take into account how activist video practices are intrinsically intertwined in a web of different media technologies and online platforms, and work across an assemblage of social and political practices.[1]

This chapter has two main objectives. The first is to critically review and thematize existing research in the area of video activism by bringing together the diverse but often dispersed literature on this topic. By synthesizing scholarship on historical and contemporary forms of video activism, I identify three distinct foci in the literature, each adding valuable but essentially isolated insights to the phenomenon by considering video as either or primarily technology, text, or testimony. Based on this review, I then demonstrate how a more holistic, practice-based approach allows us to appreciate this form of citizen media as not one, but all of these. Such an exercise enables us to identify and attend to gaps in the literature on video activism specifically, while at the same time exploring the opportunities and limitations of putting practice theory at the heart of a unifying framework for research in this area. I argue that an analytical approach anchored in practice theory puts us in a position to ask holistic questions. Rather than repeating conceptual dichotomies such as online/offline, digital/analogue, old/new, mainstream/activist, a practice-based approach addresses the rich ways in which these categories impinge and encroach on each other (Treré & Mattoni, 2016). For these purposes, I draw on the concepts of 'activist media practices' (Mattoni, 2012) and 'citizen media practices' (Stephansen, 2016) as theoretical orientations for further developing a holistic understanding of video activism as the things activists do, think and say in relation to video for social and political change.

Understanding video activism within the broader field of citizen media

Video and other visual artefacts are important resources for self-expression, collective identities, framing and diffusion of protest and social movements, and for affecting and attracting audiences and target groups. Yet scholars tend to refer to the visual realm of social movement politics not as a site of struggle in its own right, but as a site with which to exemplify and illustrate arguments. Only rarely do we engage in systematic analyses of the visual, or integrate visual analyses in our frameworks. Calls have therefore been made for scholars to consider more explicitly the role of images, video, and other visual artefacts in the study of contemporary social movement media (cf. Doerr, Mattoni, & Teune, 2013; Mattoni &

Teune, 2014). Responding to these calls, this research places activist video – as a particular 'scene of action' (Nicolini, 2017) – at the heart of inquiries into the field of citizen media and the growing body of scholarly work on media-movement dynamics. In doing so, I seek to forefront video and its increasing importance to debates on citizen media, challenging the tendency to treat video and the audio-visual as mere illustrations, documentation or auxiliary texts that complement other more 'important' forms of activism (Philips, 2012). I consider how video practices such as documenting, bearing witness, or mobilizing overlap and interact with other activist media practices such as networking and organizing, or building trust, identity, and solidarity. The strict focus on video activism thus does not imply that this is considered an isolated practice; or to necessarily, in all cases, represent the chief mode of engaging in activism. Nor should the focus on and importance assigned to the medium be seen as an expression of uncritical media-centrism, reducing everything to the workings of the moving image or the steady stream of new technologies by which they travel. Rather, the proposed framework should put us in a position to understand the fine-grained detail of how activist video practices are embedded within broader 'repertoires of communication' (Mattoni, 2012) and modes of organizing. In this sense, the focus on video activism as a distinct area of citizen media serves as an empirical, not an intellectual and theoretical, starting point.

When I use the term video activism to describe and analyse a certain form of citizen media, I position myself in a jungle of competing concepts and labels seeking to understand the place of images and moving images in political activism, and their role in creating political authority and argument more broadly. Video activism can thus be thought of alongside similar concepts including 'camera-mediated-activism' (Andén-Papadopoulos, 2014), 'image activism' (Pantti, 2013), and even terms carrying military connotations such as 'image operations' and 'image wars/warfare' (Eder & Klonk, 2016). Some scholars use 'social media image activism' (Moore-Gilbert, 2018) to signal efforts to capture the role of this new generation of technologies in the diffusion of images in conflicts and contentious politics. When using the term 'video activism', I mean to signal that I am addressing something much more specific. I understand the term to describe media produced for and by groups of organized/networked citizens, and *not* media produced by the military or the state, as is the case with terms such as 'image operations' and 'image wars'. With this label, I also consider the continued contributions of some 'outdated' formats/media such as VHS cassettes and camcorders, rather than focusing solely on social media (albeit this might, in the majority of cases, be where videos circulate and are watched today). This chapter is therefore an attempt to propose a term and a framework which is less occupied with the latest technology (presentism), a bias that is reflected in labels such as 'social media image activism'. Video can thus be analogue, digital, moving image, or still images compiled into a stream of moving images. It can take on the shape of raw unedited footage, carefully crafted documentaries, or mash-up/remixes (for an exploration of taxonomies of genres see Askanius,

2013b). A final proviso concerns the fact that the present chapter addresses video activism in the context only of what we may loosely refer to as social justice movements. 'Social justice movements' is best considered an umbrella term comprising environmental and climate change movements, feminist and gender justice movements, and humanitarian and human rights movements, including immigration rights movements. In this sense, the proposed framework is not necessarily suitable for capturing citizen media in the context of reactionary, anti-democratic, or extremist forces such as ultra-nationalist or white pride movements (although these actors are certainly diligent producers of video towards which some scholarly attention has been directed, e.g. Ekman, 2014). Studying these movements entails very different challenges in terms of access and ethics in which the practice approach, with all of its propositions of personal, inside/in-depth and multi-sited analyses, would prove difficult to fully observe.

Video activism as ...

Video activism is increasingly addressed in social movement media research, but rarely defined and theorized in any rigorous or systematic way. Representing some of the more practitioner-oriented literature, Harding (2001, p. 1) offers a straightforward definition of video activism as 'the use of video as an essential tool in social justice activism'. From the perspective of professionalized human rights activism, Gregory et al. (2005, p. 8) use the term 'video advocacy' to describe 'the process of integrating video into an advocacy effort to achieve heightened visibility or impact in your campaigning'. Video in these definitions is thus considered largely as add-on or auxiliary text to the 'real' campaign or activist effort. Further, the emphasis on use reflects a somewhat narrow, functionalist approach. In sum, such conceptualizations largely fall short on the ability to understand video as more than texts with mimetic, symbolic, aesthetic, and affective potential, and more than the sum of their use, function, and effects.

In the following, I identify and unpack tendencies in how activist video has been defined and scrutinized as either technology (analogue, digital or hybrid; industry); text (content, aesthetic, or rhetorical form); or testimony (visual evidence, mode of bearing witness, sousveillance). Addressing the limitations and pitfalls in this body of work (including my own), which for the past decade has been preoccupied with bringing digital video into perspectives on social movement media practices, sets the stage for a discussion of the main contributions that a practice lens can bring to this field. The following review by no means offers an exhaustive account of research on this topic. Further, the categorization proposed builds on a fairly crude grouping and in some cases the authors and work discussed could be understood as working across categories. The three t's of video activism research should therefore be considered broad conceptual containers that serve to sharpen our analytical categories and bring clarity into the growing body of literature addressing the intersections between video, citizen media practices, and social movements.

... technology (techno-political infrastructure and industry)

Scholars within the 'video-as-technology' strand pose questions such as: What techno-material environments are videos embedded in, and how are they inter-linked with other elements online? How do they depend on content delivery networks or the activities of social bots? How are they connected with and inte-grated into corporate social media? How do the features of commercial and non-commercial services influence production, distribution, reception, and participation around videos? What are the risks activists face (in terms of surveillance, data and personal security, censorship, unpaid labour) as they increasingly move action repertoires into the mechanisms of social networking in corporate online spaces? How have video recording and distribution technologies changed over time? How do these technological changes translate into changes in activism and social move-ment politics?

From this vantage point, scholars approach video activism by drawing on social media analysis or platform analysis, often with an interest in techno-political aspects of video activism, or in video as a form of hacktivism. For example, video tech-nology and specific platforms take centre stage in Fish's (2016) study of Anon-ymous activism in which practices of 'mirroring' videos to evade the systematic take-down of videos and retain visibility online are traced across Twitter, YouTube, and Internet Relay Chat (IRC) chat rooms. Despite a proliferation of studies taking an interest in social media, efforts have been made to historically contextualize the latest video technologies, by putting recent findings in dialogue with the longer trajectory of alternative television industries, activist film-making practices, and political documentary (Chanan, 2012), and addressing questions about how changes in technology create changes in the narrative framings of video, its political uses, agency, and audience experiences (Gregory, 2016). Those probing the histories and legacies of previous modes of video activism often conduct case studies of particular groups, drawing on archival material and in-depth interviews to understand how a shared understanding of a set of production practices, including an ethics of filming, is developed in relation or opposition to commercial and public film industries. Such perspectives are offered, for example, in my case study of *TV Stop* in Denmark (Askanius, 2018) and by Presence (2015) on the historical trajectory of the alternative video scene in the UK from the 1990s onwards. While these studies offer rich details about the activist groups and video collectives in question, they tell us little, beyond the time-and-space-bound speci-ficities of the cases in question, of the broader practice fields in which these groups operated, and to which they contributed.

... text (content, aesthetics, and art form)

Within the second strand, scholars have addressed questions such as: What are the different types, taxonomies, genres, and subgenres of video activism? (Askanius, 2013b); and how can we understand their aesthetics and artistic dimensions (Juhasz,

2006) or intertextual and trans-medial qualities? (Constanza-Chock, 2014) Others have probed the rhetorical strategies with which video stimulates affects, debate, and action (Arévalo Salinas, 2014). This strand also includes questions such as: What creative strategies are implemented to mobilize different audiences and how do different textual strategies position the viewer/audience in different spaces of action? How do different narrative, discursive, rhetorical, and visual strategies relate to truth claims and ideas of authenticity? How do video activists create counter-frames challenging those produced by mainstream media or political opponents/antagonists?

Scholars working in this tradition often draw on content analysis, visual analysis, narrative analysis, and various other combinations of text-oriented tools with which to empirically study the ways in which 'texts' – broadly conceived – engage strategies of *storytelling* (Gregory, 2012) to galvanize change/action in the viewer. Others focus on remix aesthetics and strategies examining how footage, images, animations, or songs are combined to create new hybrid texts (e.g. Askanius, 2013b; Gregory & Losh, 2012). Further, video-as-text also include perspectives on counter-framing vis-à-vis mainstream media, which is often considered an inherent feature of social movement media more generally. Mateos & Gaona (2015), for example, see video activism as an *audio-visual discursive practice* that sets out to 'counter a discursive abuse or gap and is carried out by actors outside the dominant power structures' (p. 1).

When isolating video as a discernible type of text that can be classified by reference to form, mode of address, or subject matter, however, we largely neglect the contexts involved in establishing a genre, including the 'work' of audiences. Well aware of the considerable limitations of deploying merely text-centred approaches, scholars have sought to include an audience perspective by combining textual analysis with an analysis of online comments or discussion threads (Askanius & Uldam, 2013; McCosker, 2015) to provide some indication of reception/interpretations/impact and – although more rarely – interviews with audiences. Predominantly, however, when we take an interest in the rhetorical and aesthetical strategies with which videos operate and appeal to certain target grouops, we tend to be undergirded by an often-unarticulated assumption about audiences based on analytical constructs of an imagined or ideal audience, rather than actual reception or audience studies.

The focus on video as text inevitably touches upon the functions video fills within a broader repertoire of communication strategies in activist organizations, and thus addresses the close links between content/modes of address and function/functionality and impact (e.g. education, awareness, mobilization, empowerment, evidence).

... testimony (evidence, visibility, sousveillance)

This leads us to one of the chief ways in which function(s) has been treated in the literature, namely video as a means of bearing witness and providing visual evidence, which we might pull together and discuss under the rubric of 'video as testimony'. Common to this body of work then is that video is considered 'a direct will to visibility' (Fish, 2016, p. 97). Conceptual frameworks are built around notions such as citizen camera-witnessing (Andén-Papadopoulos, 2014); strategic witnessing (Ristovska, 2016) counter-surveillance (Wilson & Serisier, 2010), or sousveillance (Bock, 2016).

Important insights in this area also concern work highlighting the systematic efforts of activist and citizen organizations in producing video materials that work as legal evidence for specialized audiences, directed to courtrooms or in semi-juridical settings such as international war tribunals (e.g. Pillay, 2005). Of critical importance to understanding such professional human rights video activism is the work of Gregory (2016), written from within and often about the US-based organization WITNESS.

More often, however, scholars have turned attention to the less professional, organized, and formalized modes of creating visibility around political or social justice issues. In the work of Hermida & Hernández-Santaolalla (2018), for example, video activism is considered a form of counter-surveillance (or sousveillance) against the abuse of power committed by state forces. Drawing on a case study of in the riots in Burgos, Spain in January 2014, they show how video distributed through Twitter is used to expose and provide evidence of police violence. Bock (2016) and Robé (2016) also consider cop-watching a specific form of sousveillance. Bock (2016), however, complicates the idea of video as visual evidence, arguing that the social value of cop-watching is only partly tied to its images, as the routines of purposeful witnessing present a unique form of activism that combines text and practice, resulting in embodied narratives that give voice to longstanding, previously marginalized concerns (p. 14). Others have turned their attention to the flip side of social media in this matter, focusing on how these platforms are increasingly used not by activists to document the power-abuse of authorities, but as tools in the hands of both states and corporate actors engaging in systematic surveillance of activists in the name of reputation and image management (Uldam, 2017).

Despite the undeniable virtues of this body of work, especially when considered in concert, the conceptualization of video-as-testimony constrains us in the sense that it offers insights solely on *one* aspect of video and does not allow us to understand how media practices intended to create and maintain visibility work in other contexts and for different purposes, let alone to understand how such practices arrange, combine, and intersect with other social practices (Couldry, 2012). Having outlined and unpacked the three dominant ways of conceptualizing and addressing video activism as either or primarily technology, text or testimony, I now move on to suggest a fourth and more open-ended understanding of video activism rooted in practice theory.

... practices

When Couldry (2004), now more than a decade ago, made a much-cited call for media research to enter a new paradigm turning towards practices, he urged scholars to focus on what people are actually *doing* with media instead of assuming that technological affordances necessarily enable or empower citizens in specific ways. In social movement scholarship, numerous studies have since sought to marry media studies and practice theory, proposing concepts such as activist media practices (Mattoni, 2012) or social movement media practices (Constanza-Chock, 2014) to approach the movement–media relationship analytically and conceptually. Stephansen (2016), too, proposes that we shift focus and terminology from citizen media to 'citizen media practices' in order to capture broader issues related to mediation beyond those directly concerned with the production and circulation of *content*. The re-orientation towards practices becomes a way of embracing *all* of the processes involved in citizen media (production, content/text, receptions, appropriations, re-circulation/mediation, archival practices, memory-work, etc.) in ways that challenge reductive accounts of citizen media as *one* of these. On a more fundamental level, we might consider a practice-based approach as a means of avoiding communicative reductionism and bringing a non-media-centric framework into the analysis of citizen media. These efforts, however, have yet to be applied to the specific area of video activism.

In the context of video activism, the practice approach helps us steer clear of a one-sided focus on the video 'texts' themselves, or of focusing exclusively on the camcorder, mobile device, YouTube, or whatever technology is being used to record or distribute. As a preliminary step in outlining the approach, we may consider the framework to primarily re-focus our attention on the actual *uses* of video and the underlying practices of these performative *doings*. In this final section, I seek to further develop practice approaches to citizen media, but also to complicate and challenge the definitions and frameworks that media scholars subscribing to this so-called practice turn have been working with so far. I do so primarily drawing on perspectives proposed by Nicolini (2017), who argues that we should not limit the practice approach to dimensions of use/doings. Instead, a comprehensive and convincing perspective challenges the idea that practice theory 'just' chronicles what people *do* and 'only what is in sight counts' (p. 31).

As a first step in this argument, I therefore begin by illustrating how the performative dimension of 'doing' might be accompanied by those of 'thinking' and 'saying' as proposed by Stephansen (2016) drawing on Schatzki (2002) to include a range of practices that form a bundle of overlapping practices around which video activism evolves. I then unpack how, in a practice-based definition of video activism, these dimensions all need to be put to work in relation to a set of 'common understandings, teleology (ends and tasks) and rules' (Schatzki, 2002, p. 86) that are specific to this particular field of citizen media.

Dovetailing on the framework proposed by Stephansen (2016), we might apply her broad definition of citizen media practices to help understand what a practice-based approach to video activism might entail. In her analysis of the agents, processes, and publics involved in World Social Forum process, she suggests an analytical framework built around four main pillars: practices of collaboration, capacity-building, networking, and movement-building. Unpacking these four practice fields, we might think of video activism as a prism of different entwined and at times overlapping practices, as illustrated in Figure 7.1.

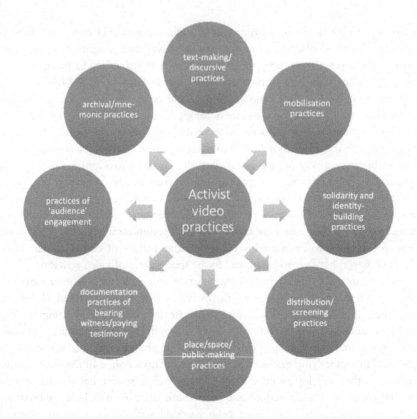

FIGURE 7.1 'Bundled' practices of video activism

We may usefully understand social phenomena, large and small, as 'bundles of practices and arrangements' (Schatzki, 2011, p. 6). If we shift focus to what activists 'do, think, and say' in relation to video, a broad range of practices and arrangements are brought into view. These include, but are not limited to, the bundle of discursive, material, and social practices outlined in Figure 7.1. Without digressing into the details of each of these practice-forms, for the purpose of the present argument it suffices to say that we, in our empirical studies, tend to pigeonhole one or perhaps, at best, combine two of these areas. For example, video activism in the realm of protest movements involves specific place/space-making practices in which meanings travel back and forth between urban places and digital spaces (Askanius, 2013a). Such space-making practices relate not only to the text-making practices in the bundle, but also to the practices of creating counter-publics, and public-making practices involved in citizen media production more generally (Stephansen, 2016). Further, archival and mnemonic practices are essential aspects of activist video practices, as for example demonstrated by Kaun (2016) in her study of activists involved in the Occupy Wall Street protests, or as articulated by former activists of video and television collectives, who appropriate social media as historical video repository and databases (Askanius, 2018).

However, Nicolini (2017) reminds us that while, for analytical purposes, practices can be isolated for examination, empirically we always encounter multiplicities or arrays of practices (p. 27). Video activism then is most productively conceptualized and approached as a particular scene of action – where several practices intersect and are knotted together in what we might understand as bundles (Nicolini, 2017). The crux of the matter being that we, when approaching our objects of analysis, should avoid isolating one particular filament in the bundle as exemplified above, and instead tune in on the intricate relations in and between the array of practices that constitute a certain field.

A practice-based definition of video activism

Returning to Schatzki's (2002) definition, he understands practices to be open, spatially and temporally dispersed *sets of doings and sayings* organized by common understandings; teleology (ends and tasks); and rules. With this definition of practices, let us unpack how this translates into a revised and slightly more wordy definition of video activism as *the things activists do, think and say in relation to video for social and political change – all of which are organized by common understandings, teleology, and rules specific to this field.*

Video activism is obviously characterized by the material arrangements or *artefacts* involved (videos – be they digital or analogue) and the *technologies* with which they are made, disseminated or watched (be it mobile phones, video-sharing sites, streaming or screening technologies). But in line with the definition proposed above, we may also bring attention to the broader dimensions of not just the doing but also the saying and thinking around such artefacts and technologies. The dimension of saying might include what is said *about* (e.g. in conversations, meetings, online fora, or screenings) and *on* those artefacts (e.g. in the video itself, in the context of a broader advocacy campaign); and *about* and *on* those technologies (e.g. Vimeo, YouTube, Bambuser). Finally, the 'thinking' dimension of the definition brings to the forefront the *lived experience* of media–movement dynamics. Drawing on in-depth interviewing or diary-based methods, for example, this realm is addressed by probing how activists reflect upon media and media-related practices (Couldry, 2004; Stephansen, 2016).

The three dimensions of doing, saying, and thinking are in turn all informed by *common understandings* shared by actors in the field. In the context of social justice movements, we might think of these shared ideological, cultural, or cognitive frameworks as rooted in largely left-leaning beliefs and principles, although new social movements do not fit comfortably within the traditional left–right classification system.

Secondly, practices of video activism are informed by specific *ends* and *tasks*. Such ends might include furthering gender justice, raising awareness of climate change, or fighting for Indigenous rights; ends that are sought obtained through concrete tasks (such as protesting, organizing direct actions, civil disobedience, sit-ins, occupations). The ends in this sense can be concrete political goals of creating policy changes, for example, or concern more abstract aspirations of social change and justice, just as the tasks might be placed on a spectrum between radical and reformist repertoires of contention.

Finally, this is done according to specific informal *rules*, which leads us to the normative and ethical dimensions of film-making and spectatorship inherent to video activism. When practices as a set of object-oriented doings and sayings have a history and a constituency, they acquire normativity over time and 'a sense emerges and is sustained that there is a right way of doing things' (Nicolini, 2017, p. 22). In this context, the rights and wrongs involve questions of what to film and how; the ethics of bearing witness, of documenting civil disobedience or human rights violations, for example; and how to ensure the anonymity and safety of subjects. These longstanding concerns for the ethics of film-making are increasingly complicated by technological developments that challenge some of the principles of ensuring the integrity of subjects as well as the role of 'the ethical witness', which has underpinned video activism and political film-making across generations (Gregory, 2010). Addressing how the 'rules' of video activism are changing, Gregory (2010, 2012), for example, argues that the audio-visual image – whether it displays public trauma, torture, police brutality, or human suffering – is burdened with an immense ethical responsibility in a time of ubiquitous camera technologies, accessible editing, and remixing software and live-streaming apps. An inherent feature of the framework thus requires us to bring attention to the ethics of what, where, and how to film to ensure the anonymity, dignity, and security of those filming and those being filmed.

Concluding remarks: virtues and limits of the practice-based approach

As scholars of citizen media and contemporary forms of activism, our objects of analysis are notoriously fickle, interchangeable, and motley entities that are situated across multiple sites of analysis. These features sit well with the prismatic approach offered by practice theory, which requires attention to context and perspectives across time and space. It asks us not to isolate certain filaments in the bundle of practices at the expense of the bigger picture, to avoid focusing exclusively on the outcomes of the practices in question (the manifest forms they take in terms of concrete, tangible artefacts through which we can infer meaning about a certain set of practices), or to de-historicize them. The trans-situated nature of practices forces us to adjust and widen our analytical lens accordingly. Such an ambitious proposition has consequences for the methods and resources we direct at social phenomena. In short, the practice lens, as proposed by Nicolini (2017), requires us to up our game in terms of research design and mixed-methods approaches. In the context of video activism, this entails refraining from (merely) conducting textual analysis. Nor are interviews, if applied in isolation, necessarily the best means to study activist practices as they tend to produce second-order accounts providing no 'direct' access to practices themselves. In order words, scholars of video activism and any other form of citizen media need to leave their desk and screen behind and, whenever possible, place themselves 'in the midst of the scene of action' (Nicolini, 2017, p. 29). Ideally, we should engage several methods in tandem with prolonged and sustained field work (just as sustained engagement over time is preferred over historical contextualization), as has been proposed by scholars in media anthropology (e.g. Bräuchler & Postill, 2010).

Further, the practice perspective is strongly connected to, and might fruitfully be combined with, that of media ecology (Treré & Mattoni, 2016), which in a similar manner suggests we focus on the symbiotic relationships between and across culture, communication, and technology over time. In communication scholarship, media ecology has been used to study media as environments so as to emphasize the complex and multidimensional interactions between people, their media, and other social forces (Lum, 2014). To Dahlberg-Grundberg (2015), the concept of ecology allows us move beyond specific media instances and technologies to unpack the 'overall, encompassing networks of communication and interaction between several forms of communication technology, which actors are immersed within' (p. 4). From a similar vantage point, Mattoni (2017) has explored the connections and potential synergies between practice and ecology perspectives in social movement studies, arguing that this pairing orients us towards a more holistic research agenda in three key ways: by situating the use of digital technologies in the broader palette of activist media practices; by taking account of temporal, diachronic dimensions of the relationship between social movements and media technologies; and by developing an 'in-depth analysis of social movement actors' appropriation of media technologies, hence bringing back activists' agency with regard to media and considering how other, non-media-related social practices order activist media practices' (pp. 496–497). In this sense, the two perspectives are rooted in the same dissatisfaction with media centrism and monocausal explanations on these matters. Together, the two perspectives might help us stay clear of these pitfalls and offer ways of understanding actual media use and appropriations, and how these are situated within the broader historical, cultural, political, and temporal contexts in which citizen media operate. In the present context, putting the concept of media ecology to work in dialogue with a practice-based approach thus seems particularly fruitful as a way of further exploring analytical frameworks with which to get at the intertwined, multi-layered, and complex dynamics between contemporary (and historical) social movements and moving image technologies.

A practice approach is obviously not without its limitations and pitfalls. One of the most common criticisms is that it does not offer a grand theory narrative. To Mattoni and Treré (2014), for example, social practices are considered useful starting points for discussing actions performed at the micro-level of social movement processes at specific moments in time, whereas they prove less fruitful for meso- or meta-level theorizing of broader processes related to media and movements over time (see Bräuchler & Postill, 2010 for a similar critique). Others have pointed out that the perspective misses out on important power aspects in regard to the technologies and techno-commercial materialities of social media, which dominate the online spaces in which citizen media practices are performed today. Finally, one might also raise critical questions as to the feasibility of the big-picture ambitions and the 'all-or-nothing ethos', that underlines its proposals. In this sense, Hobart (2010) might be right to assume that 'a strong and workable account of practices is far more demanding that its proponents appreciate' (p. 57).

These limitations notwithstanding, this chapter offers a productive and holistic approach with which we might begin to fully understand all of the intertwined social and political practices involved in video activism and citizen media more generally. It has demonstrated how the approach enables a scrutiny of video activism *across* the mediation process of the text – its properties, production, and reception – *and* positions these in relation to a wider bundle of social and political practices. Addressing some of the criticisms directed at the perspective, Nicolini (2017) argues that the practice approach might usefully be understood to provide an ontology rather than a self-contained framework with pillars carved in stone. Practice theory from this vantage point, then, is not a theoretical project in the traditional sense, but a methodological orientation supported by a vocabulary and grammar with which to approach the social world. It is, in other words, a 'package of theory, method and literary genre' (2017, p. 26); an approach that is systematic and consistent, while open-ended and flexible enough to remain faithful to the situated and contingent nature of the social world.

Note

1   See Treré (2012) and Mattoni & Treré (2014) for discussions on the one-medium bias in social movement media studies more generally.

References

Andén-Papadopoulos, K. (2014). Citizen camera-witnessing: crisis testimony in the age of 'mediated mass self-communication'. *New Media & Society*, 16(5), 753–769.

Andrews, C., Cox, L., & Wood, L. (2015). Movement practice(s): how do we 'do' social movements? *Interface: A Journal For and About Social Movements*, 7(1), 1–7.

Arévalo Salinas, A. (2014). El movimiento social 15-M de España y la promoción de la protesta a través de sus vídeos en YouTube. *Historia y Comunicación Social*, 19 (Núm. Especial Marzo), 153–163. Downloaded from revistas.ucm.es/index.php/hics/article/download/45122/42485.

Askanius, T. (2013a). Protest movements and spectacles of death: From urban places to video spaces. In N. Doerr, A. Mattoni & S. Teune (eds), *Advances in the Visual Analysis of Social Movements*. Research in Social Movements, Conflicts and Change, Vol. 35 (pp. 105–133). Bingley: Emerald.

Askanius, T. (2013b). Online video activism and political mash-up genres. *JOMEC Journal: Journalism, Media and Cultural Studies*, 4. Retrieved from https://jomec.cardiffuniversitypress.org/articles/abstract/10.18573/j.2013.10257/

Askanius, T. (2014). Video for change. In K. G. Wilkins, T. Tufte, & R. Obregon (eds), *Handbook on Development Communication and Social Change* (pp. 453–470). Malden, MA: Wiley-Blackwell.

Askanius, T. (2019). (Social) media time, connective memory and activist television histories: the case of TV Stop. In M. Mortensen, C. Neumeyer, & T. Poell (eds), *Social Media Materialities and Protest: Critical Reflections* (pp. 59–71). London: Routledge.

Askanius, T., & Uldam, J. (2013). Online civic cultures? Debating climate change activism on YouTube. *International Journal of Communication*, 7, 1185–1204. Retrieved from https://ijoc. org/index.php/ijoc/article/viewFile/1755/920.

Bock, A. (2016). Film the police! Cop-watching and its embodied narratives. *Journal of Communication*, 66(1), 13–34.

BräuchlerB., & Postill, J. (2010). *Theorising Media and Practice*. Oxford and New York: Berghahn Books.

Chanan, C. (2012). Video, activism and the art of small media. *Transnational Cinemas*, 2(2), 217–226.

Constanza-Chock, S. (2014). *Out of the Shadows, into the Streets: Transmedia Organizing and the Immigrant Rights Movement*. Cambridge, MA: MIT Press.

Couldry, N. (2004). Theorising media as practice. *Social Semiotics*, 14(2), 115–132.

Couldry, N. (2012). *Media, Society, World: Social Theory and Digital Media Practice*. Cambridge: Polity Press.

Dahlberg-Grundberg, M. (2015). Technology as movement on hybrid organizational types and the mutual constitution of movement identity and technological infrastructure in digital activism. *Convergence*, 22(5), 524–542.

Doerr, N., Mattoni, A., & Teune, S. (eds) (2013). *Advances in the Visual Analysis of Social Movements*. Bingley: Emerald

Eder, J., & Klonk, C. (eds) (2016). *Image Operations. Visual Media and Political Conflict*. Manchester: Manchester University Press.

Ekman, M. (2014). The dark side of online activism: Swedish right-wing extremist video activism on YouTube. *MedieKultur: Journal of Media and Communication Research*, 30(56).

Fish, A. (2016). Mirroring the videos of Anonymous: cloud activism, living networks, and political mimesis. *Fibreculture Journal*, 26(191), 85–107. Retrieved from http://fibreculturejournal.org/wp-content/pdfs/FCJ-191AdamFish.pdf

Gregory, S. (2010). Cameras everywhere: Ubiquitous video documentation of human rights and considerations of safety, security, dignity and consent. *Journal of Human Rights Practice*, 2(2), 191–207.

Gregory, S. (2012). Kony 2012 through a prism of video advocacy practices and trends. *Journal of Human Rights Practic*e, 4(3), 1–6.

Gregory, S. (2016). Human rights in an age of distant witnesses: remixed lives, reincarnated images and live-streamed co-presence. In J. Eder & C. Klon (eds), *Image Operations: Visual Media and Political Conflict* (pp. 184–196). Manchester: Manchester University Press.

Gregory, G., & Losh, E. (2012). Remixing human rights: rethinking civic expression, representation and personal security in online video. *First Monday*, 17(8).

GregoryS., Caldwell, G., Avni, R., & HardingT. (eds) (2005). *Video for Change. A Guide for Advocacy and Activism*. London: Pluto Press.

Haluza-DeLay, R. (2008). A theory of practice for social movements: Environmentalism and ecological habitus. *Mobilization*, 13(2), 205–218.

Harding, T. (2001). *The Video Activist Handbook*. London: Pluto Press.

Hermida, A., & Hernández-Santaolalla, V. (2018). Twitter and video activism as tools for counter-surveillance: The case of social protests in Spain. *Information, Communication & Society*, 21(3), 416–433.

Hobart, M. (2010). What do we mean by 'media practices'? In B. Bräuchler & J. Postill (eds), *Theorising Media and Practice* (pp. 55–75). New York: Berghahn Books.

Holland, D., & Lave, J. (2009). Social practice theory and the historical production of persons. *Actio: An International Journal of Human Activity Theory*, 2, 1–15. Retrieved from http://www.chat.kansai-u.ac.jp/publications/actio/pdf/no2-1.pdf

Juhasz, A. (2006). Video remains. Nostalgia, technology and queer archive activism. *GLQ Archive*, 12(2), 319–328.

Juris, J. S., & Khasnabish, A. (2015). Immanent accounts: ethnography, engagement, and social movement practices. In D. della Porta & M. Diani (eds), *The Oxford Handbook of Social Movements* (VI, 38). Oxford: Oxford University Press.

Kaun, A. (2016). *Crisis and Critique: A Brief History of Media Participation in Times of Crisis*. London: Zed Books.

Lum, C. M. K. (2014). Media ecology: contexts, concepts, and currents. In R. Fortner & M. Fackler (eds), *The Handbook in Media and Mass Communication Theory* (pp. 137–153). Hoboken, NJ: Wiley-Blackwell.

Mateos, C., & Gaona, C. (2015). Video activism: a descriptive typology. *Global Media Journal*, 2, 1–25. Retrieved from http://www.globalmediajournal.com/open-access/video-activism-a-descriptive-typology.php?aid=62532.

Mattoni, A. (2012). *Media Practices and Protest Politics. How Precarious Workers Mobilise*. Farnham: Ashgate.

Mattoni, A. (2017). A situated understanding of digital technologies in social movements. Media ecology and media practices approaches. *Social Movement Studies*, 16(4), 494–505.

Mattoni, A., & Teune, S. (2014). Visions of protest. A media-historic perspective on images in social movements. *Sociology Compass*, 8(6), 876–887.

Mattoni, A., & Treré, E. (2014). Media practices, mediation processes and mediatization in the study of social movements. *Communication Theory*, 24(3), 252–271.

McCosker, A. (2015). Social media activism at the margins: Managing visibility, voice and vitality affects. *Social Media+Society*, 1(2), 2056305115605860.

Moore-Gilbert, K. (2018). A visual uprising: Framing the online activism of Bahrain's Shi'i opposition. *Media, War & Conflict*, 1750635217741913.

Nicolini, D. (2017). Practice theory as a package of theory, method and vocabulary: affordances and limitations. In M. Jonas et al. (eds), *Methodological Reflections on Practice-Oriented Theories* (pp. 19–34). Cham: Springer International.

Pantti, M. (2013). Getting closer? Encounters of the national media with global images. *Journalism Studies*, 14(2), 201–218.

Pillay, S. (2005). Video as evidence. In S. Gregory et al. (eds), *Video for Change* (pp. 209–232). London: Pluto Press.

Philips, A. (2012). Visual protest material as empirical data. *Visual Communication*, 11(1), 3–21.

Presence, S. (2015). The contemporary landscape of video-activism in Britain. In E. Maziersk & L. Kristensen (eds), *Marxism and Film Activism: Screening Alternative Worlds* (pp. 186–212). New York: Berghahn Books.

Ristovska, S. (2016). Strategic witnessing in an age of video activism. *Media, Culture & Society*, 38(7), 1034–1047.

Robé, C. (2016). Criminalizing dissent: Western state repression, video activism, and counter-summit protests. *Framework: The Journal of Cinema and Media*, 57(2), 161–188.

Schatzki, T. (2002). *The Site of the Social: A Philosophical Exploration of the Constitution of Social Life and Change*. University Park, PA: Pennsylvania State University Press.

Schatzki, T. R. (2011). *Where the Action Is (On Large Social Phenomena such as Sociotechnical Regimes)*. Working Paper 1. Sustainable Practices Research Group. Retrieved from http://www.sprg.ac.uk/uploads/schatzki-wp1.pdf

Stephansen, H. C. (2016). Understanding citizen media as practice. In M. Baker & B. Blaagaard (eds), *Citizen Media and Public Spaces: Diverse Expressions of Citizenship and Dissent* (pp. 25–41). London: Routledge.

Treré, E. (2012). Social movements as information ecologies: Exploring the coevolution of multiple Internet technologies for activism. *International Journal of Communication*, 6, 19.

Treré, E., & Mattoni, A. (2016). Media ecologies and protest movements: main perspectives and key lessons. *Information, Communication & Society*, 19(3), 290–306.

Uldam, J. (2017). Social media visibility: challenges to activism. *Media, Culture & Society*, 40(1), 41–58.

Wessels, J. I. (2017). Video activists from Aleppo and Raqqa as 'Modern-Day Kinoks'?: An audiovisual narrative of the Syrian Revolution. *Middle East Journal of Culture and Communication*, 10(2/3), 159–174.

Wilson, D. J., & Serisier, T. (2010). Video activism and the ambiguities of counter-surveillance. *Surveillance & Society*, 8(2), 166–180.

8

ACTIVIST MEDIA PRACTICES, ALTERNATIVE MEDIA AND ONLINE DIGITAL TRACES

The case of YouTube in the Italian *Se non ora, quando?* movement

Alice Mattoni and Elena Pavan

Introduction

Early in February 2011, a call for action began to circulate online in the form of a short video in which a well-known Italian actress, Angela Finocchiaro, stated that

> Italy is not a country for women. But women, girls and young girls constitute half of Italy. [...] Men, please, could you say that you do not want to live in a country that looks like a bad movie from the 50s? And, women, let's go out of our homes all together and show our faces, naked. We will wait for you on the 13th to claim 'Italy is a country for women'.[1]

The video was directed by Francesca Comencini, an Italian movie and documentary director, and published online to promote the incoming nationwide demonstration *Se non ora, quando?* ('If not now, when?').

A group of activists from the gender-oriented organizations *Filomena* and *DiNuovo!*, some of whom were artists, movie directors, actresses, and photographers, also journalists and academics, took the initiative to realize and circulate the video. The video was originally released and then mostly disseminated within the commercial video-sharing platform YouTube, uploaded in the TalunaFilm channel managed by Carlotta Cerquetti, an Italian photographer and director who was involved in the preparation of the February demonstration. It was only after the demonstration took place, and the groups of activists behind its organization were structured as a national network of committees, that an official YouTube channel was opened to express the movement's voice through a set of videos, among which, the one that initiated the protest.

The story of the video call for action for the *Se non ora, quando?* demonstration is an emblematic example of how alternative media content is produced and circulated today in a media environment that is highly digitalized and offers activists a myriad of communication possibilities. In this chapter, we seek to understand what happens to alternative media when they intertwine with corporate platforms like YouTube. To this aim, we employ the lens of media practice theory to understand the activist media practices that result from the interplay between social media platform affordances and activists' alternative media. More specifically, we elaborate on activist media practices performed through mainstream corporate platforms by starting from the traces that movement actors and supporters leave behind when they exploit specific affordances to produce and circulate alternative content.

The chapter is organized as follows. In the first section, we discuss the notion of alternative media, arguing that today hybrid forms of mediation occur that are neither completely mainstream nor entirely alternative. In the second section, we present our analytical framework that revolves around the broad notion of activist media practices, as well as the methods and data that we employed to explore our case study. We then present our empirical findings related to the types of subjects and interactions that characterize activist media practices in YouTube to sustain the *Se non ora, quando?* (SNOQ) movement. We conclude by discussing our results and reflecting on the potentials as well as the limitations of our methodological approach to studying alternative media from a media practice perspective.

Theoretical framework

Alternative media have a long history and a relevant place within the repertoire of communication that social movements display. As literature on this topic also signals (Atton, 2015; Downing, 2001), alternative media might vary to a great degree with regard to the communication technologies through which they take shape: from posters to radio, from television to theatre, from graffiti to stickers, the long road of alternative media is characterized by a strong plurality and diversity. To take this richness into consideration, Chris Atton (2002) proposes to understand alternative media as an 'area of cultural production' where various processes of creation and distribution might coexist and have different levels of radicalization. In this regard, della Porta & Mattoni (2012) suggest that alternative media might vary along three main axes: the degree of possession, the degree of collectiveness, and the degree of openness.

The *degree of collectiveness* refers to the subjects who create alternative media content and/or infrastructures. Extant literature underlines that in many cases alternative media rest on the efforts of collective actors such as media-activist collectives (Ardizzoni, 2010; Howley, 2005; Rodríguez, 2001). Still, due to the capillary diffusion of digital technologies, the creation of alternative media content might be based on the work of individual activists as well as of lay citizens with no prior connection to social movements. The *degree of possession* denotes the extent to which the subjects who create alternative media own the infrastructure on which the alternative media is based. Some media-activists appropriate the technologies that will then allow the production of alternative media outlets and their content (cf. Milan, 2013). In other cases, however, alternative media might rest on technological infrastructures that are not directly controlled by the subjects who produce the alternative outlets and content. The *degree of openness* relates instead to the possibility of taking part in the making of alternative media content. Once created, some alternative media outlets might be open to a variety of contributions, as in the case of Indymedia: an informational website created at the dawn of the Global Justice Movements that adopted an anonymous and uncensored open-publishing system (cf. Morris, 2004). Other alternative media outlets, instead, might be more tightly linked to specific media-activist collectives, grassroots activist groups, or movement organizations that purposefully publish only their own materials.

Alternative media have always been 'impure', and a virtually infinite range of alternative media existed in the past and continue to exist today all over the world (Gumucio-Dagron, 2007). However, with the widespread use of social media, microblogging, and content sharing corporate platforms in contemporary social movements, the very notion of alternative media has become more blurred and difficult to define. This is because, as much of the literature shows, activists employ such platforms extensively to share their own content and to mitigate the lack of visibility from which they suffer in the more traditional mainstream media such as the printed press or television newscasts. Movement organizations and other grass-roots collective formations employ Facebook, Twitter, and YouTube to share their own views of the social world and to represent themselves, and in an attempt to mobilize other potential supporters. While these corporate platforms cannot be equated with alternative media *stricto sensu*, particularly because they are owned by private companies oriented to profit and not to the promotion of activists' causes, it is also true that activists' appropriation of Facebook, Twitter, and YouTube makes of them spaces in which alternative media content circulate to a great extent.

Thus, these corporate platforms can be read through the lens of alternative media, and their alternative potential assessed at the crossroads of the three above-mentioned axes. First, these corporate platforms are characterized by an *intermediate degree of collectiveness*: they were constructed with individual users in mind as their primary concern, but activists frequently appropriate and manage these platforms in a collective way. Second, they show a *low degree of possession*: activists might use them to create and spread alternative media content, but they do not own the technological infrastructure on which they rest. Finally, corporate platforms show a *high degree of openness*: even when activists link their accounts to one movement organization, any other user, even if external to the movement, can contribute to the formation of its public discourse in manifold ways – e.g. posting and reposting content, circulating hashtags, sharing content. In this chapter, we focus on such hybrid forms of mediation to go beyond the binary dichotomy that traditionally opposes mainstream commercial media to alternative non-profit media (cf. Aska-nius & Gustafsson, 2010).

Investigating the digital traces of activist media practices in YouTube

Our analytical framework relies on the notion of 'activist media practices' (Mattoni, 2012) defined as

> routinized and creative social practices in which activists engage and which include, first, interactions with media objects – such as mobile phones, laptops, pieces of paper – through which activists can generate and/or appropriate media messages, therefore acting either as media producers or media consumers; and, second, interactions with media subjects – such as journalists, public relations managers, but also activist media practitioners – who are connected to the media realm.
>
> *(Mattoni & Treré, 2014, p. 259)*

In light of their encompassing nature, scholars have usually employed a media practice approach to go beyond the focus on a single communication technology, appreciating instead the interconnectedness that characterizes media environments today, and the emergence of hybrid forms of mediation in both institutional and grassroots politics (cf. Mattoni, 2012; Postill, 2013; Barassi, 2015; Stephansen 2016). However, in this chapter we will show that activist media practices can also work as a powerful heuristic device to explore in detail what happens to activist media practices with regard to specific platforms, services, and devices.

More specifically, we investigate activist media practices that emerged in the SNOQ movement's YouTube channel, a space that the movement set up on a commercial social media platform and that was central in the communication strategy of activists. We focus our analysis on two dimensions that we argue are central to understanding the development of activist media practices within the framework of the hybridization between alternative and corporate media. First, the *types of subjects* who engage with activist media practices, and therefore who create and share alternative media content in the corporate platform. Looking at the *types of subjects* allows us to understand more closely how activist media practices that rest on new forms of collectiveness develop in corporate social media platforms, mixing up the traditional agency and points of view of social movement organizations with those of individual activists, old and new media organizations, and concerned citizens, among other actors. Second, we look at the *types of interactions* that sustain activist media practices when these subjects appropriate the technical affordances of the corporate platforms to create and share alternative media content. Focusing on the types of interactions allows us to reflect on how the absence of direct possession of platforms is compensated by the strategic appropriation of platform affordances to share personal points of view so that they become part of a collective discourse.

Scholars who adopt a media practice approach to study social movements' mediation processes usually employ an ethnographic approach to gathering data (e.

g. Foellmer, Lünenborg, & Raetzsch, 2018; Barassi, 2015; Postill, 2013). In this chapter, we show that non-ethnographic digital methods can also provide valuable materials to elaborate on activist media practices, particularly those that are carried out within sparse and networked collective endeavours and beyond the core of the mobilization. The SNOQ movement was not present in just one physical space in a stable way: while activists organized one-day demonstrations, the movement revolved around groups of activists, which were dispersed across Italy and that engaged in activist media practices from different locations and with different rhythms. There was not, therefore, one central place where one could go to see activist media practices occur live, unlike in the case of other coeval protests like Occupy Wall Street in the USA or the Indignados movement in Spain (cf. della Porta & Mattoni, 2014). In this respect, commercial social media platforms proved to be the online spaces around which the wide range of activist groups gathered. Moreover, scholars who investigate media practices through ethnographic methods are usually able to gather relevant data on the core activists who experience a more intense participation in the organization of movements and, therefore, who are also more visible in them. However, in social media platforms core activists are not the only ones participating in the creation and the sharing of alternative media content. Activist media practices are dispersed across many spaces that change continuously and it would be difficult to reconstruct them through the ethnographic method.

Since we aimed at analysing the activist media practices of an emergent yet dispersed protest movement from the perspective of the different actors with a role in the creation and sharing of its alternative media, we started from a multilayered analysis of the digital traces that activists and other users leave behind when engaging in activist media practices via digital media platforms. More precisely, we look at some of the metadata that specify YouTube videos pertaining to the 2011 SNOQ mobilizations.

Investigations centred on YouTube are typically performed starting from videos, which provide the *conditio sine qua non* for users to become active and visible on this platform (Rotman & Goldbeck, 2011). While some characteristics of videos, such as the number of views (e.g. Nahon & Hemsley, 2013), are systematically taken into consideration as an indicator of their viral diffusion, or attention is paid to videos' visual rhetoric and content (Askanius, 2013), elements such as public usernames or tags are often considered 'exhaust data', 'a byproduct of the main function [of the platform] rather than the primary output' (Manyika et al., 2011). On one hand, usernames are poor indicators of identity even when, as a result of the platforms' names policies, they are adherent to real names.[2] On the other hand, attribution of tags is not mandatory to complete uploading procedures and, even when specified, tags do not appear among videos' public information.

Nonetheless, we argue that metadata, particularly usernames and tags, can be considered a fruitful entry point to reconstruct *ex post* activist media practices that are performed on commercial social media platforms. On one hand, usernames open a window on the type of subjects who engage in activist media practices. Indeed, if triangulated with other information sources – profile descriptions, video lists, etc. – usernames provide a first element to understand users' public presence and how individual disintermediated political agencies are progressively accompanying those of social movement organizations or other political organizations such as parties or trade unions. On the other hand, tags are entry points to reflect on the modes in which subjects interact with the commercial social media platforms. Research has shown that users purposively employ tags with the explicit intention of making their content retrievable and to further characterize the content shared (Geisler & Burns, 2007). In this sense, we consider the action of tagging as a part of the activist media practices of content sharing, and this can be explored to unveil how different subjects create and put into circulation alternative content. Moreover, as they have an inherent semantic value, tags can also be considered as proxies to investigate the meanings that users convey to the experience they share through a platform like YouTube.

Through an *ad hoc* developed script, we extracted usernames, tags, and other key information (number of views, titles, and unique video IDs) from a collection of videos related to the SNOQ mobilization. Pertinent videos were identified according to a twofold strategy. On one hand, we mined the official channel of the movement on YouTube (i.e., snoqtube) and pulled out the 179 videos contained within it.[3] On the other hand, using a clean browser (DMI 2015), we exploited the YouTube internal search engine through the exact query 'se non ora quando'. Of the total results (approximately 12,700), we retained only videos actually dealing with the movement and that were displayed in the first five pages, to focus on the most prominent results proposed by the platform.[4] Overall, we composed a dataset containing 265 videos, which represent the most visible part of the public discourse on SNOQ in the YouTube platform, the names of users who uploaded them, the number of views they received up to the moment of data collection, their unique URL, and related tags (510).[5]

We first investigated our dataset looking at the *types of subjects* of activist media practices, namely the actors involved in the creation of visual content about the SNOQ movement. To this end, we triangulated information on usernames with information available on users' YouTube personal pages as well as on Google. On this base, we classified each user according to a partially adapted version of the users' classification scheme proposed by Lotan et al. (2011) to study users' effectiveness in initiating information cascades on Twitter, and examined which subjects, beside SNOQ itself, contributed to circulating content about the movement and its initiatives.[6] Secondly, in order to investigate the *types of interactions* that emerge when users appropriate YouTube's affordances in the framework of their activist media practices, we explored the network that results from tagging behaviours exerted by SNOQ activists managing the snoqtube channel as well as by other users sharing videos about the movement. More precisely, looking at the overall network structure as well as at nodes centrality scores, we elaborate on the different media practices through which SNOQ activists and other users contributed to the creation and circulation of a collective discourse on the movement; and the meanings that were conveyed to the SNOQ collective endeavour thanks to these media practices.

The boundaries of activist media practices in commercial social media platforms

While activist media practices refer to activists' engagement with media, our analysis shows that when it comes to commercial social media platforms, the understanding of what activists do to create alternative media messages also passes through media practices that are performed beyond the realm of activism and, also, independently from collective actors like social movement organizations.

Different types of actors engaged in the (activist) media practices of sharing politically oriented videos in a commercial social media platform, which, in turn, nurtured the creation of an alternative public discourse around the SNOQ movement and its main concerns. The SNOQ organizing committee took the lead in this regard: it created and shared about 68% of the videos collected through the management of the SNOQ YouTube channel. As has been the case in other recent mobilizations, including Occupy Wall Street and the uprisings in the Middle East and North Africa region (Bennett & Segerberg, 2013), the public presence of the movement was directly related to the activist media practices that originated from the collective social movement organization behind it.

While the majority of the video content was uploaded by one social movement organization, the visibility of the SNOQ movement within YouTube, and thus the emergence of an alternative public discourse on its concerns, was also in the hands of other actors. It is important to note that the remaining 32% of the visual content was created and then shared outside the boundaries of core movement organizers. This means that activist media practices that involved the use of YouTube exceeded the boundaries of the SNOQ movement and/or were complemented by media practices performed by subjects other than collective movement actors, which nonetheless contributed to expanding and enriching the alternative public discourse about the movement itself.

Figure 8.1 demonstrates that among these contributions, the involvement of individuals was more relevant than the engagement of collective actors: 55 videos out of 86 were circulated by concerned citizens not linked to any movement organization: citizens (39), individual activists (11), artists (3), and bloggers (2).[7] To a lesser extent, collective actors took part in the creation of alternative public discourses along with the SNOQ movement. Among them, the majority were media actors engaging in their routine creation of media content to be shared in YouTube. A further distinction among these actors can be made between new media organizations with an online-only presence (14), such as Web TVs and university radios, and the online channels of mainstream media organizations (6), such as the Italian daily newspaper *Il Fatto Quotidiano*. To a lesser extent, other types of collective actors related to the realm of politics (e.g. institutional political organizations, parties, and unions, 4) and to the realm of culture (e.g. cultural/professional organizations, 3) were also producing their own SNOQ-related content. When it comes to collective actors, therefore, what seems to be particularly relevant is the role of other media organizations that take part in the construction of meanings

FIGURE 8.1 Types of actors and videos uploaded

and narratives about the movement. More specifically, new media organizations that exist only online were particularly active in producing and circulating content related to the SNOQ movement.

In sum, our analysis shows that the types of subjectivities that engaged in activist media practices to create alternative public discourse on the SNOQ movement were diverse: while activist media practices of collective social movement actors had a central role for the visibility of the SNOQ movement and the creation of the related alternative public discourse, media practices performed by individuals outside the realm of social movements were also relevant in this regard. The outcome was a specific type of collectiveness, radically different from the traditionally considered alternative media outlets and content strictly linked to social movement organizations, that mixed individual contributors and collective subjects, politicized actors and concerned citizens not necessarily involved in any type of political activity. In this respect, our analysis suggests that it is the very media practice of sharing politically oriented videos in a commercial social media platform that connects many individual users to the realm of politics rather than, as in the case of social movement actors, the connection to the realm of politics that orients the type of media practice at stake. This point seems particularly important to appreciate the features of alternative media when they combine with commercial social media platforms: the high degree of openness that characterizes the latter contributes to the combination of (activist) media practices that are oriented by activists' political engagement with others that, on the contrary, nurture the political engagement of concerned individuals and organization actors.

Furthermore, our analysis shows that in commercial social media platforms like YouTube, activist media practices that can be directly linked to social movement actors should be read in the context of the broader range of practices that other actors, be they individual or collective, develop. This means that when considering the creation of alternative media messages in commercial social media platforms, the boundaries of activist media practices become more fluid with regard to their locus, that is neither necessarily collective nor exclusively political. Activist media practices combine with other media practices that originate outside the realm of social movements and that become political exactly because they are oriented towards the provision of visibility to the SNOQ movement.

Activist media practices and users' interactions with technological affordances

At the crossroads between these diverse subjectivities, the public sharing of experiences of mobilization under the SNOQ umbrella was sustained by multiple and differentiated interactions between users and YouTube's technical affordances. This means that, in performing media practices that sustained the visibility of the SNOQ movement in the YouTube channels, activists and users also had to make choices with regard to the opportunities and constraints that the commercial social media platforms offered to them. Thus, activist media practices might also be retraced looking at the levels and type of activists' and users' appropriation of the technological affordances that characterize YouTube.

One of these affordances is the opportunity to attach tags to the video content that activists and users share on the commercial social media platform. The action of tagging is an example of the appropriation of one specific technological affordance − that is, the possibility of attaching a tag to the video content − which can contribute to several media practices related to visibility: it can be used as a way to render certain topics (more) visible; to provide (more) visibility for a certain actor; or to connect a movement campaign to other contentious issues. As mentioned above, the analysis of the tags that users attributed to their videos during the uploading procedure lays the ground for reflecting on the types of activist media practices that developed within and about the SNOQ movement.

Figure 8.2 illustrates the networked system of videos (black squares) and tags (empty triangles) that users created when uploading their content. In this network, a triangle connects to a square whenever a tag was attached to a video: as it shows, a large number of videos and tags are joined together in the network 'main component'.[8]

Some black squares lay at the bottom of the picture and are not connected to other nodes, indicating that not all videos have been tagged during the uploading procedure. In this case, the activist media practices of sharing politically-oriented video leaned on the simple action of uploading video content, without any further engagement with the technological affordances of tagging. Out of these 52 tagless videos, 49 come from the snoqtube channel and belong to the video campaign *Le*

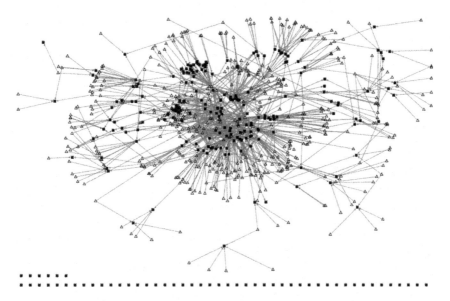

FIGURE 8.2 YouTube network of *Se non ora, quando?* videos and related tags (*N* = 775) Note: Created with NodeXL Basic (http://nodexl.codeplex.com). Triangles = tags; squares = videos. Visualization algorithm: Harel–Koren Fast Multiscale.

parole per dirlo ('The words to say it'), which was aimed at raising awareness on the complexities and difficulties of women's daily routines. The other three were posted by two activists and by a local TV channel; in these three cases, the link between the content published and overall collective endeavour passes through the title that these users chose while uploading their videos, which does always contain the name of the movement *Se non ora, quando?* Conversely, tagless videos from the snoqtube channel are all titled following a tactic of the video campaign – joining the name of the campaign with the first name of the woman interviewed (e.g. '*Le parole per dirlo* – Ambra').

Disconnected from the main component, and again laying at the bottom of the figure, are 24 small-scale groups formed by one video and its unique tags. In all these cases, videos are still part of the snoqtube channel and are either instances of the video campaign *Le parole per dirlo* or testimonies recorded during the first coordination event held by the movement in Siena in July 2011. In all these cases, even if SNOQ activists have indeed tagged their videos, they have done so choosing to specify its content with only the name of the speaker and, possibly, her job.

The presence of many videos that were not linked to any tags while having been uploaded by the SNOQ activists seems to suggest that activist media practices, particularly the creation and circulation of politically-oriented videos, did not entail the appropriation of a key YouTube technological affordance. Indeed, isolated nodes and small-scale components are indicative of activist media practices performed within the official SNOQ YouTube channel. Thus, SNOQ activists managing the channel did not contribute to the creation of an alternative discourse on SNOQ solely by sharing politically-oriented video. They also engaged in a systematic practice of media content curation – they actively engaged in the selection, organization, and display of videos (Gehl, 2009). In almost half of the cases in which SNOQ activists uploaded videos, their core interaction with the YouTube platform did not necessarily pass through a strategic tagging, but rather consisted of capitalizing on activist media practices that included the production of testimonies for the SNOQ movement campaign *Le parole per dirlo*.

Conversely, unaffiliated individuals and other collective actors mobilizing outside the SNOQ core of activists produced and shared their movement-related videos first outside of the YouTube channel space. Then, having to find a way to build a connection between their media content and the political experience and discourse of SNOQ, they leaned strategically on tagging. Thus, they did not solely share politically-oriented videos, but they engaged actively in the media practice that we name 'political characterization of media content'. Through the action of tagging, these users assigned a clear political meaning to their YouTube visual content that was openly connected to the SNOQ mobilizations.

Looking at the most frequently used tags tell us about the different meanings that substantiate this practice of political characterization of media content. As shown in Table 8.1, tagging defines a twofold set of meanings for the SNOQ collective endeavour. On one hand, there is the recognition of SNOQ as a collective actor struggling for gender equality. Not only is the most frequently used tag *se non ora quando*, the very name of the movement, but the four units composing the name itself and the movement acronym *snoq* are among the most employed tags. Moreover, the tag *donne* (women), representing the very object of the mobilization, ranks second.

TABLE 8.1 Ten most used tags in the SNOQ video-tags network

Tags	Frequency
se non ora quando	62
donne	54
ora	37
quando	36
se	35
non	35
manifestazione	33
Berlusconi	24
snoq	21
Febbraio	15

On the other hand, there is a collective recognition of SNOQ's contentious nature. Indeed, a second group of highly applied links to the big demonstration occurred in February 2011: *manifestazione* and *Febbraio* (respectively, 'demonstration' and 'February') are the seventh and tenth most used tags. Interestingly, the tag Berlusconi is also much used. While SNOQ organizers declared on several occasions that the 13 February demonstration was not against the ex-prime Minister, but rather, against the overall degradation of women and women's image, tagging actions explicitly connect the movement and Berlusconi as an individual, not as the representative of a discriminating and degrading *modus operandi*. In fact, motivations that led to the February demonstration, such as women's dignity (tags *dignità*, 'dignity', or *paese per donne*, 'a country for women'), or the claim to change the leading class (tag *dimissioni*), are used to a much lower, almost paltry, extent (see Table 8.2 in Appendix).

Conclusions

This chapter has discussed the mainstreaming of alternative media content through YouTube. More specifically, it has focused on the reconstruction of activist media practices within the commercial content-sharing platform starting from the traces that these media practices leave behind them – specifically, metadata on usernames and tags. In so doing, we were able to assess two main aspects of activist media practices – the types of subjectivities that perform them, and the types of interactions between the subjectivities and the platform technical affordances.

Our analysis suggests that the mainstreaming of alternative media content through YouTube gave rise to hybrid forms of activist media practices. First, activist media practices only partially rested on the efforts of collective actors linked to the SNOQ movement, with individual activists and concerned citizens also participating in the production of alternative media content. Thus, activist media practices combined with other media practices that originated outside the realm of social movements and that became political exactly because of their being oriented towards the provision of visibility to the SNOQ movement. Second, interactions with platform affordances revealed the different media practices through which activists and other subjects mobilizing outside the SNOQ core contributed to shaping a collective discourse on the movement. On one hand, SNOQ activists made their contributions mainly by curating the content of the snoqtube channel. Other mobilized subjects instead engaged in the political characterization of the media content they produced and shared. Moreover, through this practice of political characterization, a twofold set of meanings was collectively attributed to the SNOQ endeavour: first, the recognition of the existence of a collective actor struggling for gender equality; and second, the recognition of its contentious nature.

Finally, our chapter also illustrates yet another way to tackle activist media practices in hybrid media systems, through the use of metadata related to social media, microblogging, and content-sharing platforms. By digging into the otherwise invisible traces that movement organizations, individual activists, concerned citizens, and other actors leave behind when interacting with the video-sharing platform, we were able to render visible the multifaceted features of alternative media in hybrid media systems. Of course, as in any type of empirical investigation, the choice of focusing on digital traces related to one specific platform to reconstruct activist media practices has its trade-offs. First, such an approach allows in-depth understanding of how a specific platform is used in the context of mobilizations; but it does not take into consideration the whole media ecology in which alternative media content travels, reshaping meanings and remediating forms (cf. Treré & Mattoni, 2016; Lievrouw, 2011). Second, this platform-centred approach makes it possible to go beyond activist media practices performed by core organizers, hence also capturing the engagement of actors who are not linked to the movement; but is not able to grasp the activist media practices in their live context and thus to provide a full picture of the conditions and situations in which people interact with the platform in the framework of a movement mobilization. To go beyond these limitations, we suggest that further research on activist media practices in regard to alternative media should combine platform-centred approaches based on metadata with activist-centred approaches based on in-depth interviews and participant observations.

Notes

1 Transcription from the video 'Se Non Ora Quando.mov' available at https://www.you tube.com/watch?v=zma-HI-yF3w
2 YouTube has changed its Names Policy over time passing from allowing anonymity to requiring real-names (after its integration with Google+) to then loose constraints after massive protests from users.
3 https://www.youtube.com/user/snoqtube. Data for this study were extracted in May 2013.
4 Among results generated by the YouTube internal search engine, only five were videos from the snoqtube channel and were not considered twice in the construction of the database. Pertinence of videos was assessed after screening their content.
5 In this phase, we eliminated from the list of tags all articles and prepositions, although we kept the single words composing the string 'se non ora quando'.
6 The users' classification scheme proposed by Lotan et al. (2011) includes 11 categories: mainstream media organizations, web news organizations, non-media organizations, journalists, bloggers, activists, opinion leaders in the digital technology culture and economy, political actors, celebrities, researchers, bots, and a residual 'other' category. Every user was classified within one category.
7 We define concerned citizens are people who are concerned by the contentious issue at stake, while not having a clearly identifiable role on it in any social movement organization and/or digital media outlet. Conversely, activists and bloggers are not only concerned, but also engaged to fight the contentious issue either as participants in social movement organizations (activists) or because they run a blog on the contentious issue at stake (bloggers).
8 In network analysis, the main component is defined as 'the larger subset of nodes that are connected, hence reachable, either directly or indirectly' (Wasserman & Faust, 1994, p. 109)

References

Ardizzoni, M. (2010). Neighborhood television channels in Italy: the case of Telestreet. In M. Ardizzoni & C. Ferrari (eds), *Beyond Monopoly: Globalization and Contemporary Italian Media* (pp. 171–184). Lanham, MD: Lexington Books.

Askanius, T. (2013). Protest movements and spectacles of death: from urban places to video spaces. *Research in Social Movements, Conflicts and Change*, 35, 105–136.

Askanius, T., & Gustafsson, N. (2010). Mainstreaming the alternative: the changing media practices of protest movements. *Interface*, 2(2), 23–41.

Atton, C. (2002). *Alternative Media*. London: Sage.

Atton, C. (2015). *The Routledge Companion to Alternative and Community Media*. London: Routledge.

Barassi, V. (2015). *Activism on the Web: Everyday Struggles against Digital Capitalism*. London: Routledge.

Bennett, W. L., & Segerberg, A. (2013). *The Logic of Connective Action: Digital Media and the Personalization of Contentious Politics*. Cambridge: Cambridge University Press.

Clauset, A., Newman, M. E. J., & Moore, C. (2004). Finding community structure in very large networks. *Physical Review E*, 70, 066111. Retrieved from https://arxiv.org/abs/cond-mat/0408187.

Couldry, N. & Hepp, A. (2017). *The Mediated Construction of Reality*. London: Polity. Downing, J. (2001). *Radical Media: Rebellious Communication and Social Movements*. Thousand Oaks, CA: Sage.

Foellmer, S., Lünenborg, M., & Raetzsch, C. (2018). *Media Practices, Social Movements, and Performativity: Transdisciplinary Approaches*. London: Routledge.

Gehl, R. (2009). YouTube as archive: who will curate this digital Wunderkammer? *International Journal of Cultural Studies*, 12(1), 43–60.

Geisler, G., & Burns, S. (2007). Tagging video: conventions and strategies of the YouTube community. In *JCDL '07: Proceedings of the 7th ACM/IEEE–CS Joint Conference on Digital Libraries* (pp. 480–480). New York: Association for Computing Machinery.

Gumucio-Dagron, A. (2007). Call me impure: myths and paradigms of participatory communication. In L. K. Fuelled (ed.), *The Power of Community Media* (pp. 197–207). New York: Palgrave Macmillan.

Howley, K. (2005). *Community Media: People, Places, and Communication Technologies*. Cambridge: Cambridge University Press.

Lievrouw, L. (2011). *Alternative and Activist New Media*. Cambrdige: Polity.

Lotan, G., Graeff, E., Ananny, M., Gaffney, D., Pearce, I., & boyd, d. (2011). The revolutions were tweeted: information flows during the 2011 Tunisian and Egyptian Revolutions. *International Journal of Communication*, 5, 1375–1405.

Mattoni, A. (2012). *Media Practices and Protest Politics: How Precarious Workers Mobilise*. London: Ashgate.

Mattoni, A., & Treré, E. (2014). Media practices, mediation processes, and mediatization in the study of social movements. *Communication Theory*, 24(3), 252–271.

Manyika, J., Chiu, M., Brown, B., Bughin, J., Dobbs, R., Roxburgh, C., & Hung Byers, A. (2011). *Big Data: The Next Frontier for Innovation, Competition, and Productivity*. McKinsey Global Institute.

Milan, S. (2013). *Social Movements and their Technologies: Wiring Social Change*. London: Palgrave Macmillan.

Morris, D. (2004). Globalization and media democracy: the case of Indymedia. In D. Schuler & P. Day (eds), *Shaping the Network Society: The New Role of Civil Society in Cyberspace* (pp. 325–352). Cambridge, MA: MIT Press.

Nahon, K., & Hemsley, J. (2013). *Going Viral*. Cambridge: Polity.

della Porta, D., & Mattoni, A. (2012). Cultures of participation in social movements. In A. Delwiche & J. Jacobs Henderson (eds), *The Participatory Cultures Handbook* (pp. 170–181). London: Routledge.

della Porta, D., & Mattoni, A. (2014). *Spreading Protest: Social Movements in Times of Crisis*. Colchester, UK: ECPR Press.

Postill, J. (2013). Democracy in an age of viral reality: a media epidemiography of Spain's Indignados Movement. *Ethnography* 15(1), 51–69.

Rodríguez, C. (2001). *Fissures in the Mediascape. An International Study of Citizens' Media*. Creskill, NJ: Hampton Press.

Rotman, D., & and Goldbeck, J. (2011). YouTube. Contrasting patterns of content, interaction, and prominence. In D. L. Hansen, B. Shneiderman, & M. A. Smith, (eds), *Analysing Social Media Networks with NodeXL. Insights from a Connected World* (pp. 225–246). Burlington, MA: Morgan Kaufmann.

Stephansen, H. C. (2016). Understanding citizen media as practice. agents, processes, publics. In M. Baker & B. B. Blaagaard (eds), *Citizen Media and Public Spaces* (pp. 25–41). London: Routledge.

Treré, E., & Mattoni, A. (2016). Media ecologies and protest movements: main perspectives and key lessons. *Information, Communication & Society* 19(3), 290–306.

Wasserman, S., & Faust, K. (1994). *Social Network Analysis: Methods and Applications*. Vol. 8. Cambridge: Cambridge University Press.

APPENDIX

TABLE A8.1 Tags used more than once to characterize SNOQ-related videos on YouTube

Tag	Freq
se non ora quando	62
donne	54
ora	37
quando	36
non	35
se	35
manifestazione	33
Berlusconi	24
snoq	21
13	15
Febbraio	15
2011	11
Roma	11
Siena	9
dignità	8
Firenze	8
Piazza	8
Torino	8
donna	7
Genova	7
Verona	7
Italia	6
Maria	6

Tag	Freq
Palermo	6
ruby	6
13 febbraio 2011	5
dimissioni	5
parole per dirlo	5
politica	5
spot	5
Catania	4
femminismo	4
intervista	4
Milano	4
mobilitazione	4
paese per donne	4
protesta	4
senonoraquando	4
11	3
Bologna	3
bunga bunga	3
Cagliari	3
CGIL	3
corteo	3
diritti	3
e se domani?	3
Emma	3
Francesca	3
Lunetta	3
Napoli	3
per	3
rete	3
Roberta	3
rubygate	3
Savino	3
uomini	3

PART IV

Acting on media

INTRODUCTION

Andreas Hepp

The phrase 'acting on media' has seen a rise in use in media and communication research that is oriented towards practice theory. In essence, the term emphasizes the fact that, as Kannengießer and Kubitschko argue, 'a wide range of actors [...] take an active part in the moulding of media organizations, infrastructures and technologies that are part of the fabric of everyday life' (2017, p. 1). It leans toward thinking about 'media as practice' more broadly than originally intended. In his original intervention on the issue of practice, Nick Couldry (2004, p. 117) was concerned with describing media practice 'as the open set of practices relating to, or oriented around, media'. His focus was mainly on understanding *communication with, and the use of, media* as a practice. While the phrase acting on media is within the scope of such a concept of media practice, it extends our perspective: it is not only about practices of communication and the use of media, but also about practices of shaping the media infrastructure and technologies – of what is called in German *Gestaltung*. [1] Therefore, the expression acting on media now broadens our scope as media are becoming so fundamental in today's deeply mediatized societies – as institutions and as materialities – and as they increasingly come to represent an object of social struggle.

This view inevitably stumbles upon what we have called elsewhere 'deep mediatization' (Couldry & Hepp, 2013, pp. 7, 34). Mediatization refers to an experience everybody knows from his or her everyday life: media saturate more and more domains of society, and these domains are changing as a result. *Deep* mediatization is an advanced stage of mediatization in which, through digitalization, all elements of our social world are intricately related to digital media and their overarching infrastructures. In times of deep mediatization, diverse collectivities consider that media and media infrastructures can themselves be identified as an object of engagement – with the expectation that they might have an influence on processes of societal transformation. Examples of these 'collectivities for media change' can be seen in social movements such as the Open Data movement (Baack, 2015), think tanks such as the Inter-American Dialogue (Neubauer, 2012), and pioneer communities such as the Maker Movement (Hepp, 2016). As diverse as these collectivities may be, they share the conviction that media are fundamental to contemporary societal formations and, much like actors from the worlds of politics and economics, they consider media and media infrastructures as an object within which political engagement can thrive.

It is often the case that a change in the present gives us a different view of the past. This is the case with the idea of acting on media. While deep mediatization has directed our attention to this broader form of media-related practice, we find that – once we adopt this point of view – this has been a general phenomenon throughout media history and, in particular, a key characteristic of more recent digital media. We can even go so far as to write the history of digital media and their infrastructures as that of acting on media. Fred Turner (2006) presented an important draft for just such a perspective in his account of the history of Silicon Valley in *From Counterculture to Cyberculture*. Through a detailed historical analysis, he demonstrated how the network that developed around the *Whole Earth Catalog*, curated by Stuart Brand, had a significant influence on the development of digital technologies long before economists and politicians even gave them a moment's thought. Examining it with the benefit of hindsight, as a hybrid of social movement and think tank, the Whole Earth Network could be described as an early pioneer community (and later as a network of various pioneer communities). The point is that the Whole Earth Network was able to define itself by acting on media. After the countercultural utopias had failed, the network turned to digital media technology as a means of shaping society according to its ideas and values. It is remarkable that we can attribute many media-related social movements, such as the hacker movement, directly to the Whole Earth Network (Levy, 1984); that the early technology designs of MIT Media Lab cannot be detached from the network's broader discourse (Brand, 1987); and that today's pioneer communities, such as the Quantified Self movement, can be attributed directly to Stuart Brand's legacy (Kelly, 2016, pp. 237–252). In other words, we understand the 'making' of deep mediatization not only by starting from a political economy of prominent media corporations (Murdock, 2017), but by considering the 'making' of deep mediatization as a much lengthier historical process. We can only fully grasp it if we understand it historically and as a process of acting on media.

It is, therefore, important to consider the phenomenon of acting on media in a historical context. Nevertheless, with today's deep mediatization, it has manifested itself as a much broader phenomenon. This is well demonstrated by Sigrid Kannengießer in Chapter 9, which discusses media practices that address challenges of 'sustainability'. In looking at the various 'collectivities for media change', it is noticeable that the sustainability of media-related developments is an important connective element between them. Kannengießer uncovers the ambivalences that exist in this context by means of critical media practices on the Utopia platform, at repair cafés, and in the production of the Fairphone. In Chapter 10, using the example of the World Forum of Free Media as an umbrella organization for various social movements, Hilde Stephansen shows us which different forms of knowledge production are associated with acting on media. In doing so, she demonstrates how far knowledge practices are an integral part of media practices in general. As a consequence, media practice researchers should make knowledge practices an explicit focus of their analysis. It is also important to note Stefania Milan's contribution (Chapter 11 in Part Five), which points out that with datafication – as one of several trends of deep mediatization – acting on media is also 'acting on data'. As digital media have become not only means of communication but also means of data generation, it is important to consider to what extent data is intrinsic to media practices. This is the focus of the various (critical) data initiatives that currently exist in both the Global North and the Global South.

We can see that the term acting on media exposes a certain perspective, both historically and in relation to our present. The core element of this perspective can be seen to broaden our understanding of media practice. 'Acting on media' not only encompasses actual media 'use' in the act of communication, it also deals with any 'doing' in reference to media and their infrastructures. Due to their increasing relevance, a growing number of individual, corporate, and collective actors are concerned with gaining influence on developments in media technology. This is what the phrase acting on media sets out to emphasize.

Theoretically, then, we are dealing with an extension of the concept of media practice. We should not only see media-related practice as mediated *communication*; media-related practice is also present if there is a broader process of 'doing' in relation to media. This can take many forms. It can concern *practices of creation* of (alternative) media technologies and infrastructures, as exemplified by Civic Tech whose communication platforms are created for the improvement of the general welfare of civil society (Schrock, 2018); it can involve *practices to improve and restore* existing media technologies and infrastructures such as repair cafés (Kannengießer, 2017) or infrastructure initiatives in the Global South (Parks & Starosielski, 2015); or it can be about *practices of public discourse*, such as when the regulation of digital media is criticized by the Chaos Computer Club (Kubitschko, 2018).

When systematizing the various possible types of practices involved in acting on media, however, it is important to keep in mind that they are empirically intertwined with each other. For example, the British non-profit social enterprise mySociety is not only concerned with developing and making accessible technology, research, and relevant data that help people to be active citizens, it also concerns itself with questions of improvement. Even if this company does not consider itself an 'advocacy organization' (Baack, 2018, p. 47), it exists to promote a public debate with and about Civic Tech. Furthermore, different forms of contemporary pioneer journalism can be understood as examples of acting on media in that data journalism or sensor journalism is not only about communicating by means of such technologies but is, first and foremost, about designing and developing them to make such communication possible (Hepp & Loosen, 2018). In addition, research on pioneer communities shows that very normative value orientations can prevail in these practices of acting on media. It is not necessarily a question of left-wing, alternative movements and organizations. A pioneer community like the Maker Movement is positioned 'in between' left and right political orientations when it critiques the globalized economy with its vision of local creative manufacturing using the latest technology (Hepp, 2018). Meanwhile, the Inter-American Dialogue think tank acts on media to progress their neoliberal views (Neubauer, 2012). 'Acting on media' is, therefore, not necessarily critical, it can also act within hegemonic discourses and even maintain them.

In short, we can see that addressing the processes of acting on media is an important extension of the approach to understanding media as practice. This extension is both theoretical and empirical. It is theoretical in that it is associated with a more differentiated concept of media practice, and empirical in that it is observable as the view of a multitude of highly engaged actors both in the present day and in the past.

Note

1 *Gestaltung* as a German term means to give something a form, a shape. The corresponding verb is *gestalten*. Due to the diversity of its implications, the term is difficult to translate directly into English. *Gestalten* does not just mean 'to design', 'to make' or 'to craft', it is much more about forming something in a positive way and this can also be meant in a figurative sense.

References

Baack, S. (2015). Datafication and empowerment: how the open data movement re-articulates notions of democracy, participation, and journalism. *Big Data & Society, 2*(2). doi:10.1177/2053951715594634

Baack, S. (2018). Civic tech at mysociety: how the imagined affordances of data shape data activism. *Krisis*, (1), 43–56.

Brand, S. (1987). *The Media Lab: Inventing the Future at MIT*. New York: Viking.

Couldry, N. (2004). Theorising media as practice. *Social Semiotics*, 14(2), 115–132.

Couldry, N., & Hepp, A. (2017). *The Mediated Construction of Reality*. Cambridge: Polity.

Hepp, A. (2016). Pioneer communities: collective actors of deep mediatisation. *Media, Culture & Society*, 38(6), 918–933.

Hepp, A. (2018). What makes a maker? Curating a pioneer community through franchising. *Nordisk Tidsskrift for Informationsvidenskab og Kulturformidling*, 7(2), 3–18. Retrieved from: https://tidsskrift.dk/ntik/article/view/111283

Hepp, A., & Loosen, W. (2018). *'Makers' of a Future Journalism? The Role of 'Pioneer Journalists' and 'Pioneer Communities' in Transforming Journalism*. Communicative Figurations Working Paper 19. Bremen: Universität Bremen. Retrieved from https://www.kommunikative-figurationen.de/fileadmin/user_upload/Arbeitspapiere/CoFi_EWP_No-19_Hepp-Loosen.pdf

Kannengießer, S. (2017). Repair cafés. Reflecting on materiality and consumption in environmental communication. In T. Milstein, M. Pileggi, & E. Morgan (eds), *Pedagogy of Environmental Communication*. London: Routledge.

Kannengießer, S., & Kubitschko, S. (2017). Acting on media: influencing, shaping and (re) configuring the fabric of everyday life. *Media and Communication*, 5(3), 1–4. doi:10.17645/mac.v5i3.1165

Kelly, K. (2016). *The Inevitable: Understanding the 12 Technological Forces that will Shape Our Future*. New York: Viking.

Kubitschko, S. (2018). Chaos computer club: the communicative construction of media technologies and infrastructures as a political category. In A. Hepp, U. Hasebrink, & A. Breiter (eds), *Communicative Figurations* (pp. 81–100). London: Palgrave Macmillan.

Levy, S. (1984). *Hackers: Heroes of the Computer Revolution*. New York: Doubleday.

Murdock, G. (2017). Mediatisation and the transformation of capitalism: the elephant in the room. *Javnost – The Public, 24*(2), 119–135.

Neubauer, R. J. (2012). Dialogue, monologue, or something in between? Neoliberal think tanks in the Americas. *International Journal of Communication*, 6, 2173–2198. Retrieved from http://ijoc.org/index.php/ijoc/article/download/1481/789

Parks, L., & Starosielski, N. (eds) (2015). *Signal Traffic: Critical Studies of Media Infrastructures*. Champaign, IL: University of Illinois Press.

Schrock, A. R. (2018). *Civic Tech. Making Technology Work for People*. Long Beach, CA: Rogue Academic Press.

Turner, F. (2006). *From Counterculture to Cyberculture: Stewart Brand, the Whole Earth Network, and the Rise of Digital Utopianism*. Chicago, IL: University of Chicago Press.

9

ACTING ON MEDIA FOR SUSTAINABILITY

Sigrid Kannengießer

Introduction

Faced with ecological crisis and unjust globalization processes, growing numbers of people change their consumption behaviour by consuming fewer products or buying fair trade alternatives. Media play a crucial role in this context, as a source of information about fair consumer options and by providing platforms for selling, buying, or exchanging goods. But media themselves also become the focus of changing consumption practices as people become aware of the socio-ecological effects of the production, consumption, and disposal of media technologies. In response to this, some people try to develop alternative forms of production and appropriation of media devices; such alternatives can be referred to as *consumption-critical media practices*.

I define consumption-critical media practices as practices that involve either using media to criticize (certain forms of) consumption, or (consciously practiced) alternatives to the consumption of media technologies; these include repairing or exchanging media technologies and the production of durable media technologies (Kannengießer, 2016, p. 198).[1] While the former involves production and circulation of media content, the latter focus on production and appropriation. Consumption-critical *media practices* occur where people act in relation to media, either by using media content to inform about or advertise sustainability, or by producing and appropriating media technologies in alternative ways to contribute to a sustainable society. In some of these practices, people act by themselves; in others, they form communities or movements.

In this chapter, I discuss the concept of consumption-critical media practices using examples relating to media content, appropriation, and production. I present the results of a study of three cases of consumption-critical media practices. First, Utopia (www.utopia.de), a platform that advertises for sustainability, is analysed as an example of consumption-critical media practices at the level of media content. Second, the repairing of media technologies in Repair Cafés (public events where people meet to repair their everyday objects together) is examined as an example of appropriation. Third, the Fairphone and 'the Fair Mouse', media technologies produced under fair and sustainable working conditions, are examined as examples of alternative production practices.

Discussing these cases using a media practice approach, I argue for a broad understanding of the term media practice as referring not only to practices in which people use media, but also to practices in which media (technologies) themselves are the focus of action; practices that involve reflecting on media (technologies) and engaging with media (technologies). In other words, people *act on media* (Kannengießer & Kubitschko, 2017) when adapting, modifying, and politicizing media technologies themselves – in this case, as part of a broader practice of striving for sustainability.

Following this argumentation, the chapter is structured as follows. First, relevant theories of media practice are outlined and linked to the field of media and sustainability. The case studies are then described, and the methods used in this study presented. In the third part, the findings of the three case studies are explained, and the different examples of consumption-critical media practices on the levels of media content, appropriation, and production are discussed. Concluding the chapter, the argument for a broad understanding of the term media practice, which embraces ways in which people use media content but also *act on* media technologies, is explicated.[2]

The media practice approach: using and acting on media

Sociological practice theory defines practices as

> a routinized type of behaviour which consists of several elements, inter-connected to one another: forms of bodily activities, forms of mental activities, 'things' and their use, a background knowledge in the form of understanding, know-how, states of emotion and motivational knowledge.
>
> *(Reckwitz, 2002, pp. 249–250).*

Inspired by sociological practice theory, the practice approach has also become established in media and communication studies in the past 15 years, focusing on how people appropriate media.

Couldry (2004, p. 119) posed a central question for the practice paradigm: 'What, quite simply, are people doing in relation to media across a whole range of situations and contexts?'. This question has been applied to the study of media practices in different fields. Scholars working at the intersection of social movement research and media and communication studies have asked what people do with media to form movements and create social change (e.g. Mattoni, 2012; Mattoni & Treré, 2014; Foellmer, Lünenborg, & Raetzsch, 2018). Lünenborg and Raetzsch

(2018, p. 14) argue: 'Through practice theory, we can understand how negotiations allow different actors – let them be single actors or groups like (emerging) social movements – to participate, articulate themselves and challenge dominant viewpoints'. Mattoni (2012, p. 159) defines *activist* media practices as

(1) both routinised and creative social practices that; (2) include interactions with media objects (such as mobile phones, laptops, pieces of paper) and media subjects (such as journalists, public relations managers, other activists); (3) draw on how media objects and media subjects are perceived and how the media environment is understood and known.

While media and communication studies in general and social movement studies in particular usually analyse how people *use* media for their (political) purposes, recent research has also asked how people and activists *act on media* (Kannengießer & Kubitschko, 2017b). 'The notion of acting on media denotes the efforts of a wide range of actors to take an active part in the molding of media organizations, infrastructures and technologies that are part of the fabric of everyday life' (Kannengießer & Kubitschko, 2017b, p. 1). The concept *acting on media* refers to media practices in which people *consciously* and *actively* seek to *transform* media technologies and in doing so try to change not only the devices but also society. Often, though not always, *acting on media* is therefore an act of political participation (Kannengießer, 2016) that politicizes media technologies themselves. 'Acting on media, like other forms of political action, is best characterized as a set of practices that are embedded in and at the same time produce constellations of power (related, amongst others, to gender, class, age and education)' (Kannengießer & Kubitschko, 2017b, p. 2).

The empirical case studies comprising a special issue about *acting on media* (Kannengießer & Kubitschko, 2017a) hint at the broad and complex research field that examines media practices in which people, communities, or organizations reflect on and seek to shape, form, and impact media. Social movements make media themselves the focus of their action (Stephansen, 2017); fan communities try to transform existing media texts (Reißmann et al., 2017); collectives in social networks put pressure on media companies (Myers West, 2017); and media companies themselves try to transform media infrastructures (Möller & von Rimscha, 2017).

The examples of consumption-critical media practices discussed in this chapter show that people not only *use* media content to criticize (certain types of) consumption and advertise for sustainability, but they also *act on media* (on their own and in collectives) while reflecting on the consumption of media technologies (defined here as buying new devices) and developing sustainable alternatives in the production and appropriation of media technologies. People reflect on the socio-ecological effects of the production (Bleischwitz et al., 2012; Maxwell & Miller, 2012; Chan & Ho, 2008) and disposal (Kaitatzi-Whitlock, 2015, pp. 71–73) of media technologies, and try to avoid contributing to these effects with their media practices, for example by repairing media technologies or by producing fair media devices.

The materiality of media technologies therefore becomes relevant for the way people act in relation to media. Magaudda (2011) stresses the relevance of the materiality of media technologies when analysing digital music consumption. As the empirical study presented below shows, the materiality of media technologies is also highly relevant in consumption-critical media practices, although here it is especially the *awareness* of how media devices are produced and disposed of that motivates people to act on media in a consumption-critical way.

Nicolini (2017, p. 22) argues that practices have a normative dimension as 'there is a right and wrong way of doing things'. The normative dimension of consumption-critical media practices becomes obvious in the analysis presented here, especially in the second and third case studies, which show that people judge the production and appropriation of media normatively, and try to perform 'good' media practices that contribute to sustainability (repairing media technologies and producing fair media technologies).

On the one hand, this chapter contributes to the media practice paradigm by elaborating, through empirical examples, the concept of consumption-critical media practices, and arguing for a broad understanding of the term 'media practice'. On the other hand, it contributes to the research field of media, communication, and sustainability, which deals with sustainability on the levels of media content, production, and appropriation. This field focuses on media content, examining consumption-critical campaigns (Baringhorst et al., 2010; Micheletti & Stolle, 2007) or media representations of sustainability (Schäfer & Schlichting, 2014). It deals with media production and journalism by analysing the conditions in which journalists covering environmental topics work, how they cover those topics, with whom they work (e.g. politicians or members of non-governmental organizations, NGOs), and how journalists perceive media content relating to issues of sustainability and the environment (Engesser & Brüggemann, 2016; Adolphsen & Lück, 2012; Berglez, 2011). A third area within the field of media, communication, and sustainability considers media recipients' and users' perceptions of media content dealing with sustainability (Neverla & Taddicken, 2012). However, the issue of what people do in relation to media to contribute to sustainability has not yet been addressed within this field. This chapter addresses this gap by applying the media practice approach to the study of media, communication, and sustainability.

Case studies and methods

To explore the question of what people do with media to contribute to sustainability, three case studies were conducted. These were chosen to cover consumption-critical media practices on the levels of content, appropriation, and production. In the first case study, the focus was on media content; specifically, websites advertising for sustainability. I chose the most prominent example in Germany: the platform www.utopia.de. I conducted a qualitative content analysis of the platform as well as a virtual ethnography (Hine, 2000) of the social networking site that was originally integrated into the platform and the online forums that later replaced it. This case study shows how people use media to criticise consumption and promote sustainability. The second and third case studies show how people act on media to contribute to sustainability. The second case study focuses on media appropriation: I analysed the repairing of media technologies in Repair Cafés, public events in which people come together to repair their everyday objects – media technologies being among the goods that are brought most often to these events (Kannengießer, 2017, p. 78). I conducted observations in three Repair Cafés in Germany, and 40 qualitative interviews with organizers and participants of these events. I was interested in finding out how people act in relation to media in the context of Repair Cafés and what the motivation and aims of their actions are. The third case study focused on the production of media technologies, specifically media technologies produced under fair and sustainable conditions. I chose two initiatives: the Dutch company Fairphone, which develops and sells a smartphone produced under fair and sustainable conditions; and the German NGO NagerIT, which develops and sells the Fair Mouse, a computer mouse produced under fair and sustainable conditions. In this case study, it is not the production process *per se* that is analysed, but the producers' perspectives on the fair and sustainable production of media technologies and their aims in doing so. Therefore, I conducted a qualitative content analysis of the Fairphone and NagerIT websites, and of newspaper interviews with the Fairphone founder Bas van Abel. The data from all three case studies were analysed using the three-step coding process of grounded theory (Corbin & Strauss, 2008). The core category that was developed is the concept of consumption-critical media practices, discussed in this chapter as the ways in which people use and act on media to contribute to sustainability.

Consumption-critical media practices

Media content

On the level of media content, people and organizations *use* media to advertise for sustainability. They spread consumption-critical opinions and ideas, and network with like-minded consumption-critical people. One example of an initiative using internet media to spread information about (critical) consumption and sustainability is the German company Utopia. The company's overall aim is to bring together people, organizations, and companies who 'want to contribute together with us to a sustainable development in economy and society'.[3] It aims at 'informing and inspiring millions of consumers to change their consumer behaviour and lifestyle into sustainable ones'. What the company mainly does is spread information about consumer products and consumer practices on its platform and in its email newsletters. In different sections of the website, products and companies that are seen as non-sustainable are named and criticized, and companies and products, as well as practices, that are judged as sustainable are introduced. Moreover, the platform advertises sustainable alternatives on the media technology market, such as the Fairphone.

Utopia also provided a social network (since replaced by online forums), integrated into its platform, for 'utopian people' to give their opinions and hints on sustainable consumption in forums and blogs. By offering this social network, Utopia tried to construct a community of consumption-critical people. The company claims to have an independent editorial staff, but cooperates closely with companies to generate content. Therefore, the platform is one way for companies that Utopia judges as being sustainable to advertise their products.

Utopia uses its platform, email newsletter, and online forums to influence consumer behaviour. The media practice in this case is related to the production of media content. Couldry's central question, which asks what people are doing in relation to media (Couldry 2004, p. 119), can easily be answered here: Utopia uses media (its platform and email newsletters) to criticize certain forms of consumption and advertise for sustainability. Moreover, it enables networked communication among the registered members. Though consumption itself is not criticized, certain consumer products and consumption behaviours are. In this way, Utopia supports certain forms of consumption by advertising consumer goods and consumption practices that the company classifies as sustainable.

Media appropriation

The consumption of media technologies itself is criticized by initiatives and people *acting on* media at the level of appropriation. Here, people reflect on the materiality of media technologies and develop alternatives to buying new devices such as repairing, exchanging, or giving away their old ones. While repairing is itself an old practice, it is nowadays becoming visible and politicized in Repair Cafés. Repairing can be defined as 'the process of sustaining, managing, and repurposing technology in order to cope with attrition and regressive change' (Rosner & Turner, 2015, p. 59). Repair Cafés are new events where people meet to repair their everyday objects such as electronic devices, textiles, or bicycles – media technologies being among the goods that are brought most often to these events (Kannengießer, 2017, p. 78). While some people volunteer to help with the repair process, others seek help with repairing their things. The Dutch foundation Stichting Repair Café claims to have invented the concept of Repair Cafés in 2009. Whether or not this was the origin, Repair Cafés have spread throughout Western European and North American countries in recent years.[4]

Following the media practice paradigm, we can ask what people actually do in Repair Cafés in relation to media. On one hand, organizers of Repair Cafés use media to advertise the events (Kannengießer, 2018, pp. 112–114). On the other hand, and this is my focus here, people act in relation to media by *repairing* broken media devices. The motivations and aims of people repairing their devices are what make the media practice of repairing consumption-critical. My case study identified six main aims of the actors involved in Repair Cafés: conservation of resources, waste prevention, valuing the device, having fun while repairing, economic pressure, and becoming part of a community. The former three can be characterized as consumption-critical and will be discussed in the following, drawing on quotes from selected interview partners.[5]

People involved in Repair Cafés are aware of the harmful consequences of the production of media technologies: 'I think especially the repairing of computers is important as they contain resources, because of which people in other countries die', stated one of the male organizers (50-year-old) of a Repair Café. Many Repair Café organizers and participants point to the harmful and polluting circumstances and situations of war under which the resources needed for digital media technologies (such as coltan) are extracted (for the socio-ecological effects of extraction, see e.g. Bleischwitz et al., 2012).

A second dominant motivation for people repairing their devices is waste prevention: 'We would have a better world if more people repair their things [...] because our planet would be less polluted', said one 60-year-old woman, trying to repair her old mobile phone. Several interviewees pointed to the circumstances on waste dumps, for example in Ghana, where people (often children) burn broken media technologies to extract reusable resources, damaging their health and polluting the environment in the process as poisonous substances end up in the soil and groundwater (for the socio-ecological effects of e-waste, see e.g. Kaitatzi-Whitlock, 2015).

Reflecting on the socio-ecological effects of the production and disposal of media technologies, participants in Repair Cafés try to reduce the need to produce new media technologies and dispose of existing ones by prolonging the lifespan of the devices they own. They stress the value of their existing devices and their personal relationship to the technologies they possess: 'I befriend my smartphone', said one young male participant trying to repair his device. A 58-year-old male volunteer helping to repair media technologies underlined the amount of work that is invested in each apparatus: people inventing, developing, and designing the products, and others constructing them, were a reason for him to value his goods and try to maintain them.

The media practice of repairing can be characterized as consumption-critical in the sense that the frequent consumption of media technologies (replacement of existing media technologies through the purchase of new ones), as well as the harmful and polluting nature of production and disposal processes, are criticized. When repairing broken media devices, people *act on media* as they reflect on the materiality of media technologies and the production and disposal of devices. Moreover, they politicize the technologies as well as their media practices. People involved in Repair Cafés strive for a transformation of dominant media practices in everyday life: they want to prolong the lifespan of their devices to avoid buying new ones, and try to spread their consumption-critical ideas by repairing publicly and staging Repair Cafés as consumption-critical events. For them, repairing media technologies is an alternative to the consumption of (new) devices and therefore an alternative media practice.

In Repair Cafés, communities (*Vergemeinschaftungen*) are built in Max Weber's sense (1972, p. 21): People meet because of a shared aim and sense a feeling of belonging. One 68-year-old volunteer helping to repair computers explained:

> People who are participating in something of this kind [Repair Cafés] have a different societal and political attitude. [...] For me, it is much nicer to get involved in something cooperative than in economy, because there is a sense of belonging. I do not belong to Saturn,[6] I buy at Saturn, but actually I do not give a shit about Saturn.

Repair Cafés enable the gathering of a consumption-critical community, whereby the practice of repairing anchors other practices (Couldry, 2004), such as practices of chatting with other participants, consuming beverages, and listening to music played in the cafés.

However, there are also ambivalences regarding consumption-critical media practices in Repair Cafés. People stressed in the interviews that they repair their media devices to contribute to sustainability by prolonging the lifespan of their technologies. But at the same time, many Repair Café participants are technophiles and have a big media repertoire (Hasebrink & Domeyer, 2012), meaning that they own many media devices and buy innovations frequently – which might conflict with their ambitions regarding sustainability. Nevertheless, repairing media technologies can be understood as an *effort* to contribute to a sustainable society.

Production

A third area in which consumption-critical media practices can be observed is the production of media technologies. Here, people *act on* media at the level of production. Examples of such practices are efforts to develop media technologies that are produced under fair working conditions with sustainable resources. In the following, two examples of consumption-critical media production are analysed.

The first is the Fair Mouse, a computer mouse developed by the German NGO NagerIT ('rodentIT' in English), which is supposed to be produced under fair working conditions with sustainable resources such as bioplastic made out of wood leavings by the paper industry.[7] NagerIT aims at producing 'a mouse without damaging anyone who is involved in the production'. The NGO wants to 'kickstart a fair trade electronics market so that one day caring customers have the possibility to choose the fair option for every product they need'. For NagerIT, fair means restricted working hours (relying on the standards of the International Labour Organization), appropriate pay, health protection, social security, freedom of association, and exclusion of exploitative child and forced labour.

NagerIT and the Fair Mouse are similar in their argumentation and self-representation to the Fairphone – a smartphone produced by an Amsterdam-based company. The smartphone was first developed in 2010, the second-generation phone was available in December 2015, and the third generation went on sale in August 2019.[8] Fairphone aims at producing a smartphone that is manufactured under safe working conditions with fair wages and with sustainable resources extracted in conflict-free areas. It strives not only to offer a fair alternative to other smartphones but also to influence debate. The company indirectly criticizes frequent consumption of new media technologies: it produces a modular, repairable smartphone, and thereby strives to change the 'relationship' between people and their smartphones, giving consumers more control over their phone. Interestingly, in 2017 the company stopped the production of spare parts for the first-generation Fairphone, meaning that it is no longer repairable (or at least that the company does not support these repairing processes any more). After announcing the abandonment of spare part production, the founder of the company, Bas van Abel, claimed in media interviews that durability was not the focus of the company, or the previous smartphone (Tricarico, 2017). This is one of the ambivalences that can be identified in this case.

Another ambivalence lies in the contradiction between the ambition of being fair and its implementation: neither the Fairphone nor the Fair Mouse is completely fair – as both initiatives admit on their websites. Only one-third of the Fair Mouse is claimed to be produced under fair conditions and, even now, only a few minerals in the Fairphone are actually produced under conflict free working conditions. The Fairphone company claims that a '100% fair phone is in fact unachievable' but it (as well as NagerIT) stresses that it follows a 'step-by-step process' trying to make its products more 'fair' in future.

The production of fair media technologies can be defined as a media practice in which people and organizations *act on* media. People reflect on the materiality of media technologies, criticize the socio-ecological effects of the production and appropriation of media apparatuses, and try – by designing and producing fair (and repairable) media devices – to develop alternatives. In this way, they put media technologies at the centre of their actions, politicizing the devices as well as their practices.

The production of fair media technologies can be characterized as consumption-critical insofar as it implies a critique of (certain forms of) consumption of media technologies. While both initiatives analysed here criticize bigger companies on their websites and try to offer alternatives with their products, they still support the consumption of specific media technologies – framing it as 'good' consumption. Therefore, it is not consumption itself that is being criticized, but the consumption of non-fair and non-sustainable media technologies – as well as non-fair production itself. Still, both initiatives discussed here can be understood as efforts to contribute to a sustainable society.

Both examples show that people act on media in organizations. The Fairphone company is even trying to build a movement: it uses Facebook, Twitter, and Instragram to build a 'Fairphone community'.[9] People are invited to become part of the 'Fairphone movement' by buying the device and/or becoming part of the social networks used by the company: 'Buy a phone, join a movement'. The company is trying to construct a community, in Max Weber's (1972: 21) sense, of people who share the aim of sustainability by creating a feeling of belonging: #WeAreFairphone.

Consumption-critical media practices: acting on media for sustainability

By introducing the theoretical concept of consumption-critical media practices and discussing empirical examples of such practices at the levels of media content, appropriation, and production, this chapter has achieved two aims. First, it has introduced the media practice paradigm into the research field of media, communication, and sustainability through case studies of what people do in relation to media to contribute to a sustainable society. Second, the chapter has argued for a broad understanding of the term 'media practice': as the empirical case studies that unfold the concept of consumption-critical media studies show, people not only *use* media (as in the case of Utopia) but also *act on* media by repairing media technologies or producing fair media devices.

The concept of *acting on media* (Kannengießer & Kubitschko, 2017b) refers to media practices in which individuals, organizations, or collectives place the focus of their action on media technologies themselves: they reflect on media devices and their materialities, engage with apparatuses, modify and transform them. Repairing media technologies in Repair Cafés and producing fair media technologies are examples of media practices in which people act on media, as both cases involve reflection on the materiality of media technologies and the implementation of alternatives. Both the technologies and the practices are politicized – as acts against consumer society and as media practices for sustainability. In this way, through consumption-critical media practices, people follow the normative goal of contributing to sustainability. They try to act in a 'good' way in relation to media by repairing their broken media devices or producing fair technologies. The motivation for these practices lies in the awareness of the socio-ecological effects of current production and disposal processes. Thus, the materiality of media technologies becomes relevant for the way people act in relation to media (see also Kannengießer, 2019).

The notion of *acting on media* adds a further dimension to existing media practice theory, as it acknowledges the ways in which different actors put media at the centre of their action. This term grasps and underlines how people *consciously* and *actively* seek to *transform* media technologies and in doing so try to change not only the devices, but also society. If we want to understand how people act in relation to media to transform society, scholars need to analyse not only how people, collectives, and organizations *use* media, but also how they *act on* media.

In the example of consumption-critical media practices, though, people do not act on media alone, but become part of communities: initiators like the companies Fairphone and Utopia strive to build communities among people sharing consumption-critical attitudes, and Repair Cafés generate a feeling of belonging to an 'alternative' community. The (consumption-critical) media practices and their shared aims are what bring people together. Therefore, when analysing how people *act on media*, research also has to ask if people act alone, in communities or collectives, or in networks or organizations.

Alongside the ambivalences that I have pointed to, consumption-critical media practices are also limited in terms of their influence on society. For example, the public debate generated on the website Utopia is restricted to this online platform; only a small, although growing, number of people participate in Repair Cafés; and only a small number of Fairphones and Fair Mice are sold on the huge smartphone market. Nevertheless, the examples of consumption-critical media practices discussed here can at least be judged as *attempts* to act on media for sustainability.

Notes

1 The term consumption-critical media practice is a translation of the German term *konsumkritische Medienpraktiken* and might be a clumsy translation. Still, I want to introduce this term as a *terminus technicus*, stressing with this adverb that through these media practices people criticize (certain types of) consumption itself.
2 The results of this study and the concept of consumption-critical media practices have been discussed as means of political participation before, see Kannengießer (2016).
3 The quotes were taken from the company's website, which exists only in German, and have been translated by the author. 'Über Utopia', https://utopia.de/ueber-utopia/; various articles retrieved from https://news.utopia.de/tag/fairphone/; 'Neu anmelden bei Utopia und Utopia City', https://utopia.de/registrieren/, retrieved 30 November 2015 and 8 August 2019.
4 'About Repair Café', retrieved from https://repaircafe.org/en/about/, retrieved 8 August 2019. See a map of locations at www.repaircafe.org.
5 For a more detailed discussion of the results, see Kannengießer (2017, 2018). All quotes were previously in German and have been translated by the author.
6 Saturn is one of the biggest stores selling electronic goods in Germany.
7 NagerIT: 'Fair electronics', https://www.nager-it.de/en/projekt; 'What does "fair trade" mean at NagerIT?', https://www.nager-it.de/en/maus/umsetzung/details; 'The Fair Mouse', https://www.nager-it.de/en/maus, all retrieved 29–30 November 2015.
8 Fairphone: 'About us', https://www.fairphone.com/about/; 'History', https://www.fairphone.com/en/how-we-work/?ref=header; 'Fairphone 2 cost breakdown', http://fairphone.com/costbreakdown/; 'Fairphone 2, an ethical phone with a modular design', http://shop.fairphone.com/; 'Fairphone fact sheet', https://www.fairphone.com/wp-content/uploads/2016/08/Fairphone-factsheet_EN.pdf; 'Our roadmap to a fairer phone. Creating lasting change one step at a time', https://www.fairphone.com/en/our-goals/; 'A smart phone with social values', https://www.fairphone.com/; 'Welcome to the movement', https://www.fairphone.com/we-are-fairphone/, retrieved 15 January and 30 November 2015, and 8 August 2019.
9 https://www.facebook.com/fairphone; https://twitter.com/fairphone; https://www.instagram.com/wearefairphone/.

References

Adolphsen, M., & Lück, J. (2012). Non-routine interactions behind the scenes of a global media event: how journalists and political PR professionals co-produced the 2010 UN climate conference in Cancún. *Medien- & Kommunikationswissenschaft*, Special Issue 2, 'Grenzüberschreitende Medienkommunikation', H. Wessler & S. Averbeck-Lietz (eds), 141–158.

Baringhorst, S., Kneip, V., März, A., & Niesyto, J. (2010). *Unternehmenskritische Kampagnen*. Wiesbaden: VS Verlag für Sozialwissenschaften.

Barrett, M., & Brunton-Smith, I. (2014). Political and civic engagement and participation: towards an integrative perspective, *Journal of Civil Society*, 10(1), 5–28.

Baumer, E., Ames, M., Burrell, J., Brubaker, J., & Dourish, P. (eds) (2015). Non-use of technology: perspectives and approaches, *First Monday Special Issue*, 20(11).

Berglez, P. (2011). Inside, outside, and beyond media logic: journalistic creativity in climate reporting. *Media, Culture & Society* 33(3), 449–465.

Bleischwitz, R., Dittrich, M., & Pierdicca, C. (2012). Coltan from Central Africa, international trade and implications for any certification. *Rescources Policy* 37(1), 29–29.

Chan, J., & Ho, C. (2008). *The Dark Side of Cyberspace: Inside the Sweatshops of China's Computer Hardware Production*. Berlin: World Economy, Ecology and Development (WEED). Retrieved from http://goodelectronics.org/publications-en/Publication_2851/.

Corbin, J., & Strauss, A. (2008). *Basics of Qualitative Research Techniques and Procedures for Developing Grounded Theory*. Thousand Oaks, CA: Sage.

Couldry, N. (2004). Theorising media as practice. *Social Semiotics*, 14(2), 115–132.

Engesser, S., & Brüggemann, M. (2016). Mapping the minds of the mediators: the cognitive frames of climate journalists from five countries. *Public Understanding of Science*, 25(7), 825–841.

Foellmer, S., Lünenborg, M., & Raetzsch, C. (eds) (2018). *Media Practices, Social Movements, and Performativity. Transdisciplinary Approaches*. New York: Routledge.

Hasebrink, U., & Domeyer, H. (2012). Media repertoires as patterns of behaviour and as meaningful practices: a multimethod approach to media use in converging media environments. *Participations: Journal of Audience & Reception Studies*, 9(2), 757–783.

Hine, C. (2000). *Virtual Ethnography*. London: Sage.

Kaitatzi-Whitlock, S. (2015). E-waste, human-waste, inflation. In R. Maxwell, J. Raundalen, & N. L. Vestberg (eds), *Media and the Ecological Crisis* (pp. 69–84). Milton Park/New York: Routledge.

Kannengießer, S. (2016). Conceptualizing consumption-critical media practices as political participation. In L. Kramp et al. (eds), *Politics, Civil Society and Participation* (pp. 193–207). Tartu: Tartu University Press.

Kannengießer, S. (2017). 'I am not a consumer person' – political participation in Repair Cafés. In C. Wallner, J. Wimmer, & K. Schultz (eds), *(Mis)Understanding Political Participation. Digital Practices, New Forms of Participation and the Renewal of Democracy* (pp. 78–94). London: Routledge.

Kannengießer, S. (2018). Repair Cafés as communicative figurations: consumer-critical media practices for cultural transformation. In A. Hepp, U. Hasebrink, & A. Breiter (eds), *Communicative Figurations. Rethinking Mediatized Transformations* (pp. 101–120). London: Palgrave.

Kannengießer, S. (2019): Reflecting on and engaging with the materiality of media technologies: repairing and fair producing. *New Media & Society*. DOI: 10.1177/1461444819858081

Kannengießer, S., & Kubitschko, S. (eds) (2017). Acting on media: influencing, shaping and (re)configuring the fabric of everyday life. *Media and Communication*, 5(3).

Lünenborg, M., & Raetzsch, C. (2018). From public sphere to performative publics: developing media practice as an analytic model. In S. Foellmer, M. Lünenborg, & C. Raetzsch (eds), *Media Practices, Social Movements, and Performativity. Transdisciplinary Approaches* (pp. 13–35). New York: Routledge.

Magaudda, P. (2011). When materiality 'bites back': digital music consumption practices in the age of dematerialization. *Journal of Consumer Culture*, 11(1), 15–36.

Mattoni, A. (2012). *Media Practices and Protest Politics: How Precarious Workers Mobilise*. London: Routledge.

Mattoni, A., & Treré, E. (2014). Media practices, mediation processes, and mediatization in the study of social movements. *Communication Theory*, 24(3), 252–271.

Maxwell, R., & Miller, T. (2012). *Greening the Media*. Oxford: Oxford University Press.

Micheletti, M., & Stolle, D. (2007). Mobilizing consumers to take responsibility for global social justice. *Annals of the American Academy of Political and Social Science*, 611(1), 157–175.

Möller, J., & von Rimscha, B. (2017). (De)Centralization of the global informational ecosystem. *Media and Communication*, 5(3), 37–48.

MyersWest, S. (2017). Raging against the machine: network gatekeeping and collective action on social media platforms. *Media and Communication*, 5(3), 28–36.

Neverla, I., & Taddicken, M. (2012). Der Klimawandel aus Rezipientensicht: Relevanz und Forschungsstand. In I. Neverla & M. Schäfer (eds), *Das Medien-Klima. Fragen und Befunde der kommunikationswissenschaftlichen Klimaforschung* (pp. 215–232). Wiesbaden: Springer VS.

Nicolini, D. (2017). Practice theory as a package of theory, method and vocabulary: affordances and limitations. In M. Jonas, B. Littig, & A. Wroblewski (eds), *Methodological Reflections of Practice Oriented Theories* (pp. 19–34). Dordrecht: Springer.

Reckwitz, A. (2002). Toward a theory of social practices: a development in culturalist theorizing. *European Journal of Social Theory*, 5(2), 243–263.

Reißmann, W., Stock, M., Kaiser, S., IsenbergV., & Nieland, J.-U. (2017). Fan (fiction) acting on media and the politics of appropriation. *Media and Communication*, 5(3), 15–27.

Rosner, D. K., & Turner, F. (2015). Theaters of alternative industry: hobbyist repair collectives and the legacy of the 1960s American counterculture. In H. Plattner, C. Meinel, & L. Leifer (eds), *Design Thinking Research: Building Innovators* (pp. 59–69). Heidelberg: Springer International.

SchäferM. S., & Schlichting, I. (2014). Media representations of climate change: a meta-analysis of the research field. *Environmental Communication*, 8(2), 142–160.

Stephansen, H. C. (2017). Media activism as movement? Collective identity formation in the world forum of free media. *Media and Communication* 5(3), 59–66.

Tricarico, T. (2017). Mängel des Fairphone 1. Letzte Chance Secondhand. Die Tageszeitung. Retrieved from https://www.taz.de/!5426933/.

Weber, M. (1972). *Wirtschaft und Gesellschaft*, Tübingen (5th ed). Heidelberg: Mohr Siebeck Verlag.

Widmer, R., Oswald-Krapf, H., Sinha-Khetriwal, D., Schnellmann, M., & Böni, H. (2005). Global perspectives on e-waste. *Science of the Total Environment*, 25, 436–458.

10

CONCEPTUALIZING THE ROLE OF KNOWLEDGE IN ACTING ON MEDIA

Hilde C. Stephansen

Introduction

The media practice approach has been widely adopted among scholars of citizen and social movement media, and has proved a productive framework for analysing the social contexts in which media are produced, consumed, and circulated. According to Couldry's (2012, p. 35) widely adopted definition, media practices can be understood as 'what people are doing in relation to media in the contexts in which they act': this might include actions that are *directly oriented* to media, actions that *involve* media, and actions whose *preconditions* are media (Couldry, 2012). Highlighting the ubiquity and embeddedness of media in contemporary social life, this definition encompasses a very broad range of practices, and the ethnographic openness it generates is a key strength of the media practice approach. Thus far, however, research within the media practice literature has focused primarily on the *use* and *impact* of media; 'how actors use specific tools, platforms or devices and what consequences this use has for their ability to engage with politics' (Kubitschko, 2018, p. 631). Although this focus on what people *do with* media has generated important insights into the ways that activists use media to organize and mobilize, it does not capture the full range of practices involved in media activism. Though media activists *use* media for other substantive ends, they also mobilize *around* media, making media technologies, infrastructures, and policies the explicit focus of their activism (Hackett & Carroll, 2006; Milan, 2013; Stein, Kidd, & Rodríguez, 2009; Stephansen, 2017). Recognizing the importance of media for social change struggles, media activists create autonomous alternatives to state and corporate media (Milan, 2013), campaign to democratize existing media (Hackett & Carroll, 2006), and work to raise awareness about the political nature of media technologies (Kubitschko, 2015). Such media-focused activism is not new – it dates back at least to the 1970s and the New World Information and Communication

Order (NWICO) debates within UNESCO – but it arguably takes on increased urgency and significance in an age of 'deep mediatization' (Couldry & Hepp, 2017). As activists increasingly mobilize *around* media, we need to expand the definition of media practices to include practices aimed at thematizing, problematizing, and *politicizing* media and communication.

The term 'acting on media' has been proposed (Kannengießer & Kubitschko, 2017; Kubitschko, 2018) as a way to capture the wide range of practices that make media technologies and infrastructures sites of political struggle. 'Acting on media denotes the efforts of a wide range of actors to take an active part in the molding of media organizations, infrastructures and technologies that are part of the fabric of everyday life' (Kannengießer & Kubitschko, 2017, p. 1). Kubitschko (2018, p. 631) cites examples ranging from citizen media to data activism (Milan & van der Velden, 2016), Repair Cafés where people fix everyday media objects (Kannengießer, 2017), and hacker practices that involve modifying and deconstructing media technologies. Taking up Couldry's key question, 'how is people's media-related practice related [...] to their wider agency?' (2012, p. 37), Kubitschko (2018, p. 632) argues that the concept of 'acting on' media needs to be incorporated as 'a central analytical dimension of media as practice research'.

The conceptual reorientation offered by acting on media opens up media practice research to a wider range of practices beyond those that involve doing things *with* media. In what follows, I further draw out the implications of this conceptual move by problematizing the role of *knowledge* in media practices. While, arguably, many media practices are so embedded in everyday life as to be largely habitual and unreflexive, acting on media involves the 'articulation of viewpoints, interests, experiences and knowledge' (Kubitschko, 2018, p. 633). Citizen media practices (Stephansen, 2016), which are our concern in this volume, involve 'act[ing] in public space(s) to effect aesthetic or socio-political change' (Baker & Blaagaard, 2016, p. 16). They are *intentional* and involve mobilizing knowledge: about specific technologies, about the wider media environment, about other actors in the field, and more. If we expand the concept of 'media practices' to include practices that thematize and politicize media, we need to consider the role of knowledge in such practices.

The aim of this chapter is to critically explore how we might understand the role of knowledge in media practices – particularly those that involve acting on media. As I show in the first section, knowledge has been conceptualized as integral to media practices. However, as I go on to discuss, knowledge has a contested status among practice theorists, who reject the 'mentalism' and rationalist assumptions of much modern social thought. While some see practices as governed largely by tacit 'know-how' and skill, others insist on the importance of perceptions, reasons, and propositional knowledge. Siding with the latter, I argue that knowledge is a core dimension of media practices, but that activities such as theorizing, reflecting, and analysing should themselves be treated as social practices rather than subjective mental activities (Schmidt, 2016). Thus conceived, 'knowledge practices' can be analysed as an important dimension of media practices. In the latter parts of the chapter, I draw on literature on knowledge production in social movements to develop a framework for analysing such knowledge practices, and illustrate the utility of this framework through a brief case study of the World Forum of Free Media, a global gathering of NGOs and activist groups that mobilize around media and communication.

Knowledge in the media practice literature

The literature on media practices already offers some resources for conceptualizing the role of knowledge. Couldry (2004, p. 121) suggested that media practice research involves posing two key questions: 'what types of things do people do in relation to media? And what types of things do people say in relation to media?' – adding in a footnote that this also implies 'studying what people believe and think' (ibid.). Couldry's (2004, p. 124) core question – 'what types of things do people do/say/think that are oriented to media?' – clearly, then, includes a concern with cognitive processes. Cognitive processes also figure prominently in Mattoni's defi- nition of 'activist media practices' as 'both routinized and creative social practices that [...] draw on how media objects and media subjects are *perceived* and how the media environment is *understood and known*' (2012, p. 159, emphasis added). More specifically, Mattoni makes the point that activist media practices 'rest on the pro- duction of perceptions and knowledge about the broader context in which and with which social actors interact' (2012, p. 66). She goes on to define 'media knowledge practices' – practices 'related to the development of knowledge about the media environment' (ibid.) – as a central component of activist media practices. Mattoni shows how activists construct 'semantic maps' of the media environment as they decode media texts, engage in their own media production, and interact with journalists and other media subjects. Media knowledge practices thus 'play an important role in shaping interactions between social movement actors and the media environments in which they are embedded' (Mattoni, 2013, p. 48).

McCurdy (2013) similarly argues that activists' media practices are informed by 'lay theories of media': 'theories or understandings, expressed and/or enacted by social movement actors, concerning the functions and motivations of news media, how news media operate, what drives them, and theories concerning how the logic of news influences the representation of reality' (2013, p. 62). McCurdy suggests that such lay theories of media, which are often informed by academic theories, can be situated as part of the 'background knowledge' (Reckwitz, 2002) informing a broader practice of activism. Like Mattoni, McCurdy points out that activists' knowledge of media is informed by their experiences as both audiences and producers of media: this knowledge 'reflexively informs and translates to media-oriented practices' (2013, p. 69).

These perspectives resonate with research that has explored the role of political cultures and imaginaries in media activism (Barassi, 2015; Barassi & Treré, 2012; Fotopoulou, 2017; Juris, 2008; Kavada, 2013; Treré, Jeppesen, & Mattoni, 2017; Treré, 2018, 2019; Wolfson, 2014). A key insight to be drawn from this literature is that activists' media imaginaries – the ways in which they perceive and imagine digital media technologies – together with their broader political visions and ideals, contribute to shaping political cultures, organizational structures, and media practices. As empirical research has shown, the ways in which activists imagine and perceive digital technologies have 'material consequences for political practice' (Treré, 2018, p. 144). For example, Juris (2008) and Wolfson (2014) show, from different perspectives, how ideals of horizontality and networked participation – derived from widely shared beliefs about the internet – came to constitute a powerful political 'logic' within the Global Justice Movement. Barassi (2015) shows how cultural variations in media imaginaries among activist groups in Spain, Italy, and the UK inspired different social media practices, while Fotopoulou (2017) shows how the media practices of feminist groups are differently shaped by widely circulating social imaginaries of connectivity, participation, and networked politics.

There is considerable overlap between this literature and the previously outlined approaches, which focus explicitly on the role of *knowledge* in media practices. As I discuss below, imaginaries figure among the mental activities that many practice theorists see as integral to practices, and form part of the broad understandings of 'knowledge' deployed by social movement scholars. Without digressing into an extended discussion of definitions, we might conceptualize 'knowledge' here as a broader category that includes values and imaginaries as well as analytical and reflexive knowledge, knowledge about social relations, and practical know-how. Knowledge, in other words, can be understood as the 'broader cognitive praxis that informs all social activity' (Eyerman & Jamison, 1991, p. 49). Together, these perspectives make clear that we cannot study what activists *do* with media without also exploring the various forms of knowledge that underpin their media practices. They show that media practices involve not just the tacit know-how required to *use* media, but also imaginaries and analytical knowledge. The relevance of the latter forms of knowledge is accentuated by practices that make media explicit objects of struggle. These kinds of media practices clearly involve knowledge production – about 'media-related injustice' (Milan, 2013), media policy, and media institutions, to name a few – and they are usually informed by broader visions of social change based on shared values and ideals.

Knowledge in practice theory

From a practice theory perspective, however, this focus on knowledge and intentionality raises complex questions regarding subjectivity, the relationship between structure and agency, and social change. While most practice theorists agree that practices involve some form of knowledge, its exact role and nature is contested. There is basic agreement that practices depend on shared skills and understanding (Schatzki, 2001, p. 12), and definitions of practice typically include reference to practical know-how and embodied capacities. Summarizing widely shared understandings, Schatzki defines practices as 'embodied, materially mediated arrays of human activity centrally organized around shared practical understanding' (2001, p. 11). Spaargaren, Weenink, & Lamers (2016, n.p.), in an introductory text, define social practices as 'shared, routinized, ordinary ways of doings and sayings enacted by capable human agents who – while interacting with the material elements that co-constitute the practice – know what to do next in a non-discursive, practical manner'. In these definitions, the emphasis is on tacit, practical, and embodied 'know-how' – the largely unreflexive forms of knowledge that enable social actors to 'go on' within any given social situation and perform routine social practices with skill.

But how might we understand the role of more reflexive forms of knowledge in social practices? Practice theorists differ on this question. While for Bourdieu, the practical understanding and embodied norms implied by the concept of habitus provide a sufficient basis for explaining social reproduction, others emphasize the importance of perceptions, goals, reasons, and propositional knowledge (Schatzki, 2001). Barnes (2001), who argues that practice, by itself, forms an insufficient basis for explaining social life, conceptualizes such forms of knowledge as extrinsic to social practices: 'It is always necessary to ask what disposes people to enact the practices they do, how and when they do; and their aims, their lived experience and their inherited knowledge will surely figure amongst the factors of interest here' (2001, p. 29–30). Others incorporate reflexive and motivational knowledge as part of broader definitions of practice that recognize the role of cultural meanings and socially shared bodies of knowledge. Reckwitz (2002, p. 249) defines practice as

> a routinized type of behaviour which consists of several elements, inter-connected to one another: forms of bodily activities, forms of mental activities, 'things' and their use, a background knowledge in the form of understanding, know-how, states of emotion and motivational knowledge.

Along similar lines, Shove, Pantzar, & Watson (2012, p. 12) develop an understanding of practices as consisting of three main elements: materials (objects, technologies, tangible physical entities), competences (skill, know-how, and technique), and meanings (symbolic meanings, ideas, and aspirations).

The contested status of knowledge and intentionality can be linked to practice theory's rejection of rationalist traditions that explain action and social order by reference to the motivation and reasoning of individuals. Having emerged as an attempt to chart a middle ground between methodological individualism and holism, practice theory rejects the voluntarism and 'mentalism' associated with such approaches, while at the same time seeking to avoid the constrictions of structuralist models. 'Whereas philosophers and social investigators once cited mental entities such as beliefs, desires, emotions, and purposes, practice theorists instead highlight embodied capacities such as know-how, skills, tacit understanding, and dispositions' (Schatzki, 2001, p. 16). Shifting the focus away from individuals, their backgrounds and motivations, practice theory instead turns attention towards the practices they engage in (Spaargaren, 2016), and conceptualizes the social as 'a field of embodied, materially interwoven practices centrally organized around shared practical understandings' (Schatzki, 2001, p. 12). Prioritizing practices over mind, practice theory sees intelligibility, meaning, and purpose as features of practices themselves rather than located in the minds of individuals (Schatzki, 2001). According to Reckwitz, individuals act as 'carriers' of practices – as carriers not only of 'patterns of bodily behaviour, but also of certain routinized ways of understanding, knowing how and desiring' (2002, p. 250). Such 'mental' activities are therefore better understood as qualities of practices rather than of the individuals that participate in such practices (Reckwitz, 2002, p. 250).

This emphasis on practices rather than individual mental activities implies a transformed understanding of knowledge. From a practice perspective, knowledge and truth 'are no longer automatically self-transparent possessions of minds' but rather 'mediated by interactions between people and by arrangements in the world' (Schatzki, 2001, pp. 20–21). Practice theory, in brief, seeks to account for knowledge by placing it decisively in the social realm, and conceptualizing it as intrinsically bound up with material practices and relations. However, some (e.g. Schmidt, 2016) argue that this ontological and epistemological reorientation has led to a neglect among practice theorists of the mental features (such as sense-making and reflexive, analytical knowledge) that are bound up with practice. To understand 'precisely how reflexive, analytical and theoretical knowledge processes contribute to practices' (Schmidt, 2016, n.p.), practice theory needs to make theoretical and analytical practices themselves the object of empirical–praxeographic research (ibid.). Activities such as analysing, reflecting, and theorizing should thus be treated not as subjective mental activities but rather as 'empirically accessible, observable sets of organised doings and sayings (Schatzki) that are intertwined with artefacts and technologies' (Schmidt, 2016, n.p.). In other words, knowledge production should itself be treated as a social practice. Returning to the topic of citizen media practices, this means asking questions about *how* media-related knowledge is produced, *what* kinds of knowledge are produced (and by whom), and how such knowledge is mobilized to effect change. Some useful conceptual resources for asking these questions can be found in a growing literature on knowledge production in social movements.

Knowledge practices in social movements

One of the first (and theoretically most comprehensive) accounts of social movements as sites for knowledge production is Eyerman & Jamison's (1991) *Social Movements: A Cognitive Approach*. Operating with a view of knowledge production as a fundamentally social endeavour and emphasizing the creative role of consciousness and cognition in all human action, Eyerman and Jamison see social movements as privileged agents in the social production of knowledge: as breeding grounds for innovations in thought and bearers of new ideas, which are subsequently diffused in wider society. The significance of a social movement thus lies in the historical project it articulates at the level of ideas. Eyerman and Jamison advocate studying social movements as 'cognitive praxis', which means focusing on the collective processes of knowledge production through which the identity of a movement is articulated, and thinking about the contribution they make in the long term to human knowledge and the civilizational paradigms that guide human action.

Such an understanding of social movements as sites for knowledge production has been taken up in more recent scholarship, which sees studying knowledge production in social movements as crucial to understanding their broader social significance and political 'effects' (Casas-Cortés, Osterweil, & Powell, 2008; della Porta & Pavan, 2017). Social movements are conceptualized as privileged sources of knowledge because they 'have long been bearers of knowledge about forms of oppression and injustice' (Chesters, 2012, p. 153) that is not accessible from dominant viewpoints, and are uniquely placed to develop critiques of – and alternatives to – the current social order to effect social change (Chesters, 2012; Cox, 2014).

The relevance of such approaches for theorizing citizen media and practice lies in their understanding of knowledge *as practice*. Casas-Cortés et al. (2008, p. 19) use the hyphenated term 'knowledge-practices' to emphasize the 'concrete, embodied, lived, and situated' character of knowledge. Knowledge-practices refers to the 'creation, modification and diverse enactments' of movement knowledges, which might take the form of 'stories, ideas, narratives, and ideologies, but also theories, expertise, as well as political analyses and critical understandings of particular contexts' (ibid., p. 20). Similarly, della Porta and Pavan define the concept of 'repertoires of knowledge practices' as

> the set of practices that foster the coordination of disconnected, local, and highly personal experiences and rationalities within a shared cognitive system able to provide movements and their supporters with a common orientation for making claims and acting collectively to produce social, political, and cultural changes.
>
> *(della Porta & Pavan, 2017, p. 300)*

A common argument within this literature is that what makes movement knowledges unique and politically important is their situated, material, and place-based nature (Casas-Cortés et al., 2008; Cox, 2014; della Porta & Pavan, 2017). Grounded in everyday experiences of inequality, oppression, and struggle against the status quo, movement knowledges are often contrasted to more abstract and 'objective' forms of knowledge produced by academics and policy experts, who seek to establish categories, patterns and generalities (Esteves, 2008). From a postcolonial perspective, de Sousa Santos (2006) conceptualizes the diversity of knowledges produced by the world's social movements as expressive of an 'epistemology of the South'. Challenging the universalism and abstraction of Western modern thought and the subalternization of alternative knowledges wrought by histories of colonialism, the epistemology of the South asserts the validity and existence of a global 'ecology' of knowledges as well as the potential for translation and partial connection between them. This is not to say that movements only produce situated and place-based knowledge – they *also* engage in the production of more abstract analytical knowledge including technical/scientific expertise – but if we are to take movements seriously as knowledge producers, we need to value the situated and contextual character of their knowledge production in its own right (Chesters, 2012).

To better understand the diverse forms that movement knowledge practices might take – and in turn be able to analyse the different forms of knowledge practices involved in acting on media – it is useful to review different typologies of movement knowledge. Eyerman & Jamison (1991) identify three dimensions of the 'knowledge interests' of social movements. The *cosmological* dimension refers to a movement's basic assumptions or beliefs – its fundamental worldview. The *technological* dimension relates to specific topics of protest and alternative technologies, and can also incorporate new institutions created by movements (Cox, 2014). The *organizational* dimension relates to a movement's organizational paradigm, i.e. knowledge about strategies and tactics, or how to mobilize – in brief, how to 'do' social movements.

Adopting a slightly different angle, della Porta & Pavan (2017) propose three categories of knowledge production within social movements. The first, *knowledge about the collective self*, is concerned with the construction of a collective subject and is produced through activists' collective self-reflection, often during events such as social forums and protest camps. The second, *knowledge about the action network*, involves 'the effort of creating "strategic collectivities" by fostering the circulation of information about diverse agendas, competences, and resources, thus generating large-scale and coordinated networks of strategic action and collaboration between different movements or parts of them' (della Porta & Pavan, 2017, p. 306). The third, *knowledge as production of (political) alternatives*, involves knowledge practices 'oriented to develop critique of the status quo and substantiate alternative proposals to overcome it' (ibid., p. 307).

Integrating these schemes, the following typology of knowledge produced by social movements can be constructed:[1]

1. *Worldview.* This category corresponds to Eyerman and Jamison's cosmological dimension and refers to the kinds of knowledge production involved in the creation of a movement's broad vision and worldview.
2. *Knowledge about collective identity.* This refers to practices of knowledge production involved in collective identity formation. It corresponds to della Porta and Pavan's 'knowledge about the collective self', but also incorporates elements of their second category, 'knowledge about the action network', as knowledge about the actors that form part of wider networks beyond a movement's immediate milieu is arguably also central to processes of collective identity formation (Melucci, 1996).

3.   *Organizational knowledge.* This incorporates Eyerman and Jamison's organizational dimension and elements of della Porta and Pavan's 'knowledge about the action network'. It refers to knowledge about mobilization and strategy, as well as the organizational structures of the movement itself.
4.   *Knowledge about alternatives.* This final category incorporates Eyerman and Jamison's technological dimension and della Porta and Pavan's 'knowledge as production of (political) alternatives'. It can take different forms, ranging from forms of knowledge production that involve expert or analytical knowledge, such as the creation of alternative technologies and policy proposals, to more embodied forms of knowledge involved in prefigurative politics.

Knowledge practices in the World Forum of Free Media

To illustrate how this typology might be used to analyse knowledge involved in acting on media, I draw on a case study of the World Forum of Free Media (FMML for the Portuguese *Fórum Mundial de Mídia Livre* and its French/Spanish equivalents), a thematic forum for media activists and media advocacy organizations linked to the World Social Forum (WSF).[2] The FMML was first held in 2009 in conjunction with the WSF in Belém, Brazil and there have since been four further global editions (Rio de Janeiro 2012, Tunis 2013 and 2015, Montréal 2016) alongside a number of regional meetings. The FMML emerged out of a longer history of media activism within the WSF, which since 2001 has provided a space for media activists from around the world to gather, exchange knowledge and experiences, and produce collaborative coverage of forum events. Though activists were initially concerned primarily with the production of alternative media content, the physical co-presence afforded by the WSF also encouraged political debate. Since 2003, media activists have organized seminars and workshops at every WSF to discuss issues such as internet governance, freedom of speech, alternative technologies, and community media. The FMML has emerged out of this process, providing a thematic forum dedicated to media and technology issues. Over its five editions, it has brought together hundreds of very diverse participants – ranging from citizen media producers and tech activists to media reform groups, development NGOs, and academic researchers – all of whom have in common that they seek to thematize and politicize media. The FMML is therefore a highly appropriate case study for analysing knowledge practices involved in acting on media.

The typology outlined above provides a useful tool for analysing the diverse kinds of knowledge involved in FMML participants' media practices. *Knowledge about alternatives* is produced in several ways. First, the FMML provides a space for activists to experiment with and share knowledge about media technologies. At most editions, hackers and tech activists have organized hacklabs – spaces dedicated to hands-on experimentation with, and knowledge sharing about, technologies ranging from lo-fi FM radio transmitters to alternative social media. The FMML also regularly hosts seminars about alternative technologies. Second, several forum participants are engaged in media policy advocacy, and use the FMML as a space to discuss and share policy alternatives. Third, many FMML participants work actively, on an everyday basis, to construct new institutions in the form of alternative, citizen, and community media based on principles of cooperation, participation, and non-hierarchical organization.

The FMML also provides a site for the production of *organizational knowledge*. It offers a space for participants to share knowledge about strategy and mobilization, whether through informal conversations or organized activities – thus enabling participants to build knowledge about 'what works' and expand their repertoires of contention. The FMML also enables members of the organizing committee to gain knowledge about how to mobilize at a global scale, ranging from awareness of the need for cultural and linguistic translation to technical knowledge about the use of videoconferencing software for online meetings. The FMML also acts as a laboratory for experimentation with non-hierarchical ways of organizing media production, giving activists concrete experience of 'another communication'.

As a global gathering of media activists from different cultural and political backgrounds, who work in diverse contexts, the FMML has played a fundamental role in supporting the production of *knowledge about collective identity* (see Stephansen, 2017 for a detailed analysis of collective identity in the FMML). Successive face-to-face gatherings have enabled participants to get to know one another and develop mutual recognition through 'knowledge production about the shared characteristics, principles and aims of "free media"' (Stephansen, 2017, p. 62). Alongside these more organic processes of collective identity formation, FMML organizers have also engaged in deliberate efforts to develop a shared definition of 'free media' – which has involved working across cultural and linguistic boundaries to arrive at a plural, inclusive definition (Stephansen, 2017). One of the ways that they have done so is through the creation of the World Charter of Free Media (FMML, 2015), which was adopted in 2015 following a two-year consultation process via online forums and face-to-face meetings. The process of negotiating the Charter was explicitly conceived by organizers as an effort to create knowledge about collective identity: as one organizer suggested in 2013, 'this [negotiating the Charter] is going to help us define and identify ourselves' (quoted in Stephansen, 2017, p. 62). Accordingly, the Charter opens with a statement of who 'we' – free media – are, which appears as an attempt to set out a comprehensive definition:

> We are communicators, activists, journalists, hackers, community media associations and free media, social movements and popular organizations. We are bloggers, audiovisual producers, free and open technology developers, associations, networks, unions, journalism schools, research centers on information and communication, and NGOs supporting access to information and communication.
>
> *(FMML, 2015, n.p.)*

The Charter also provides insights into the *worldview* – or worldview*s* – that signatories hold, and its construction can be viewed as a process of knowledge production about the FMML's vision. At a basic level, this worldview is succinctly expressed by the statement in one of its opening paragraphs: 'democratization and the right to communicate for all are essential if we are to build a just and sustainable world'. FMML participants share a broad vision of media democratization as essential to social justice and an understanding of media and communication as *political* issues. Beyond this broad general vision, however, the Charter is also evidence of processes of knowledge production that involve efforts to consolidate different visions. As Eyerman & Jamison (1991) pointed out, the development of a movement's cosmology always draws on the visions and knowledge of previous mobilizations, and this is also true in the case of the FMML. In a detailed analysis of the Charter (Stephansen, 2017), I have shown that this document is in fact a composite of different worldviews: the Charter brings together several different ways of framing free media, with different historical and political trajectories. These include a 'right to communicate' frame, which draws on human rights discourse and can be traced back to previous international mobilizations such as the Communication Rights in the Information Society (CRIS) campaign in the early 2000s and the NWICO debates in the 1970s and 1980s; frames that emphasize the media's role in supporting cultural diversity and intercultural dialogue, which can be linked to the WSF's ideals of horizontality and respect for epistemic plurality; and a social justice frame that locates media activism within broader struggles against colonialism, racism, sexism, and other forms of oppression (Stephansen, 2017). The development of the Charter has involved a process of knowledge production aimed at consolidating these different visions.

Discussion and conclusion

The value of the typology of social movement knowledge proposed here is that it offers analytical purchase on the range of knowledge practices involved in acting on media. While it is not a typology of *how* knowledge is produced, but rather a typology of different forms of knowledge, it provides a lens through which a range of seemingly disparate practices – organizing a seminar about media policy, working collaboratively to produce media content, negotiating a joint declaration, etc. – can be analysed as *knowledge practices*. A key argument in this chapter has been that such knowledge practices should be conceptualized as integral to media practices – especially those that involve thematizing and politicizing media – and that media practice researchers should make knowledge practices an explicit focus of their analysis. While much media practice research has focused on the habitual and unreflexive nature of everyday media use, citizen media practices often involve intentional efforts to effect change and, arguably, a greater degree of reflexive and analytical knowledge, as well as creativity. A focus on knowledge practices is therefore important for our broader understanding of agency in the context of citizen media.

By analysing knowledge practices in this way, media practice researchers will be better placed to address questions about how citizen media practices might contribute to social change. A common criticism of practice theory is that it is better at accounting for social reproduction than it is at explaining social change (Shove et al., 2012). If, as in some versions of practice theory, individuals are conceptualized as carriers of practices, and practices conceptualized as routinized forms of behaviour, how can we account for innovation? Part of the answer to this question lies in Shove et al.'s (2012, ch. 7) insight that '[p]ractices change when new elements are introduced or when existing elements are combined in new ways'. I would add that in order to understand how and why such instances of recombination occur, it is essential to understand the knowledge practices that underpin them. The literature on knowledge production in social movements suggests that we should look to media activists as sources of new ideas and innovation in media practices.

Taking social movements seriously as knowledge producers also involves rethinking hierarchies of academic knowledge production, which position movement activists and their media practices as objects of knowledge to be analysed by academic researchers. If we conceptualize media activists as reflexive and knowledgeable agents, academic researchers cannot claim to occupy a privileged vantage point for analysing their media practices. Instead, we need to develop our analyses in conversation with activists, treating them not just as sources of ethnographic data, but as interlocutors with a distinct contribution to make to our understanding of contemporary media practices. This involves developing an ethics of engagement and co-production of knowledge (Chesters, 2012) and opening up the canon of (Western) academic knowledge to the critical perspectives offered by movements of marginalized and oppressed groups (Cox, 2014).

A focus on knowledge practices has been introduced in this chapter to rectify the relative lack of attention to cognitive processes within the media practice literature – and practice theory more generally. While the ethnographic openness that results from asking what people *do* with media has produced important insights into the ways that citizens use media to organize, campaign, and gain visibility, my argument has been that it is important to also pay attention to the different forms of knowledge that underpin their media practices. As discussed above, such an understanding of knowledge as integral to agency does not necessitate a return to the mentalism and voluntarism that practice theory has sought to refute. By treating activities like theorizing, analysing, and reflecting about media as *practices*, rather than as subjective mental processes located in the minds of individuals, knowledge production can be situated decisively within the social realm as a material and embodied set of practices and subjected to empirical research. This is an important task for media practice scholars, working in collaboration with media activists.

Notes

1 The categories presented here are ideal types; different types of knowledge might overlap in practice. Nonetheless, they are useful for gaining analytical purchase on the range of

knowledge practices that take place among individuals and groups that are acting on media. My typology excludes the tacit knowledge that forms part of all social practice, as this is already accounted for by the notions of know-how and competence in practice theory.

2 See http://www.fmml.net. The empirical examples used here are drawn from a larger ethnographic study of media activism in the WSF, conducted between 2008 and 2018 (see Stephansen, 2013a, 2013b, 2016, 2017). During this period, I attended numerous social forums (including the WSF 2009 in Bélem, Brazil, the WSF 2011 in Dakar, Senegal, the WSF 2013 in Tunis, and the WSF 2018 in Salvador, Brazil – as well as several local, regional, and thematic social forums); conducted 100 in-depth interviews; and accompanied online organizing processes between forum events.

References

Baker, M., & Blaagaard, B. (2016). Reconceptualising citizen media: a preliminary charting of a complex domain. In M. Baker & B. Blaagaard (eds), *Citizen Media and Public Spaces: Diverse Expressions of Citizenship and Dissent* (pp. 1–22). London: Routledge.

Barassi, V. (2015). *Activism on the Web: Everyday Struggles against Digital Capitalism*. London: Routledge.

Barassi, V., & Treré, E. (2012). Does Web 3.0 come after Web 2.0? Deconstructing theoretical assumptions through practice. *New Media & Society*, 14(8), 1269–1285.

Barnes, B. (2001). Practice as collective action. In T. R. Schatzki, K. Knorr-Cetina, & E. von Savigny (eds), *The Practice Turn in Contemporary Theory* (pp. 25–36). London: Routledge.

Casas-Cortés, M. I., Osterweil, M., & Powell, D. E. (2008). Blurring boundaries: recognizing knowledge-practices in the study of social movements. *Anthropological Quarterly*, 81(1), 17–58.

Chesters, G. (2012). Social movements and the ethics of knowledge production. *Social Movement Studies*, 11(2), 145–160.

Couldry, N. (2004). Theorising media as practice. *Social Semiotics*, 14(2), 115–132.

Couldry, N. (2012). *Media, Society, World: Social Theory and Digital Media Practice*. Cambridge: Polity.

Couldry, N., & Hepp, A. (2017). *The Mediated Construction of Reality*. Cambridge: Polity.

Cox, L. (2014). Movements making knowledge: a new wave of inspiration for sociology? *Sociology*, 48(5), 954–971.

Esteves, A. M. (2008). Processes of knowledge production in social movements as multi-level power dynamics. *Sociology Compass*, 2(6), 1934–1953.

Eyerman, R., & Jamison, A. (1991). *Social Movements: A Cognitive Approach*. Cambridge: Polity.

FMML (2015). World Charter of Free Media. Forum Mondial des Médias Libres/World Forum of Free Media. Retrieved from http://www.fmml.net/spip.php?article146

Fotopoulou, A. (2017). *Feminist Activism and Digital Networks: Between Empowerment and Vulnerability*. Basingstoke: Palgrave Macmillan.

Hackett, R. A., & Carroll, W. K. (2006). *Remaking Media: The Struggle to Democratize Public Communication*. London: Routledge.

Juris, J. S. (2008). *Networking Futures: The Movements Against Corporate Globalization*. Durham, NC: Duke University Press.

Kannengießer, S. (2017). Repairing of media technologies as unconventional political participation. In C. Wallner, J. Wimmer, & K. Schultz (eds), *(Mis)Understanding Political Participation*. London: Routledge.

Kannengießer, S., & Kubitschko, S. (2017). Acting on media: influencing, shaping and (re) configuring the fabric of everyday life. *Media and Communication*, 5(3), 1–4.

Kavada, A. (2013). Internet cultures and protest movements: the cultural links between strategy, organizing and online communication. In Cammaerts, B., Mattoni, A., & McCurdy, P. (eds), *Mediation and Protest Movements*. London: Intellect, pp. 75–94.

Kubitschko, S. (2015). Hackers' media practices: demonstrating and articulating expertise as interlocking arrangements. *Convergence*, 21(3), 388–402.

Kubitschko, S. (2018). Acting on media technologies and infrastructures: expanding the media as practice approach. *Media, Culture & Society*, 40(4), 629–635.

Mattoni, A. (2012). *Media Practices and Protest Politics: How Precarious Workers Mobilise*. Abingdon: Taylor & Francis.

Mattoni, A. (2013). Repertoires of communication in social movement processes. In B. Cammaerts, A. Mattoni, & P. McCurdy (eds), *Mediation and Protest Movements* (pp. 39–56). Bristol: Intellect.

McCurdy, P. (2011). Theorizing 'lay theories of media': a case study of the Dissent! network at the 2005 Gleneagles G8 Summit. *International Journal of Communication*, 5, 619–638.

McCurdy, P. (2013). Mediation, practice and lay theories of media. In B. Cammaerts, A. Mattoni, & P. McCurdy (eds), *Mediation and Protest Movements* (pp. 57–74). Bristol: Intellect.

Melucci, A. (1996). *Challenging Codes: Collective Action in the Information Age*. Cambridge: Cambridge University Press.

Milan, S. (2013). *Social Movements and their Technologies: Wiring Social Change*. Basingstoke: Palgrave Macmillan.

Milan, S., & van der Velden, L. (2016). The alternative epistemologies of data activism. *Digital Culture & Society*, 2(2), 57–74.

della Porta, D., & Pavan, E. (2017). Repertoires of knowledge practices: social movements in times of crisis. *Qualitative Research in Organizations and Management*, 12(4), 297–314.

Reckwitz, A. (2002). Toward a theory of social practices: a development in culturalist theorizing. *European Journal of Social Theory*, 5(2), 243–263.

Schatzki, T. R. (2001). Introduction: practice theory. In T. R. Schatzki, K. Knorr Cetina, & E. von Savigny (eds), *The Practice Turn in Contemporary Theory* (pp. 1–14). London: Routledge.

Schmidt, R. (2016). Reflexive knowledge in practices. In A. Hui, T. Schatzki, & E. Shove (eds), *The Nexus of Practices: Connections, Constellations, Practitioners* (ch. 10). London: Routledge.

Shove, E., Pantzar, M., & Watson, M. (2012). *The Dynamics of Social Practice: Everyday Life and How it Changes*. London: Sage.

de Sousa Santos, B. (2006). *The Rise of the Global Left: The World Social Forum and Beyond*. London: Zed Books, pp. 13–34.

Spaargaren, G., Weenink, D., & Lamers, M. (2016). *Practice Theory and Research: Exploring the Dynamics of Social Life*. Abingdon: Taylor & Francis.

Stein, L., Kidd, D., & Rodríguez, C. (2009). *Making our Media: Global Initiatives toward a Democratic Public Sphere. Vol. 2: National and Global Movements for Democratic Communication*. Cresskill, NJ: Hampton Press.

Stephansen, H. C. (2013a). Connecting the peripheries: networks, place and scale in the World Social Forum process. *Journal of Postcolonial Writing*, 49(5), 506–518.

Stephansen, H. C. (2013b). Starting from the Amazon: communication, knowledge and politics of place in the World Social Forum. *Interface*, 5(1), 102–127.

Stephansen, H. C. (2016). Understanding citizen media as practice: agents, processes, publics. In M. Baker & B. Blaagaard (eds), *Citizen Media and Public Spaces: Diverse Expressions of Citizenship and Dissent* (pp. 25–41). London: Routledge.

Stephansen, H. C. (2017). Media activism as movement? Collective identity formation in the World Forum of Free Media. *Media and Communication*, 5(3), 59–66. doi:10.17645/mac.v5i3.1034

Treré, E. (2018). The sublime of digital activism: hybrid media ecologies and the new grammar of protest. *Journalism & Communication Monographs*, 20(2), 137–148.

Treré, E. (2019). *Hybrid Media Activism: Ecologies, Imaginaries, Algorithms*. London: Routledge

Treré, E., Jeppesen, S., & Mattoni, A. (2017). Comparing digital protest media imaginaries: anti-austerity movements in Spain, Italy & Greece. *triple C*, 15(2), 404–422.

Wolfson, T. (2014). *Digital Rebellion: The Birth of the Cyber Left*. Champaign, IL: University of Illinois Press.

PART V

Citizen data practices

INTRODUCTION

Helen Kennedy

It is now widely accepted that, as data gathering and tracking become increasingly ubiquitous, 'datafication' is transforming our social world. The quantification of aspects of life previously experienced in qualitative, non-numeric form, such as health and fitness, transport and mobility, democratic participation, leisure and consumption, and, important for this collection, media and communication practices, is having wide-ranging effects. These include alleged benefits, such as greater efficiencies in service provision, and also widespread harms, such as more surveillance, less privacy, and new forms of inequality and injustice. It is these harms that have been the focus of the emerging field of data studies (sometimes also called critical data studies, precisely because of the focus on harms). For example, surveillance is said to be much more ubiquitous, opaque, and speculative in datafied times, as social media and other kinds of data mining make it possible to surveil aspects of life once private and intimate (Andrejevic & Gates, 2014; Dencik & Cable, 2017) and thus deny people their basic right to privacy, itself a contested issue (Cohen, 2013). Another harm of datafication, it is argued, is that it reproduces old inequalities and creates new ones. One of boyd & Crawford's much-cited 'six provocations for big data' is that 'limited access to big data creates new digital divides' (2012, p. 673). Relatedly, and emerging from these debates, the discriminatory consequences of the rise of big data have also been noted. Data mining, analysis, and subsequent discrimination result in certain groups having better access to resources, it has been claimed (Andrejevic, 2013; Taylor & Richter, 2017; see Kennedy (2018) for a longer discussion).

Concern about these potential harms has led to measures to influence the governance of digital data mining and usage, such as the establishment of a Centre for Data Ethics and Innovation (CDEI) by the UK Government, the consultation document of which claims that understanding public views and acting upon them will be at the heart of its work. The mission of another body, the newly-formed

Ada Lovelace Institute, established by the Nuffield Foundation and partners, is to ensure 'that data and AI work for people and society' (Ada Lovelace Institute, 2019, n.p.). However, understanding of what is described here as 'public views' is somewhat limited. Not much is known about how data gathering, analysis and use, and increasingly everyday technologies like AI, are experienced and perceived by the people whose lives they affect. Things are slowly starting to change, as some scholars attempt to fill this gap. These include researchers investigating the datafication of health, such as Lupton (2018), Neff and Nafus (2016), Pink et al. (2017) and Ruckenstein (2016). There is also growing attention to users' responses to the data analytics that takes place on social media and other platforms, such as Bucher's (2017) small-scale project on algorithmic imaginaries, and the work of Kollyri & Milioni (2017) on attitudes to the gendering of algorithmic identity.

These examples notwithstanding, there is still something of an empirical gap in relation to *experiences* of datafication, and it is here that practice theory approaches can make a contribution. We might say that too much structure, not enough agency, has been the focus of data studies to date. The contributions gathered together in this section provide a welcome antidote to that trend, transcending 'dualisms of structure and agency' which Shove, Pantzar, & Watson (2012) argue is a defining characteristic of practice theory. In the first chapter in this section, Stefania Milan's discussion of data activism (Chapter 11) uses practice theory to highlight the human agency that activist practices necessarily involve. Aristea Fotopoulou characterizes everyday life data practices as both experiential and often embodied in Chapter 12, on citizen data practices, thus also mobilizing practice theory to foreground experience. In Chapter 13, on the use of social media intelligence (or socmint) in policing, Lina Dencik identifies how visions of datafication from above are 'decoupled' from the implementation of socmint 'on the ground' (citing Christin, 2017). In these ways, the authors mobilize practice theory to contribute much needed analyses of datafication 'from the bottom up' (Couldry & Powell, 2014), analyses which take account of both agency and experience.

Alongside these 'bottom-up' analyses of datafication that are beginning to emerge, there is also a growing recognition that research into the new roles played by data in society need to be grounded in specific material contexts, times, and places (Kennedy & Bates, 2017). This is because the material contexts in which datafication takes place, has effects, and is experienced are not all the same. This might seem an obvious point, but in a field that has been dominated by structural critique, it needs making. In particular, we need to attend to the specific ways in which already-disadvantaged populations are more likely than others to be discriminated against within data assemblages, as a number of writers have recently pointed out (such as Eubanks, 2018 and Noble, 2018). In other words, material implementations of datafication are shot through with specific, unequal power relations. Again, practice theory is useful for engaging with this fact. As Fotopoulou states in Chapter 12, developing the notion of data practice makes it possible to attend to such political issues as they pertain to big data and permeate the specificities of distinct everyday lives. Dencik, likewise, sees a practice theory approach as a way of connecting questions of agency with questions of political economy in the particular context of predictive policing, in order to understand the ways in which datafication contributes to new power relations in this specific context.

To sum up the argument thus far: increasingly, everything is datafied, understanding of how datafication is experienced is limited, and in researching data experiences, we need to attend to the distinct, power-laden, material contexts in which datafication unfolds, which are often shaped by social inequalities. In my own writing, I have turned to sociology and philosophy for the conceptual and methodological tools with which to do this. In writing about the emotional dimensions of everyday engagements with data and their visual representations, together with my co-author Rosemary L. Hill, we have built on the sociology of emotions to explore the epistemological value of feelings in knowing, deciding, engaging, and being with data (Kennedy & Hill, 2018). In this and in other work, I have also mobilized a sociology of everyday life approach to understand data experiences, conceiving of the everyday as contingent and situational and therefore of datafication as not simply constitutive of social life, but rather as 'made and unmade' (Neal & Murji 2015, p. 812) through everyday practices (Kennedy, 2018). I have considered how the capabilities approach advocated, for example, by philosophers Amartya Sen and Martha Nussbaum, might help us make sense of how people live, and how they might live better, with datafication (Nussbaum, 2006, 2011; Sen, 1973, 1992, 2009). I have also drawn on work within the philosophy of technology tradition (e.g. Feenberg, 1999) to explore whether technological ensembles of all kinds can be appropriated as tools of democratization, enablement, and action, despite their origins within the belly of the beast (Kennedy, 2016). Across all of this work, I have explored the agentic practices that constitute social life under the 'new data relations' that emerge in times of datafication (see Kennedy, 2016 for an elaboration of this concept).

A practice theory approach not only adds to this mix, it brings together these converging concerns – with the emotional, the everyday, and with agency. As Stephansen and Treré put it Chapter 1 of this volume, theorizing media as practice means attending to what people are 'doing in relation to media across a wide range of situations and contexts' (citing Couldry, 2012, p. 37). Today, media are data and media practices are data practices. Therefore, and as I hope is apparent in this short introduction, I think we need to attend to what people are doing in relation to *data* across a wide range of situations and contexts, to paraphrase Couldry. To take the parallel yet further, also drawing on Stephansen and Treré's use of Couldry in Chapter 1, we need to distinguish between 'acts aimed specifically at [data], acts performed through [data], and acts whose preconditions are [data]' (Couldry, 2012, p. 57; [media] replaced with [data] by me). Indeed, we might think of the three chapters in this section in these ways, with Milan's chapter on data activism focusing on acts aimed specifically at data; Fotopoulou's chapter on everyday data practices focusing on acts performed through data; and Dencik's chapter on the use of socmint in policing focusing on acts whose preconditions are data.

But we also need to move beyond a focus on what people are doing in relation to data in their everyday lives, because there is a pressing need for thinking about how the conditions of datafication could be improved. With research into data harms under way, it is now important to reflect on how datafied systems might operate in ways that are not harmful and oppressive, and that instead contribute to well-being and justice. This proposal is emerging in a broad range of fields. For example, David Lyons (2018), a founding figure in surveillance studies, spoke of the need to think about how we might arrive at human flourishing and the common good in a recent talk about user agency in dataveillance cultures. Data practitioners call for 'responsible data' practices (see for example Oxfam's Responsible Data guide), and the Data Justice Lab at the University of Cardiff, set up by Dencik and colleagues, would seem to be committed to just that – data justice. Furthermore, the Centre for Data Ethics and Innovation, the Ada Lovelace Institute, and other actors and activists all suggest, in various ways, that studies of data in society need to address the question of how data arrangements can be improved, as critical commentary on data harms suggests they need to be. Thinking about how data assemblages can be crafted in ways that are just, fair, good, ethical, or responsible means moving beyond existing data practices and imagining new and different ones. Whether practice theory, with its emphasis on the here-and-now, provides the tools to do this remains to be seen.

In the meantime, datafication continues apace. As Couldry & Mejias (2019) note, also using the concept of data relations, datafication is productive of a new social order. This new social order, they argue, is best understood through the concept of colonialism, given that new data relations normalize 'the exploitation of human beings through data, just as historic colonialism appropriated territory and resources and ruled subjects for profit' (Couldry & Mejias, 2019, p. 1). The models and concepts we use to think about citizen practices, whether these are data, media, or other practices, need to be able to take account of this reality.

References

Ada Lovelace Institute (2019). About. Retrieved from https://www.adalovelaceinstitute.org.

Andrejevic, M. (2013). *Infoglut: How Too Much Information is Changing the Way we Think and Know*. London: Routledge.

Andrejevic, M., & Gates, K. (2014). Big data surveillance: introduction. *Surveillance and Society*, 12(2), 185–196.

boyd, d., & Crawford, K. (2012). Critical questions for big data: provocations for a cultural, technological and scholarly phenomenon. *Information, Communication & Society*, 15(5), 662–679.

Bucher, T. (2017). The algorithmic imaginary: exploring the ordinary affects of Facebook algorithms. *Information, Communication & Society*, 20(1), 30–44.

Cohen, J. (2013). What is privacy for? *Harvard Law Review*, 126, 1904–1933. Retrieved from www.harvardlawreview.org/wp-content/uploads/pdfs/vol126_cohen.pdf. Couldry, N. (2004). Theorising media as practice. *Social Semiotics*, 14(2), 115–132.

Couldry, N. (2012). *Media, Society, World: Social Theory and Digital Media Practice*. Cambridge: Polity. Couldry, N., & Mejias, U. A. (2019). Data colonialism: rethinking big data's relation to the contemporary subject. *Television & New Media*, 20(4).

Couldry, N., & Powell, A. (2014). Big data from the bottom up. *Big Data and Society*, 1(1), 1–5.

Dencik, L., & Cable, J. (2017). The advent of surveillance realism: public opinion and activist responses to the Snowden leaks. *International Journal of Communication*, 11, 763–781.

Eubanks, V. (2018). *Automating Inequality: How High-Tech Tools Profile, Police and Punish the Poor*. New York: St Martins Press.

Feenberg, A. (1999). *Questioning Technology*. London: Routledge.

Kennedy, H. (2016). *Post, Mine, Repeat: Social Media Data Mining Becomes Ordinary*. Basingstoke: Palgrave.

Kennedy, H. (2018). Living with data: aligning data studies and data activism through a focus on everyday engagements with data. *Krisis: Journal for Contemporary Philosophy*, 1. Retrieved from http://krisis.eu/living-with-data/

Kennedy, H., & Bates, J. (2017). Data power in material contexts: Introduction. *Television & New Media*, 18(8).

Kennedy, H., & Hill, R. (2018). The feeling of numbers: emotions in everyday engagements with data and their visualisation. *Sociology*, 52(4).

Lupton, D. (2018). Lively data, social fitness and biovalue: the intersections of health self-tracking and social media. In J. Burgess, A. Marwick, & T. Poell (eds), *The Sage Handbook of Social Media*. London: Sage.

Lyons, D. (2018). Data and social transformations. Data Justice Conference, Data Justice Lab, Cardiff University, Cardiff, UK, May 2017.

Kollyri, L., & Milioni, D. (2017). 'fuck ur fucking gender construct!': The construction of algorithmic gender identity through users' narratives. Digital Democracy: Critical Perspectives in the Age of Big Data Conference, European Communication Research and Education Association (ECREA),Södertörn, Sweden, November 2017.

Neal, S., & Murji, K. (2015). Sociologies of everyday life: editors' introduction to the special issue. *Sociology*, 49(5), 811–819.

Neff, G., & Nafus, D. (2016). *Self-Tracking*. Cambridge, MA: MIT Press.

Nussbaum, M. (2006). *Frontiers of Justice*. Cambridge, MA: Harvard University Press.

Nussbaum, M. (2011). *Creating Capabilities*. Boston, MA: Harvard University Press.

Pink, S., Sumartojo, S., Lupton, D., & Heyes La Bond, C. (2017). Mundane data: the routines, contingencies and accomplishments of digital living. *Big Data and Society*, doi:10.1177/2053951717700924.

Ruckenstein, M. (2016). Keeping data alive: talking DTC genetic testing. *Information, Communication & Society*, 20(7), 1024–1039.

Sen, A. (1973). *On Economic Inequality* (expanded edition). Oxford and New York: Clarendon Press.

Sen, A. (1992). *Inequality Reexamined*. Oxford and New York: Clarendon Press.

Sen, A. (2009). *The Idea of Justice*. London: Penguin.

Shove, E. (2016). Matters of practice. In Hui, A., Schatzki, T., & Shove, E. (eds), *The Nexus of Practices: Connections, Constellations, Practitioners*. London: Routledge.

Shove, E., Pantzar, M., & Watson, M. (2012). *The Dynamics of Social Practice: Everyday Life and How it Changes*. London: Sage.

Taylor, L., & Richter, C. (2017). The power of smart solution: knowledge, citizenship and the datafication of Bangalore's water supply. *Television & New Media*, 18(8).

11

ACTING ON DATA(FICATION)

Stefania Milan

Introduction

The ongoing process of datafication turns numerous aspects of social life, such as emotions and relationships, into quantifiable and monetizable data points (Mayer-Schönberger & Cukier, 2013). It represents a fundamental paradigm shift in the way we organize societies and make sense of the world around us (Kitchin, 2014a). On one hand, it allows corporations to monetize social interactions and funnel social behaviour, while enabling state institutions to monitor and police citizens (c. f. Lyon, 2014). On the other hand, it encourages and empowers users to engage in innovative forms of civic engagement and political action that critically interrogate such a paradigm shift. These pioneering instances of collective action variably contesting and/or exploiting datafication are slowly changing the way we conceive of citizenship, participation, and civic life (Milan & van der Velden, 2016).

This chapter explores grassroots data politics seen as emerging 'data practices', defined as 'the open set of practices relating to, or oriented around' (Couldry, 2004, p. 117) data and the infrastructure supporting data production, consumption, and sharing (e.g. databases, collaborative data visualization software – henceforth, 'data infrastructure'). In particular, it opens up the emancipatory effects often associated with bottom-up data practices (Milan & Gutierrez, 2017), building on the notion of 'emancipatory communication practices' (Milan, 2013). To do so, the chapter promotes a dialogue between the sociology of social movements, media studies, and the emerging discipline of critical data studies – concerned with the study of datafication and its impact on culture and society (Kitchin & Lauriault, 2015b; Dalton, Taylor, & Thatcher, 2016) – on the assumption that only a cross-disciplinary perspective can produce a nuanced understanding of the situated uses of data and data infrastructure.

The chapter is organized as follows. First, it explores the notions of media practice (see, among others, Couldry, 2004, 2012; Lünenborg & Raetzsch, 2017) and of 'acting on' media and technology (Kubitschko, 2018) as they apply to the analysis of datafication. Secondly, it illustrates tactics, technical identities, and the relation between software and the prefigurative politics of 'data activists', in view of probing whether the focus on data and data infrastructure prompts us to rethink the notion of media practices. It then moves to analyse how we ought to adapt our understanding of media practice to capture contemporary changes in the nature of technology and information, broadening our understanding of 'acting on' datafication by grounding it on software and a novel understanding of information – both crucial to understanding today's engagement with media practice beyond data activism. It concludes by reflecting on the notion of 'data assemblages' (Kitchin & Lauriault, 2015b) as a fruitful addition to our interpretation of (media) practice in the age of datafication.

(Media) practice in times of datafication

'Practice' can be understood as 'a coherent set of activities that are commonly engaged in, and meaningful in particular ways, among people familiar with a certain culture', and it includes 'thinking and talking about those activities in particular ways' (Craig, 2006, p. 38). Media practices, more specifically, embrace the 'complex and socially situated "pattern" of acting with media' (Couldry, 2012, p. 34), including both routine and self-reflexive activities (Couldry, 2004, p. 117). The concept weaves together the material and the symbolic dimensions (Couldry & Hepp, 2017), and allows us to include in the analysis 'interactions with both media objects […] and media subjects' (Mattoni, 2012, p. 159). Within contemporary social movements, media practices emerge when media technologies are 'appropriated and transformed by activists' (Kubitschko, 2018). In the context of this chapter, the notion of practice refers to what people do with data and data infrastructure, and what in turn these do to them – or 'data practice'.

To be sure, datafication, with its corollary of mass surveillance and citizen policing (Haggerty & Ericson, 2000; Andrejevic, 2012; Murakami Wood, 2013; Treré, 2016; Dencik, Hintz, & Carey, 2017) but also empowerment and appropriation (Couldry & Powell, 2014; Baack, 2015, 2018; Schrock, 2016; Kennedy, 2018; Gutierrez, 2018), yields itself to be approached through the conceptual lenses of (media) practice. A practice-oriented approach allows us to 'capture and analyse quotidian routines of' datafication 'in their relevance for the emergence of publics' (Lünenborg & Raetzsch, 2017, p. 23; see also Stephansen, 2016). If, as Lünenborg and Raetzsch argue, publics are brought into existence by the very same practices they engage in, a practice-oriented analysis brings into focus the *datafied subject and its making*, observing such a datafied subject not as a given, but in a dynamic fashion able to bring agency back (cf. Kennedy, Poell, & van Dijck, 2015). The spotlight is thus simultaneously on human subjects *and* their (critical) engagement with datafication – with its repercussions in terms of mobilization dynamics and novel publics.

A practice-oriented approach alone, however, is not able to fully account for those activities that, for example, explicitly include a critique *of* technology. To this end, Kubitschko's invitation to pay attention to how social actors engage in 'acting on' rather than merely 'by means of' digital technology is particularly valuable, for it reveals political engagement that has technology at its core (Kubitschko, 2018; see also Kannengießer & Kubitschko, 2018). Specifically, it sheds light on the 'efforts of a wide range of actors belonging to different fields to take an active part in the moulding of the media technologies and infrastructures that have become part of the fabric of everyday life' (Kubitschko, 2018, p. 633).

People who 'act on' datafication question the social life of data, including its production and mobilization by institutions such as states and corporations. Kubitschko rightly argues that 'looking beyond what actors *do with media* and including why and how they *act on media* allows for more adequate recognition of power structures as it emphasises and at the same time scrutinises the role of actors' practices in contemporary media environments' (2018, p. 634, original emphasis). In this respect, his notion resonates with my earlier work on 'emancipatory communication practices' as forms of hands-on, radical engagement with technology infrastructure such as internet servers and radio transmitters, which signal that 'media and communication technologies have become a site of struggle in their own right' (Milan, 2013, p. 2). Recognizing the deeply political nature of technological artefacts (Winner, 1999) and inviting us to consider at once the 'technological' and the 'social' of infrastructure (cf. Bijker & Law, 1992), the notion of emancipatory communication practices foregrounds *the politics of technology* as well as how people make sense of and act upon it. It also gives prominence to the self-determination and autonomy ethos of practitioners questioning and engaging with the materiality of infrastructure, in view of seeking ways out of the determinism of the commercial grid. In particular, emancipatory communication practices promote 'reform from below of the current communication system' (Milan, 2013, p. 2); their 'liberated technologies' (Milan, 2016) extend 'also to non-experts the possibility of controlling communicative actions and bypassing commercial platforms' (Milan, 2013, p. 2). In the words of a practitioner, the imperative is 'by-pass[ing] the mainstream by creating living alternatives to it. [...] we have "to do", "keep doing" and keep building working structures and alternatives that are diametrically opposed to the ways capitalism forces us to function in our everyday lives' (p. 130). But what does 'acting on' data with emancipatory goals mean in practice?

Experiences and features of grassroots data practices

Maria, a mother of two in the rural area of Magdalena Medio (Colombia), decided to fight the looming environmental degradation of her region by gathering and visualizing detailed histories and geographies of the area surrounding the Magdalena River. Rich in natural resources and until recently subject to widespread political violence, the region is called home by a number of communities living primarily from subsistence farming and fishing. Over the decades, the aggressive exploitation by the extractive industry and the poor accountability of local authorities have resulted in dramatic alternations of the river basin and the ecosystem of the neighbouring *ciénagas* (marshlands). Maria realized that local administrations relied on outdated satellite maps unable to account diachronically for the impact of policies on communities. But advocates needed new, different maps. In a series of workshops, Maria and the local fishermen documented ecosystem alterations and generated maps on sheets of paper, which were then transposed to large canvases by Maria and her two teenage children. The production and visualization of 'small data' (Kitchin & Lauriault, 2015a) and 'actionable data' (Jasanoff, 2017) served the local community as an advocacy tool to demand better policies.[1] Adopting a similar tactic in a radically distinct sociocultural context, the technologists of the Syrian Archive (syrianarchive.org) leverage the 'big data' of social media user-generated content to document and preserve visual evidence of human rights violations in the Syrian conflict, for advocacy, reporting, and accountability purposes. The collective develops open-source machine learning techniques typical of 'open source intelligence', also adopted by law enforcement (see Kazansky et al., 2019).

But individuals and groups also mobilize to resist the expansion of a 'computational politics' characterized by 'individualized targeting, the opacity and power of computational modeling (…) and the growth of new power brokers who own the data' (Tufekci, 2013). To name but one, the global CryptoParty network seeks to 'pass on knowledge about protecting yourself in the digital space'. Asking 'party-goers' to 'bring your laptop or smartphone', CryptoParty organizers hold workshops to teach non-experts 'encrypted communication, preventing being tracked while browsing the web, and general security advice regarding computers and smartphones' (CryptoParty, n.d.). CryptoParties have been equaled to 'Tupperware parties for learning crypto' (Doctorow, 2012) because they replicate the knowledge-sharing dynamics of housewives' home-shopping gatherings. Also using software to empower people, the nongovernmental organization Guardian Project has developed a phone app that strengthens verification of citizen-generated data around conflicts: InformaCam allows individuals and groups gathering visual clues about human rights violations to use the footage in the court of law (Holmes, 2012).

These disparate cases illustrate the diversity of projects and tools 'acting on' datafication today and centring the politics of data and data infrastructure in activism and advocacy efforts. They are examples of social mobilizations taking a critical approach towards datafication and/or massive data collection – an emerging form of collective action going under the name of 'data activism' (Milan, 2014). In its crudest form, 'data' indicates information, which is today increasingly quantified, processed through computational means, and transmuted into value.[2] Data does not necessarily equal 'big', digitized datasets: as the Colombian case shows, data activism is often a matter of 'small data' or 'good enough data' (Gabrys, Pritchard, & Barratt, 2016, p. 12).

From a media studies perspective, data activism can be included in the broader category of citizen media, of which it represents an evolution (Milan, 2019).

Citizen media are defined as 'the physical artefacts, digital content, practices, performative interventions and discursive formations of affective sociality produced by unaffiliated citizens as they act in public space(s) to effect aesthetic or socio-political change or express personal desires and aspirations' (Baker & Blaagaard, 2016, p. 16). Not unlike other, earlier recorded forms of citizens' media (Rodriguez, 2001), data activism helps in *making spaces* for individuals and groups to enact their democratic agency beyond traditional means of civic participation such as voting. As such, it contributes 'values and agendas' to the 'creation of diverse publics' (Baker & Blaagaard, 2016, p. 16), which come to constitute 'spaces of political and pedagogic *practice*' (Stephansen, 2016, p. 37; original emphasis). In its most uncompromising manifestations, data activism can be assimilated to radical media practices, whose activists 'express an alternative vision to hegemonic politics, priorities, and perspectives'; their tactics might as well occasionally 'break[ing] somebody's rules, although rarely all of them in every aspect' (Downing, 2001, pp. v–ix). Data activism signals the need to think of liberation as an everyday process that disrupts immediate realities (Downing, 1984), where both the narratives associated with datafication and the dynamics of datafication *per se* are to be disrupted.

Sociologically speaking, data activism identifies an emerging, composite, collective identity increasingly shared by a number of individuals and groups (Gutierrez, 2018). All in all, this resembles a 'technical identity' associated with earlier forms of citizen media, such as radio broadcasting: emerging in interaction with engagement with infrastructure and 'technical' activities like soldering and software development, it 'marks the boundaries' between data activists and other groups (Dunbar-Hester, 2012, p. 149). In this respect, data activism can be understood as an 'emergent movement praxis' (Hackett & Carroll, 2006, p. 84). Within the contemporary social movement ecology, it represents the newest manifestation of media activism, in that it appropriates information – in its newest forms and formats – *and technological innovation* to achieve political goals such as social change (Milan, 2017). Reminiscent of the media activism of the turn of the century, seizing the nascent digital technology to give voice to the streets and bypass mainstream media (Meikle, 2002; van de Donk et al., 2003), data activism seeks to uncover stories of injustice or change. It, too, emerges from the fringes of contemporary mobilizations, and 'taps on the broker and sense-making role of a relatively small group of tech-savvy activists' (Milan, 2017, p. 152). It exercises self-determination in the datafied society, embracing the do-it-yourself and hands-on approach typical of emancipatory communication practices. Its novelty, however, is to be found in its ability to speak to the general public, rapidly spreading to ordinary users, thanks to novel software that also enables non-experts to engage in data analysis and obfuscation activities. Similarly to the media democracy movement of the early 2000s, rather than coalescing as a movement in its own, data activism is 'more about constructing a "politics of connections" than it is about constructing its own composite action system' (Carroll & Hackett, 2006, p. 93). Its activists 'spread across the field of movement politics, thriving in the empty spaces "in between"', and contributing to 'strengthen the counterhegemonic capacity' of present-day mobilizations (Hackett & Carroll, 2006, p. 189).

Tactics of data activism are variably positioned and dynamically moving along a continuum where projects, events, software tools, and people are variably positioned. At the opposite ends of this continuum are two ideal-types, which help guide our understanding of datafication 'from the bottom up' (cf. Couldry & Powell, 2014). At one end of the spectrum is what we may call 'reactive data activism', embracing initiatives oriented to resist – usually by means of technical fixes – the threats derived from government and corporate snooping. Examples include the development and use of encryption (Gürses, Kundnani, & van Hoboken, 2016); the organization of security training for human rights defenders (Kazansky, 2016); projects oriented to reinstate 'data justice' and fight algorithmic discrimination (Dencik, Hintz, & Cable, 2016); or promoting obfuscation in data collection techniques (Brunton & Nissenbaum, 2015). At the opposite end of the spectrum we find instead 'proactive data activism', whereby people seek to take advantage of the possibilities for civic engagement, advocacy, and campaigning that the datafication of social life might offer. Examples include open data-related initiatives (Schrock, 2016); the development of 'civic technologies' to tackle governance shortcomings (Russon Gilman, 2016); crowdsourced mapping exercises (Gutierrez, 2018); as well as the incorporation of data visualization techniques in advocacy efforts (Tactical Tech Collective, 2013). The reactive and proactive ideal-types identify two facets of the same phenomenon: both take information as a constitutive force in society capable to shape social reality (cf. Braman, 2009), questioning and/or seeking to subvert the mainstream 'politics of representing events in the world in the form of data points, data sets, or data associations' (Jasanoff, 2017, p. 1). Most importantly, they are typically (but not exclusively) *enabled (and constrained) by software* – or the lack thereof – which is at the core of data activism and its tension towards prefigurative politics. Using software to increasingly involve average users, proactive and reactive data activism signals a fundamental change in perspective and attitude towards 'big data' emerging within the organized civil society, increasingly engaged in 'acting on' datafication rather than merely enduring its consequences.

With information, but also software and software development, being so central to grassroots data practices, one might ask what datafication, and data activism in tow, add to our understanding of (media) practices.

What is new in (data) practices?

Taking a practice perspective to understand how people engage politically with – or 'act on' – datafication forces us to perform two operations, which, I argue, are also of central relevance to understand citizen media *practices* today (Stephansen, 2016). The first operation concerns our understanding of information, which is at the heart of data activism, but also of citizen media practices more generally. However, the 'classical' definitions of citizen media (Rodriguez, 2001, 2011;

Downing, 1984, 2001; Baker & Blaagaard, 2016; and to some extent Gordon & Mihailidis, 2016) tend to underscore the role *and nature* of the information conveyed by citizen media, paying attention almost exclusively to the discursive dimension. According to Baker and Blaagaard, media are 'endowed with expressive power by human agents and used to communicate information as well as emotions, values, narratives' (2016, p. 15) but 'information' is not further examined. However, information today *takes different forms and formats* – including 'small' and 'big' data in the shape of numbers, percentages, maps, infographics – and these mould discourses, publics, and practices in completely novel ways. In other words, if the nature of information changes – and, most fundamentally, our ways of relating to it and creating publics around and through it evolve – probably our understanding of (media) practices should change, too.

I argue that to be able to understand what people do with data(fication), we ought understand information, and data, *as a technology in itself*. To understand this claim, I mobilize the etymology of the noun, namely its ancient Greek antecedent *techné*. Rather than merely designating machinery and tools as the contemporary use usually suggests, *techné* indicates the 'human ability to make and perform [...] as interpretation' (Shiner, 2001, pp. 19–20), or the craft or 'making' that art and engineering have in common (Braman, 2004, p. 4). In other words, *techné* captures the realm of 'embodied knowledge' (Sterne, 2006, p. 92), allowing us to take into account that data are not neutral (Dalton & Thatcher, 2014; see also Gitelman, 2013), nor are their infrastructure, formats, uses, and applications.

If information is embodied knowledge, there is a second move we ought to make. This concerns the role of software. The 'tech factor' is central in grassroots data politics and, I contend, is increasingly important in citizen media practices as well. Practitioners operate in an extremely commercialized ecosystem monopolized by a handful of corporations including Google and Facebook – the 'monopolists of mind' (Foer, 2017) – which dramatically alter the 'discursive terrain in which meaning contests occur' (Snow, 2004, p. 405). These leave little space for actual autonomous action of the type evoked by emancipatory communication practices and most citizen media initiatives. Digital life is mediated by proprietary algorithms whose 'machine logic' (Powles, 2016) is not accessible nor transparent, let alone accountable, to final users (Pasquale, 2015). Furthermore, digital technologies – think of social media platforms – are the product of particular value systems and tend to perpetuate the power structure within which they are developed (Feenberg, 2002). They must be seen 'as techno-cultural constructs and as organized socioeconomic structures' (van Dijck, 2013, p. 25), rather than as neutral 'pipes' conveying information.

Not surprisingly, software also mediates today's grassroots data practices, enabling activists to make sense of large quantities of data, or to protect themselves from government and corporate snooping. The critique of commercial software and the collaborative development of open-source alternatives are taken very seriously by these communities, in recognition of the fact that, in a society highly reliant on algorithms, code 'pervade[s] and format[s] our action' (Berardi, in Cox, 2013, p. ix). By developing software tools to resist massive data collection or engage creatively with 'small' and 'big' data, data activists take software as 'line of escape from the determinism of code' itself (Cox, 2013, p. x). Software becomes then a crucial symbol of, and tool in, the struggle for emancipation from the grinder of datafication, and a step towards the creation 'here and now' of 'data justice' (Dencik et al., 2016). Event series such as the Internet Freedom Festival in Valencia, Spain (internetfreedomfestival.org), and funding entities such as the Berlin-based nonprofit Center for the Cultivation of Technology (techcultivation.org), are exactly built around this idea.

As a result scholars, too, should acknowledge that in the citizen media equation, *information and software are no longer inconsequential variables*. The increased attention to the critique of commercial infrastructure and to the development of 'activist' alternatives forces us to also include software in our analyses. This means paying adequate attention to the politics (Gillespie, 2010) and the political economy of infrastructure (Mosco, 2009, 2014), investigating, for example, the 'object conflicts' that influence the decisions of developers in matter of design and usability (Hess, 2005, p. 516), as they largely set the boundaries for data and citizen media activism alike.

Assemblages as complementary to practices

The scenario described above prompts us to rethink our notion of (media) practice. Invitations to give careful consideration to the 'material, embodied and social aspects of processes of public-formation' (Stephansen, 2016, p. 38) are not new. But public formation has been profoundly altered by datafication, as many have argued (Marres, 2012; Papacharissi, Hunsinger, & Selft, 2014; Isin & Ruppert, 2015; Milan, 2018). And looking at grassroots data practices urges to take a couple of additional conceptual steps forward. I argue that we need to broaden our understanding of media practice by connecting and grounding it on software, and by giving careful attention to the contemporary ontologies of information and their evolution. The notion of (data) assemblage might be of help here. Data assemblages are 'complex socio-technical systems' encompassing 'all of the technological, political, social and economic apparatuses and elements that constitutes and frames the generation, circulation and deployment of data' (Kitchin & Lauriault, 2015b, p. 1). Furthermore, '[d]ata and their assemblage are mutually constituted, bound together in a set of contingent, relational and contextual discursive and material practices and relations' (2015b, p. 7).

The notion of (data) assemblages helps us to give adequate consideration to the materiality of both information and infrastructure as they mediate our actions and interactions (Gillespie, 2010; Bucher & Helmond, 2017). It is a reminder of the need to understand digital artifacts by looking at the whole 'supply chain', from the creator to the user experience, incorporating both machine and non-human agency. Elements to be considered include, for example, the systems of thought and forms of knowledge, historical conditions, business models, governmentalities, practices, subjectivities, and communities associated with (media) practice today (Kitchin, 2014b).

Looking at (data) assemblages allows us to safeguard the emphasis on the socio-logical processes at the core of 'acting on' and citizen media practices more gen-erally, while at the same time teasing out the complex relationships that move beyond the mere bi-directional relations between people and technology. It com-plexifies and 'thickens' our understanding of the 'material, embodied and social aspects' (Stephansen, 2016, p. 38), opening up fruitful new directions of inquiry. It contributes a sensibility towards the ontologies of information and infrastructure, analysing the evolution of our systems of knowing and its consequences on the practitioners' epistemologies (Milan & van der Velden, 2016). It allows us to cap-ture the magmatic and ever-changing nature of the complex media- and data-scapes in which practitioners operate today, disallowing the pervasive temptation to ignore the fabrics of technology and information.

In conclusion

This chapter has explored critical data practices emerging at the grassroots level, combining inputs from citizen media analysis, the sociology of social movements, and critical data studies. Taking inspiration from the works of Couldry (2004, 2012), Lünenborg and Raetzsch (2017), and Stephansen (2016), it builds on notions of 'acting upon' (Kubitschko, 2018) and 'emancipatory communication practices' (Milan, 2013) to emphasize both the political nature and the emancipa-tory ethos of bottom-up involvement with information and infrastructure. It asks how datafication alters the dynamics as well as our understanding of (media) prac-tice(s), and what this can this teach us in relation to citizen media today.

In order to do so, the chapter explored contemporary forms of data activism, including forms of affirmative engagement with data such as open data activism and data-based advocacy, as well as resistance and subversion of massive data collection by means of encryption and obfuscation. We noticed how grassroots data practices tend to be rooted in software and in an understanding of information as con-tinuously evolving and embedded in complex, highly political systems shaping activists' actions. We have seen how the changing nature of information and the centrality of software encourage us to rethink the notion of (citizen) media prac-tice, wiring into it a more nuanced understanding of the dynamics associated with the ontologies of information and infrastructure.

The notion of (data) assemblage – although in itself rather fuzzy – might prove useful to overcome the potential blind spots of the notion of media practice. It offers a way forward to tease out the growing *complexity* of the landscape that citi-zen media practitioners inhabit today, and the dynamic relations between its different parts. This shift in the research agenda is, I argue, particularly urgent: not only is the nature of information and infrastructure changing; so is the ubiquity of the phenomena people are constantly invited (or forced) to interact with. We can safely argue that datafication by nature is far more pervasive and surreptitious in its mechanisms than what we have known historically as 'media'. Observers have gone as far as announcing the advent of a specific logic of capitalist accumulation termed 'surveillance capitalism' (Zuboff, 2015), an extractive variant of information capitalism made possible by 'a distributed and largely uncontested new expression of power [...] constituted by unexpected and often illegible mechanisms of extraction, commodification, and control that effectively exile persons from their own behavior while producing new markets of behavioral prediction and modification' (2015, p 75). Others have announced the rise of data colonialism, a 'new social order, based on continuous tracking, and offering unprecedented new opportunities for social discrimination and behavioral influence' and promoting 'the capitalization of life without limits' (Couldry & Mejias, 2019, p. 1). No matter what one wants to call the complex set of socio-technical and cultural-economical phenomena at hand, they have a dramatic effect on citizens' agency, and on people's ability to act meaningfully in the world. To be sure, the notion of assemblages is merely an invitation to consider the (much more) complex socio-technical systems enabling and constituting datafication, and the changing fabrics of information and the digital. It is certainly evocative, yet more work is needed in order to make from the notion of assemblage a research programme able to contribute fruitfully to the 'strong programme' within the 'practice turn' in the analysis of citizen media (see Chapter 1 in this volume).

Finally, if we are to consider the 'multiple articulations with media in everyday life' (Bird, 2010, p. 85) in the era of datafication, we might want to explore new epistemological and methodological venues for our work. Epistemologically, it makes little sense to talk about solid borders between disciplines: to understand datafication and its consequences for today's citizens and social movements, we ought to dialogue with fields of inquiry as diverse as science and technology studies, political economy, law, and informatics – to name but a few. As far as research methods are concerned, we might want to consider expanding our methodological toolbox. Studies on citizen media practices have been, for the most part, qualitative in nature and have often adopted ethnographic or quasi-ethnographic approaches able to tease out the complexity of contextual and motivational factors. While this line of work probably remains the most fruitful, it might be integrated with computational methods able to shed light on, for example, software-mediated dynamics (such as interactions on platforms), which lend themselves to be investigated in an automatized fashion. Computational methods may also complement qualitative fieldwork by bringing to our attention those routinized performances that escape human awareness – think for instance of the 'hidden' influence of personalization algorithms on social media platforms. It is only by taking these challenges seriously that we might be able to do justice to the media practice paradigm in the age of datafication, and make the best of the prospects it has to offer. 'Acting on' datafication, after all, will only get more intricate – and more urgent – with artificial intelligence increasingly oiling the cogs of social life.

Notes

1 Author's fieldnotes, Barranca, Colombia, July 2017.
2 Together with Mayer-Schönberger & Cukier, I define (big) data as 'things that one can do at a large scale, that cannot be done at a smaller scale, to extract new insights or create new forms of value, in ways that change markets, organizations, the relationship between citizens and governments, and more' (2013, p. 6). Rather than focusing on magnitude, this definition emphasizes the transformative potential of data and the role of human agency.

Acknowledgement

This research has received funding from the European Research Council (ERC) under the European Union's Horizon 2020 research and innovation program (grant agreement No 639379-DATACTIVE and grant agreement No. 825974-ALEX).

References

Andrejevic, M. (2012). Ubiquitous surveillance. In D. Lyon, K. D. Haggerty, & K. S. Ball (eds), *Routledge Handbook of Surveillance Studies*. New York and London: Routledge.

Baack, S. (2015). Datafication and empowerment: how the open data movement re-articulates notion of democracy, participation, and journalism. *Big Data & Society*, July–December, 1–11. doi:10.1177/2053951715594634

Baack, S. (2018). Civic tech at mysociety: how the imagined affordances of data shape data activism. *Krisis: Journal for Contemporary Philosophy*, 1. Retrieved from http://krisis.eu/civic-tech-at-mysociety-how-the-imagined-affordances-of-data-shape-data-activism/

Baker, M., & Blaagaard, B. B. (2016). Reconceptualizing citizen media. In M. Baker & B. B. Blaagaard (eds), *Citizen Media and Public Spaces. Diverse Expressions of Citizenship and Dissent* (pp. 1–24). Abingdon and New York: Routledge.

Bijker, W. E., & Law, J. (1992). *Shaping Technology/Building Society. Studies in Sociotechnical Change*. Cambridge, MA and London: MIT Press.

Bird, S. E. (2010). From fan practice to mediated moments: the value of practice theory in the understanding of media audiences. In B. Bräuchler & J. Postill (eds), *Theorising Media and Practice* (pp. 85–104). New York and Oxford: Berghahn Books.

Braman, S. (2004). The meta-technologies of information. In S. Braman (ed.), *Biotechnology and Communication: The Meta-Technologies of Information* (pp. 3–36). Mahwah, NJ: Lawrence Erlbaum Associates.

Braman, S. (2009). *Change of State: Information, Policy, and Power*. Cambridge, MA: MIT Press.

Brunton, F., & Nissenbaum, H. (2015). *Obfuscation: A User's Guide for Privacy and Protest*. Cambridge: MIT Press.

Bucher, T., & Helmond, A. (2017). The affordances of social media platforms. In J. Burgess, T. Poell, & A. Marwick (eds), *The Sage Handbook of Social Media*. London and New York: Sage.

Carroll, W. K., & Hackett, R. A. (2006). Democratic media activism through the lens of social movement theory. *Media, Culture & Society*, 28(1), 83–104.

Couldry, N. (2004). Theorising media as practice. *Social Semiotics*, 14(2), 115–132.

Couldry, N. (2012). *Media, Society, World: Social Theory and Digital Media Practice*. Malden, MA: Polity.

Couldry, N., & Hepp, A. (2017). *The Mediated Construction of Reality*. Cambridge: Polity.

Couldry, N., & Mejias, U. A. (2019). Data colonialism: rethinking big data's relation to the contemporary subject. *Television & New Media*, 20(4).

Couldry, N., & Powell, A. (2014). Big data from the bottom up. *Big Data & Society*, 1(2), 1–5.

Cox, G. (2013). *Speaking Code. Coding as Aesthetic and Political Expression.* Cambridge, MA and London: MIT Press.

Craig, R. T. (2006). Communication as a practice. In G. J. Shepherd & J. St John (eds), *Communication As ...: Perspectives on Theory* (pp. 38–47). Thousand Oaks, CA: Sage.

CryptoParty (n.d.). About. Retrieved from https://www.cryptoparty.in

Dalton, C. M., & Thatcher, J. (2014). What does a critical data studies look like, and why do we care? *Society & Space*, 12 May. Retrieved from http://societyandspace.org/2014/05/12/what-does-a-critical-data-studies-look-like-and-why-do-we-care-craig-dalton-and-jim-thatcher/

Dalton, C. M., Taylor, L., & Thatcher, J. (2016). Critical data studies: a dialog on data and space. *Big Data & Society*, 3(1), 1–9. doi:10.1177/2053951716648346

Dencik, L., Hintz, A., & Cable, J. (2016). Towards data justice? The ambiguity of anti-surveillance resistance in political activism. *Big Data & Society*, 3(2), 1–12. doi:10.1177/2053951716679678

Dencik, L., Hintz, A., & Carey, Z. (2017). Prediction, pre-emption and limits to dissent: Social media and big data uses for policing protests in the United Kingdom. *New Media & Society*, 20(4), 1433–1450. doi:10.1177/1461444817697722

van Dijck, J. (2013). *The Culture of Connectivity: A Critical History of Social Media.* Oxford: Oxford University Press.

van de Donk, W., Loader, B. D., Nixon, P. G., & Rucht, D. (eds). (2003). *Cyberprotest: New Media, Citizens and Social Movements.* London: Routledge.

Doctorow, C. (2012, October 12). CryptoParty: like a Tupperware party for learning crypto. Retrieved from http://boingboing.net/2012/10/12/cryptoparty-like-a-tupperware.html

Downing, J. D. H. (1984). *Radical Media: The Political Experience of Alternative Communication.* Boston, MA: South End Press.

Downing, J. D. H. (2001). *Radical Media. Rebellious Communication and Social Movements.* Thousand Oaks, CA: Sage.

Dunbar-Hester, C. (2012). Soldering toward media democracy technical practice as symbolic value in radio activism. *Journal of Communication Inquiry*, 36(2), 149–169.

Feenberg, A. (2002). *Transforming Technology: A Critical Theory Revisited.* New York: Oxford University Press.

Foer, F. (2017). *World Without Mind: The Existential Threat of Big Tech.* New York: Penguin.

Gabrys, J., Pritchard, H., & Barratt, B. (2016). Just good enough data: figuring data citizenships through air pollution sensing and data stories. *Big Data & Society*, 1(14). doi:10.1177/2053951716679677

Gillespie, T. (2010). The politics of platforms. *New Media & Society*, 12(3), 347–364.

Gitelman, L. (2013). *Raw Data is an Oxymoron.* Cambridge, MA: MIT Press.

Gordon, E., & Mihailidis, P. (eds). (2016). *Civic Media: Technology, Design, Practice.* Cambridge, MA: MIT Press.

Gürses, S., Kundnani, A., & van Hoboken, J. (2016). Crypto and empire: the contradictions of counter-surveillance advocacy. *Media, Culture & Society*, 38(4), 576–590.

Gutierrez, M. (2018). *Data Activism and Social Change.* Cham: Palgrave Macmillan.

Hackett, R. A., & Carroll, W. K. (2006). *Remaking Media: The Struggle to Democratize Public Communication.* New York and London: Routledge.

Haggerty, K. D., & Ericson, R. V. (2000). The surveillance assemblage. *British Journal of Sociology*, 51(4), 605–622.

Hess, D. J. (2005). Technology- and product-oriented movements: approximating social movement studies and science and technology studies. *Science, Technology & Human Values*, 30(4), 515–535.

Holmes, H. (2012). Introducing InformaCam. *Guardian Project*, 20 January. Retrieved from https://guardianproject.info/2012/01/20/introducing-informacam/

Isin, E., & Ruppert, E. (2015). *Becoming Digital Citizens*. Lanham, MD: Rowman & Littlefield.

Jasanoff, S. (2017). Virtual, visible, and actionable: data assemblages and the sightlines of justice. *Big Data & Society*, 4(2). doi:10.1177/2053951717724477

Kannengießer, S., & Kubitschko, S. (2017). Acting on media: influencing, shaping and (re) configuring the fabric of everyday life. *Media and Communication*, 5(3), 1–4. doi:10.17645/mac.v5i3.1165

Kazansky, B. (2016). *Digital Security in Context: Learning How Human Rights Defenders Adopt Digital Security Practices*. Berlin: Tactical Technology Collective. Retrieved from https://secresearch.tacticaltech.org/media/pages/pdfs/original/DigitalSecurityInContext.pdf?1459444650

Kazansky, B., Torres, G., van der Velden, L., Wissenbach, K. R., & Milan, S. (2019). Data for the social good: toward a data-activist research agenda. In A. Daly & M. Mann (eds), *Good Data* (pp. 244–259). Amsterdam: Institute of Network Cultures.

Kennedy, H. (2018). Living with data: aligning data studies and data activism through a focus on everyday experiences of datafication. *Krisis: Journal for Contemporary Philosophy*, 1. Retrieved from http://krisis.eu/living-with-data/

Kennedy, H., Poell, T., & van Dijck, J. (2015). Data and agency. *Big Data & Society*, 2(2). doi:10.1177/2053951715621569

Kitchin, R. (2014a). Big Data, new epistemologies and paradigm shifts. *Big Data & Society*, 1(1). doi:10.1177/2053951714528481

Kitchin, R. (2014b). *The Data Revolution: Big Data, Open Data, Data Infrastructures and their Consequences*. London: Sage.

Kitchin, R., & Lauriault, T. (2015a). Small data in the era of big data. *GeoJournal*, 80(4), 463–475.

Kitchin, R., & Lauriault, T. (2015b). Towards critical data studies: charting and unpacking data assemblages and their work. The Programmable City Working Paper 2. Retrieved from https://papers.ssrn.com/sol3/papers.cfm?abstract_id=2474112

Kubitschko, S. (2018). Acting on media technologies and infrastructures: expanding the media as practice approach. *Media, Culture & Society*, 40(4), 629–635.

Lünenborg, M., & Raetzsch, C. (2017). From public sphere to performative publics: developing media practice as an analytic model. In *Media Practices, Social Movements, and Performativity: Transdisciplinary Approaches* (pp. 13–35). London: Routledge.

Lyon, D. (2014). Surveillance, Snowden, and Big Data: capacities, consequences, critique. *Big Data & Society*, 1(2). doi:10.1177/2053951714541861

Marres, N. (2012). *Material Participation. Technology, the Environment and Everyday Publics*. Basingstoke, UK: Palgrave Macmillan.

Mattoni, A. (2012). *Media Practices and Protest Politics. How Precarious Workers Mobilise*. Farnham, UK: Ashgate.

Mayer-Schönberger, V., & Cukier, K. (2013). *Big Data: A Revolution That Will Transform How We Live, Work, and Think*. Boston, MA: Houghton Mifflin Harcourt.

Meikle, G. (2002). *Future Active: Media Activism and the Internet*. New York: Routledge.

Milan, S. (2013). *Social Movements and Their Technologies: Wiring Social Change*. Basingstoke, UK: Palgrave Macmillan.

Milan, S. (2014). Between datafication and encryption: media activism in times of Big Data. Presented at the Scholars Program Symposium on Media Activism, Annenberg School of Communication, University of Pennsylvania, Philadelphia, PA. Retrieved from https://www.asc.upenn.edu/news-events/events/scholars-program-symposium-media-activism

Milan, S. (2016). Liberated technology: inside emancipatory communication activism. In E. Gordon & P. Mihailidis (eds), *Civic Media: Technology, Design, Practice* (pp. 107–124). Cambridge MA: MIT Press.

Milan, S. (2017). Data activism as the new frontier of media activism. In V. Pickard & G. Yang (eds), *Media Activism in the Digital Age* (pp. 151–163). New York: Routledge.

Milan, S. (2018). Political agency, digital traces and bottom-up data practices. *International Journal of Communication*, 12, 507–527.

Milan, S. (2019). Citizen media and big data. In B. Blaagaard, L. Pérez-González, & M. Baker (eds), *Routledge Encyclopedia of Citizen Media*. New York: Routledge.

Milan, S., & Gutierrez, M. (2017). Technopolitics in the age of Big Data. In F. Sierra Caballero & T. Gravante (eds), *Networks, Movements & Technopolitics in Latin America: Critical Analysis and Current Challenges* (pp. 95–109). London: Palgrave Macmillan.

Milan, S., & van der Velden, L. (2016). The alternative epistemologies of data activism. *Digital Culture & Society*, 2(2), 57–74.

Mosco, V. (2009). *The Political Economy of Communication* (2nd edn). London: Sage.

Mosco, V. (2014). *To the Cloud: Big Data in a Turbulent World*. New York: Paradigm Publishers.

Murakami Wood, D. (2013). What is global surveillance? Towards a relational political economy of the global surveillant assemblage. *Geoforum*, 49, 317–326.

Papacharissi, Z., Hunsinger, J., & Selft, T. (2014). On networked publics and private spheres in social media. In *The Social Media Handbook* (pp. 144–158). New York: Routledge.

Pasquale, F. (2015). *The Black Box Society: The Secret Algorithms that Control Money and Information*. Cambridge, MA: Harvard University Press.

Powles, J. (2016). Machine logic: our lives are ruled by big tech's "decisions by data." *The Guardian*, 8 October. Retrieved from https://www.theguardian.com/technology/2016/oct/08/algorithms-big-tech-data-decisions

Rodriguez, C. (2001). *Fissures in the Mediascape. An International Study of Citizens' Media.* Cresskill, NJ: Hampton Press.

Rodriguez, C. (2011). *Citizens' Media Against Armed Conflict: Disrupting Violence in Colombia.* Minneapolis, MN: University of Minnesota Press.

Russon Gilman, H. (2016). *Participatory Budgeting and Civic Tech: The Revival of Citizen Engagement.* Washington, DC: Georgetown University Press.

Schrock, A. R. (2016). Civic hacking as data activism and advocacy: a history from publicity to open government data. *New Media & Society*, 18(4), 581–599.

Shiner, L. (2001). *The Invention of Art. A Cultural History.* Chicago, IL: University of Chicago Press.

Snow, D. A. (2004). Framing process, ideology, and discursive fields. In D. A. Snow, S. A. Soule, & H. Kriesi (eds), *The Blackwell Companion to Social Movements* (pp. 380–412). Oxford: Blackwell.

Stephansen, H. (2016). Understanding citizen media as practice: agents, processes, publics. In M. Baker & B. B. Blaagaard (eds), *Citizen media and Public Spaces: Diverse Expressions of Citizenship and Dissent* (pp. 25–40). London: Routledge.

Sterne, J. (2006). Communication as Techné. In G. J. Shepherd & J. St John (eds), *Communication as …: Perspectives on Theory* (pp. 91–97). Thousand Oaks, CA: Sage.

Tactical Tech Collective (2013). *Visualising Information for Advocacy*. Bangalore: Tactical Tech Collective.

Treré, E. (2016). The dark side of digital politics: understanding the algorithmic manufacturing of consent and the hindering of online dissidence. *IDS Bulletin*, 47(1). Retrieved from http://goo.gl/MEFYhn

Tufekci, Z. (2013). Big Data: pitfalls, methods and concepts for an emergent field. Retrieved from http://papers.ssrn.com/sol3/papers.cfm?abstract_id=2229952

Winner, L. (1999). Do artefacts have politics? In D. MacKenzie & J. Wajcman (eds), *The Social Shaping of Technology* (pp. 28–40). Maidenhead and New York: Open University Press.

Zuboff, S. (2015). Big other: surveillance capitalism and the prospects of an information civilization. *Journal of Information Technology*, 30, 75–89.

12

UNDERSTANDING CITIZEN DATA PRACTICES FROM A FEMINIST PERSPECTIVE

Embodiment and the ethics of care

Aristea Fotopoulou

Introduction: understanding data practices

The spread of data-driven systems and technologies such as social media and tracking apps has meant that citizen media have also become saturated by data. Community organizations learn to use open data for advocacy and to reflect on their own 'data burden' (Darking et al., 2016). Young, unemployed women are algorithmically categorized as not in education, employment, or training (NEET) by a digital bureaucratic system that appears as gender-free and apolitical (Thornham & Gómez Cruz, 2017). Open governmental data are used for advocacy and campaigning, or are used otherwise politically for activism and social change, for example in humanitarian aid (Milan & Gutiérrez, 2015; Gutiérrez, 2018). At the same time, the issue of privacy, sharing, and access to personal data is a hot matter of legal and cultural negotiations such as the EU General Data Protection Regulation (GDPR). And feminists use hashtags to coordinate street protests, but also to evaluate cultural changes around gender equality at a global scale (Mendes et al., 2018). These are only a few examples of data-saturated citizen media practices in the past decade. These citizen media practices are complemented by data practices of communities and groups that do not necessarily see themselves as political in any way, such as those of early adopters of emerging technologies, especially the Quantified Self. At the same time, the standardization of self-measuring practices, especially in relation to productivity, health and fitness among ordinary people, makes everyday lived experience a site of analytical interest from a data practice perspective.

Why focus on practices, and what might a practice-based understanding of data entail? There are good reasons for focusing on data practices. Critical data studies and other disciplines have approached critical questions around data, but have mainly considered the production and employment of data (Iliadis & Russo,

2016; Neff et al., 2017). So far in scholarly work around big data and artificial intelligence (AI), the focus remains on data – defining data, understanding data, framing data, and making sense of data. The object of study remains *data* even in Pink et al's (2017) anthropological take on mundane everyday contexts of self-tracking cycling commuters. Scholars have studied the measurable aspects of data (Kitchin & McArdle, 2016); the experiential or 'lived' aspects of data (Lupton, 2016); and the ontological status of data (Thornham & Gómez Cruz, 2017). But here I am arguing for a shift of focus to *practices*, and further, a theorization of data practices informed by feminist science and technology studies (STS) thinking on 'matters of care'. As Wajcman (1991) explained in an early account of science, technologies, and gender, technologies are both what people do and what they know. They form a part of human activities and practices, they are not just textual or material. Of course, when Wajcman was writing, computer technologies were bits of silicon, plastic, and metal. Today, technologies of data seem to have lost their materiality as physical objects, and cultural representations celebrate their longevity and immateriality (Fotopoulou, 2018). The challenge is thus to reinstate the materiality of data, to think about labouring bodies, invisible human practices, and social relations and activities. This change of focus is of key epistemological importance for critical thought that prioritizes the agency of humans and the significance of sociocultural contexts over accounts of object-oriented ontologies of data.

This chapter traces how practice theory is relevant to critical data studies from a feminist STS perspective. Drawing from social practice and media practice theory, it conceptualizes data practices as those sets of dynamic actions and materialities, competencies, and meanings that entail data, digital technologies, and human and non-human actors. The first section starts by showing how the practice paradigm, as it has been developed in the social sciences, and specifically in media studies, can be applied in the study of data practices. It does so by thinking through the idea of data practices as media and communicative practices. Here I argue that a focus on *data practices* is needed because it incorporates a wider range of practices than those designated by the term 'data activism' and thus allows us to analyse the politics and power relations inherent in seemingly mundane, everyday practices. To illustrate the advantages of using a practice perspective for data practices that may not be deemed or intended to be explicitly political, the chapter then moves on to present three key examples: algorithmic disobedience, self-tracking, and the collection of data by community organizations. Then the chapter takes a step further. It introduces the notion of care, as developed by feminist STS scholars (Puig de la Bellacasa, 2011; Murphy, 2015) to think about the political and epistemological implications of conceptualizing data practices as practices of care. In this final section, I argue that data practices are material and embodied, as they involve human labour and power relations. In this way the chapter draws a theoretical roadmap for a media practice theory as it intersects with a feminist data studies, which is committed to unsettling the power relation of race, class, gender, and ability in datafied worlds.

Data and practice theory: data practices as media practices

The concept of practice has been developed by social theorists and has met interesting applications and expansions in a range of disciplines, including media studies. As I argue next, this paradigm, and specifically the framework of media practices, can be valuable when applied to the study of data practices, especially when we consider data practices to be intrinsically communicative.

Thinking with social practice theory

Social theorists of 'practice', and especially Shove, Pantzar, & Watson (2012), define social practices as constituted through three main elements: 'meanings' (ideas, values, and affects); 'materials' (such as devices, technological objects, and generally 'stuff'); and 'competences' (skills, literacies, and knowledges). This triple axis is useful in theorizing data practices because 'practices' cannot be studied in isolation – they form wider constellations (Hui et al., 2016). Hui and colleagues think of social practices as a nexus, which can add an important element of dynamics and complexity to the conceptualization of data practices, especially since it also accounts for practitioners. We can thus understand the nexus of data practices to consist of:

- wider constellations of practitioners (users, subjects, citizens);
- meanings and understandings of data technologies and systems (think for instance of reactions to algorithmically informed advertising and predictive analytics);
- the materiality of data (such as the environmental impact of data storage and smart city infrastructures, as well as technological objects such as drones and wearable sensors);
- the competencies that are necessary in order to participate in these data practices (for example, the critical skills and data literacies that are required for personal data safety).

It is important to also stress the dynamic aspect of data practices. Williams and colleagues' analysis of self-tracking as a communicative and social practice highlights the temporal and dynamic aspects of practices, and defines them as 'embedded social forms that emerge (and die) over long periods during which they must be constantly renewed and reproduced' (2018, p. 2). Similarly to self-tracking, other practices involving data also change, as the technologies, skills, and meanings of data change, and people play an active part in this process of shaping ideas about data practices. It is thus essential to incorporate a consideration of the dynamics of data practices through this quadruple analytical prism, which can help us reveal wider structures of power in a context of rapidly changing technologies and innovation. As I argue in the following subsections, putting communication and human actors (as users, producers, consumers, and citizens) at the heart of understanding data practices is crucial in this task.

The usefulness of media practice theory

In media studies, practice theory scholars have tried to reconcile the difficult divide between representation, meanings and affects, and media artefacts and technologies, and have focused on what people do with the media. Media practice theory is key to critically approaching everyday practices and the domestication of data-related technologies and systems (Couldry, 2004; Postill, 2010). Communicative practices and digital media practices have been thought to encompass not only the transfer of information between activists and audiences, but also knowledge-making practices and learning spaces for media production (Mattoni, 2012). They are therefore pivotal in the formation of publics and civil society. They have been shown, for instance, to facilitate thick social bonds between actors in the case of the World Social Forum, and to help citizens form networks of solidarity across national borders that shape their social realities and everyday lives (Stephansen, 2016). In this work, media practice theory moves beyond thinking of the media in terms of publicizing matters of concern, to think about social production and the material forces and relations that surround the use of media technologies in micro-spaces (such as activist and citizen spaces of political organizing). Media practices have also been understood to bring feminist and queer activists together in shared spaces in order to learn and experiment with digital technologies, but also with political concepts and ideas, and serve as opportunities for forming networks, community, and political subjectivity (Fotopoulou, 2017). An exploration of activist media practices in these examples involves both the symbolic and the material. To develop a framework of social and media practice theory for data practices, we thus need first to frame data practices as communicative and media practices, encompassing social lives and everyday realities.

Alongside media practice theory, citizen media scholarship is particularly relevant to thinking about data-related activist and citizen practices because it focuses on everyday practices and spaces of empowerment beyond conventional understandings of citizenship such as voting rights (Rodríguez, 2001). Citizen participation in local governance programmes encompasses smart cities (Kitchin, 2014) and open data and journalism (Baack, 2015). For example, Emiliano Treré (2018) has researched the role of algorithms in politics and analysed practices of algorithmic resistance of the Spanish Indignados, noting the significance of advanced digital media competencies. Milan & Gutiérrez (2015) have examined the empowering elements of people's active engagement with data in the Amazon region. In these cases, participation in data-related practices is crucial for enacting citizenship. As the same authors have argued elsewhere, pro-active data activism can be thought as a new form of citizens' media because it critically approaches big data and attempts to alter the relationships of citizens to automated data collection (Milan & Gutiérrez, 2015). However, the notion of citizens' media cannot absorb the tension between 'the individual and the collective dimension of organized collective action' (Milan & Gutiérrez, 2015, p. 124). In other words, there is often too much emphasis on how new media and data technologies enable participation for individual citizens, rather than how these can be the means for collective action. But can we think about politics and spaces of empowerment beyond the study of activists' practices and engagement with data? Although applying a citizens' media framework is relevant and useful, there is wider scope in developing data practice as a conceptual tool beyond the study of resistances to top-down data collection or explicitly political engagement with data for advocacy purposes.

Beyond activists and citizens

The premise of advancing the notion of *data practice* in this chapter (rather than, say, data activism), and understanding citizens' media beyond its application to the study of data activists, is to avoid marginalization of the political issues that pertain to big data. Data practices allow the political ecology to re-enter everyday life and maintain big data as a wider political issue in contemporary societies – not just an issue to be resolved by data activists. For instance, it has been noted how anti-surveillance resistance practices such as encryption and anonymization are limited among civil society organizations, and activists' interest in privacy and data protection is very narrow (Dencik et al., 2016). This indicates the extent to which top-down data-based systems and practices are culturally and socially accepted. Changes in the structure of labour and changing understandings of joy and work with the introduction of digital tools for self-management (Moore, 2017), the commercialization of leisure time and the transformation of body exercise into labour (Till, 2014), and the acceleration of time with digital technologies (Wajcman, 2018), along with widespread data-based surveillance seem to dovetail with a remodelled ideology of participation and empowerment. As voluntary data sharing complements automated data collection and data surveillance, understandings of digital participation and the boundaries of what constitutes citizenship, agency, and social justice also shift. These are relevant beyond the study of grassroots and civil society organizations that resist automated data collection or manipulate big data for activism. They are relevant in the study of social and cultural practices that use data systems beyond collective action, and where the individual is implicated through occupying identities different from that of 'activist' or 'active citizen'.

Applying the lessons of media practice theory and Shove et al.'s (2012) framework of social practices, we may adopt an analogous emphasis on the social and cultural significance of data-related practices, which implicates human actors from a variety of positions and identities: as users, producers, consumers, and citizens. These practices usually include standard data collection practices – those of individuals, and those of businesses and governance. They can be empowering, such as the practices of data activism (Milan & Van der Velden, 2016) or practices of algorithmic disobedience that are mentioned next in this chapter. They may be hurtful practices, such as those of data discrimination and inequality (Crawford, 2016; Metcalf & Crawford, 2017; Eubanks, 2018); or mainly mundane, everyday practices that appear seamless and normalized, and take place in both public and private spaces, such as skimming through a dating site like Grindr or Tinder (see Wilken et al., 2017) or logging a run using a mobile phone or other wearable device.

Data practices: can the mundane be subversive?

Self-tracking

A mundane everyday activity such as self-tracking is a good example for understanding data practices as communicative and media practices. This is because self-tracking not only aims at communicating achievements to a wider social network, but it also mediates professional and family life, health, and wellbeing. So although self-tracking has been approached as a means for the collection of health data, and for motivating behavioural changes through self-care and wellbeing practices, it is predominantly a media and communications practice (Lomborg & Fradsen, 2016; Fotopoulou & O'Riordan, 2017). Similarly, other data-related practices such as those of hackathons and citizen science are predominantly cultural and social, aiming at forming groups of affinity and belonging, learning from each other and sharing ideas and information, while also enacting 'entrepreunerial citizenship' (Irani, 2015). The practices of the quantified self movement and the spaces they enable do not link to advocacy in any explicit way; they do, however, enable spaces of knowledge sharing and technical expertise, while they facilitate public debate around data privacy, ownership, and innovation policies (Fotopoulou, 2018a). Meet-ups are spaces of meaning making, of forming subjectivity and a thick web of relations between the commercial industry of sensors and other technologies, users of these technologies, and designers and other professionals. They are also gendered places where patriarchal and heteronormative exclusions are reproduced (Fotopoulou, 2017; Sanders, 2017). Thus, applying a media practice lens to data-related everyday activities and routines should start from the proposition that data practices are communicative, and that they are also practices of mediation – mediating complex social and power relations.

Algorithmic disobedience

One interesting example of data practices that ostensibly cannot be categorized as 'data activism' are various forms of manipulation of data practised by consumers and employees as a form of disobedience to automated data collection. These are less spectacular than organized anti-state activism or organized citizen action, and they are practised by ordinary people as part of their everyday activities.

Data collection permeates our everyday life, through advertising's targeting of specific social groups and user profiles on Facebook for example. But these uses of our data by certain media technologies, platforms, and their algorithms are not transparent; at the same time, they are socially blind, and reproduce social inequalities. Many artists and designers have tried to experiment with these problematic aspects of data collection. For example, The Library of Missing Data is a project that comments critically on citizen data practices and specifically the interplay between data collection and missing data sets – where there is an expectation for the data to be there (Onuoha, 2016). Other artists and practitioners actively try to resist data collection and to take back control by developing devices, apps, and other media that spoof data. *Unfit Bits* (http://www.unfitbits.com) is an online DIY fitness data spoofing website that aims to help users mislead insurance companies. It guides users through simple tricks that help them fake an active lifestyle by producing a wealth of data. The slogan 'Free Your Fitness from Yourself' on the website sums up how the project problematizes the use of fitness tracking by insurance companies to incentivize health insurance premiums. According to one of the creators, Surya Mattu,[1] fitness tracking devices like Fitbit are technologically plain: they are essentially accelerometers. However, their marketing campaigns make huge claims about their role in advancing consumer health and wellbeing. Here the subversive data practices of spoofing fitness data reveal the role of meanings and ideas about innovation that are communicated about the technological object. Engaging in data-spoofing practices allows users to question ideas of innovation in science and technology in relation to commercial devices, but also, importantly, to challenge the meanings of self-care that are embedded in such commercial self-tracking devices. *Unfit Bits* highlights the role of trust, in both the device and the data collection process, which is required for these devices to actually operate as an aid to a healthier life.

'Imagine a future where incentivization is replaced by punishment', provokes Mattu. Such a scenario does not seem too far off, as all aspects of our everyday lives are targeted by AI and the data industry more generally. In this context, data practices of data and algorithmic disobedience seem necessary. Disobedient data practices involve the active refusal to conform to predicated use patterns of data-collecting devices and platforms, for example. Thus, such practices of disobedience manifest how data practices are dynamic and how they can be changed when their meanings, competences, and materiality shift. These disruptive practices can be as simple as changing a user name on Facebook or adopting a persona avatar. In this case, the meaning of providing personal data to the platform changes, and this alters the experience of use. Mattu urges: 'Don't just engage in the way that the device is designed, but ask it to give you a bad experience.' Although in cases like *Unfit Bits* the inspiration comes from artists, algorithmic disobedience and other kinds of resistances, such as plain disengagement, are important strategies that 'ordinary' people use in order to survive the changing management practices of increasingly quantified workplaces (see Moore, 2018).

Data practices and care

Everyday life data practices and what people do with data are experiential and often embodied. Helen Kennedy has argued for a data studies informed by emotions and the everyday in what she calls the 'phenomenology of datafied agency' (Kennedy, 2018) in order to understand the conditions and possibilities for data activism. My approach here, however, seeks to make media practice scholarship politically relevant beyond the study of citizens' media and data activism. For this I will now turn to the productive exchange between media and critical studies with feminist STS, because I would like to underline the indispensable contribution of a feminist perspective to the study of data practices, as they are informed by frameworks of media and social practice, and to critical data studies more generally.

Feminist STS and critical care

Feminist STS has a long trajectory of unsettling hegemonic narratives and histories of ableism, colonialism, gender, and race. It is committed to situatedness and embodiment and has highlighted the importance of subjective and partial perspectives (Haraway, 1991; Harding, 1991). What is more, STS has long addressed the conundrum of materiality of technologies by establishing the social, cultural, and political factors that shape technologies, and by focusing on the practices, knowledges, and networks of actors and things. In Barad's framework of posthumanist performativity (2007), the discursive, social, and material are overlapping rather than conflicting elements of certain technoscientific practices. For Barad, meanings and matter are both present in practices, while bodies are discursive. Applying new materialism to digital health technologies research has analysed the material relations that surround the collection of data and the interplay of material forces within unstable assemblages that emerge around bodies and technologies (Fox, 2017). This work has been taken up to discuss dynamic human–data assemblages and the 'liveliness' of data (Lupton, 2018). However, my interest is more in how data come to matter from an ethical and political perspective.

I am intrigued by frameworks of critical care practice as they have developed in feminist STS (Martin, Myers, & Viseu, 2015) and particularly inspired by Puig de la Bellacasa (2011), and later Murphy's (2015, p. 721) provocation that we need to move from '"matters of fact" to "matters of concern" to "matters of care", the affective entanglements through which things come to matter'. Puig de la Bellacasa (2011) describes what an ethos of care in studying science and technology may entail. '[C]are connotes attention and worry for those who can be harmed by an assemblage but whose voices are less valued, as are their concerns and need for care – for example, trees and flowers, babies in prams whose noses stroll at the level of [sports utility vehicle] SUV's exhaust pipes, cyclists or older people' (2011: 92). Because of the embodied, experiential, and material character of data practices, a materialist analysis cannot leave out invisible forms of labour, such as emotional and caring labour, but also what has been termed as immaterial, free, or affective labour in relation to digital media.

Three considerations for an ethos of care when analysing data practices

An ethos of care when studying the affective and material elements that constitute practices of data, data rights, and citizen media includes accounting for the often invisible and devalued ordinary human labour involved in producing data in everyday contexts or analysing data within organizations. The narratives of data and the language of data compel us to translate all everyday activities and experiences into measurable activities, and potentially into generating value activities. The materialities of productive activity are however 'messy' (Lupton, 2016). We may think of those of the productive labouring body that gets tracked using biosensors, for example, or all the material processes of setting up infrastructures and maintaining them in terms of technical expertise. It is important to make visible the labour involved in sustaining data systems and how indispensable the human labourer is in implementing their use.

First, we may ask, as Sheila Jasanoff (2017) urges us to, whose views, standpoints, and framing questions shape data collection and analysis, and what is the extent of what is represented or remains invisible or underrepresented. Critical AI studies have also recently documented problems of gender discrimination, for example, voice recognition systems that have problems 'hearing' women; Google searches not showing highly managerial job listings to women; and Siri giving inadequate instructions about women's health (Campolo et al., 2017). From a practice perspective, however, an analysis of bias should not be limited to datasets but should include practices and infrastructures of data collection, and particularly the power asymmetries between data collector and generator (Dalton, Taylor, & Thatcher, 2016), but also within data analysis teams. As Hanna Wallach (an AI researcher and cofounder of the Women in Machine Learning Conference) reports, such teams are still male-dominated and conditioned by white privilege, with only 13.5 per cent of women working in machine learning (Snow, 2018). Feminist Marxist critiques of affective labour (Jarrett, 2015; Terranova, 2000; Weeks, 2007) are mostly useful when thinking about women's value-producing activity beyond work. To further follow the gesture of historical feminist critiques of science and technology, emerging technologies are shaped by the interests of professionals whose matters of concern get represented. When it comes to data, this is the systematic, ordered, rational, and detailed forms of knowledge (Kitchin, 2017). With such a small number of women and other people from disadvantaged social groups working in the development of data systems, there is pressing need for work that focuses on care and messiness.

Second, care practices and affective labour have been shown to be key within citizen media practices and activist organizing (Boler et al., 2014). But beyond noting the social elements and the communicative practices of activist groups, and as data practices meet citizen media practices, we should be asking: what and who is involved in collecting, cleaning, accessing, and maintaining datasets among civil society actors? Data analysis practices have now become an increasing 'community data burden' for voluntary and community organizations, which often need to collect excessive information in order to seek funding (Darking et al., 2016). In their position statement, Darking et al. suggest the implementation of a community data agreement between local government and other funding bodies and grant professionals that 'recognises and takes action to change methods of data collection which place undue strain on organisations and citizens', but also 'recognises examples of good community data practice that ensure compassion and dignity within the sector' (2016, 5). This focus of the research team on affect (compassion), on hearing the experiences of volunteers and citizens, and on dignity introduces the central aspect of care in approaching citizen data practices. It also indicates how a care ethos allows us to understand temporality differently from those expected by data collection regimes and productive time, and a different conceptualization of timescales.

Third, a care ethos also entails analysing the changing relations within numerous social systems (health and social care, family units, education, governments, advocacy organizations) where data-based systems increasingly mediate social and financial relations but remain largely invisible. This is important because often critical examinations of datafication, data systems, and societies err towards technological determinism, blaming the apps, algorithms, and mobile phones instead of looking closely at institutional contexts and the problematic power relations within them. As Wajcman (2018, p. 6) notes

> The speed, convenience and flexibility provided for the users of the multitude of service apps on offer require human labour to operate. Those who actually drive the Uber taxis, who deliver the pizzas for Deliveroo, who clean your clothes when you use a laundry app, who do the DIY when you use TaskRabbit.

In this example, it is not just the affective and care labour of the Uber taxi driver whilst in the workplace that we would need to attend to, but also the challenging working conditions in the sharing economy and the way affluent people's privilege relates to the taxi driver's precarious status.

Thus, and as Puig de la Bellacasa (2011) also reminds us, drawing from Latour and Haraway, we need to care for the technologies we are critical about in order to remain responsible for their social justice impact and to really affect their use, no matter how passionate, angry, and critical we may be. This is particularly important when we think of the powerful interests of the industries that relate to AI and big data.

> Representing matters of fact and sociotechnical assemblages as matters of care is to intervene in the articulation of ethically and politically demanding issues. The point is not only to expose or reveal invisible labours of care, but also to generate care. In strongly stratified technoscientific worlds, erased concerns do not just become visible by following the articulate and assembled concerns

composing a thing, nor does generating care happen by counting the participants present in an issue. In the perspective proposed here, generating care means counting in participants and issues who have not managed or are not likely to succeed in articulating their concerns.

(Puig de la Bellacasa, 2011, p. 94)

Linnet Taylor (2017) provides an interesting example of how data technologies of control co-evolve with empowering uses. She describes how refugees use satellite-based GPS and mapping technologies on their phones to find their way through Europe, the same technologies that are used by border agencies to control migration. Counting in migrants' empowering data practices here is important because the study of data practices involves exclusions and objectifications that come with using data in different social arrangements.

Data, social justice, and feminist care ethics

Although ethnographies of media practices have been particularly useful in the past in bringing forward how alternative media production can empower citizens, with the power asymmetries and epistemological problems that are inherent in studying data critically, ethnographic and phenomenological studies of data practices are simply not enough. *We need a production of standpoints.* As Puig de la Bellacasa (2011) notes, standpoints come with the question: Why do we care? Why do we care about data practices and social justice? And for whom?

'Data justice' has been proposed as a new conceptual tool for analysing the implications of data-driven systems and data assemblages for social transformations beyond individual privacy (Dencik et al., 2016). Care and justice have often been thought to counter each other and to represent different approaches to moral reasoning, as feminist ethics evolved over the years. Thus, care has been thought to encompass the empathetic and relational approaches to moral issues, while justice tends to value rational action, impartiality, and universality, favouring discourses of rights and responsibilities (Held, 2006). However, we need both justice and care, for different domains. 'A care perspective relies centrally on a conception of human good and entails a deep commitment to a transformative politics' (Deveaux in Held, 2006, p. 64). As well as seeing data governance, regulating the data-driven economy, and data privacy laws as the essential components for a just society, a social and media practice approach to data that is guided by feminist ethics of care and is committed to the production of standpoints may focus on a plethora of issues and aspects. For instance, on how we bring up children in societies where face recognition technologies are routinely used even for babies (Barassi, 2018); on intervening actively to make the breastpump not suck (d'Ignazio et al., 2016); on taking a standpoint to enhancing critical and creative capacities of audiences and communities when implementing education and data literacies (Bhargava et al., 2016; Fotopoulou, 2018b); and problematizing how people interact in a world increasingly populated by drones (Suchman, 2015), wearable devices, and other 'unreal' technoscientific objects (O'Riordan, 2017). Such work not only demonstrates how to adopt a care perspective in the production of knowledge and scholarship, or a 'critical care practice' as a researcher, but also seeks to incite their readers to care (Martin et al., 2015, p. 12). Turning to 'matters of care' instead of matters of fact, or *a priori* notions of social justice, 'suggests that we make of them what is needed to generate more caring relationships' (Puig de la Bellacasa, 2011, p. 100) for a more just world. I have already discussed how citizens' media and practice theory scholarship have encouraged thinking about social bonds, trust, relationships, and particularities, although citizenship and justice have been defined mainly in terms of rights and responsibilities. A framework of care through a feminist ethics lens further helps us understand the political potential of connections and situations in the data practices of people occupying a variety of identities and within ordinary contexts.

Conclusion

To close this chapter, there is no doubt that 'care' is a slippery concept and has been misused in colonial and other contexts of subordination (Martin et al., 2015). Self-care is also a strong narrative circulating in the media and in health policy, and alongside the discourse of the 'common good', it heavily underpins the moral economy of sharing data for research purposes (see Fotopoulou, 2018a,b). By foregrounding the politics of care and invoking groundbreaking work in feminist STS, here I have been attentive to the various ways in which 'care' can be a productive analytical and critical approach, especially when we scrutinize how power relations manifest in data practices. Guided by the question 'Why do we care?' the notion of care inserts particularity and empathy in social justice frameworks, but notably draws a theoretical roadmap of a data practice theory that is focused on materiality and embodiment.

Thinking through Shove et al.'s (2012) social practice theory, and media practice theory, in this chapter I have conceptualized data practices as entities of actions and materialities, competencies, and meanings that entail data technologies, and human and non-human actors. I have then shown how data practices are social and communicative practices that can be studied with the application of media practice theory. Building on this work, the chapter makes two key interventions in understanding data practices. First, I argue that attention to 'data practices' allows us to analyse the power relations and political significance of seemingly mundane everyday practices that are not explicitly political or usually classified as activism. The politics of big data go beyond the efforts of data activists and organized citizen action. I have thus suggested that a data practice approach can help us study the power relations of self-tracking in the workplace, for example, but also disengagement, unintended use patterns, and non-organized data manipulation. What is more, data practice incorporates a wider range of practices of human actors who are dynamic and occupy a range of identities (citizens, users, consumers, and employees).

The second key argument that this chapter makes is that data practices are material and embodied, and therefore need to be understood through the lens of a feminist ethics of care. Approaching the political issues and power relations inherent in data practices as 'matters of care' allows us to account for their affective, embodied, and material aspects, including the habitually devalued human labour of data users, activists, producers, consumers, and citizens. Through a close reading of feminist STS care ethics, I have discussed how an ethos of care in studying data practices can be focusing on, but not limited to, gender and other power assymetries within data analysis teams; care and affective labour in data collection within voluntary sector and civil society organizations; and changing power relations within institutions, including work, family, and education. Following Puig da la Bellacasa's (2011) prompt, I have suggested that a social and media practice approach to data that is additionally guided by a feminist ethics of care needs to move beyond ethnographic and phenomenological accounts of everyday practices. It needs to be committed to the production of standpoints; in other words, to actively seek to incite readers to care for a more just world.

Note

1 Interview with the author, 10 January 2017.

References

Baack, S. (2015). Datafication and empowerment: how the open data movement re-articulates notions of democracy, participation, and journalism. *Big Data & Society*, 2(2). doi:10.1177/2053951715594634

Barad, K. (2007). *Meeting the Universe Halfway: Quantum Physics and the Entanglement of Matter and Meaning*. Durham, NC: Duke University Press.

Barassi, V. (2018). The data in our faces, blog post, *Child Data Citizen*. Retrieved from http://childdatacitizen.com/data-in-our-faces/

Bhargava, R., Kadouaki, R., Bhargava, E., Guilherme, C., & d'Ignazio, C. (2016). Data murals: using the arts to build data literacy. *Journal of Community Informatics*, 12(3), 197–216.

Boler, M., Macdonald, A., Nitsou, C., & Harris, A. (2014). Connective labor and social media: women's roles in the "leaderless" Occupy movement. *Convergence*, 20(4), 438–460.

Campolo, A., Sanfilippo, M., Whittaker, M., & Crawford, K. (2017). *AI Now 2017 Report*. New York: AI Now Institute, New York University. Retrieved from https://assets.ctfassets.net/8wprhhvnpfc0/1A9c3ZTCZa2KEYM64Wsc2a/8636557c5fb14f2b74b2be64c3ce0c78/_AI_Now_Institute_2017_Report_.pdf

Couldry, N. (2004). Theorising media as practice. *Social Semiotics*, 14(2), 115–132.

Crawford, K. (2016). Artificial intelligence's white guy problem. *The New York Times*, 26 June. Retrieved from https://www.nytimes.com/2016/06/26/opinion/sunday/artificial-intelligences-white-guy-problem.html

Dalton, C., Taylor, L., & Thatcher, J. (2016). Critical data studies: a dialog on data and space. *Big Data & Society*, 3(1). doi:10.1177/2053951716648346

Darking, M., Marino, A., Prosser, B., & WalkerC. (2016) Monitoring, evaluation and impact: a call for change. Position statement. Blog post, *Monitoring, Evaluation & Impact:*

Making Data Work, January. Retrieved from http://blogs.brighton.ac.uk/meicomm unity/mei-position-statement/

Dencik, L., Hintz, A., & Cable, J. (2016). Towards data justice? The ambiguity of anti-sur-veillance resistance in political activism. *Big Data & Society*, 3(2). doi:10.1177/2053951716679678

Eubanks, V. (2018). *Automating Inequality*. New York: St Martin's Press.

Fotopoulou, A. (2017). *Feminist Activism and Digital Networks: Between Empowerment and Vulnerability*. Cham: Springer.

Fotopoulou, A. (2018a). From networked to quantified self. In Z. Papacharissi (ed.), *A Networked Self and Platforms, Stories, Connections* (ch. 10). London: Taylor & Francis.

Fotopoulou, A. (2018b). Creativity and critical data literacy for advocacy. Presented at MeCCSA Annual Conference, London South Bank University, 11 January 2018.

Fotopoulou, A., & O'Riordan, K. (2017). Training to self-care: fitness tracking, biopeda-gogy and the healthy consumer. *Health Sociology Review*, 26(1), 54–68.

Fox, N. J. (2017). Personal health technologies, micropolitics and resistance: a new materi-alist analysis. *Health*, 21(2): 136–153.

Gutiérrez, M. (2018). *Data Activism and Social Change*. Basingstoke: Palgrave Macmillan.

Hansen, M., Roca-Sales, M., Keegan, J., & King, G. (2017). *Artificial Intelligence: Practice and Implications for Journalism*. New York: Tow Center for Digital Journalism, Columbia University.

Haraway, D. (1991) *Simions, Cyborgs and Women*. New York: Free Association Books.

Harding, S. (1991). *Whose Science? Whose Knowledge?*Ithaca, NY: Cornell University Press.

Held, V. (2006). *The Ethics of Care: Personal, Political, and Global*. Oxford: Oxford University Press.

Hui, A., Schatzki, T., & Shove, E. (2016). *The Nexus of Practices: Connections, Constellations, Practitioners*. London: Routledge.

d'Ignazio, C., Hope, A., Michelson, B., Churchill, R., & Zuckerman, E. (2016). A feminist HCI approach to designing postpartum technologies: "When I first saw a breast pump I was wondering if it was a joke". In *Proceedings of the 2016 CHI Conference on Human Factors in Computing Systems* (pp. 2612–2622). San Jose, CA: Association for Computing Machinery.

Iliadis, A., & Russo, F. (2016). Critical data studies: an introduction. *Big Data & Society*, 3(2), 2053951716674238.

Irani, L. (2015). Hackathons and the making of entrepreneurial citizenship. *Science, Technol-ogy, & Human Values*, 40(5), 799–824.

Jarrett, K. (2015). *Feminism, Labour and Digital Media: The Digital Housewife*. Abingdon: Routledge.

Jasanoff, S. (2017). Virtual, visible, and actionable: data assemblages and the sightlines of justice. *Big Data & Society*, 4(2), 2053951717724477.

Kennedy, H. (2018). Living with data: aligning data studies and data activism through a focus on everyday engagements with data. *Krisis: Journal for Contemporary Philosophy*, 1. Retrieved from http://krisis.eu/living-with-data/

Kennedy, H., Poell, T., & van Dijck, J. (2015). Data and agency. *Big Data & Society*, 2(2). doi:10.1177/2053951715621569

Kitchin, R. (2014). The real-time city? Big data and smart urbanism. *GeoJournal*, 79(1), 1–14.

Kitchin, R., & McArdle, G. (2016). What makes Big Data, Big Data? Exploring the onto-logical characteristics of 26 datasets. *Big Data & Society*, 3(1). doi:10.1177/2053951716631130

Kitchin, R., Lauriault, T. P., & McArdle, G. (2017). Data and the city. In *Data and the City* (ch. 1). London: Routledge.

Lomborg, S., & Frandsen, K. (2016). Self-tracking as communication. *Information, Communication & Society*, 19(7), 1015–1027.

Lupton, D. (2016). *The Quantified Self*. Cambridge: Polity.

Lupton, D. (2018). How do data come to matter? Living and becoming with personal data. *Big Data & Society*, 5(2). doi:10.1177/2053951718786314

Martin, A., Myers, N., & Viseu, A. (2015). The politics of care in technoscience. *Social Studies of Science*, 45(5), 625–641.

Mattoni, A. (2012). *Media Practices and Protest Politics: How Precarious Workers Mobilise*. Abingdon: Taylor & Francis.

Mendes, K., Ringrose, J., & Keller, J. (2018). #MeToo and the promise and pitfalls of challenging rape culture through digital feminist activism. *European Journal of Women's Studies*, 25(2), 236–246.

Metcalf, J., & Crawford, K. (2017). Where are human subjects in Big Data research? The emerging ethics divide. *Big Data & Society*, 3(1). doi:10.1177/2053951716650211

Milan, S., & Gutiérrez, M. (2015). Citizens' media meets big data: the emergence of data activism. *MEDIACIONES*, 11(14), 120–133. doi:10.26620/uniminuto.mediaciones.11.14.2015.120-133

Milan, S., & van der Velden, L. (2016). The alternative epistemologies of data activism. *Digital Culture & Society*, 2(2), 57–74.

Moore, P. V. (2018). Tracking affective labour for agility in the quantified workplace . *Body & Society*, 24(3), 39–67.

Moore, P., & Robinson, A. (2016). The quantified self: What counts in the neoliberal workplace. *New Media and Society*, 18(11), 2774–2792.

Moore, P., Piwek, L., & Roper, I. (2017). The quantified workplace: A study in self-tracking, agility and change management. In B. Ajana (ed.), *Self-Tracking*. Cham: Palgrave Macmillan.

Murphy, M. (2015). Unsettling care: troubling transnational itineraries of care in feminist health practices. *Social Studies of Science*, 45(5), 717–737.

Neff, G., Tanweer, A., Fiore-Gartland, B., & Osburn, L. (2017). Critique and contribute: a practice-based framework for improving critical data studies and data science. *Big Data*, 5(2), 85–97.

Onuoha, M. (2016). The library of missing datasets. Retrieved from http://mimionuoha.com/the-library-of-missing-datasets

O'Riordan, K. (2017). *Unreal Objects: Digital Materialities, Technoscientific Projects and Political Realities*. London: Pluto Press.

Pink, S., Sumartojo, S., Lupton, D., & Heyes La Bond, C. (2017). Mundane data: the routines, contingencies and accomplishments of digital living. *Big Data & Society*, 4(1), 2053951717700924.

Postill, J. (2010). Introduction: theorising media and practice. In B. Bräuchler & J. Postill (eds), *Theorising Media and Practice* (pp. 1–32). New York: Berghahn Books.

Puig de la Bellacasa, M. (2011). Matters of care in technoscience: assembling neglected things. *Social Studies of Science*, 41(1), 85–106.

Rodríguez, C. (2001). *Fissures in the Mediascape. An International Study of Citizens' Media*. Cresskill, NJ: Hampton Press.

Ruckenstein, M., & Schüll, N. D. (2017). The datafication of health. *Annual Review of Anthropology*, 46, 261–278.

Sanders, R. (2017). Self-tracking in the digital era: biopower, patriarchy, and the new biometric body projects. *Body & Society*, 23(1), 36–63.

Shove, E., Pantzar, M., & Watson, M. (2012). *The Dynamics of Social Practice: Everyday Life and How it Changes*. London: Sage.

Snow, J. (2018) The AI world will listen to these women in 2018. *MIT Technology Review*, 9 January. Retrieved from https://www.technologyreview.com/s/609637/the-ai-world-will-listen-to-these-women-in-2018/

Stephansen, H. C. (2016). Understanding citizen media as practice: agents, processes, publics. In M. Baker & B. Blaagaard (eds), *Citizen Media and Public Spaces: Diverse Expressions of Citizenship and Dissent* (pp. 25–41). London: Routledge.

Suchman, L. (2015). Situational awareness: deadly bioconvergence at the boundaries of bodies and machines. *Media Tropes*, 5(1), 1–24.

Taylor, L. (2017). What Is Data Justice? The Case for Connecting Digital Rights and Freedoms Globally. *Big Data & Society*, 4(2). doi:10.1177/2053951717736335

Terranova, T. (2000) Free labour: producing culture for the digital economy. *Social Text*, 2(18): 33–58.

Thornham, H., & Gómez Cruz, E. (2017). [Im]mobility in the age of [im]mobile phones: Young NEETs and digital practices. *New Media and Society*, 19(11), 1794–1809.

Till, C. (2014). Exercise as labour: quantified self and the transformation of exercise into labour. *Societies*, 4(3), 446–462.

Treré, E. (2018). *Hybrid Media Activism: Ecologies, Imaginaries, Algorithms*. Abingdon: Routledge.

Wajcman, J. (1991). *Feminism Confronts Technology*. Cambridge: Polity.

Wajcman, J. (2018). Digital technology, work extension and the acceleration society. *German Journal of Human Resource Management*, 32(3/4), 168–176.

Weeks, K. (2007). Life within and against work: affective labour, feminist critique, and postfordist politics. *Ephemera*, 7(1): 233–249.

Wilken, R., Albury, K., Light, B., Race, K., & Burgess, J. (2017). Data cultures of mobile dating and hook-up apps: emerging issues for critical social science research. *Big Data & Society*, 4(2). doi:10.1177/2053951717720950

Williams, R., Weiner, K., Henwood, F., & Will, C. (2018). Constituting practices, shaping markets: remaking healthy living through commercial promotion of blood pressure monitors and scales. *Critical Public Health*, 17 July.

13

SITUATING PRACTICES IN DATAFICATION – FROM ABOVE AND BELOW

Lina Dencik

Introduction

The collection and analysis of massive amounts of data has become a significant feature of contemporary social life; what has been described as the 'datafication' of society (Mayer-Schönberger & Cukier, 2013). These processes are part of a significant shift in governance, in which big data analysis is used to predict, pre-empt, explain, and respond to a range of social issues. Yet we still struggle to account for the ways in which different actors make use of data, and how data is changing the ways actors understand and act in relation to social and political issues. Overwhelmingly, focus has been on data as a technical artefact, abstracted from social context, and analysed in relation to its functionalist design. This has meant that discussions on big data have often neglected the *social* dimension of datafication, instead confining it to a question of technology, and – with that – not fully engaged with the *politics* of data, instead presenting it as a neutral account of social life. As Ruppert et al. (2015) contend, emphasis needs to be placed on the social significance of big data, in terms of both its social composition (a subject's data is a product of collective relations with other subjects and technologies) and its social effects. From this, we can begin to explore *data politics* as the performative power *of* or *in* data that includes a concern with how data is generative of new forms of power relations and politics at different and interconnected scales (Ruppert, Isin, & Bigo, 2017).

Drawing on research on uses of social media data in the policing of protests and activists in the UK, this chapter outlines how researching data-driven decision-making in relation to other social practices can provide crucial insights into the dynamics of datafication, and highlight significant areas of tension and struggle. A practice approach invites us to ask 'what people are doing' in relation to resources (in this case data) in the contexts in which they act (Couldry, 2012, p. 35). It therefore provides an opportunity to *situate* data practices in *relation* to other social practices that can illuminate a much-needed focus on dynamics of power and organizational context in analysing datafication. A practice approach thus allows us to overcome a prominent *data centrism* in studies of big data. By focusing on practices – at both the level of those creating and/or acting on data profiles, and the level of those subjected to such data profiles – we can begin to uncover key questions about the values and interests that pertain to data in different contexts, how citizens are reconfigured within these constellations, and how, they in turn, might engage with such configurations. In this regard, a situated approach to datafication speaks to the long-standing concerns of citizen media research and practice by (re)asserting the political dimension of datafication, beyond techno-centric accounts, that, in turn, points to both the (re)construction of citizens in data systems and the emerging opportunities for citizen intervention and resistance.

A practice approach to datafication

According to Mayer-Schönberger & Cukier (2013, p. 8), datafication refers to 'a modern technological trend turning many aspects of our life into computerized data'. At its core, they argue, is the pursuit of predictions based on the premise that it is possible to infer probabilities by feeding systems lots of data. 'Big data is about *what*, not *why*. We don't always need to know the cause of a phenomenon; rather, we can let data speak for itself' (Mayer-Schönberger & Cukier, 2013, p. 14). While the advancement of this 'technological trend' has at times been hailed as the onslaught of a 'new industrial revolution' (Hellerstein, 2008), many have also argued that what we are witnessing with the increasing mass collection and analysis of data across our social life is the emergence of a *paradigm* (van Dijck, 2014). Grounded in what van Dijck refers to as 'dataism', datafication is rooted in assumptions not just about (objective) data that flows through neutral technological channels, but also that there is 'a self-evident relationship between data and people, subsequently interpreting aggregated data to predict individual behaviour' (van Dijck, 2014, p. 199). In other words, the drive towards datafication is rooted in a belief in the capacity of data to interpret social life, sometimes better or more objectively than pre-digital (human) interpretations. It is on this premise that uncertainties about the future can be rendered apparent, what McQuillan (2017) compares to the neoplatonism that informed early modern science in the work of Copernicus and Galileo: 'That is, it resonates with a belief in a hidden mathematical order that is ontologically superior to the one available to our everyday senses' (McQuillan, 2017, p. 2).

The trend is to reduce social identities, mobilities, and environments to mere data that can be managed and sorted as abstractions without a clear understanding of the embodied power relations and social effects produced by those activities (Monahan, 2008; Leistert, 2013). This datafication paradigm therefore relies on particular epistemological and ontological assumptions, underpinned by its own specific set of values and logics – and politics. Big data refers not only to very large data sets and the tools used to manipulate and analyse them, but also to a 'computational turn' in thought and research (Burkholder, 1992; boyd & Crawford, 2012) that reinforces some lines of reasoning and argumentation over others, with significant social and political consequences (Redden, 2015). However, in order to examine these in full, we need to situate this paradigm within the specific contexts where it is being played out. As Christin (2017) argues, the discussion to date has largely focused on the instruments themselves – how algorithms are constructed and how their models operate. We are therefore familiar with *general* (largely technical) critiques of big data that highlight issues such as lack of transparency, bias, and discrimination, and emerging social stratifications between data profilers and data subjects (e.g. boyd & Crawford, 2012; Pasquale, 2015; Barocas & Selbst, 2016). We know less about the practices, representations, and imaginaries of the people who rely on data systems in their work and lives (Christin, 2017). By advancing a practice approach to datafication we can move from a general critique of societal implications, to a more particular and *process*-focused analysis that 'decentres' (Couldry, 2004, p. 117) data and algorithms. In Couldry's terms when advancing a theory of media practice, the decentring of the 'text' (algorithm) provides a way to sidestep insoluble problems over how to prove 'effects' through a focus on either the text itself or the institutional structures that produce that text, and makes us instead consider the *uses* to which data systems are put in social life. As such, it places the study of data firmly within a broader sociology of action and knowledge.

Such an approach re-situates the significance of materiality at the centre of social research, in conjunction with meanings, assumptions, and representations (Stephansen & Treré, Chapter 1 in this volume). Moreover, it provides an avenue to combine questions of agency together with questions of political economy, as the focus is on the *organizing* properties of distinct practices (Schatzki, 2001) that incorporate a significant degree of *intentionality* (Couldry, 2012). In line with Bourdieu, agent and social world form a relation between two dimensions of the social – a 'habitus' – rather than two separate sorts of being (Calhoun, 1995, p. 144). Bourdieu's notion of practices attempts to delineate the practical logic of social activity in any given field as central to the constitution of power (Bourdieu, 1977, 1990). That is, Bourdieu seeks to extrapolate the structural constraints and discursive meanings that dialectically constitute the 'immanent laws' (Bourdieu, 1990, p. 59) inscribed in the practices of a given field.

When drawing on insights from a theory of media practice, a practice approach to datafication, therefore, would go beyond a focus on the data and algorithms themselves (the text) or the institutions that produce data systems (political economy), and instead combine concerns with both these aspects to look at the uses to which data systems are put within a given context. In doing so, it seeks to understand underlying social mechanisms within that context (e.g. organizational constraints, allocation of resources, ideology) in relation to tendencies among agents working and living within such context (e.g. imaginaries, discretion, resistance). The aim of such an approach is not only to emphasize the social dimensions

of data as a response to the predominantly technical and functionalist understandings that have prevailed in many discussions so far (Ruppert et al., 2015), but
also to *situate* data in a way that can illuminate its *relation* to dominant agendas and
potentials for resistance. It invites us to reject datafication as a 'natural' or 'inevitable' development, and instead see it as a continuously constructed project, shaped
by multiple, converging and conflicting forces, across data life-cycles. In this, it
leads us to points of contention and intervention, including by citizens, practitioners, and data subjects in general. Thus, the concern is with the active *politicization* of data systems as they appear as sites of struggle in social life.

The case of predictive policing

As a way to demonstrate the value of a practice approach to datafication, I now
turn to the specific case of 'predictive policing' to illustrate how data systems are
situated in relation to other social practices. The focus here is particularly on policing practices, with the aim to identify how citizens 'fit' in data-driven policing,
both as subjects and as potential interveners or participants; a perspective on the
citizen–data nexus we might think of as 'researching up' (Feigenbaum, 2016). I will
therefore start with outlining the logic of 'predictive policing' as a data-driven
practice, before going on to explore the way this practice is situated within specific
institutional contexts, and then finally discuss what implications this has for citizens
and citizen practices.

The advent of predictive policing is indicative of how promises of data-driven
predictions have taken root, and how data systems are proliferating, along with
their values and logics, across sectors and government agencies. Early versions were
developed in the 1990s in the United States, with programmes such as 'PredPol'
designed to deliver predictions about 'crime hotspots' to police on the street in real
time, based on amassing data from various surveillance networks relating to events,
places, environmental factors, and information about individuals (Mohler et al.,
2011; Howard, 2012; Koehn, 2012; Badger, 2012). Following 9/11 and attacks in
Madrid in 2004 and London in 2005, the use of big data for predictive policing
increased precipitously. In recent years, it has become a decisively prominent
avenue for British police (Dencik, Hintz, & Carey, 2018). For this chapter, I draw
on findings from a research project I worked on called 'Managing threats: uses of
social media for policing domestic extremism and disorder in the UK'[1] that
explored how social media data, in particular, is used to inform pre-emptive strategies in relation to the policing of protests and demonstrations (in the UK, this
falls under the remit of the National Domestic Extremism and Disorder Intelligence Unit, NDEDIU). For this we interviewed leading police officers in the UK
working in the area of digital intelligence and engagement, and examined uses of
'socmint' (social media intelligence) in the form of big data in the lead-up to, and
during, protests.

Predictive policing is a significant example of the ways in which datafication is
permeating the contours of established understandings of citizenship and the nature

of state–citizen relations (Hintz, Dencik, & Wahl-Jorgensen, 2018). Partly, as Lyon (2015) suggests, data-driven decision-making is a continuation of the bureaucratization that has been long-standing in public administration. But used in conjunction with an onus on anticipation, it also seeks to place more weight on managing consequences rather than seeking to understand underlying causes of social ills – as noted above, the focus is on the 'what' and not the 'why'. Indeed, for Andrejevic (2017) the shift that has become emblematic with predictive policing is one from prevention to pre-emption, a shift that also undermines how we have previously understood the democratic process. With pre-emption we are confronted with the 'rapid shrinking of the space and time for deliberation – a diminution heralded by automated forms of sorting, decision-making, and response that promise (or threaten) eventually to subtract the human element altogether' (Andrejevic, 2017, p. 879). Insofar as politics is a site of both struggle and deliberation, the logic of data-based pre-emption comes to appear as decidedly 'post-political' (Andrejevic, 2017).

Yet, when situated in the context of existing institutional and organizational practices, it becomes apparent how data systems in policing are also continuously negotiated, repurposed, advanced, and resisted in the face of alternative logics, (re)humanization, resource constraints, and wider political culture. In British 'domestic extremism and disorder' policing, social media became a core focus following the 'riots' that took place in a number of English cities (most notably London) in the summer of 2011. Reports have suggested that since 2012 a dedicated team working specifically with social media intelligence has been established (Wright, 2013). Police collect social media data leading up to any event, such as a protest or demonstration, and monitor social media activity during the event. Social media data therefore informs both pre-emptive as well as real-time police strategies. However, our research indicated that the organizational culture of policing is not one that is immediately receptive to the integration of digital technologies, and one interviewee expressed that the use of social media data has been a 'learning curve' among a workforce that has not 'grown up' with social media. Yet the further integration of these technological systems has been reasoned partly as a way to practise intelligence-gathering in a way that is seen as having more 'legitimacy' among the public than other intelligence-gathering tactics (e.g. infiltration and undercover policing, which has received a lot of criticism) as well as a more efficient way of garnering 'situation awareness' for any protest or event. At the same time, there is recognition among some of the police we spoke with that the nature of the data that is collected blurs the lines between what is public and what is private information, creating some hesitations as to how it is or should be used specifically for policing.

Beyond these broader questions of workforce and political culture, data practices are anchored in policing by other social practices that are manifest in organizational dynamics and institutional structures. By taking a practice approach we can begin to distinguish (crudely) how data practices are situated within different contexts, and get a better grip on the distinctive types of *social process* enacted *through* data-related practices (Couldry, 2012, p. 44). This speaks to Swidler's (2001) suggestion to consider the *hierarchy* of practices in a given context, and how some practices organize, anchor, or constrain others. Data systems themselves can be thought to enact 'constitutive rules' that acquire power 'to structure related discourses and patterns of activity because they implicitly define the basic entities or agents in the relevant domain of social action' (Swidler, 2001, p. 95) As Couldry (2004) has argued in relation to the media, we might think of media practices as having a *privileged* role in anchoring other types of practice because of the privileged circulation of media representations and images of the social world. We can extend this argument to big data as well. As noted above, datafication strives to order the social world in particular ways through the reduction of environments into data points for the purposes of classification, categorization, sorting, and profiling. Data practices might therefore be seen as part of a hierarchy between data practices and other sorts of practice, as they have consequences for how other practices are defined and ordered (Couldry, 2004).

While considering such a hierarchy adds to the complexity of how data practices can be understood on a large scale, we can also identify specific practices internal to a given institutional context that are central or more determinative than others for understanding how data systems are situated. Here I briefly mention two forms of anchoring practices from my case study on predictive policing as a way of illustration: integration and out-sourcing. Firstly, in the institutional structure of NDEDIU, big data analysis sits alongside other forms of intelligence-gathering practices. In what is described as an 'all source hub', big data is integrated into police strategies together with human intelligence and existing databases; a context police described as a form of 'cross-checking' of big data. This is significant as it suggests that protests and actions are never *solely* understood through data systems, but that social media data is, in the words of a chief police officer, 'just one tool in the box of many'. Secondly, the systems that are implemented for data analytics in policing are not developed in-house. Rather, the design, development, and training of software used for protest policing come predominantly, if not exclusively, from private companies. That means that the software police rely on for data analysis is developed externally, either in the form of 'off-the-shelf' tools developed by different companies that police then use, or in the form of procuring specific systems through contracts with private companies. There is some scope for police to make suggestions for changes and amendments to these systems to better suit their needs, but there is no active involvement in the design or development of the actual software. Developers or private 'accredited training companies' train police in using the software, as well as in how to use social media data more generally. Therefore, the police do not necessarily have any knowledge or understanding of the algorithms they employ for collecting and analysing social media data. As one member of police put it, police only know that they are 'looking for A if it's associated with B and also has C in it [...] the actual algorithm [that] sits behind it [is] beyond us'. As many of the already-available tools police employ are commercially developed, they are overwhelmingly market-driven, repurposed for policing.

Both the emphasis on integration and the out-sourcing of data systems to external (commercial) actors are significant in understanding the social processes of predictive policing and how citizenship is (re)constructed within this mode of governance. We see this in the different (sub-) data practices that all form part of the practice of data-driven policing. In our research we identified five prominent sets of practices in police uses of social media data: i) identification of 'threat words' with a view to 'filter the noise' and focus on particular (potential) activities; ii) risk assessment and resourcing outlining who ('risk' individuals or groups) and how many people are likely to attend an event; iii) identification of organizers and 'influencers'; iv) sentiment analysis to gauge the 'mood' of people, particularly in relation to feelings about the police; and v) location analysis of potential crowds through geo-location data.

While these (sub-) data practices are intended to aid what police refer to as 'situation awareness' for any protest or event, they also indicate a significant reliance on marketing-driven discourses and non-technical information and knowledge. The outsourcing of data systems to commercial actors, through either procurement or off-the-shelf tools, becomes manifest in the focus on market-driven categories such as 'influencers' and positive or negative 'sentiment', which have migrated into policing and by extension into the configuration of the 'threatening', 'bad', or 'criminal' citizen. Furthermore, the identification of keywords and threat words or 'risky' individuals and groups relies significantly on pre-existing or external knowledge gathered from sources outside data analytics. This illustrates a continued dependence on institutional memory and non-data narratives to inform and attribute meaning to data practices and the configuration of citizens as they become visible through data points. Indeed, the assertion of such knowledge is translated into a privileging of professionalism that occasionally spills over into a level of scepticism towards data-driven policing. In our research, this was in some cases based on concerns with the technology itself not being developed enough yet (e.g. for geo-location data to detect crowds and for language detection to inform sentiment analysis), while in other cases it was rooted in a lack of experience or intuition in data systems that is otherwise perceived as being key to the professionalism of police officers. That is, an assessment of genuine risk requires knowledge and expertise that cannot be learnt by computers.

Outlining and distinguishing these (sub-) data practices in data-driven policing therefore suggests a complex interaction between what we might think of as discretion and quantification. On one hand, the emphasis on integration in uses of data analytics in combination with a prevalent perception of professionalization significantly shapes any interpretation of results and suggests an important space for human agency. On the other, data analysis introduces particular forms of knowledge that shift the terrain for what might be interpreted as 'risk' based on the productions of categories and networks, driven by 'measurable' activity and communication. In this way, therefore, understanding the *practice* of predictive policing entails a necessary emphasis on *negotiation* with regard to the *relation* of data practices to other social practices. Such negotiation points to a political dimension in data practices in which data systems not only prefigure, but are also *embedded* within, a set of interests and agendas that shape their uses and significance in policing.

Situating data practices in context

The research on uses of social media data in predictive policing highlights the importance of moving beyond a *data-centric* analysis of how the advance of datafication is shifting the governance of citizens. It is certainly the case that big data and the perceptions around the 'epistemic capabilities of algorithms' (Aradou & Blanke, 2015, p. 6) that underpin the datafication paradigm are premised on particular logics that have significant implications for citizenship in and of themselves. The assumed abstraction in the relationship between data and people allows for a version of citizenship that is rooted in a 'digital doppelgänger logic' in search of our data double (Harcourt, 2015). This suggests a mode of governance that relies on decision-making informed by 'measurable-type' categories (Cheney-Lippold, 2017) about what people *like* us *tend* to do. These predictions seek to bypass any intentionality in the constitution of both the data profiler and the data subject. That is, citizenship becomes an assertion of quantified calculations based on a series of data points. What this means is not that citizens are governed according to new risks, necessarily, but rather, as Amoore (2013) argues, that the calculus of risk is new. She goes on to argue that we see a shift in practices of authorization that enable software engineering (and other agents of data science) to flourish as expert knowledges, to act as though they were 'sovereign'. The advent of predictive policing is emblematic of this shift.

Yet, at the same time, our research also suggests that a significant power dynamic plays out in the assertion of technical authority in relation to the professionalism of the police. This power dynamic is shaped by a combination of structural constraints and discursive meanings within the field of policing. Importantly, as Couldry (2012, p. 37) points out, a key question that emerges with a practice approach is how people's media (or data)-related practice is, in turn, related to their wider agency. In this context, we need to consider how the organizing properties of distinct policing practices stand in both tension and alignment with the datafication paradigm. While in some instances the spaces for discretion, interpretation, and cross-checking of data might lead to hesitation towards or rejection of algorithmic decision-making, in other cases, algorithms provide an avenue for extending institutional logics and desire to expand intelligence-gathering for pre-emptive strategies.

In her ethnographic study of uses of algorithms in the fields of criminal justice and journalism, Christin (2017) similarly found instances where the vision 'from the top' in implementing data systems is 'decoupled' from practices 'on the ground'. She contends that the 'algorithmic imaginary' meaning 'ways of thinking about what algorithms are, what they should be and how they function' (Bucher, 2017, p. 30) differs within fields, depending on questions of profit concerns (and, we might add, the stability of resources within the organization more broadly), level of professionalization, and the immersion in technological innovation historically in that field (Christin, 2017). As discussed above, some of these questions are also pertinent to the field of policing. Thus, the significance of data systems in policing cannot be understood purely through the nature of the data systems themselves, but only in relation to their situated context.

Approaching datafication in this way is significant in several respects. By moving beyond an analysis of the algorithms and data sources, we are confronted with a broader understanding of data politics. As Ruppert, Isin, & Bigo (2017) have pointed out, the performative power *of* or *in* data is hugely significant in explaining the transformation of the social fabric that emerges with datafication. Similarly, Couldry & Hepp (2017) have stressed the altering social ontology that occurs in a context where what comes to pass for social knowledge is held not by persons but by automated processing. As they go on to argue, 'when governments' actions, *whatever* their democratic intent, become routinely dependent on processes of automated categorization, a dislocation is threatened between citizens' experience and the data trajectory on the basis of which they are judged' (Couldry & Hepp, 2017, p. 212). But the politics of data can also be found in the way these processes of automated categorization are situated in different contexts. That is, we have to consider the political dimension of data also in how data practices *relate* to other social practices, including people's wider agency. Here we have considered it in the practices of protest policing, where data systems are integrated in a way that both extends and transforms the governance of citizens. The nature of this integration is a *political* question, embedded in existing and emerging power relations.

In 'researching up', the focus in this chapter has so far been on the ways in which law enforcement and citizenship are (re)configured through emerging data practices, and how 'risky' citizens are constructed through a combination of complex socio-technical systems, institutional structures, and forms of discretion that creates a distinctly political abstraction of citizens into algorithmic processes (despite post-political promises/threats). This, in turn, introduces a significant question as to how this form of (data) politics comes to implicate citizen practices 'from below' and the potential for intervention and resistance. As noted above, despite the logic of abstraction between data and people that permeates the datafication paradigm, automated categorization is threatened by a dislocation between citizens' lived experience and their perceived data double. The politics of data, in this sense, emerges in what we might think of as the 'distance' (Goriunova, 2016) between a citizen and its constructed data subject, the human and the digital. The extent to which citizens are able to challenge, avoid, or mediate their data double – that is, the *relation* between data practices and other social practices – becomes a key political question of our time. The aggregation of combined data produces correlations of group traits and in turn informs predictions about the individual, making tracing any data life-cycle, let alone identifying direct impact, very difficult. This is further convoluted by the state-corporate nature of many data systems and the fact that the algorithmic means by which profiling, sorting, categorizing, and scoring citizens are carried out are predominantly proprietary entities. Such power asymmetries suggest a dislocation that is fundamentally stifling to citizen agency and intervention.

At the same time, the 'distance' between a citizen and its data projection is also suggestive of a productive space where (new) forms of citizen practices may emerge. While this often remains confined to those who have the resources or expertise, and can be limited in the long-term, here we might think of forms of data activism (Milan & van der Velden, 2016) that seek to minimize citizen-generated data points, such as using anonymization tools or alternative platforms that make citizens less 'visible' to corporate and state actors. Or, alternatively, we can think of forms of activism that aim to obfuscate (Brunton & Nissenbaum, 2015) the production of data doubles, such as mass solidarity 'check-ins' on social media in certain locations, as we saw in the case of the Standing Rock protest camp on Facebook. This action was presented as a direct response to knowledge that police used such location data to identify and arrest activists. We can also consider the subversion of dominant data profiler–data subject relations as part of this productive space of intervention, such as citizens profiling police activity using similar data-driven practices (e.g. https://mappingpoliceviolence.org).

These are just a few examples of how we might consider how data-driven policing might interplay with citizen data practices, in both restrictive and productive ways. More broadly, however, situating datafication within a practice approach shifts the focus away from data as the entry point for citizen intervention and resistance. While such data practices may form part of revealing the capacity for citizen agency, a practice approach points to the importance of understanding data practices in relation to other social practices, and suggests that struggles – and interventions – also emerge in the negotiations that permeate different institutional contexts with regard to data. Indeed, it suggests a need to look to the interests and agendas in which data systems are embedded as the basis for any analysis of citizenship in relation to data-driven governance and the datafication paradigm in general. This is the crux of situating practices in datafication from both above and below and for getting to grips with data politics as it plays out across social life.

Conclusion – beyond data centrism

In situating practices in debates on datafication, we can begin to have a better understanding of the actual transformations that are emerging in the governance of citizens. Discussions on datafication have often been limited by focusing the analysis on the algorithms and collection of data in order to understand social shifts. There is no question that the 'computational turn' (Burkholder, 1992) raises important political questions in itself, and that the current datafication paradigm is premised on a particular belief system with ideological ramifications. The reduction of social life to mere data that can be managed and sorted as abstractions is a trend embedded in particular epistemological and ontological assumptions that have profound implications for society. Yet the nature of these implications requires us to look beyond data as our entry point, and to focus, instead, on data practices in relation to other social practices. For example, by approaching pertinent issues such as the way data systems perpetuate or introduce social inequalities and forms of discrimination through the lens of algorithms and data systems, there is an implicit danger that we begin to understand social injustice as a technical matter – and, by extension, one that has a 'technical fix'. Instead, by 'decentring' data, and moving beyond data centrism in our investigation of how data relates to questions of social justice, we are forced to actively politicize data processes and outline how they are situated in relation to interests, power relations, and particular agendas.

This chapter has illustrated the relevance of a practice approach by briefly outlining how data systems are integrated in protest policing in the UK. This case study highlights how the mass collection of social media data fits with an agenda to move from a 'reactive' to a more 'proactive' form of governance that places an onus on pre-emptive strategies, and that facilitates more extensive intelligence-gathering without necessarily jeopardizing perceived legitimacy. At the same time, uses of social media data are informed by external commercial logics that interact with a particular algorithmic imaginary rooted in a high level of professionalization, a historical hesitation towards technological innovation, and a considerable prevalence of other forms of knowledge and narratives. The advent of predictive policing is a significant development in shifting notions of citizenship, and these negotiations between different forces and actors play a pertinent part in this context. These negotiations are important not only for a more nuanced understanding of how citizens are governed through data systems, but a practice approach also raises crucial questions about the potentials for citizens to enact agency, mediation, and resistance in relation to such data systems through different points of intervention. As the datafication paradigm continues to manifest itself across our social life, this becomes a key question for our time.

Note

1 This project was funded by the Media Democracy Fund, Ford Foundation, and Open Society Foundations. The full project report can be accessed here: http://orca.cf.ac.uk/85618/1/Managing-Threats-Project-Report.pdf

References

Amoore, L. (2013). *The Politics of Possibility: Risk and Security Beyond Probability*. Durham and London: Duke University Press.

Andrejevic, M. (2017). To pre-empt a thief. *International Journal of Communication*, 11, 879–896.

Aradou, C., & Blanke, T. (2015). The (Big) Data-security assemblage: knowledge and critique. *Big Data & Society*, 2(2). doi:10.1177/2053951715609066

BadgerE. (2012). How to catch a criminal with data. *CityLab*, 14 March. Retrieved from: http://www.citylab.com/tech/2012/03/how-catchcriminal-data/1477/

Barocas, S., & Selbst, A. (2016). Big Data's disparate impact. *California Law Review*, 10, 672–732.

Bourdieu, P. (1977). *Outline of A Theory of Practice*. Cambridge: Cambridge University Press.

Bourdieu, P. (1990). *The Logic of Practice*. Cambridge: Polity.

boyd, d., & Crawford, K. (2012). Critical questions for big data. *Information, Communication & Society*, 15(5), 662–679.

Brunton, F., & Nissenbaum, H. (2015). *Obfuscation: A User's Guide for Privacy and Protest*. Cambridge, MA: MIT Press.

Burkholder, L. (ed.) (1992). *Philosophy and the Computer*. Boulder, San Francisco and Oxford: Westview Press.

Calhoun, C. (1995). *Critical Social Theory*. Malden and Oxford: Blackwell.

Cheney-Lippold, J. (2017). *We Are Data*. New York: New York University Press.

Christin, A. (2017). Algorithms in practice: comparing web journalism and criminal justice. *Big Data & Society*, 4(2). doi:10.1177/2053951717718855

Couldry, N. (2004). Theorising media as practice. *Social Semiotics*, 14(2), 115–132

Couldry, N. (2012). *Media, Society, World: Social Theory and Digital Media Practice*. Cambridge and Malden, MA: Polity

Couldry, N., & Hepp, A. (2017). *The Mediated Construction of Reality*. Cambridge and Malden, MA: Polity.

Dencik, L., Hintz, A., & Carey, Z. (2018). Prediction, pre-emption and limits to dissent: social media and big data uses for policing protests in the United Kingdom. *New Media & Society*, 20(4), 1433–1450.

van Dijck, J. (2014). Datafication, dataism and dataveillance: big data between scientific paradigm and ideology. *Surveillance & Society*, 12(2), 197–208.

Feigenbaum, A. (2016). Investigative Research for Academics and Campaigners: A Skill Share Workshop, London, 2 May.

Goriunova, O. (2016). Data subjects. Paper presented at Social Media and Politics Symposium, Ulster University, 3 June.

Harcourt, B. E. (2015). *Exposed: Desire and Disobedience in the Digital Age*. Cambridge, MA: Harvard University Press.

Hellerstein, J. (2008). The commoditization of massive data analysis. *Radar*, 19 November. Retrieved from: http://radar.oreilly.com/2008/11/the-commoditization-of-massive.html

Hintz, A., Dencik, L., & Wahl-Jorgensen, K. (2018). *Digital Citizenship in a Datafied Society*. Cambridge: Polity.

Howard, A. (2012). Predictive data analytics is saving lives and taxpayer dollars in New York City. *Radar*, 26 June. Retrieved from: http://radar.oreilly.com/2012/06/predictive-data-analytics-big-data-nyc.html

Koehn, J. (2012). Algorithmic crimefighting. *San Jose.com*, 22 February. Retrieved from: http://www.sanjose.com/2012/02/22/sheriffs_office_fights_property_crimes_with_predictive_policing/

Leistert, O. (2013). *From Protest to Surveillance – The Political Rationality of Mobile Media*. Frankfurt Am Main: Peter Lang.

Lyon, D. (2015). *Surveillance After Snowden*. Cambridge, MA: Polity Press.

Mayer-Schönberger, V., & Cukier, K. (2013). *Big Data: A Revolution That Will Transform How We Live, Work and Think*. New York: John Murray.

McQuillan, D. (2017). Data science as machinic neoplatonism. *Philosophy & Technology*, 31(2), 253–272. doi:10.1007/s13347-017-0273-3

Milan, S., & van der Velden, L. (2016). The alternative epistemologies of data activism. *Digital Culture & Society*, 2(2), 57–74.

Mohler, G. O., Short, M. B., Brantingham, P. J., Schoenberg, F. P., & Tita, G. E. (2011). Self-exciting point process modeling of crime. *Journal of the American Statistical Association*, 106(493), 100–108.

Monahan, T. (2008). Editorial: Surveillance and inequality. *Surveillance and Society*, 5(3), 217–226.

Pasquale, F. (2015). *The Black Box Society: The Secret Algorithms that Control Money and Information.* Cambridge, MA: Harvard University Press.

Redden, J. (2015). Big data as system of knowledge: investigating Canadian governance. In G. Elmer, G. Langlois, & J. Redden, (eds), *Compromised Data: From Social Media to Big Data* (pp. 17–39). London: Bloomsbury.

Ruppert, E., Harvey, P., Lury, C., Mackenzie, A., McNally, R., Baker, S. A., Kallianos, Y., & Lewis, C. (2015). *Background: A Social Framework for Big Data.* Project Report. CRESC, University of Manchester and Open University. Retrieved from: http://research.gold.ac.uk/13484/1/SFBD%20Background.pdf

Ruppert, E., Isin, E., & Bigo, D. (2017). Data politics. *Big Data & Society,* 4(2). doi:10.1177/2053951717717749

Schatzki, T. R. (2001). Introduction: Practice theory. In T. R. Schatzki, K. Knorr Cetina, & E. von Savigny (eds), *The Practice Turn in Contemporary Theory* (pp. 1–14). London: Routledge.

Swidler, A. (2001). What anchors cultural practices. In T. R. Schatzki, K. Knorr Cetina, & E. von Savigny (eds), *The Practice Turn in Contemporary Theory* (pp. 83–101). London: Routledge.

Wright, P. (2013). Meet Prism's little brother: Socmint. *Wired,* 26 June. Retrieved from: http://www.wired.co.uk/news/archive/2013-0 6/26/socmint

INDEX

Entries in *italics* denote figures; entries in **bold** denote tables.